MUSIC, MODERN

When the story of modernity is told from a theological perspective, music is routinely ignored—despite its pervasiveness in modern culture and the mani-fold ways it has been intertwined with modernity's ambivalent relation to the Christian God. In conversation with musicologists and music theorists, in this collection of essays Jeremy Begbie shows that the practices of music and the discourses it has generated bear their own kind of witness to some of the pivotal theological currents and counter-currents shaping modernity. Music has been deeply affected by these currents and in some cases may have played a part in generating them. In addition, Begbie argues that music is capable of yielding highly effective ways of addressing and moving beyond some of the more intractable theological problems and dilemmas which modernity has bequeathed to us.

Music, Modernity, and God includes studies of Calvin, Luther, and Bach, an exposition of the intriguing tussle between Rousseau and the composer Rameau, and an account of the heady exaltation of music to be found in the early German Romantics. Particular attention is paid to the complex relations between music and language, and the ways in which theology, a discipline involving language at its heart, can come to terms with practices like music, practices which are coherent and meaningful but which in many respects do not operate in language-like ways.

Jeremy Begbie is the inaugural holder of the Thomas A. Langford Research Professorship in Theology at Duke Divinity School, North Carolina.

Music, Modernity, and God

Essays in Listening

JEREMY BEGBIE

OXFORD
UNIVERSITY PRESS

OXFORD
UNIVERSITY PRESS

Great Clarendon Street, Oxford, OX2 6DP,
United Kingdom

Oxford University Press is a department of the University of Oxford.
It furthers the University's objective of excellence in research, scholarship,
and education by publishing worldwide. Oxford is a registered trade mark of
Oxford University Press in the UK and in certain other countries

First published 2013
First published in paperback 2015

Published in the United States of America by Oxford University Press
198 Madison Avenue, New York, NY 10016, United States of America

British Library Cataloguing in Publication Data
Data available

Library of Congress Cataloging in Publication Data
Data available

ISBN 978–0–19–929244–8 (Hbk.)
ISBN 978–0–19–874503–7 (Pbk.)

For A. J. T.

Acknowledgements

This book has emerged over many years, and is to a large extent the result of numerous conversations, debates, letters, and email exchanges, both formal and informal. I owe much to the unique stimulation provided by my colleagues at Duke Divinity School, a number of whom have generously read drafts of these chapters and offered penetrating comments—my heartfelt thanks go to Richard Hays, Douglas Campbell, Stephen Chapman, Ellen Davis, Stanley Hauerwas, Sujin Pak, Kavin Rowe, Allen Verhey, and Norman Wirzba. A remarkable group of doctoral students has played a large part in keeping me intellectually alert to issues I would never have considered otherwise—Carole Baker, Tanner Capps, Brian Curry, Joelle Hathaway, Bo Helmich, Jacki Price-Linnartz, and David Taylor. When in Cambridge, I have been fortunate to enjoy a superb research environment at Wolfson College, and an outstanding network of wisdom in the University, which includes Imogen Adkins, Stephen Cleobury, Sarah Coakley, Francis Coburg, David Ford, Malcolm Guite, and Christopher Page. Further afield, I am immensely grateful for the scholarly insights of Nick Adams, Oliver Crisp, Mark Husbands, Mareque Ireland, Tony Lane, Mickey Mattox, Murray Rae, Kevin Vanhoozer, Tom Wright, as well as the formidable musico-theological dynamism of Alan Torrance. I have benefited enormously from the stimulation and encouragement of numerous scholars and practitioners in the world of music, some of whom have kindly read portions of the developing manuscript; particular gratitude is due to Peter Bannister, Andrew Bowie, John Butt, Christina Carnes, Daniel Chua, Thomas Christensen, Nicholas Cook, Stephen Crist, Ian Cross, Guy Damann, Elizabeth Eichling, Julian Johnson, Nathan Jones, Daniel Trocmé-Latter, Elizabeth Linnartz, Andreas Loewe, James MacMillan, Michael Marissen, Markus Rathey, Férdia Stone-Davis, Bettina Varwig, Geoffrey Webber, and Cordelia Williams. Nonetheless, I take full responsibility for any infelicities in the script.

My sincere thanks go to Lizzie Robottom and her predecessors at OUP for their diligence and long-standing patience.

I am hugely indebted to Dona McCullagh, my industrious and highly gifted research assistant: with graciousness and gentle humour, she has undertaken a vast amount of book-hunting, proofreading, and indexing, and her wise guidance at many turns of the project has massively improved the quality of the essays that follow.

My greatest debt, as always, is to my wife, Rachel, who, by the way she lives, has taught me more than anyone else about the energetic faithfulness of God in the world.

Contents

List of Figures

1

Introduction: Listening to Music

> He wrote about important universal issues such as exile, politics, integration. However, the most surprising thing for me, as his friend and great admirer, was the realisation that, on many occasions, he formulated ideas and reached conclusions through music; and he saw music as a reflection of the ideas he had regarding other issues.
>
> *The conductor Daniel Barenboim, writing about Edward Said*[1]

This book is an invitation to theologians, and to any with a lively interest in theology, to listen to music—to its sounds, to those who make and enjoy them, and to the extraordinary literature this beguiling art form has generated.

But the invitation is to listen in a particular way, to be attuned to particular trajectories. My aim is to demonstrate that the practices of music and its discourses can bear their own kind of witness to some of the pivotal theological currents and counter-currents that have shaped modernity—that music has been affected in distinctive ways by those currents, and in some cases may have contributed to forming them. Music, in other words, is capable of providing a kind of 'theological performance' of some of modernity's most characteristic dynamics. In addition, and perhaps more unusually, I hope to show that the world of music is capable of yielding highly effective ways of addressing and moving beyond some of the intractable theological aporias that modernity has bequeathed to us.

These are bold claims, and may at first seem odd. After all, music has not been a prominent player in contemporary theology, and certainly not in theology's narrations of modernity. Recent years have witnessed several major studies, which offer detailed and lengthy accounts of the rise and development of the modern sensibility, with particular attention to its theological determinants.[2]

---

[1] Daniel Barenboim, 'Sound and Vision', *The Guardian* [online newspaper], Monday 25 October 2004: <http://www.guardian.co.uk/music/2004/oct/25/classicalmusicandopera1>, accessed 28 September 2012.

[2] e.g. Hans Blumenberg, *The Legitimacy of the Modern Age* (Cambridge, MA: MIT Press, 1983); Amos Funkenstein, *Theology and the Scientific Imagination: From the Middle Ages to the Seventeenth Century* (Princeton: Princeton University Press, 1986); Charles Taylor, *A Secular*

These have been widely discussed, and rightly so. But it is noticeable that when it comes to the practices or disciplines thought to be relevant for constructing such a narrative, attention is focused largely on the natural sciences (including their history and philosophies), the history of philosophy, economics, politics, and sociology. Of the arts, fictional literature and poetry may make brief illustrative appearances, 'high' visual art may be given a passing glance, perhaps even film. But music is largely conspicuous by its absence.

Doubtless, there are some good reasons for this neglect. One of the most obvious is the weakness of music's powers of depiction and assertion, its struggle to 'say' or 'picture' anything with precision and consistency. Music finds it hard to articulate even something as simple as 'There is a tree', let alone portray a tree in a widely recognizable way. How, then, can it *tell* us anything of worth? Another probable reason for the disregard of music among theologians is the way in which the vocabulary of musical analysis seems to be in danger of imprisoning music in a forbidding terminological fortress, and this in turn may raise the suspicion that elitist ideological drives are at work, shoring up the power interests of the privileged few, especially if the object of interest is so-called 'classical' music. A further reason is the common (but often unspoken) assumption that music is no more than a gloss, a trivial, diversionary froth thrown to the surface of cultural streams whose driving ideological currents operate at much deeper levels. Further still, there is the sheer difficulty of speaking and writing about music in ways that actually advance our understanding and enjoyment of it; George Steiner remarks that 'In the face of music, the wonders of language are also its frustrations.'[3]

Despite all this, it remains the case that music has been a major player in the shaping of European and North American (and virtually every other) culture, and in ways that call out for theological attention. It has been ubiquitous in modern social life, and of considerable importance in framing and articulating ethnic, political, and economic identities. It has been intimately intertwined with many of modernity's most significant ideological upheavals and dilemmas, and its practitioners have at various times been pivotal agents of cultural change. So, for example, the musicologist John Butt can make the passing observation that although the intellectual study of time-consciousness did not begin in earnest until the nineteenth and twentieth centuries, 'modern novelists and philosophers undoubtedly built their systems on much that had already been articulated through the arts, and especially in music'.[4] In a similar vein, historian John Toews tellingly observes that in the nineteenth century,

Age (Cambridge, MA: Harvard University Press, 2007); Michael Allen Gillespie, *The Theological Origins of Modernity* (Chicago: University of Chicago Press, 2008).

[3] George Steiner, *Errata: An Examined Life* (London: Phoenix, 1997), 65.

[4] John Butt, *Bach's Dialogue with Modernity: Perspectives on the Passions* (Cambridge: Cambridge University Press, 2010), 31.

the production, performance and consumption of classical music was not just an important element in the history of aesthetic and cultural forms but also a privileged site for imagining and enacting the organization of individuals into historical subjects (the *Bildung* of modern individuals) and for the integration of individuals into collectivities through processes of subjective identification.[5]

In addition, the modern age has generated a vast corpus of scholarly writing on the making and hearing of music, often of considerable intellectual sophistication, and engaging some of life's most momentous philosophical and theological (or quasi-theological) challenges. Any theologian with more than a passing interest in cultural dynamics and their development through history can hardly discount this cloud of witnesses, however demanding the field might at first appear.

Moreover, whatever the hesitations of the theologian, from the musicological side there have been significant stirrings which may signal new opportunities for a musico-theological engagement with modernity's history and legacy. The current stress in the corridors of academic music departments on the cultural situatedness of music, and on the ways in which it has been intrinsically bound up with ideological ambitions, is one example—cultural approaches to music constitute a rapidly expanding field.[6] The so-called 'new musicology',[7] with its resolute attention to music's social, cultural, and political embeddedness, may have been prone to reductionist cul-de-sacs, but it has at least served to widen the playing field in music studies, opening up fresh kinds of questions, including those of directly theological import. Certainly, in writing this book I have been fortunate to benefit greatly from contemporary scholars of music who profess no theological commitment or expertise but who are nonetheless prepared to enter theological territory with intellectual serious and generosity.[8]

---

[5] John Toews, 'Integrating Music into Intellectual History: Nineteenth-Century Art Music as a Discourse of Agency and Identity', *Modern Intellectual History* (2008): 309–31, 309. However, Toews goes on to observe that 'music has not fully entered the mainstream of intellectual and cultural history'. Toews, 'Integrating Music': 310. The same could certainly be said of music vis-à-vis historical theology.

[6] Martin Clayton, Richard Middleton, and Trevor Herbert (eds), *The Cultural Study of Music: A Critical Introduction*, 2nd edn. (London: Routledge, 2012). Among numerous examples, see Butt, *Bach's Dialogue with Modernity*; J. P. E. Harper-Scott, *Edward Elgar, Modernist* (Cambridge: Cambridge University Press, 2006); Mark Evan Bonds, *Music as Thought: Listening to the Symphony in the Age of Beethoven* (Princeton: Princeton University Press, 2006); Daniel Beller-McKenna, *Brahms and the German Spirit* (Cambridge, MA: Harvard University Press, 2004).

[7] See David Fallows, 'New Musicology', in Alison Latham (ed.), *The Oxford Companion to Music* (Oxford: Oxford University Press, 2002), 834.

[8] Michael Steinberg remarks that historians 'have not been as receptive to the musical dimensions of history as the musicologists have increasingly been to historical contexts': Michael P. Steinberg, *Listening to Reason: Culture, Subjectivity, and Nineteenth-Century Music* (Princeton: Princeton University Press, 2004), 3. The comment could surely be widened to apply to theologians with historico-cultural interests.

'MODERNITY'?

Anyone foolhardy enough to include 'modernity' in a book title will need to set down at least some markers about the meaning of this greatly contested term. For our purposes, I am understanding modernity to refer primarily to a cluster of attitudes or mindsets inextricably bound up with social and cultural practices, which include, for example, particularly strong and prominent concepts of autonomy and human freedom; the notion of humans as standing 'over against' their physical environment; linear understandings of time and associated notions of progress; the privileging of a distinctive form of reasoning allied to bureaucratization, technological mastery, and industrialization; and an inclination to favour post-religious, even anti-theological, 'metanarratives'. As such—we should note—modernity should be clearly distinguished from what music historians speak of as 'modernism', a stylistic term used of music that first took shape in the late-nineteenth and early-twentieth centuries, associated especially with innovative figures such as Arnold Schoenberg (1874–1951) and Igor Stravinsky (1882–1971).

Needless to say, modernity can be (and often is) understood in a related, secondary sense as identifying a chronological phase or period—as in 'the modern era'. There has been much dispute about where the border between pre-modern and modern should be assumed to lie, and even more about where the so-called 'postmodern' or 'late modern' might begin. Establishing neat and universally applicable temporal demarcations is notoriously hard, and a dubious enterprise in any case; much depends, after all, on the kind of story one wishes to recount when making such distinctions. Mercifully, precise line-drawing is unnecessary here. It is enough to say that the decisive changes of sensibility evident with the advent of the Renaissance and Reformation can usefully be interpreted as marking a shift from pre-modern to modern, and among the most crucial of these changes of outlook was a 'disembedding' of humankind from its previously assumed place in an interconnected and harmonious cosmic order.

In what follows, we will deploy the term 'modernity' in both these senses, depending on the context. As to the question of the nature and significance of the instabilities and disturbances dubbed 'postmodern', this is not a matter we explore in any detail. Some propose that cultures in the West are experiencing an overlap of 'conditions' in which marks of the modern interweave with features of a decidedly new ethos, which is still emerging. Some see postmodernity not so much as a 'turn' but as a regression, or even an imploding of modernity; others as an intensification of the modern condition that exposes its internal incongruities. Still others believe genuinely new and fruitful forms of thought, social organization, and culture are currently being born. In any case, if 'postmodern' is to be taken with any seriousness as describing phenomena or aspects of phenomena that are in some sense distinctive and impossible to ignore theologically, this will surely entail not a disregarding of modernity, but a deeper understanding of it. This book is intended more as a contribution to discerning what has flowed into the postmodern—if that is the right way of putting it—than an account of the postmodern itself.

A TALE OF ORIGINS

It is probably worth commenting briefly on a particular narrative concerning modernity that has attracted considerable interest and attention in recent scholarship. Although it takes different forms, it is essentially a narrative of origins: at its core lies an attempt to trace modernity's philosophical ills more than anything else to certain metaphysical and theological moves to be found in late medieval thinking.[9] The work of John Duns Scotus (*c*.1266–1308) is usually pinpointed as marking a critical shift away from analogical modes of understanding and articulating God's relation to the world, towards a metaphysics that favoured a category of 'being' univocally applicable to all that is, including God. The consequence, it is said, was a conceptual assimilation of the Creator to the order of creation, an ontological domestication of divine transcendence. This was reinforced and advanced by an inordinate stress on the absolute freedom of God's will, which, in addition to the nominalist 'razor' of William of Ockham (*c*.1287–1347) led (whatever intentions to the contrary) to an outlook that posited a bifurcation of creation and Creator, an exclusion of God's presence and involvement in the finite world. The desultory effects,

[9] As presented by the movement known as Radical Orthodoxy, see e.g. Catherine Pickstock, *After Writing: On the Liturgical Consummation of Philosophy* (Oxford: Blackwell Publishing, 1998), 121–35, and for discussion see: James K. A. Smith, *Introducing Radical Orthodoxy: Mapping a Post-Secular Theology* (Grand Rapids, MI: Baker Books, 2004), ch. 3; Richard Cross, 'Duns Scotus and Suárez at the Origins of Modernity', in Wayne J. Hankey and Douglas Hedley (eds), *Deconstructing Radical Orthodoxy: Postmodern Theology, Rhetoric and Truth* (Aldershot: Ashgate, 2005), 65–80. For related versions: Hans Urs von Balthasar, *The Glory of the Lord: A Theological Aesthetics*, vol v. *The Realm of Metaphysics in the Modern Age*, trans. Oliver Davies et al. (Edinburgh: T & T Clark, 1991), 9–29; Graham Ward, 'The Future of Protestantism: Postmodernity', in Alister E. McGrath and Darren C. Marks (eds), *The Blackwell Companion to Protestantism* (Oxford: Blackwell Publishing, 2006), 453–67, 457–60; Hans Boersma, *Heavenly Participation: The Weaving of a Sacramental Tapestry* (Grand Rapids, MI: Eerdmans, 2010), ch. 4; Brad S. Gregory, *The Unintended Reformation: How a Religious Revolution Secularized Society* (Cambridge, MA: Belknap Press of Harvard University Press, 2012), ch. 1; Louis K. Dupré, *Passage to Modernity: An Essay in the Hermeneutics of Nature and Culture* (New Haven: Yale University Press, 1993), esp. ch. 7.

which have pervaded modernity, can be found today in various forms of secular naturalism and atheism, according to which God 'no more needs room to act than he needs room to exist'.[10]

None of the chapters in this book depend on accepting (or denying) this identification of the intellectual roots of modernity's 'secularization'. The battles for and against such a reading will have to be fought elsewhere. Having said that, one area where we are clearly out of step with at least some renderings of this story is with respect to the Reformation. Brad Gregory, for example, implicates Reformation thought heavily in the extension of univocal sensibilities into the modern age, believing that the Reformers fostered a retreat from Roman conceptions of the world's 'sacramentality', resulting in an (albeit unintended) imagining of the world as devoid of God's active presence. As will be clear in Chapter 2, it is by no means obvious to me (or to many others) that Calvin, to take one central Reformation figure, was complicit in propagating or encouraging such an outlook, whatever the exact lines of influence of Scotist and nominalist thought were on his theology.[11]

Clearly, however, it would be foolish to ignore or downplay the massive theological and metaphysical upheavals associated with the advent of the Renaissance and Reformation, and with the move from late medieval to early modern patterns of cultural life and thought. There is also little doubt that univocal metaphysics (whatever its particular genealogy) has played a decisive part in the development of some dominant—and destructive—strands of modern theology. (Indeed, this is central to my argument in Chapter 6.) Further, it may well be that a fruitful field of research would be opened up if one were to enquire about the extent to which musical modes of imagining the world under God (intertwined with musical practices) encouraged or resisted the habits of thought implicated in the changes that this narrative highlights. But that is for another place and another time.

---

[10] Gregory, *The Unintended Reformation*, 33. Gregory's is probably the most vigorous presentation along these lines to appear over the past few years. Examining the emergence of 'methodological naturalism' under the impact of the natural sciences of the seventeenth and eighteenth centuries, he highlights the two cardinal tenets he believes were at work: 'The first was the metaphysically univocal concept of God as a highest being among others: this brought God within the same ontological and causal order as his creation. The second was Occam's razor: if God was unneeded to account for causal explanations of natural phenomena, there was no reason to invoke him.' Gregory, *The Unintended Reformation*, 52.

[11] See e.g. J. Todd Billings, *Calvin, Participation, and the Gift: The Activity of Believers in Union with Christ* (Oxford: Oxford University Press, 2007); Carl Trueman, 'Metaphysics, the Middle Ages and the Birth of Protestantism', on *Reformation 21* [website] (2 April 2012): <http://www.reformation21.org/blog/2012/04/metaphysics-the-middle-ages-an.php>, accessed 31 December 2012; Euan Cameron, 'Living with Unintended Consequences', *Historically Speaking* 13, 3 (June 2012): 11–13.

SETTING THE SCENE

Three further preliminary comments are in order. First, it is presumed throughout that 'music' is to be considered chiefly as a set of material practices, immersed in dynamic and changing communities, inextricably tied to humanly shaped purposes and drives, and deeply embedded in the physical constitution of the world (including our bodies). To 'listen to music' implies being attentive to this manifold matrix. At the same time, it is appropriate, and indeed necessary, to acknowledge that however entwined with its various contexts, musical practices and the formations of sound they entail possess an irreducibility, giving them certain distinctive capacities. As Andrew Bowie puts it, 'why does music exist at all if what it "says" could be said just as well in other ways?'[12] Scott Burnham puts the matter thus:

> ...precisely because music is musical, it can speak to us of things that are not strictly musical. This is how we hear music speak: not by reducing it to some other set of circumstances—music is simply not reducible to any other circumstances, whether cultural, historical, biographical, or sexual, and any attempt to make it so has only a cartoonish reality—but by allowing it the opacity of its own voice, and then engaging that voice in ways that reflect both its presence and our own, much as we allow others a voice when we converse with them.[13]

This book is an attempt to allow music the 'opacity of its own voice' in the midst of theological renderings of the story of modernity.

Second, the ensuing chapters are undoubtedly weighted strongly towards what is sometimes called 'the history of ideas' or 'intellectual history'. However, there is no attempt to underplay the importance of the immensely complex and reciprocal intertwinings of ideas (musical or otherwise) with material conditions, human agency, political and economic forces, social institutions, and cultural currents. In this respect, I find the kind of approach outlined by Jonathan Israel, prefacing his massive tome on the Enlightenment, largely persuasive.[14] Against what he calls the 'old intellectual history' (with its bifurcation of ideas from social context), the French sociocultural *histoire de mentalités*, the 'Cambridge School' (concerned with the textual and linguistic context of ideas), and German 'conceptual history' (Koselleck and Reichardt), Israel argues for a method that acknowledges a 'two-way interaction between

---

[12] Andrew Bowie, *Music, Philosophy, and Modernity* (Cambridge: Cambridge University Press, 2007), 3.

[13] Scott Burnham, *How Music Matters: Poetic Content Revisited* (Oxford: Oxford University Press, 2009), 215.

[14] Jonathan Irvine Israel, *Enlightenment Contested: Philosophy, Modernity, and the Emancipation of Man, 1670–1752* (New York: Oxford University Press, 2006).

basic concepts and society',[15] one which refuses to assume that 'ideas must be subordinate to supposedly deeper social realities'.[16]

I also have no wish to underplay the dangers of projecting false continuities onto historically extended cultural phenomena. The perspective advocated by the Harvard historian David Armitage is especially promising in this regard, cutting as he does a subtle and judicious path through the tangle of debates concerning the viability of intellectual history.[17] He wants to avoid, on the one hand, the kind of materialist reductionism to which he believes some purveyors of 'big' history are prone, where a suspicion of the notions of meaning and intention threaten to erase all recognition of human agency; and on the other, the tendency of contemporary intellectual historians to abandon long-range perspectives and focus entirely on the local and short-term, eschewing the kind of abstraction from sociocultural contexts that marks some earlier attempts at the genre. With this in mind, Armitage regrets what he calls the 'mutual repulsion' between an interest in the 'long-term view' and a commitment to the history of ideas: '*longue-durée* intellectual history remained until recently an oxymoron'.[18] However, he believes there have lately been signs of a rapprochement between the two outlooks—he cites Charles Taylor's *Sources of the Self* (1989) as one example among others.[19] He delineates a type of intellectual history that he calls 'transtemporal'—one that stresses linkage and comparisons across time 'while maintaining the synchronic specificity' of particular contexts.[20] It proceeds by means of a 'serial contextualism'—distinct and temporally separated contexts can be set in sequence, producing 'longer-range histories which are neither artificially punctuated nor deceptively continuous'.[21] And the result is 'a history *in* ideas', in which the ideas that hold the history together are 'focal points of arguments shaped and debated episodically across time with a conscious—or at least a provable—connection with both earlier and later instances of such struggles'.[22]

---

[15] Israel, *Enlightenment Contested*, 24.

[16] Israel, *Enlightenment Contested*, 20. Israel wishes to focus on *controversies* as 'the pivot, the means to grasp not just intellectual history in its proper perspective, but, more importantly, the real relationship between the social sphere and ideas'. Israel, *Enlightenment Contested*, 25. The fact that much of the material in the following chapters is focused on intellectual controversy is hardly accidental.

[17] David Armitage, 'What's the Big Idea? Intellectual History and the Longue Durée', *History of European Ideas* 38, 4 (2012): 493–507.

[18] Armitage, 'What's the Big Idea?': 4.

[19] See Darrin M. McMahon, 'The Return of the History of Ideas?', in Darrin M. McMahon and Samuel Moyn (eds), *Rethinking Modern European Intellectual History* (New York: Oxford University Press, forthcoming).

[20] Armitage, 'What's the Big Idea?': 6.

[21] Armitage, 'What's the Big Idea?': 6–7.

[22] Armitage, 'What's the Big Idea?': 7. For an interesting example of an attempt to do something along these lines, in relation to 'musical storytelling as a metaphoric representation of selfhood' and with attention to the twin 'moments' of the emergence and 'decay' of modernity,

It would be presumptuous in the extreme to claim that the following chapters have fully lived up to the desiderata of these scholars. But arguably, they (and other comparable writers) point to markedly fruitful ways forward for those who struggle to do justice to the intricate interlacing of ideas, contexts, and human agency, and in ways that can, I believe, advance the type of project with which we are engaged here.

Third, these chapters take the form of focused studies, which treat particular figures (composers, writers, theorists) and specific themes in depth. They are offered as samples of what can be done when we are prepared to 'listen' in a concentrated way in a few critical areas. There are thus numerous musicians and writers on music who invite intense theological attention but who are not considered at length here (Wagner would be an obvious example, Adorno another). Although Chapters 2–5 follow very roughly a chronological order, and although there are certainly recurring threads of argument, there is no attempt to provide a unified, continuous narrative or a single case. All of the chapters (apart from 7 and 8, which form a pair) should make sense on their own. They are to be read as highlighting distinct scenes in a massively intricate and endlessly fascinating drama—or, perhaps better, as leading themes in an elaborate and multi-voiced polyphony.

see Ljubica Ilic, *Music and the Modern Condition: Investigating the Boundaries* (Farnham: Ashgate, 2010). Unfortunately, Ilic's study came to my attention very late in the process of preparing this book; I have not been able to consider it at length.

2

Shifting Sensibilities: Calvin and Music[1]

John Calvin (1509–64) is hardly the most obvious person to be considering in a book like this. He is, after all, not renowned for his generosity towards music. His ban on instruments in worship, his insistence that only Psalms are to be sung, his prohibition of harmony—none of this suggests fertile territory for those keen to explore the theological possibilities of music, in worship or indeed anywhere else. The musical legacy of this notoriously austere and uncompromising Reformer, played out most clearly on the stage of Puritanism, appears to be one of radical proscription, a narrowing down of possibilities, a severe curbing of music's distinctive and potent eloquence. Far more promising, surely, is Martin Luther, a musician to his fingertips, who could declare: 'next to the Word of God, music deserves the highest praise'.[2]

But swift dismissals of Calvin are disingenuous in any field, and that certainly applies here. If we take the trouble to spend time with him, sensing something of the theological and cultural currents that shape and propel him as well as those he set in motion, and situating him against some of the prevailing contemporary debates about how music is best conceived and practised, we will discover a rather more nuanced and thought-provoking approach to music than we might first imagine, and one that is highly illuminating for our purposes.

To narrow things down, we will concentrate on a critical intellectual shift in musical discourse evident in Europe during this period, a shift that Calvin's writing on music highlights with particular clarity. It concerns the way music is perceived to relate (or not relate) to theological cosmology: to the created order at large, and through that order, to the Creator. In this respect, Calvin is

---

[1] The material of this chapter revises and expands two earlier pieces of writing: Jeremy S. Begbie, 'Music, Word and Theology Today: Learning from John Calvin', in Lyn Holness and Ralf Wüstenberg (eds), *Theology in Dialogue: The Impact of the Arts, Humanities and Science on Contemporary Religious Thought* (Grand Rapids, MI: Eerdmans, 2002), 3–27, and Jeremy S. Begbie, *Resounding Truth: Christian Wisdom in the World of Music* (Grand Rapids, MI: Baker Books, 2007), 105–12.

[2] Martin Luther, *Luther's Works*, vol. liii. *Liturgy and Hymns* (Philadelphia: Fortress Press, 1965), 323.

consistent with a major turn in late medieval–early modern music theory, in which the kind of physical and metaphysical embeddedness of music that was assumed by most medieval music theorists is sharply interrogated and rendered deeply problematic. An anthropological justification of music begins to become ever more prominent, and in particular, an appeal to verbal language in order to ground music's validity. Calvin, acutely aware of music's immense powers, is especially eager to bind them firmly to the order and realm of written and spoken words.

This shift was to raise with new force the perennial question of music's relation to language—in particular, the extent to which (if any) music's capacity for 'meaning' is dependent on the modi operandi characteristic of verbal language. In one way or another, this has become one of the critical and most-discussed issues for musicians and music theorists in modernity. The fact that the two media are so often judged to be in an uneasy tension with each other (even struggling for dominance) has been a critical determinant in the shaping of musical history over the past few hundred years.

Theological matters are implicated at every level of this shift, whether or not they are overtly acknowledged. For at issue is nothing less than the manner in which the coherence of the cosmos is to be imagined in relation to God, and, with this, what kind of ontological weight human language is to be regarded as possessing in the purposes of the Creator. Needless to say, these were pivotal concerns for the mainline Reformers of the first half of the sixteenth century, and have been subject to massive attention in the succeeding centuries. What I hope will be clear by the end of this chapter is that music, and discourse about music, from this period bears its own kind of witness to what was at stake theologically among those who wrestled with these themes, and in ways that have been largely overlooked by theologians to date.

In what follows, with these particular interests in mind, we seek to provide an account of the way Calvin conceives the place and purpose of music.[3] To be sure, nowhere does he offer a consolidated, let alone comprehensive, 'theology of music'. Most of his comments on the topic arise in the midst of highly practical concerns: to ensure adequate musical provision in the churches under his care, specifically in worship (he rarely considers music outside this setting), and

---

[3] The most useful secondary sources for understanding Calvin's theology of music are Charles Garside, 'The Origins of Calvin's Theology of Music: 1536–1543', *Transactions of the American Philosophical Society* 69 (1979): 4–35; Jeffrey T. VanderWilt, 'John Calvin's Theology of Liturgical Song', *Christian Scholar's Review* 25, 1 (1995): 63–82; John D. Witvliet, 'The Spirituality of the Psalter in Calvin's Geneva', in John D. Witvliet (ed.), *Worship Seeking Understanding: Windows into Christian Practice* (Grand Rapids, MI: Baker Books, 2003), 203–29. These surpass earlier pieces such as Émile Doumergue, 'Music in the Work of Calvin', *Princeton Theological Review* 7 (1909): 529–52; Walter Blankenburg, 'Calvin', *Die Musik in Geschichte und Gegenwart*, vol. ii (Kassel and Basel: Bärenreiter-Verlag, 1952), 653–66; and Oskar Söhngen, 'Fundamental Considerations for a Theology of Music', in Theodore Hoelty-Nickel (ed.), *The Musical Heritage of the Church*, vol. vi (St Louis: Concordia Publishing, 1963), 7–16.

especially in Geneva, where Calvin settled from 1541. As is well known, the main tangible outcome of Calvin's involvement with music was something of a liturgical best-seller, the Genevan (or Huguenot) Psalter, whose culminating edition appeared in 1562 (with 150 texts and 125 tunes). Selling tens of thousands of copies in Calvin's lifetime, it became integral to the identity of Genevan Protestants, expressing and shaping a quite distinctive spirituality, and leaving an indelible mark on subsequent Protestant worship that endures to this day.[4]

MUSIC, WORDS, AND THE WORD

In the first (1536) edition of Calvin's *Institutio*, we are given a brief comment on the subject of music in the context of a discussion of private prayer. Prominent at this time was Calvin's deep concern for the interiority of prayer as against empty, outward forms: authentic prayer is lodged within the 'heart'. Overt acts, in order to be of value, must issue from this centre. He writes: 'it is fully evident that unless voice and song, if interposed in prayer, spring from deep feeling of heart, neither has any value or profit in the least with God'.[5] Later he refers to public singing, something well established in Basel (where he completed this edition of the *Institutio*). At the Lord's Supper, after the minister has prayed that the congregation receive the sacrament with due faith and gratitude, and that they might be made 'worthy of such a feast', Calvin stipulates that if the congregation are to sing, they should sing Psalms. And at the end of the Supper, they should sing praises to God.[6]

Apart for some other fleeting and inconsequential remarks, nothing else is said about music in the 1536 *Institutio*. A year later, the contrast is striking. Co-writing the 1537 *Articles concernant l'organisation de l'Église et du culte à Genève*, we now find Calvin prepared to recommend singing as integral to public worship:

> it is a thing very expedient for the edification of the Church, to sing some psalms in the form of public devotions by which one may pray to God, or to sing his praise so that the hearts of all be roused and incited to make like prayers and render like praises and thanks to God with one accord.[7]

---

[4] For a fine and accessible discussion, see Witvliet, 'The Spirituality of the Psalter'. Also: Robert Weeda, *Itinéraires du Psautier huguenot à la Renaissance* (Turnhout, Belgium: Brepols, 2009); Daniel Trocmé-Latter, 'The Psalms as a Mark of Protestantism: The Introduction of Liturgical Psalmsinging in Geneva', *Plainsong and Medieval Music* 20, 2 (October 2011): 145–63.

[5] John Calvin, *Institutes of the Christian Religion 1536 Edition* (hereafter *IOCR 1536*), trans. Ford Lewis Battles (London: Collins, 1986), 74.

[6] Calvin, *IOCR 1536*, 122.

[7] John Calvin, 'Articles Concerning the Organization of the Church and of Worship at Geneva', in J. R. S. Reid (ed.), *Calvin: Theological Treatises* (London: SCM Press, 1954), 47–55, 48.

He urges that the Psalms alone are to be sung, for only in this way will the heart be appropriately stirred. We also find an appeal to history—he believes that psalmody was an apostolic practice, and that it now needs to be restored in the local tongue in a context where liturgical music has rendered the Word of God largely unintelligible to worshippers (we recall the common attack on the Roman Church for using Latin, and often inaudibly). The Church must sing with understanding. All Calvin's later writings on church music develop these points. Psalm-singing is thus intrinsically linked to Calvin's programme of restoring the face of the ancient Church according to the Word of God.

The shift in Calvin's attitude to music is vividly seen when we compare the 1536 and the 1539 editions of the *Institutio*. In the former, Calvin writes: 'Yet we do not here condemn speaking and singing provided they are associated with the heart's affection and serve it.'[8] The latter's version of the same sentence reads: 'Yet we do not here condemn speaking and singing but rather *strongly commend them*, provided they are associated with the heart's affection.'[9] Looking ahead to the first edition of the Genevan Psalter, Garside comments:

> . . . on the basis of what [Calvin] published in 1536 the possibility of a Calvinist liturgy employing music to any considerable degree seemed at best remote. Seven years later, however, he revealed himself as a determined, although by no means uncritical, advocate of psalmody and superintending editor as well of what eventually would be one of the most influential psalters ever created for Christian worship.[10]

What accounts for the change? Garside believes Calvin's pastoral experience had a large part to play: he took on pastoral responsibility in Geneva for the first time in 1536. William Farel's worship was devoid of music and Calvin found the situation intolerable: 'Certainly as things are, the prayers of the faithful are so cold, that we ought to be ashamed and dismayed.'[11] He would probably have remembered reports of congregational singing from Gérard Roussel and others, and he would have experienced singing Psalms himself in Basel. Moreover, Martin Bucer had already presented a case for Psalm-singing as integral to worship.[12] In any case, the solution to Geneva's 'cold' prayer is

---

[8] Calvin, *IOCR 1536*, 74.

[9] John Calvin, *Institutes of the Christian Religion*, ed. John T. McNeill, trans. Ford Lewis Battles, 2 vols, vol. ii (London: SCM Press, 1960), 894. My italics. It may well be that Calvin has anti-monastic concerns here; he tended to associate mindless or unintentional singing with that practised by monks and nuns. I owe this insight to Dr Sujin Pak.

[10] Garside, 'The Origins of Calvin's Theology of Music': 6–7.

[11] Calvin, 'Articles Concerning the Organization of the Church', 53.

[12] Garside lists the points Calvin and Bucer have in common: prayer (sung or spoken) must have its origin in the heart; liturgy (including songs) must be in the vernacular; what is said and sung must be derived from Scripture; the case for singing in worship must be grounded in scriptural evidence and the practice of the early Church; liturgical reform must be geared

Psalm-singing: 'The Psalms can incite us to lift up our hearts to God and move us to an ardour in invoking and exalting with praises the glory of his Name.'[13]

Whatever the reasons, we should not miss the significance of what has happened. Calvin has come to realize the positive contribution that music can make to the Church's appropriation of words (in this case, the words of Scripture), a contribution at once distinctive and, it would seem, critical for public worship. And he has done this without any weakening of his commitment to the authoritative primacy of the written Word—indeed, he explicitly justifies his attitude to music by reference to Scripture.

Music's Power

But just what is music's distinctive contribution? As we shall see, Calvin believes that, depending on how it is structured, music is capable of connoting dimensions of God's character or nature—specifically 'weight' and 'majesty'. But this is probably not the core of the matter. As the contrast between 'cold' prayer and prayer in which the heart is stimulated by song would suggest, more significant is music's *affective* power—and in this Calvin stands with numerous late-medieval humanist music theorists. When sung, Psalms assume a quality which greatly intensifies communal prayer and praise, appealing directly to the worshipper's heart. In the passage just quoted, Calvin's language is strongly affective—singing Psalms can arouse (*esmouyer*) and stimulate (*inciter*) our hearts, so they can be raised to ardour (*ardeur*). In his foreword to the Genevan Psalter he writes: 'we know from experience that song has great force and vigour to move (*d'esmouvoir*) and inflame (*enflamber*) people's hearts to invoke and praise God with a more vehement and ardent zeal (*zele*)'.[14] In Calvin's view, then, texts can be appropriated with a greater passionate intensity when combined with music. And this should be understood in a thoroughly corporate sense: Calvin's overarching interest is in building up the Church, and it is the affective power of *communal* singing which left such a marked impression on him.

towards a recovery of the early Church's worship. Garside, 'The Origins of Calvin's Theology of Music': 10–14. For further discussion of Bucer's impact on Calvin, see Willem van't Spijker, 'Bucer's Influence on Calvin: Church and Community', in David F. Wright (ed.), *Martin Bucer: Reforming Church and Community* (Cambridge: Cambridge University Press, 1994), 32–44.

[13] Calvin, 'Articles Concerning the Organization of the Church', 53. VanderWilt wrongly cites this passage from the *Articles* as a quotation from the 1536 *Institutio* (VanderWilt, 'John Calvin's Theology of Liturgical Song': 67).

[14] John Calvin, 'Foreword to the Genevan Psalter', in Elsie Anne McKee (ed.), *John Calvin: Writings on Pastoral Piety* (New York: Paulist Press, 2001), 91–7, 94. Notably, in the 1537 *Articles* Calvin remarks that 'we are not able to estimate the benefit and edification which will derive from this [psalmody] until after having experienced it'. As translated in Garside, 'The Origins of Calvin's Theology of Music': 10.

It is worth underlining also the role of 'experience' in his developing attitudes to music: 'we know *from experience* that song has great force . . .', he writes in the 1542 Psalter. Just as his encounter with singing Psalms in Basel probably played a significant part in the initial shift of position on church music, so his pastorate in Strasbourg (1538–41) gave him an experience of vernacular Psalm-singing (already well established there), which may well be behind the strong endorsement we find in his Foreword to the Psalter:

> Calvin had had his own congregation [in Strasbourg], and from his own parish-ioners he had quickly learned at first hand the depth of their appreciation for the singing of the psalms in their own language . . . After his years, even his first months, in Strasbourg, Calvin would and could speak of the power of music with a knowledge and a certainty which he cannot be said definitively to have possessed before.[15]

It should also be stressed that in these contexts, the 'heart' should not be assimilated to modern conceptions of 'the emotions'. The heart is not so much the seat of emotion as the seat of the affections or desires; a change of heart is profounder than a change of feeling or mood, it is a shift of basic orientation. As such, the heart is best understood as an aspect of the will. In stressing music's direct appeal to the heart, therefore, Calvin is clearly according it considerable powers: 'What enters the heart passes into daily living and so transforms life.'[16]

Delights and Dangers

For Calvin, music has been given for our recreation and pleasure; to be more specific, for our 'spiritual joy'—that we might rejoice and delight in God, which is our 'true end'.[17]

---

[15] Garside, 'The Origins of Calvin's Theology of Music': 18.

[16] James Sauer, *Faithful Ethics According to John Calvin: The Teachability of the Heart* (Lewiston, NY: E. Mellen Press, 1997), 138. According to Anthony Lane, Calvin is not consistent in his use of the term 'heart'. In some contexts he aligns it very closely with the mind, but 'normally the heart is contrasted to the mind and can be seen as an aspect of the will': Anthony N. S. Lane, 'Calvin's Doctrine of Assurance', *Vox Evangelica* 11 (1979): 32–54, 42. So Calvin can attack the 'trifling Sophists who are content to roll the gospel on the tips of their tongues when its efficacy ought to penetrate the inmost affections of the heart, take its seat in the soul, and affect the whole man a hundred times more deeply than the cold exhortations of the philosophers!' *Inst.* III:6:4, as translated by John Ford Lewis Battles in John Calvin, *Institutes of the Christian Religion*, ed. John T. McNeill, 688. For an extensive treatment of the conceptual background to the notion of 'heart', and in relation to the common charge against Calvin of 'intellectualism', see Richard A. Muller, *The Unaccommodated Calvin: Studies in the Foundation of a Theological Tradition* (New York: Oxford University Press, 2000), ch. 9.

[17] Calvin, 'Foreword', 95.

Thus then, as our nature draws us and induces us to look for all manner of demented and vicious rejoicing, so to the contrary our Lord, to distract us and withdraw us from the temptations of the flesh and the world, presents us all means possible to occupy us in that spiritual joy which he recommends to us so much.[18]

Music thus gains his high approval:

Now among the other things which are appropriate for recreating people and giving them pleasure, music is either the first or one of the principal, and we must value it as a gift of God deputed to that use.[19]

However, as with all divine gifts, music has its shadow side. As we have seen, it makes immediate contact with the heart: therein lies both its promise and its danger. Calvin has an especially vivid sense of the vulnerability of all human activity to corruption. The catastrophe of sin has turned music into a distinctly mixed blessing. Music can poison and disfigure the heart as much as help to redirect it, bringing disastrous moral consequences. Echoing Plato, he writes:

It is true that every evil word (as Saint Paul says, 1 Cor 15:33) perverts good morals, but when the melody is with it, it pierces the heart that much more strongly and enters into it; just as through a funnel wine is poured into a container, so also venom and corruption are distilled to the depth of the heart by the melody.[20]

He appeals quite openly to the Greek philosopher: 'there is scarcely anything in the world which is more capable of turning or moving morals this way and that, as Plato prudently considered it. And in fact we experience that it has a secret and almost incredible power to arouse hearts in one way or another.'[21]

Critical to turning music to good effect is a proper attitude of heart. From Calvin's first musings on music in worship to his last, this concern never leaves him. Even a fine song can be sung to evil purpose if it does not issue from a regenerate heart.

...unless voice and song, if interposed in prayer, spring from deep feeling of heart, neither has any value or profit in the least with God. But they arouse his wrath against us if they come only from the tip of the lips and from the throat, seeing that this is to abuse his most holy name and to hold his majesty in derision...Yet we do not here condemn speaking and singing but strongly commend them, provided they are associated with the heart's affection.[22]

---

[18] Calvin, 'Foreword', 95.   [19] Calvin, 'Foreword', 95.
[20] Calvin, 'Foreword', 96.   [21] Calvin, 'Foreword', 95.
[22] *Inst.* III:20:31, as translated by John Ford Lewis Battles in Calvin, *Institutes of the Christian Religion*, ed. McNeill, ii. 894. Compare his Foreword to the Genevan Psalter: 'it is necessary for us to remember what Saint Paul says, that spiritual songs can be sung truly only from the heart': Calvin, 'Foreword', 96. See also his comments on Ephesians 5:18: 'when [Paul] adds, *singing in your hearts*, it is as if he had said, "From the heart and not only on the tongue, like hypocrites."'.

Along with this emphasis on the rightly oriented heart goes a repeated accent on the participation of the entire church in worship (against Roman clericalism), and—as we have already noted—on the importance of understanding and intelligibility (against what was perceived as the obfuscation engendered by the music of the Roman Church). Again, we are reminded of the corporate dimension: the *whole* church must sing (no specially trained choirs are allowed) and if worship is to edify the whole congregation it is imperative that all singing be in the vernacular, so that everyone may understand what they are singing. If we are to sing with the heart,

> the heart requires intelligence, and in that (says Augustine) lies the difference between human singing and that of the birds. For a linnet, a nightingale, a parrot may sing well, but it will be without understanding. Now the peculiar gift of a person is to sing knowing what he is saying. The heart and the affection must follow after the intelligence, which is impossible unless we have the hymn imprinted on our memory in order never to cease from singing.[23]

Text and Music

By implication, the text and the music relate effectively. And vital here is the principle of 'moderation' or 'regulation': music is to be tempered by, shaped towards the text.[24] We must be 'diligent in regulating [music] in such a way that it may be useful to us and not at all pernicious'.[25] Applied to music in worship, Calvin's logic is clear:

> . . . surely, if the singing be tempered to that gravity which is fitting in the sight of God and the angels, it both lends dignity and grace to sacred actions and has the greatest value in kindling our hearts to a true zeal and eagerness to pray. Yet we should be careful that our ears be not more attentive to the melody than our minds to the spiritual meaning of the words.[26]

John Calvin, *The Epistles of Paul The Apostle to the Galatians, Ephesians, Philippians and Colossians*, trans. T. H. L. Parker (London: Oliver and Boyd, 1965), 203. Compare his comments on Colossians 3:16: 'as we ought to stir up others, so also we ought to sing from the heart, that there may not be merely an outward sound with the mouth. Yet we must not understand it as though [Paul] is telling everyone to sing inwardly to himself, but he wants both to be conjoined, provided the heart precedes the tongue': Calvin, *The Epistles of Paul The Apostle to the Galatians*, 353.

[23] Calvin, 'Foreword', 96.

[24] On this concept of 'moderation', see Léon Wencelius, 'L'Idée de modération dans la pensée de Calvin', *Evangelical Quarterly* 7 (1935): 87–94, 295–317.

[25] Calvin, 'Foreword', 95.

[26] *Inst.* iii:20:32, as translated by John Ford Lewis Battles in Calvin, *Institutes of the Christian Religion*, ed. McNeill, ii. 895. Compare Augustine in his *Confessions*: 'Yet when it happens to me that the music moves me more than the subject of the song, I confess myself to commit a sin

Calvin goes on to allude to Augustine's *Confessions*, specifically to where the Latin saint warns of being moved more by singing than by what is sung, and writes of wishing he could restore the ancient custom of instructing the reader to veer closer to speaking than singing. The text must always temper the music: 'when this moderation is maintained, it is without doubt a most holy and salutary practice'.[27] It is worth underlining that the principle of 'moderation' is grounded at a deeper level in what Calvin believes is an appropriate disposition before God: one marked by being content with what God has provided. Moderation and gratitude—in music, as in all parts of worship—are fitting in the presence of God the Giver.[28]

And which texts are permitted? Above all the Psalms, or more strictly, poetic, metrical reworkings of the Psalms.[29] Left to ourselves, we are prone to favour poor and damaging words, and we recall that music can intensify the harmful effects of bad words. The God-given Psalms cannot be surpassed:

> what Saint Augustine says is true, that no one is able to sing things worthy of God unless he has received from him. Wherefore, when we have looked thoroughly everywhere and searched high and low, we shall find no better songs nor more appropriate to the purpose than the psalms of David which the Holy Spirit made and spoke through him. And furthermore, when we sing them, we are certain that God puts the words in our mouths, as if he himself were singing in us to exalt his glory.[30]

What of the music? Calvin is clear that the Psalms should be set to music that possesses a dignity befitting the God of the Scriptures: the melodies must 'carry gravity (*poids*) and majesty (*majesté*) appropriate to the subject'.[31] He is clearly not open to the notion that 'any style will do' as long as the right texts are in place. The music must be sharply distinguished from secular genres that risk trivializing the divine presence. 'There must always be concern that the song be neither light nor frivolous, but have gravity and majesty.'[32] Again invoking Augustine, he argues that 'there is a great difference between the music which one makes to entertain people at table and in their homes, and

---

deserving punishment, and then I would prefer not to have heard the singer.' Augustine, *Confessions*, trans. Henry Chadwick (Oxford: Oxford University Press, 1992), bk. x, 208, ¶ 50.

[27] *Inst.* III:20:32, as translated by John Ford Lewis Battles in Calvin, *Institutes of the Christian Religion*, ed. McNeill, ii. 896. Cp. Augustine, *Confessions*, bk. x, 208, ¶ 50.

[28] I owe this point to Tanner Capps.

[29] From the 1539 Strasbourg Psalter onwards, Calvin was prepared to include sung versions of other biblical material—the Nunc Dimittis, the Ten Commandments, the Creed, and, from 1562, two table songs. In the Strasbourg collection (*Aulcuns pseaulmes et cantiques mys en chant*), Calvin includes a sung Creed (the words are arranged by Calvin himself); in the 1542 edition the words are by Clément Marot. (It was quite normal for German-speaking Psalters to include the Creed set to music—I am grateful to Daniel Trocmé-Latter for pointing this out to me.)

[30] Calvin, 'Foreword', 96.

[31] Calvin, 'Foreword', 97.

[32] Calvin, 'Foreword', 94.

the psalms which are sung in the church in the presence of God and his angels'.[33] Secular melodies are accordingly prohibited. It seems that one of Calvin's motivations was a concern to exclude certain types of obscene song, perhaps especially those associated with dancing.[34] His lively paraphrase of Paul's words in Colossians 3:16 is worth quoting in this connection:

> 'Leave to unbelievers that foolish delight which they get from ludicrous and frivolous jests and witticisms. Let your words, not merely those that are serious, but those also that are joyful and cheerful, contain something profitable. In place of their obscene, or at least barely modest and decent, songs, it becomes you to sing hymns and songs that sound forth God's praise.'[35]

In fact, Calvin wants to replace all secular vocal music with Psalm-singing. We should not be misled by his warm recommendation in the Foreword to the Psalter that we sing beyond the church in 'homes' and 'fields'. What looks like an endorsement of 'secular' song is in fact nothing of the sort: the context makes it clear he has Psalm-singing in mind.[36]

To return to music in worship, harmony and polyphony were forbidden by Calvin (though four-part Psalm arrangements could be purchased in Geneva from the 1540s, and polyphonic singing was, it seems, tolerated outside the liturgy[37]). And, as is well known, Calvin disallows instrumental music, even if it is permitted in homes and schools.[38] The topic has recently been ably researched by W. David O. Taylor, with particular attention to Calvin's commentaries on the Psalms.[39] Taylor notes both a positive and negative side to Calvin's attitude to instruments. Positively, the Psalms make it clear that instruments can stimulate a love for God and strengthen praise, in addition to helping lead worshippers 'away from those vain and corrupt pleasures to which they are excessively addicted, to a holy and profitable joy'.[40] Appropriate as this might be for pre-Christian times, however, Calvin

---

[33] Calvin, 'Foreword', 94.

[34] Garside, 'The Origins of Calvin's Theology of Music': 24–5; Witvliet, 'The Spirituality of the Psalter', 219–23.

[35] Calvin, *The Epistles of Paul The Apostle to the Galatians*, 353.

[36] Calvin, 'Foreword', 95. To many modern readers, of course, these stipulations will seem impossibly restrictive, going far beyond what could ever be gleaned from Scripture. But as John Witvliet points out, more positively, they can be read as a rejection of any sacred–secular divide: 'Whereas Roman Catholic sensibilities preferred a clear line between liturgy and secular life, the Calvinists freely sang these texts and tunes in their homes and fields': Witvliet, 'The Spirituality of the Psalter', 229.

[37] Trocmé-Latter, 'The Psalms as a Mark of Protestantism': 161.

[38] For a useful collection of references to musical instruments in Calvin, see David W. Music, *Instruments in Church: A Collection of Source Documents* (Lanham, MD: Scarecrow Press, 1998), 59–63.

[39] I am indebted to Taylor for his unpublished paper; W. David O. Taylor, 'John Calvin and Musical Instruments: An Investigation' (ThD paper, Duke Divinity School, 2010).

[40] John Calvin, *Commentary on the Book of Psalms*, trans. James Anderson, 5 vols, vol. v (Edinburgh: The Edinburgh Printing Company, 1849), 320 (Psalm 150:3).

is adamant that instruments have no place in Christian worship. In the old dispensation instruments in worship are a concession for those not yet mature, those 'yet tender and like children'[41] who are being trained under the law: they belong to the 'infancy of the Church'.[42] With the coming of Christ, all such external aids are rendered redundant; moreover, to make use of them now would in effect be to extend 'the ceremonies of the law'[43]—something of which Calvin accuses the Church of Rome.

> I have no doubt that playing upon cymbals, touching the harp and the viol, and all that kind of music, which is so frequently mentioned in the Psalms, was a part of the education; that is to say, the puerile instruction of the law: I speak of the stated service of the temple. For even now, if believers choose to cheer themselves with musical instruments, they should, I think, make it their object not to dissever their cheerfulness from the praises of God. But when they frequent their sacred assemblies, musical instruments in celebrating the praises of God would be no more suitable than the burning of incense, the lighting up of lamps, and the restoration of the other shadows of the law. The Papists, therefore, have foolishly borrowed this, as well as many other things, from the Jews.[44]

A number of factors are probably at work here—not least a deep-seated concern for simplicity in worship (in contrast to the Old Testament cult).[45] But there is good reason to believe that the major driving force in Calvin's suspicion of instruments comes from his convictions about language in God's economy, and thus about the importance of verbal articulation in worship. Clear language is needed to ensure worship's intelligibility and the engagement of the mind; without this, God cannot be honoured. 'The name of God, no doubt, can, properly speaking, be celebrated only by the articulate voice.'[46] 'The voice of man', Calvin insists, 'assuredly excels all inanimate instruments of music.'[47] Purely instrumental (inarticulate) music is like the 'unknown tongue' that Paul shuns in 1 Corinthians 14.[48]

---

[41] John Calvin, *Commentary on the Book of Psalms*, trans. James Anderson, 5 vols, vol. iii (Edinburgh: The Edinburgh Printing Company, 1847), 312 (Psalm 81:2). See also David F. Wright, 'Calvin's Pentateuchal Criticism: Equity, Hardness of Heart and Divine Accommodation in the Mosaic Harmony Commentary', *Calvin Theological Journal* (1986): 33–50.

[42] Calvin, *Commentary on the Book of Psalms*, v. 312 (Psalm 149:3).

[43] John Calvin, *Commentary on the Book of Psalms*, trans. James Anderson, 5 vols, vol. iv (Edinburgh: The Edinburgh Printing Company, 1847), 73 (Psalm 98:5).

[44] John Calvin, *Commentary on the Book of Psalms*, trans. James Anderson, 5 vols, vol. i (Edinburgh: The Edinburgh Printing Company, 1845), 539 (Psalm 33:2).

[45] Taylor makes acute observations about Calvin's treatment of 'spiritual worship' in John 4: pointed distinctions are made between outward and inward, the elaborate and the simple, together with an alignment of Roman Catholic and Old Testament worship. Taylor, 'John Calvin and Musical Instruments', 13–15, and see his comments in 18–20.

[46] Calvin, *Commentary on the Book of Psalms*, i. 538 (Psalm 33:3).

[47] Calvin, *Commentary on the Book of Psalms*, i. 539 (Psalm 33:2).

[48] Calvin, 'Foreword', 92. As Taylor notes, this sits uneasily with his comments on instruments in the Psalms: here he was content to say that instruments did have a positive role in worship. Taylor, 'John Calvin and Musical Instruments', 17.

Calvin was not a skilled musician, in contrast to Luther (and in even greater contrast to Zwingli), and did not write any of the melodies of the Psalters whose production he oversaw. But he did contribute Psalm paraphrases of his own and had a substantial influence on the various editions of the Psalter. Not surprisingly, the Psalm tunes bear out his wishes. They are metrical, monophonic (without harmony), generally syllabic (one note to each syllable), rarely exceed an octave in range (helping to make them easily learnable and singable by the untrained), and use only minims and semiminims[49] (Figure 2.1). The sense of dignity which Calvin so longed for is evident most of all in the music's metrical, melodic, and notational simplicity (as well as in the use of certain modes—a matter we return to later). Again, running through all this is a corporate concern: that the whole church may participate fully in the act of singing, and thus be edified.

It might be thought that the musical austerity of the Psalter was an innovation, drastically out of line with anything that might be found in the musical culture at large. In fact, the philosophy of word-setting that informs the Psalter was quite consistent with many strands in contemporary humanist music theory.[50] The strong impact of humanism on the Reformer has never been in doubt, though the extent of its direct influence on his approach to music is a matter needing further research.[51] In any case, in the sixteenth century, leading humanist music theorists would readily echo Plato in recommending the priority of text over music and the tightening of the word–music relation, issuing 'instructions for both the semantic and syntactic matching of music to words'.[52] This resulted in music whose features included 'the curtailment of melismatic writing for the sake of a more syllabic delivery; a new feeling for chordality; attention to the accentuation of words and their proper arrangement; and in general, simplification of musical means and clarification of textual content, a concern . . . with audibility, with

---

[49] Most of the melodies have their origin in existing models. The roots of most of the Genevan melodies are very likely in medieval church songs; the more immediate models are hard to determine. As far as the first Strasbourg Psalter is concerned, it seems that a number of the melodies originated in Strasbourg, especially in the work of the musician Matthäus Greitter. Ford Lewis Battles, *The Piety of John Calvin: An Anthology Illustrative of the Spirituality of the Reformer* (Grand Rapids, MI: Baker Books, 1978), 144–65. The musician most influential on the 1562 edition was Louis Bourgeois (*c.*1510–*c.*1559). See Frank Dobbins, 'Bourgeois, Loys' on *Grove Music Online* [website]: <http://www.oxfordmusiconline.com>, accessed 2 July 2012.

[50] Charles Garside, 'Calvin's Preface to the Psalter: A Re-appraisal', *Musical Quarterly* 37 (1951): 566–77, 575–6. For background, see Don Hárran, *Word–Tone Relations in Musical Thought: From Antiquity to the Seventeenth Century* (Neuhausen-Stuttgart: American Institute of Musicology, 1986), ch. 4.

[51] On this, see Édith Weber, 'L'Humanisme musical au XVIe siècle et ses répercussions sur le chant d'Église protestant et catholique', in Charles Kannengiesser and Yves Marchasson (eds), *Humanisme et foi chrétienne* (Paris: Beauchesne, 1976), 239–54.

[52] Jonathan King, 'Text-setting' on *Grove Music Online* [website]: <http://www.oxfordmusiconline.com>, accessed 4 July 2012.

Figure 2.1. 1919 Facsimile of Psalm 1 from the 1539 Strasbourg Psalter, *Aulcuns pseaulmes et cantiques mys en chant* (Morison.41.11). Reproduced by kind permission of the Syndics of Cambridge University Library.

intelligibility'.[53] The sixteenth-century treatises of Lanfranco, Vincentino, Zarlino, and Stoquerus all bear this out.[54] To be sure, the motivation was undoubtedly different from Calvin's. According to Garside, the humanists were intent on recovering the affectively potent marriage of word and music that had been extolled in the literature of antiquity: 'the fundamental purpose of the revival of [the humanist] . . . ideal was to reproduce what the Italians called the *maravigliosi effetti* of ancient music . . . all agreed that the best way to do so was to emphasise the text rather than the music'.[55] Calvin brings particular theological matters to the fore: music must accord with text to ensure that it truly is the power of God's Word that takes hold of the Church, so that it can worship God from the heart. But the means by which Calvin and the humanists wanted to achieve their ends, and the philosophy of music–word relations believed to secure those ends were very much the same.

The Primacy of Scripture

From what we have seen, there can be little doubt about the determinative role of Scripture in Calvin's thinking about music. As Garside puts it,

> Calvin's vernacular psalmody in the last analysis is nothing other than a formu-lation, in uniquely musical terms, of the Reformation principle of *sola scriptura*. Thus from its inception Calvin's theology of music in its textual dimension was *scriptural*. The Psalter was conceived, and always would be considered by him, as an indispensable instrument for the prosecution of his ministry of the Word of God to the city of Geneva and the wider world beyond.[56]

---

[53] Hárran, *Word–Tone Relations*, 82. It is important to note that this should not lead us to assume that a concern for reflecting the text in music was an invention of Renaissance humanism. Leo Treitler argues cogently against such an assumption: 'medieval music was made and circulated in partnership with language, and medieval witnesses make no technical distinction between "speaking" and "singing" in reference to the execution of *cantus*. These facts call for us to develop a conception of sung language as a single, unitary mode of expression': Leo Treitler, 'Medieval Music and Language', in Leo Treitler (ed.), *With Voice and Pen: Coming to Know Medieval Song and How It Was Made* (Oxford: Oxford University Press, 2003), 435–56, 437.

[54] Hárran speaks of five principles that lie behind the rules presented by the theorists. Of the first two rules, he writes: 'One is that vocal music as composed and performed should *relate in one or more ways to speech*. Another is that the *structure and content of the text should be audible*. There are different kinds of audibility: declamatory writing facilitates the apprehension of words, but their emotive content is sometimes more finely perceived in more florid styles': Don Hárran, 'Text Underlay' on *Grove Music Online* [website]: <http://www.oxfordmusiconline.com>, accessed 28 June 2012. Italics mine. Extending Hárran's work, Gary Towne has helpfully elaborated more systematically what he believes to be the principles common to the main sixteenth-century theorists; G. Towne, 'A Systematic Formulation of 16th-Century Text Under-lay Rules', *Musica Disciplina* 44 (1990): 255–87; 45 (1991): 143–68.

[55] Garside, 'Calvin's Preface to the Psalter': 576.

[56] Garside, 'The Origins of Calvin's Theology of Music': 29.

It is worth pausing to consider the different senses in which Calvin's convictions about music relate to his commitment to Scripture's primacy. First, and most obviously, he is attempting a renovation of worship in accordance with the simplicity he believed it possessed in New Testament times—as testified in Scripture. Music must be deployed in a way that corresponds to apostolic practice. Scripture therefore has a *programmatic* priority in his approach to music; it informs us of the practice of the earliest Christian communities to which contemporary practice must conform.

Second, in worship (and, it would seem, beyond worship) music is to be *subservient as far as possible to the scriptural text* being sung. At the semantic level, Calvin wants the ethos of all music in worship to be one of gravity and majesty, as is apt for the God with whom the Psalms (and all parts of worship) engage. Moreover, it has been pointed out that in his approved musical settings, different modes are used to reflect the specific qualities of different Psalms: the melody for Psalm 51 is in the 'sombre' Phrygian mode, whereas that for Psalm 19 uses the 'brighter' Mixolydian mode.[57] Along with this, the music must promote verbal audibility and intelligibility. The relative simplicity of the music, its lack of harmony and polyphony, its limited vocal range, the absence of instruments, the closeness of musical rhythms to speech rhythms—all these and other devices are designed not only to ensure the requisite sense of divine nobility, but to render the words accessible to the ear and clearly comprehensible, so that the church can attend to their 'spiritual meaning'.

The assumed ideal model of the music–text relation, then, would appear to be one of close conformity: the music must rigorously correspond to the text, serve the text, fit the text—both at the syntactic level (the level of verbal and musical structure) and the semantic (the level of meaning). This kind of position has many parallels in music theory of the time (as we have seen). The ideal being presented is of music as a kind of mirror—with a complete agreement between it and the texts; or a clear varnish, wholly transparent to the words; or, to be more accurate, an amplifier of meanings already 'contained' in the text. The Genevan Psalter would seem to achieve just this model.

And yet if we look a little closer, things are not so simple, neither in practice nor in theory. In practice, the melodies used in the Genevan Psalter frequently show a distinct rhythmic independence from the natural rhythms of the words they carry, giving them a character distinct from, say, the songs of the German Reformed churches. According to Walter Blankenburg, 'The intimate interweaving of text and melody, typical for other regions of Reform song, is replaced here by a goal of rhythmic construction, i.e. *by a certain measure of musical autonomy*. There is no other feature in church music as typically

---

[57] Witvliet, 'The Spirituality of the Psalter', 217.

Calvinist as this one.'[58] Furthermore, there is much in the texts that finds no obvious counterpart in the music. Ironically, as Albert Dunning notes, 'Contemporary secular and Catholic music, though having similar traits [to the music of the Genevan Psalter], had developed patterns of detailed textual interpretation and word-painting, but these found no place in Calvin's church.'[59] And as we have seen, different modes are used for different types of Psalm in ways that, even if they are thought of as appropriate, are appropriate *in a musical way*—modes are a distinctively musical device.

Calvin's theory is also far from being as straightforward as a simple model of conformity might suggest. He certainly wanted the words to be plainly audible and thus intelligible, but he also stipulated that the music should reflect a suitable mood (*poids et majesté*), which reflects the character of God as rendered by these words. To achieve the latter, the composers will need to deploy some formalized musical devices—such as unison singing, carefully shaped and repeated melodies with a restricted vocal range—which inevitably generate a certain structural *distance* between tones and words. As we have just indicated, in many respects the sung text is being asked to sound quite different from the way it would sound if recited, and is therefore *not* going to be as plainly audible and intelligible as it could be. (And it is worth reminding ourselves that the texts of the Genevan Psalter are not the un-adorned scriptural texts as we would read them: they are poetry. Even *before* they are set to music they have *already* been shaped according to the demands of poetic verse.)

It would seem, then, that believing in the primacy of the scriptural texts by no means precludes music being allowed, indeed encouraged, to deploy some of its most distinctive resources, even if these to some extent need to work against the natural features of the text. Music, we might say, can be employed to do *its own* kind of work *in its own* ways *in order that* the realities with which texts engage might be more fully apprehended and an appropriate 'heart' response effected. If this is so, music is not being regarded or treated merely as a mirror, a varnish, or an amplifier, but rather as a medium with its *own distinctive powers* (not possessed by language) to present to the congregation particular dimensions of the text's meanings (explicit or implicit) and to enable an apposite heartfelt engagement. It is worth recalling the shift we noted at the outset in Calvin's own stance on music in worship—from muted forbearance to enthusiastic endorsement, from considering music as a minor (and dispensable?) component in worship to insisting on it as a key element.

---

[58] Walter Blankenburg, 'Church Music in Reformed Europe', in Friedrich Blume (ed.), *Protestant Church Music: A History* (New York: W. W. Norton & Co., 1974), 509–90, 529. My italics.

[59] Albert Dunning, 'Calvin, Jean' on *Grove Music Online* [website]: <http://www.oxfordmusiconline.com>, accessed 28 June 2012.

This was a discovery (and tacit recognition) of music as a medium with at least some capacities that are not possessed by language but that nevertheless can enable a deeper engagement with the realities with which a given language deals.[60]

There is a third sense in which Scripture is accorded a primacy in Calvin's treatment of music, namely that *it is to be given primacy over every other text.* No text could surpass these writings when it comes to finding suitable words to sing in worship, and the most obvious scriptural texts to use are the Psalms, the divinely provided songbook.

Although this is not the place for an extensive account of Calvin's doctrine of Scripture, it is worth attempting to sketch at least something of the broader theological horizons against which these commitments to Scripture's primacy are set.[61] Critical to note is that for Calvin, Scripture is not an end in itself, a *terminus* or object of faith, but rather arises within and is appropriated by God's trinitarian dynamic of salvation. As part of God's 'accommodation' to our capacity,[62] the language of Scripture functions (in different ways) as the primary means through which humans discover a saving union, initiated and sustained by the Spirit, with Christ—the one in whom all parts of our salvation are contained,[63] in whose humanity our humanity finds its *telos* in the praise of God the Father.[64] Human language, and decisively the language of the Bible, though frail and fragile in itself, becomes *intrinsic* to the triune of God's redeeming work among us.[65] Bearing this in mind, together with Calvin's theological construal of corporate worship (especially his careful understanding of the Word–sacrament relation, and his trinitarian theology

---

[60] The music–language relation is a theme explored much more thoroughly in Chs 7 and 8.

[61] The issues raised here will reappear at a number of places in this book, but especially in Ch. 8.

[62] Ford Lewis Battles, 'God Was Accommodating Himself to Human Capacity', *Interpretation* 31, 1 (1977): 19–38; Edward A. Dowey, *The Knowledge of God in Calvin's Theology* (Grand Rapids, MI: Eerdmans, 1994), 4–17; David E. Wright, 'Calvin's Accommodating God', in Wilhelm H. Neuser and Brian G. Armstrong (eds), *Calvinus Sincerioris Religionis Vindex* (Kirksville, MO: Sixteenth Century Journal Publishers, 1997), 3–19: Wright, 'Calvin's Pentateuchal Criticism'.

[63] Calvin, *Institutes of the Christian Religion*, ed. McNeill, i. 527 (ii:16:19).

[64] See Trevor Hart, 'Humankind in Christ and Christ in Humankind: Salvation as Participation in Our Substitute in the Theology of John Calvin', *Scottish Journal of Theology* 42 (1989): 67–84; Philip Walker Butin, *Revelation, Redemption, and Response: Calvin's Trinitarian Understanding of the Divine–Human Relationship* (New York: Oxford University Press, 1994), 55–94.

[65] The secondary literature on Calvin's soteriological doctrine of Scripture is vast, but see e.g. Thomas F. Torrance, 'Knowledge of God and Speech About Him According to John Calvin', in Thomas F. Torrance (ed.), *Theology in Reconstruction* (London: SCM Press, 1965), 76–98; B. A. Gerrish, *Grace and Gratitude: The Eucharistic Theology of John Calvin* (Minneapolis, MN: Fortress Press, 1993), 76–86; and for an account of the specifically trinitarian structure of Calvin's understanding of revelation in relation to Scripture, see Butin, *Revelation, Redemption, and Response*, 58–60.

of the Lord's Supper),[66] we have good reason to follow Jeffrey VanderWilt when he writes:

> The project of the psalms was but a correlative extension into music of that famous, Calvinist principle of sacramental theology, his curiously compelling interpretation of the *Sursum Corda*:
>
>> 'Therefore, lift up your hearts on high, seeking the heavenly things in heaven, where Jesus Christ is seated at the right hand of the Father; and do not fix your eyes on the visible signs which are corrupted through usage. In joy of heart, in brotherly union, come, everyone, partake of our Lord's Table, giving thanks unto him for the very great love which he has shown us. Have the death of this good Saviour graven on your hearts in eternal remembrance so that you are set afire, so also that you incite others to love God and follow his holy Word.'[67]

It is no accident that Calvin makes one of his most theologically telling comments about music in worship in a context of a resolute focus on the risen High Priest at the right hand of the Father. Discussing Hebrews 2:12, a verse in which words from Psalm 22 are put on the lips of Jesus—'I will proclaim your name to my brothers and sisters, in the midst of the congregation I will praise you'—Calvin comments, 'Christ heeds our praise, and is the chief Conductor of our hymns.'[68]

In short, for Calvin, scriptural language is integral to the way in which God draws us into union and communion with Christ through the Spirit, and thus into Christ's eternal communion with the Father. Whatever proximate meanings of the text we may celebrate in song, the ultimate semantic dimension is this dynamic (or at least least a variant on it). Thus when Calvin speaks of Psalm-singing as enhancing and enriching the experience of worship, it is implicitly the *Sursum Corda* that is in play—the lifting up of our hearts in the power of the Spirit to Jesus Christ at the right hand of the Father, who is in our midst 'conducting' our hymns.

MUSIC AND COSMOS: COMPARING CALVIN AND LUTHER

Of course, many will wish Calvin had gone much further in recognizing the powers of this most controversial of art forms. Is there not a place for giving

---

[66] See Michael S. Horton, 'Union and Communion: Calvin's Theology of Word and Sacrament', *International Journal of Systematic Theology* 11, 4 (October 2009): 398–414.

[67] VanderWilt, 'John Calvin's Theology of Liturgical Song': 77. VanderWilt is quoting *La Forme des prières et chantz ecclesiastiques*.

[68] John Calvin, *The Epistle of Paul the Apostle to the Hebrews and the First and Second Epistles of St Peter*, trans. T. H. L. Parker (Edinburgh: Oliver and Boyd, 1963), 27.

music more room for manoeuvre in worship, to exalt God in its own ways, and sometimes without the direct mediation of texts? And might the same be asked of music beyond the walls of the church? And are there not good theological grounds for pressing these questions?

The matters at stake here can be usefully opened up by comparing Calvin with his renowned predecessor, Martin Luther (1483–1546).[69] Concerning music, the contrast between the two has often been overplayed: Luther's putatively boundless enthusiasm for music of all sorts supposedly meets its opposite in Calvin's austere, restrictive, and word-fixated caution.[70] This betrays a crude, unnuanced caricature of Calvin, as well as an oversimplified view of Luther. In fact, there is much that Luther holds in common with Calvin. He too is deeply impressed by music's affective powers and its capacity for moral formation, and he too is eager to ensure appropriate music in corporate worship.

Most seriously, however, the caricature obscures what are arguably the most theologically crucial and musically determinative differences between the two Reformers. For our purposes, the most significant divergence is that Calvin seems to make no overt attempt to speak of music in terms of the grand metaphysical tradition that had imbued music theory for centuries. The notion that musical sound, especially musical harmony, coincides with and gives expression to cosmic order derives pre-eminently from the half-legendary figure of Pythagoras, finding its entry into Western literature through Book X of Plato's *Republic*, and passing into Christian music theory above all through Augustine and Boethius.[71] Yet, although Calvin was undoubtedly educated in the literature of this stream, the notion that music in some manner 'sounds' the order of the universe seems to play no substantial part in his

---

[69] The scholarly literature on Luther's approach to music is by now substantial. Studies include Paul Nettl, *Luther and Music*, trans. Frida Best and Ralph Wood (New York: Russell & Russell, 1967); Patrice Veit, *Das Kirchenlied in der Reformation Martin Luthers: Eine thematische und semantische Untersuchung* (Stuttgart: Franz Steiner Verlag, 1986); Gracia Grindal, 'Luther and the Arts: A Study in Convention', *Word and World* 3 (1983): 373–81; Jean-Denis Kraage, 'Luther: Théologien de la musique', *Études théologiques et religieuses* 58 (1983): 449–63; Carl Schalk, *Luther on Music: Paradigms of Praise* (St Louis: Concordia Publishing, 1988). See also John Barber, 'Luther and Calvin on Music and Worship', *Reformed Perspective Magazine* 8, 26 (25 June to 1 July 2006): 1–16; Hans Schwarz, 'Martin Luther and Music', *Lutheran Theological Journal* 39, 2/3 (August–December 2005): 210–17 and Dietrich Bartel, *Musica Poetica: Musical-Rhetorical Figures in German Baroque Music* (Lincoln, NE: University of Nebraska Press, 1997), 3–9.

[70] See e.g. W. E. Buszin, 'Luther on Music', *Musical Quarterly* 32 (1946): 80–97. Buszin speaks of 'Calvin's indifference, or rather hostility, to music' (80).

[71] For a concise survey of this tradition from Plato to Boethius, see Wayne D. Bowman, *Philosophical Perspectives on Music* (New York: Oxford University Press, 1998), 19–68. For its appropriation in the Middle Ages, see Calvin M. Bower, 'The Transmission of Ancient Music Theory into the Middle Ages', in Thomas Christensen (ed.), *The Cambridge History of Western Music Theory* (Cambridge: Cambridge University Press, 2002), 136–67.

reflections. In Luther, it is frequently present.[72] With regard to music in worship, he is no less practically motivated than Calvin (indeed, he was famously a skilled musician and saw music as integral to a comprehensive education). And like Calvin, he shows no interest in propounding an elaborate musical metaphysics, nor in endorsing the philosophical superstructures on which at least some of the medieval cosmic tradition depended, and he too is passionate about the importance of comprehensible language for mediating the Word of God. However, as Andreas Loewe has recently argued at length, the strong influence of the ancient cosmological tradition (in addition to more contemporary humanist theory) is pronounced,[73] and it gives Luther's comments on music a markedly different flavour from Calvin's.

Traditionally, in the late medieval university, music (*musica*) had been grouped as part of the quadrivium, one of the four mathematical arts (the other three being arithmetic, geometry, and astronomy); to be studied alongside the trivium (grammar, rhetoric, and dialectic or logic).[74] *Musica* was thus properly speaking a mathematical discipline that studied proportional relationships, and, moreover, was ineluctably tied to a perception of a unified, divinely upheld cosmos.[75] At its best, the 'music' we hear from a voice or instrument engages the unheard numerical coherence of the universe, which in turn reflects and in some manner grants access to the eternal rationality of the Creator. No less a figure than Pope Emeritus Benedict XVI draws boldly and unashamedly upon this tradition:

> The courses of the revolving planets are like melodies, the numerical order is the rhythm, and the concurrence of the individual courses is their harmony. The music made by man must . . . be taken from the inner music and order of the universe . . . The beauty of music depends on its conformity to the rhythmic

---

[72] See Robin A. Leaver, *Luther's Liturgical Music: Principles and Implications* (Grand Rapids, MI: Eerdmans, 2007); Andreas Loewe, '"Musica est Optimum": Martin Luther's Theory of Music' on *academia.edu (Melbourne College of Divinity)* [website]: <http://mcd.academia.edu/loewe/Papers/1074845/Musica_est_optimum_Martin_Luthers_Theory_of_Music>, accessed 7 July 2012. In this section, I am especially indebted to Loewe's fine and illuminating article.

[73] Loewe, '"Musica est Optimum"'.

[74] For a detailed treatment, see Joseph Dyer, 'The Place of Musica in Medieval Classifications of Knowledge', *Journal of Musicology* 24, 1 (Winter 2007): 3–71.

[75] Boethius, whose influence during the high Middle Ages was extensive, had (like Augustine) a strong love for the physical sound of music but he saw this as profoundly 'instrumental': a first step (and only a first step) towards understanding the higher, universal, unheard harmonies of the soul and the universe, which have their source in the divine realm of unchanging number. As Henry Chadwick explains, 'Arithmetic directs the mind towards immutable truths unaffected by the contingencies of time and space. But music advances even further towards that "summit of perfection" for which the quadrivium is a prerequisite. The theory of music is a penetration of the very heart of providence's ordering of things . . . a central clue to the interpretation of the hidden harmony of God and nature': Henry Chadwick, *Boethius: The Consolations of Music, Logic, Theology, and Philosophy* (Oxford: Clarendon Press, 1981), 101. See also Calvin M. Bower, 'Boethius' on *Grove Music Online* [website]: <http://www.oxfordmusiconline.com>, accessed 4 July 2012.

and harmonic laws of the universe. The more that human music adapts itself to the musical laws of the universe, the more beautiful it will be.[76]

As part of his formal education, Luther would have been made familiar with at least some forms of this venerable stream of thought and its classic treatises.[77] And by the time of his mature writings there is every sign that this tradition is still playing a key part in his thinking about music, albeit in theologically modified forms. According to Loewe, Luther 'consistently classified music in strictly quadrivial terms as part of the study of the mathematical disciplines, alongside (and possibly subordinate to) arithmetic'.[78] More than that, in Leaver's words, 'in matters concerning the expression of theology—the praise and glory of God—music takes precedence over the other disciplines of the *quadrivium*'.[79] It is no accident that in his *Preface to the Symphoniae Iucundae* (1538)[80]—written to introduce a collection of motets by a variety of composers—Luther grounds his discussion of sonorous music first and foremost in a theology of creation, and in a manner consonant with established themes in medieval music theory. He distinguishes between 'natural music' (*musica naturalis*), and composed music (*musica artificialis*)—performed by instruments, singers, or both:

---

[76] Joseph Ratzinger, *The Spirit of the Liturgy*, trans. John Saward (San Francisco: Ignatius Press, 2000), 40. Again we note—this should not be taken to imply that in medieval music there is no concern for the relation between text/word and musical sounds. See n. 53.

[77] Leaver, *Luther's Liturgical Music*, 66. See also Rebecca Wagner Oettinger, *Music as Propaganda in the German Reformation* (Aldershot: Ashgate, 2001), 41–4. Boethius would have undoubtedly been known to him. Loewe argues that Luther was especially dependent on the work of the French theorist Johannes de Muris (*c.*1290–*c.*1355), as well as the late medieval writings of Adam von Fulda, Nicolaus Wollick, and Matthäus Herbenus. Loewe, '"Musica est Optimum"', 15–16.

[78] Loewe, '"Musica est Optimum"', 11. See Martin Luther, *Luther's Works*, vol. i. *Lectures on Genesis Chapters 1–5* (Saint Louis: Concordia, 1958), 126: 'We do not marvel at the countless other gifts of creation, for we have become deaf toward what Pythagoras aptly terms this wonderful and most lovely music coming from the harmony of the motions that are in the celestial spheres. But because men continually hear this music, they become deaf to it . . . [The Fathers of the Church] did not want to be understood as though sound were given off by the motion of the celestial bodies. What they wanted to say was that their nature was most lovely and altogether miraculous, but that we ungrateful and insensible people did not notice it or give due thanks to God for the miraculous establishment and preservation of His creation.'

[79] Leaver, *Luther's Liturgical Music*, 66. Leaver goes on to quote Luther: 'This is the reason why the prophets did not make use of any [quadrivial] art except music; when setting forth their theology they did it not as geometry, not as arithmetic, not as astronomy, but as music': Leaver, *Luther's Liturgical Music*, 66. According to Loewe, 'Towards the close of the sixteenth century, music would increasingly be defined in terms of its bridge-function between the trivial and quadrivial arts, a centrality among the arts that was extolled by Luther': Loewe, '"Musica est Optimum"', 12.

[80] Luther, *Luther's Works*, liii. 321–4.

from the beginning of the world [music] has been instilled and implanted in all creatures, individually and collectively. For nothing is without sound or harmony [*numero sonoro*; 'sounding number'].[81]

By convention, natural music comprises *musica mundana*—the sounds of the non-human natural world at large;[82] *musica humana*—humanly produced vocal sound in speaking, laughing, or crying; and *musica caelestis*—the heavenly music of angels and saints, the music sung in praise of God in heaven. We can see this pattern clearly in Luther. The key point to note here, however, is that for Luther music was there *ab initio mundi*, 'instilled' in the fabric of the created world. *Musica artificialis*—composed music, of which the supreme instrument is the human voice—can only be understood in the light of *musica naturalis*; it 'corrects, develops, and expands [*corrigat, excolat et explicet*] the natural music'.[83]

A particularly interesting strand in Luther's thought about music is his belief that music can drive away the devil. This goes deeper than the thought that music can provide a valuable distraction; it is rather that as a gift of God which generates joy, music will be abhorred by Satan: 'the devil, the creator of saddening cares and disquieting worries, takes flight at the sound of music almost as he takes flight at the word of theology'.[84]

> There cannot be an evil mood
> Where there are singing fellows good,
> There is no envy, hate, nor ire,
> Gone are through me all sorrows dire;
> Greed, care, and lonely heaviness
> No more do they the heart oppress.[85]

Music, it would seem, is *enacting an order* that by its very nature stands against evil—a moral order, in other words. It is not surprising to find Luther insisting that music be a major part of a child's education. Leaver notes a marked connection between music and peace for the Reformer, both civil and theological; music 'rules in times of peace'.[86] Consonant with this are some of Luther's observations on the opening chapters of Genesis, highlighted in an interesting article by Brian Horne.[87] According to Horne, Luther sees the

---

[81] Luther, *Luther's Works*, liii. 322.
[82] 'Even the air, which of itself is invisible and imperceptible to all our senses, and which, since it lacks both voice and speech, is the least musical of all things, becomes sonorous, audible, and comprehensible when it is set in motion...Music is still more wonderful in living things, especially birds...'. Luther, *Luther's Works*, liii. 322.
[83] Luther, *Luther's Works*, liii. 324. This translation renders *explicet* as 'refines'; but 'expands' or 'expounds' is almost certainly more appropriate.
[84] Letter to Ludwig Senfl, as translated and quoted in Leaver, *Luther's Liturgical Music*, 93.
[85] Luther, *Luther's Works*, liii. 319–20.
[86] Leaver, *Luther's Liturgical Music*, 95–7.
[87] Brian L. Horne, 'A Civitas of Sound: On Luther and Music', *Theology* 88 (1985): 21–8.

creation of the world's order as a revelation of order in the life and purpose of God himself: 'the entirely non-figurative, non-representational, non-verbal world of sound in which every note and rhythm finds its proper place in the whole, and is indispensable to the whole, was not only a sign of the possibility of order, but was an actual achievement of that order, a sure indication of the stability of God in a shifting and unstable world'.[88] Music, the most intensely formal of the arts, the most removed from self-expression, and thus the most dissociated from the untidiness and messiness of human life, by virtue of its embedding in cosmic order possesses a remarkable power to hold the forces of sin and chaos at bay, to remind us of the fundamental stability God has conferred upon the world. Music is a means, granted by God, through which we are given to share in and enjoy the world's God-given coherence.[89]

We must be careful not to read too much into scattered remarks and reflections, but it does appear that Luther is adopting a perspective on music that places a very considerable weight on sonorous music-making engaging with, deriving from, and even participating in a musical matrix that has already been provided in and with, the created world. Luther's stress on music as gift, as *donum Dei*,[90] seems to carry this strong sense of the contingency of human music-making on this prior generosity of the Creator God.[91] As far as Calvin is concerned, though he can certainly claim that music is God's gift to humankind, it is striking that the notion of a prior *musica naturalis* does not seem to play a noticeable part in his reflections on music's nature or purpose.

It is perhaps no surprise, then, to find Luther much more relaxed than Calvin about musical instruments. Indeed, instruments are welcomed into the worship sanctuary: 'Christian musicians should let their singing and playing to the praise of the Father of all grace sound forth with joy from their organs, symphonias, virginals, regals, and whatever other beloved instruments there are (recently invented and given by God), of which neither David nor

---

[88] Horne, 'A Civitas of Sound': 27.

[89] This is not to imply that music for Luther has the status of one of the 'orders of creation', in his fairly restricted sense (*Stiffte* or *Hierarchien*), i.e. structures (Church, home) that order and make divine–human and human–human relationships possible. Nor is it one of the 'orders of preservation' that have been given solely as a consequence of the fall. I am grateful to Dr Mickey Mattox for pointing this out to me.

[90] Leaver, *Luther's Liturgical Music*, 70.

[91] It is telling that in lectures Luther delivered on Genesis, in commenting on Genesis 4:21— '[Jabal's] brother's name was Jubal; he was the ancestor of all those who play the lyre and pipe'— he is completely silent on the second part of the verse. Unlike many commentators before him, he does not trace the origin of music itself to Jubal: Leaver, *Luther's Liturgical Music*, 67–70. Leaver explains: 'the question of the origin of music cannot be answered simply in terms of history, chronology, or human progenitors; indeed, the question cannot be understood, let alone answered, without recourse to theology, since music per se was not invented by humans but rather created by God': Leaver, *Luther's Liturgical Music*, 70.

Solomon, neither Persia, Greece, nor Rome, knew anything.'[92] Unlike Calvin, Luther was quite prepared to include polyphony in the praise of God. Indeed, Luther can revel in the polyphony of his day:

> it is most remarkable that one single voice continues to sing the tenor [the principal melody within medieval counterpoint], while at the same time many other voices play around it, exulting and adorning it in exuberant strains and, as it were, leading it forth in a divine roundelay, so that those who are the least bit moved know nothing more amazing in this world.[93]

He regarded the music of heaven as a perfect form of polyphony, and earthly musical praise as a kind of bridge between *musica humana* and *musica caelestis*: 'Whenever human beings used their voice to sing God's praises, *musica humana* and *musica caelestis* [are] conjoined.'[94]

Of a piece with this, Luther appears less anxious about the negative potential of music than Calvin, its proneness to misuse and abuse. Although he was far from carefree about the kind of music to be employed in worship, more cautious than is often thought about employing 'secular' music,[95] and certainly very aware of the danger of exploiting music for sinful ends,[96] he seems far more impressed by the capacity of music to help free us from the bondage of evil than its capacity to entrap us in it.

None of this generous enthusiasm for music should be taken as suggesting a weak commitment on Luther's part to the priority of Scripture or to the need for the specific and focused Word of the Gospel, written and preached. After all, the ability to see music *as* a good gift of creation and use it appropriately presupposes the faith that comes through responding to Jesus Christ, and this happens through hearing the life-changing *kerygma* of the Gospel. And there is little doubt Luther was influenced by late medieval humanist writers, who, like Calvin, saw music as a rhetorical tool, able to intensify the affective potency of a text.[97] For Luther, 'music had its highest purpose when it was joined with God's Word for the proclamation of the Gospel'.[98] Luther's

---

[92] As in Leaver, *Luther's Liturgical Music*, 70.

[93] Luther, *Luther's Works*, liii. 324.

[94] Loewe, '"Musica est Optimum"', 39.

[95] Begbie, *Resounding Truth*, 104–5.

[96] 'Take special care to shun perverted minds who prostitute this lovely gift of nature and of art with their erotic rantings; and be quite assured that none but the devil goads them on to defy their very nature which would and should praise God its Maker with this gift, so that these bastards purloin the gift of God and use it to worship the foe of God, the enemy of nature and of this lovely art': Luther, *Luther's Works*, liii. 324.

[97] In this connection, Loewe highlights themes in the writing of Matthäus Herbenus (1451–1538) that are plainly evident in Luther: Loewe, '"Musica est Optimum"', esp. 16–20 and 27–43.

[98] Christopher Boyd Brown, 'Devotional Life in Hymns, Liturgy, Music, and Prayer', in Robert Kolb (ed), *Lutheran Ecclesiastical Culture, 1550–1675* (Leiden: Brill, 2008), 205–58, 214. There has been much discussion of the extent to which Luther believes music *itself* could be regarded *as* a

appropriation of the medieval outlook is thus undoubtedly 'humanized' and practically oriented, not speculative.[99] Nevertheless, the clear signs are that music's powers vis-à-vis language are being set within a wider, cosmological context. Musical sound bears theological witness in its own right by virtue of its embeddedness in cosmic order, even without being directly or immediately attached to text or speech.

In short, and at the risk of drastically oversimplifying, the evidence would seem to indicate that for Luther, music finds its most immediate theological context in the doctrine of creation, whereas for Calvin it is found in anthropology. To propose this, however, is not to imply that Calvin's theology of creation plays no part in the shaping of his understanding of music. He shows every sign of regarding music in the light of strongly held convictions about the Creator–creature distinction. Indeed, the difference between him and Luther on this matter is wholly consistent with their differing estimations of music. Calvin generally operates with a more pointed accent on the indissoluble otherness of the Creator, the primacy and freedom of God's agency, and the irreducible integrity of all that is finite and creaturely. As some have surmised, *finitum non est capax infiniti* stands as something of a watchword over his theology.[100] This accounts for significant divergences between him and Luther in various theological *loci*, including the interrelation of divine and human in Christ, and the way Christ's eucharistic presence is conceived. So we find Calvin a good deal more circumspect than Luther about ascribing powers to music per se, lest this might detract from the prior and utterly free action of God. Compare the way the two theologians read the story in 1 Samuel 16, where David plays his lyre to comfort Saul (vs. 23: 'and the evil spirit would depart from him'). Luther claims that music does more than calm Saul; it 'serves to cast out Satan, the instigator of all sins'[101]—a view a good deal more daring than many of his predecessors.[102] In Calvin's eyes, music may have soothed Saul but *God* drove out the spirit. Saul 'had indeed been revived

---

form of preaching. See Joyce L. Irwin, '"So Faith Comes from What Is Heard": The Relationship Between Music and God's Word in the First Two Centuries of German Lutheranism', in Jeremy S. Begbie and Steven R. Guthrie (eds), *Resonant Witness: Conversations Between Music and Theology* (Grand Rapids, MI: Eerdmans, 2011), 65–82; Leaver, *Luther's Liturgical Music*, 282–8; Brown, 'Devotional Life', 214–19.

[99] Bartel, *Musica Poetica*, 27–8.

[100] Carlos Eire notes that the two most common phrases used to sum up Calvin's theology of worship are *soli Deo gloria* and *finitum non est capax infiniti*: Carlos M. N. Eire, *War Against the Idols: The Reformation of Worship from Erasmus to Calvin* (Cambridge: Cambridge University Press, 1986), 197.

[101] Luther, *Luther's Works*, liii. 323.

[102] Loewe describes Luther's reading as marking 'a sea change in humanist interpretation': Loewe, '"Musica est Optimum"', 37.

by David's harp, but by the Lord's doing, and by his instilling of that power within it'.[103]

WIDER MOVEMENTS AND QUESTIONS

It is time to step back a little and take stock. We have seen enough to show that Calvin's appraisal of music is one weighted heavily towards anthropology, regarding it more as a humanly grounded practice than one whose materiality and rationale is integrally embedded in the order of the physical world at large. Along with this, music is incorporated into a theological vista that gives a focal and prominent place to the written and spoken word. Music requires the presence of language. In order that there may be proper understanding, music used in congregational worship needs to be yoked to the kind of clear articulation that only language can provide. To be more specific, God-given scriptural language is mandatory: only biblical texts are to be sung, and none will be better suited than the Psalms. They will ensure that the heart is properly oriented and at the same time curb music's potentially negative effects. Properly deployed, music can evoke a 'mood' (as we might say today) appropriate to the God of the Psalms, as well as promote an appropriate affective response of the heart. In these ways the congregation is edified.

Though he shares much common ground with Luther, the distinct lack of any stress in Calvin on music resonating with the created order marks a decisive step away from the earlier Reformer, and not only from Luther but from most of the leading streams of music theory in the medieval era. Calvin is certainly not alone. The change we have detected in comparing Luther to Calvin is not simply a local ecclesiastical idiosyncrasy, but indicative of what is widely recognized as a major shift of perspective between the late medieval and early modern eras regarding music, which in turn relates to much wider changes in intellectual and cultural life.

Again to speak in very broad terms and oversimplify, for a variety of reasons the sixteenth century witnessed among many a gradual erosion of confidence in the grand cosmic perspective that in one form or another had sustained music theory for hundreds of years, and by the time we reach the early eighteenth century, it was largely abandoned except as a literary trope. The sounds of music became more and more the object of empirical investigation, according to the canons and methodological rigour of the fast-developing

---

[103] John Calvin, Sermon on 1 Samuel 16; trans. Dona McCullagh. John Calvin, 'Homiliae in primum librum Samuelis Cap. XIII–XXXI': Homilia LIX, in Guilielmus Baum, Eduard Cunitz, and Eduard Reuss (eds), *Ioannis Calvini Opera Quae Supersunt Omnia*, vol. xxx (Brunswick: C. A. Schwetschke, 1886), 171–84, 183.

natural sciences. The ancient and venerable theories of number struggled to account adequately for the materials of sound, and for the kinds of music that were emerging at the time—especially virtuosic instrumental music. Developments in keyboard music led to new methods of tuning that did not obviously match up to the supposedly 'perfect' numbers of former years.[104] Musical sounds were forced to find new grounds of validity—fresh solidities to underwrite their rationality and 'meaningfulness'.

Various strategies for dealing with instrumental music's waywardness were offered. By far the most common way of giving music semantic respectability was to subsume it in some manner under the order of spoken and written language. Thus, for example, we find the matter of text 'underlay' (the alignment of notes and syllables) becoming a particularly live issue in the early sixteenth century. To be sure, medieval composers were not unconcerned or careless about the relation of music and texts/words, or about the anthropological dimensions of music.[105] But with the Renaissance in particular, distinctive types and expressions of that relation certainly become a matter of major concern among theorists.

Sounds on their own, we might say, seem to have no capacity for signification. But that is just what language can provide. So it was instrumental music that proved the perennially awkward challenge to music theorists of early modernity—a problem that comes to the fore in Calvin. At least the vocal music of church and cathedral had words to anchor it in extra-musical reality, giving its tones something to designate, a stability of reference and thus a measure of legitimacy. But not the violin concerto, the keyboard solo, the concerti grossi—music without words. Hence among many writers instrumental music comes to be construed as something radically different from, and potentially inferior to, vocal music. Not surprisingly, some went to great lengths to demonstrate that instrumental music was an elaborate form of speech—using quasi-rhetorical devices that correspond to particular passions, for example.[106] In various strands of early Enlightenment thought, the problem of stabilizing instrumental music was answered in terms of physics and physiology.[107] What was once explained in terms of an integrally theological metaphysics could now be accounted for, some believed, by employing the categories of a rapidly burgeoning Newtonian science. This gave rise to a number of elaborate explanations of the effects of music on the body and,

---

[104] Stuart Isacoff, *Temperament: How Music Became a Battleground for the Great Minds of Western Civilization* (New York: Alfred A. Knopf, 2001); Rudolf Rasch, 'Tuning and Temperament', in Thomas Street Christensen (ed.), *The Cambridge History of Western Music Theory* (Cambridge: Cambridge University Press, 2002), 193–222.

[105] See n. 53.

[106] Bartel, *Musica Poetica*.

[107] Jean-Philippe Rameau's work is probably the most obvious example. See 'Rameau and the 'Natural'' (pp. 76–81) in this volume.

through the body, on the passions—a process typically conceived as deploying structural models borrowed from representative language. But without an ontology (or, we might say, a doctrine of creation) of sufficient depth and subtlety to embrace and integrate the human and extra-human, vocal and instrumental, it is not surprising that such attempts were widely regarded as highly strained and artificial, and were to have a relatively short shelf-life.[108]

The burgeoning of instrumental music in the seventeenth and eighteenth centuries and the development of its new auditorium, the concert hall; the development of the concept that was eventually to be dubbed 'absolute music'; the prominence of the notion of a 'work' encoded supremely in a score, and supposedly free of any 'external' connections: all of these are elements in a complex and many-stranded narrative that has been described as 'the emancipation of music from language'.[109] In this light, the eventual near-divinization of 'pure' music by the early Romantics can usefully be read as an audacious attempt to recover something of the gleam of the long-disappeared medieval vision.[110]

The Church, needless to say, was caught up in these currents and cross-currents of discourse long after Calvin had departed this life. A suspicion of instrumental music was reiterated in much Reformation and post-Reformation writing, and debates were to rage over the relative value of vocal and instrumental music. In the Lutheran churches, we find a series of often fierce and polarized disputes about the relation of music to cosmos, music to words, music to the passions, instrumental to vocal music, the judgement of theory to the judgement of the ear—disputes that bear more than a passing resemblance to the so-called 'worship wars' that have become so familiar in some sectors of the contemporary Church.[111]

---

[108] For treatments of the movements and developments we have traced in this section, see e.g. John Hollander, *The Untuning of the Sky: Ideas of Music in English Poetry, 1500–1700* (New York: W. W. Norton & Co., 1970); John Neubauer, *The Emancipation of Music from Language: Departure from Mimesis in Eighteenth-Century Aesthetics* (New Haven: Yale University Press, 1986); Daniel K. A. Chua, *Absolute Music* and the Construction of Meaning (Cambridge: Cambridge University Press, 1999), esp. chs 1–11; Daniel K. L. Chua, 'Vincenzo Galilei, Modernity and the Division of Nature', in Suzannah Clark and Alexander Rehding (eds), *Music Theory and the Natural Order from the Renaissance to the Early Twentieth Century* (Cambridge: Cambridge University Press, 2001), 17–29; Downing A. Thomas, *Music and the Origins of Language: Theories from the French Enlightenment* (Cambridge: Cambridge University Press, 1995); Suzannah Clark and Alexander Rehding, *Music Theory and Natural Order from the Renaissance to the Early Twentieth Century* (Cambridge: Cambridge University Press, 2001).

[109] Neubauer, *The Emancipation of Music*. For further discussion, see John Butt, 'The Seventeenth-Century Musical "Work"', in Tim Carter and John Butt (eds), *The Cambridge History of Seventeenth-Century Music* (Cambridge: Cambridge University Press, 2005), 27–54.

[110] See Chapter 5 (pp. 106–40) in this volume.

[111] See Joyce L. Irwin, *Neither Voice Nor Heart Alone: German Lutheran Theology of Music in the Age of the Baroque* (New York: Peter Lang, 1993); Joseph Herl, *Worship Wars in Early Lutheranism* (Oxford: Oxford University Press, 2004).

The still wider canvas against which these arguments were played out—the emergence and development of characteristically modern ontologies amidst the weakening of the medieval 'synthesis'—has received huge attention from intellectual and cultural historians. The so-called 'disenchantment' of the world and associated patterns of 'secularization' are not matters we can rehearse in detail here, but such phenomena are obviously implicated.[112] In the light of what we have uncovered in this chapter, students of this literature will surely recognize that the practices of music—including discourses about music—bear their own distinctive testimony to the theological factors bound up with these upheavals.

Returning to Geneva

We have veered away from Calvin, if only to widen our theological and cultural vantage point. In closing, however, it is worth returning to this remarkable figure to offer some final reflections.

In the first place, in urging that Calvin be situated against these wider movements of engagement with music, we are emphatically not suggesting he was a prisoner of his culture, or a singular or major 'cause' of the developments we have sketched. He can, however, be seen as representative figure, signalling a crucial turn in early modern theological evaluations of music. The precise lines of influence between him and his complex musical surroundings would require far more detailed scholarly attention than is possible here. Second, it is to Calvin's credit that at an early stage of his career he recognized that music had powers denied to language, and that he sanctioned a practice that tacitly acknowledged the irreducible differences between the two media, a practice that not only permitted but encouraged music to spread its own wings, even at the expense of certain 'natural' features of texts, albeit *while* strongly urging a strenuous faithfulness to Scripture. It is always worth recalling that Calvin's (albeit overplayed) caution about music arises from his vigorous respect for its peculiar eloquences—he has a *high*, not a low, view of music.

Having said that, and this is the third reflection, it is hard not to be disappointed that Calvin did not engage at least some strands of the medieval cosmological outlook on music that Luther drew on so readily. Of course, we need to be extremely wary of assuming that there was ever a single and secure monolithic 'medieval synthesis', and perhaps even more wary of succumbing

---

[112] The literature is legion; see e.g. Brad S. Gregory, *The Unintended Reformation: How a Religious Revolution Secularized Society* (Cambridge, MA: Belknap Press of Harvard University Press, 2012); Charles Taylor, *A Secular Age* (Cambridge, MA: Harvard University Press, 2007); Amos Funkenstein, *Theology and the Scientific Imagination: From the Middle Ages to the Seventeenth Century* (Princeton: Princeton University Press, 1986).

to a nostalgic and uncritical idealization of it. And in any case, there are vastly different theological ontologies that can be called upon to ground the validity and *raison d'être* of music, and the reasons behind early modernity's relinquishment of this overall perspective need to be taken seriously. But arguably, Calvin's interpretation of the word–music relation aligns rather too closely with those in early modernity who, in relinquishing one type of doctrine of creation, find themselves unable, albeit for understandable reasons, to set music within a viable and fruitful alternative theological scenario, and explore the myriad of musical possibilities that God's Spirit might release through human engagement with created materiality. Calvin's constant reiteration of the rhetoric of conformity (music must conform to words), without locating music clearly within a theological ontology of creation, runs the risk of driving music into a functionalism in which the links between music and the natural order are bypassed in favour of the 'efficient utility'[113] of its sounds, directly harnessed to particular words.

The irony here is that Calvin is famous for offering a rich and resplendent—indeed opulent—evocation of the universe as the 'theatre of God's glory', in which created reality is regarded as possessing its own differentiated contingent order, bestowed and sustained by God, inviting a variety of quite distinct modes of human engagement. It is a portrayal that has proved extraordinarily persuasive and fruitful, far beyond Calvinist and Reformed circles, and not least recently among those eager to promote a full-blooded participation of Christians in the arts. Elaborated carefully, such an outlook, with its stress on humans indwelling a diversely structured environment as social, embodied creatures, opens up the possibility of doing justice *both* to the immense capacities of language to engage fruitfully with the world we inhabit, *and* to a recognition that the created world possesses a rationality not wholly transparent to the ordering power of language—thus readily accommodating a practice such as music. In other words, Calvin's theology of creation can in many respects point the way to an integrated and biblical 'imaginary' of the sort that can challenge the assumed split between music and word that has generated so many difficulties in modernity.

Of course, dissatisfied as we might be with some aspects of Calvin's own approach to music, we must nonetheless always bear in mind his motivations and leading concerns, insofar as we can properly discern them. Julie Canlis, among others, has argued that his vision of creation as a whole is characterized by a marked emphasis on Christ as Mediator of creation, and on the Spirit as the one who enables and affirms creation's particularity as it is borne forward towards its eschatological consummation.[114] This gives Calvin a strong sense of the primacy of God's commitment to creation, in which God's active

---

[113] Chua, *Absolute Music*, 24.
[114] For a lucid exposition, see J. Canlis, *Calvin's Ladder: A Spiritual Theology of Ascent and Ascension* (Grand Rapids, MI: Eerdmans, 2010), ch. 2.

presence and creation's irreducible particularity are not opposed in some kind of zero-sum balance, but both wholly affirmed—something we have already touched upon. His heavy and much-cited accent on human finitude should not be read as a diminution of the creature, nor as a way of positing a gulf between God and the world, but as a way of honouring Christ's mediatorship of all finite things, and thus the Creator–creature distinction that is a prerequisite for true and full fellowship. Idolatry destroys such fellowship. As far as his approach to music is concerned, then, the absence of a fuller cosmological dimension may to some extent be a function of his belief that humans do not possess in themselves the capacity to read creation aright, that they are repeatedly tending to idolatry. Nevertheless, for Calvin the core tragedy of idolatry is that it entails a denial of God's presence, and with it a refusal to live *as creatures*, to live in humility and gratitude *coram Deo*. Calvin's repeated assault on idolatry is not driven by a concern to *distance* God *from* created reality (in a kind of abstract transcendence, as if creaturely reality was intrinsically fallen), but by a concern to restore a proper understanding of creation's relatedness *to* God.

Bringing this to a head, we close by asking: whatever he said specifically about music, could the theological trajectories we have discerned in Calvin be drawn out and carried forward in order to testify more fully to a unity of all things *prior* to word and music, which can both undergird their commonality *and* sustain their difference? That, I suggest, is the most intriguing—and demanding—question to arise from our encounter with this ever-absorbing Reformer.

3

Disquieting Conversations: Bach, Modernity, and God[1]

There are few figures in the story of music more theologically compelling than Johann Sebastian Bach (1685–1750). Yet for all that they might love his music, theologians have generally been reluctant to engage him with the specific resources of their own disciplines—and this despite the fact that the last two decades have seen musicologists in the secular academy who are not daunted by theology, who show a willingness to explore the specifically Christian dimensions of Bach and his output with scholarly seriousness.[2] From their point of view, the theologian appears to be welcome to sit at the table of the cognoscenti, to contribute as well as learn.

It would be odd not to respond. Indeed, there is much to suggest that the time is ripe for a new and rewarding conversation between theologians and musicians regarding this stupendously gifted craftsman of sound. This chapter

---

[1] This chapter conflates material, with revisions, from two earlier pieces: Jeremy S. Begbie, 'Time and Eternity: Richard Bauckham and the Fifth Evangelist', in Jonathan T. Pennington and Grant Macaskill (eds), 'In The Fullness of Time . . .': A Festschrift for Professor Richard Bauckham (forthcoming), and Jeremy S. Begbie, 'Pressing at the Boundaries of Modernity: A Review Essay on Bach's Dialogue with Modernity: Perspectives on the Passions by John Butt (CUP, 2010)', Christian Scholar's Review 40, 4 (Summer 2011): 453–65.

[2] See e.g. John Butt, 'Bach's Metaphysics of Music', in John Butt (ed.), The Cambridge Companion to Bach (Cambridge: Cambridge University Press, 1997), 46–71; Robin A. Leaver, 'Eschatology, Theology and Music: Death and Beyond in Bach's Vocal Music', in Anne Leahy and Yo Tomita (eds), Bach Studies from Dublin (Dublin: Four Courts Press, 2004), 129–47; Peter Smaill, 'Bach Among the Heretics: Inferences from the Cantata Texts', Understanding Bach 4 (2009): 101–18; Michael Marissen, 'The Theological Character of J. S. Bach's Musical Offering', in Daniel R. Melamed (ed.), Bach Studies 2 (Cambridge: Cambridge University Press, 1995), 85–106; Michael Marissen, The Social and Religious Designs of J. S. Bach's Brandenburg Concertos (Princeton: Princeton University Press, 1995); Eric T. Chafe, Tonal Allegory in the Vocal Music of J. S. Bach (Berkeley and Los Angeles: University of California Press, 1991); Eric T. Chafe, Analyzing Bach Cantatas (Oxford: Oxford University Press, 2000). New perspectives have been opening up in Bach studies in recent years, such that methods and issues traditionally thought to be outside the musicologist's purview are now discussed extensively—literary theory, metaphysics, moral philosophy, the history of ideas, the philosophy of art, and so forth. See Butt, 'Introduction', 1–2.

is a contribution to that end. Specifically, I will consider two of the finest and most stimulating studies of Bach currently available: John Butt's *Bach's Dialogue with Modernity*[3] and Karol Berger's *Bach's Cycle, Mozart's Arrow*.[4] Both come from distinguished musicologists who enter theological territory in a way that invites close and sustained attention. I want to engage them in a constructive (though critical) conversation, not only with respect to our main concerns in this book—Bach and theology in the context of an emerging modernity—but also with an eye to what we can learn more widely about how theologians and musicologists might go about their respective tasks in a late modern context. I will suggest that this music, understood in its time, rebounds on both the musicologist and the theologian in unexpected ways, making Bach a rather more disturbing figure than we might perhaps first imagine.

I have chosen to focus on three main *loci* raised by these studies, of considerable consequence to any with theological interests in the development of modernity: subjectivity and creativity, order and openness, and time and eternity.

Beginning with John Butt: this scholar's particular interest is in the features of Bach's music that seem to 'transcend' its time and place. However disturbed we might be by the chastening winds of postmodern academe, with its suspicion of any such notion as a 'classic', there do seem to be cultural texts that have a remarkable capacity to persist in their witness far beyond their time and place, and touch highly diverse social and cultural groups over the course of centuries. In what sense or senses might Bach's music have 'transcendent' significance within modernity? Butt regards 'modernity' to be primarily a mindset or cluster of mindsets associated with the culture of what is loosely called the 'Modern Age'—which include a vision of 'disembedded' humans in a 'disenchanted' universe; the accessibility and adaptability of the natural world through human reason, yielding potentially unlimited knowledge; the privatization of religion; specific and autonomous zones of knowledge; directional change and progress; the independent, individual self, wary of an unthinking reliance on past tradition.[5] While by no means uncritical of these attitudes, he is also distrustful of wholesale rejections of modernity: 'One of the most pernicious pieties of some self-proclaimed postmodernists is the assumption that everything within modernity necessarily points towards an ordered regulation of obedient, individualist subjects,

---

[3] John Butt, *Bach's Dialogue with Modernity: Perspectives on the Passions* (Cambridge: Cambridge University Press, 2010).

[4] Karol Berger, *Bach's Cycle, Mozart's Arrow: An Essay on the Origins of Musical Modernity* (Berkeley and Los Angeles: University of California Press, 2007).

[5] Butt, *Bach's Dialogue*, 20–1.

always on the brink of some new Auschwitz.'[6] He is also careful to acknowledge the entanglement of Reformation Christianity with some of modernity's dynamics.[7]

Butt's study concentrates on the St Matthew and St John Passions, particularly the musical procedures and strategies that give Bach a power and relevance far beyond his own time. The resultant picture is of Bach as a composer whose music spans both pre-modern and modern sensibilities. Indeed, Butt thinks Bach's ability to take and reconfigure elements of the pre-modern is itself an example of a process central and integral to the mindset of modernity.[8] He can thus speak of 'the productive tension between pre-modern and modern elements',[9] and, further, of Bach exercising a kind of 'prior corrective' to modernity's worst aspects.[10]

SUBJECTIVITY AND CREATIVITY

Butt's approach is thematic: he examines various strands he believes to be central to modernity and invites us to hear Bach's Passion music with these in view. Subjectivity is one such strand. Basic to modernity, Butt believes, is a proneness to conceive the self as an essentially disembodied centre of individual consciousness, a tendency in part birthed by the Reformation. Even the novice to Bach's Passions cannot help but notice how strongly they are geared towards the individual believer, something especially evident in the solo arias, where the singer stands not in the time and place of the historical narrative but very much in our present time, our world, drawing us into the drama so that each of us can make our own response. Butt relates this to 'emergent modern subjectivities' in Bach's era, noting a growing emphasis on self-discipline and self-construction, along with a conception of the self as a unique entity awaiting discovery. At the political level, this finds expression in the notion of the absolute monarch authorized by his subjects (Butt cites Thomas Hobbes in this connection), subjects who secure their autonomy through obedience to the ruler. At the individual level, Butt cites Lutheranism's stress on the believer's 'responsibility to cultivate faith internally as the means towards

---

[6] Butt, *Bach's Dialogue*, 20–1.

[7] Butt, *Bach's Dialogue*, 20–1.

[8] 'I associate this sense of a continually circulating process (i.e. nothing is absolutely fixed, nothing stands still, least of all in this type of music) with the modern.' Butt, *Bach's Dialogue*, 35. 'What is most valuable about the modern condition', he says, is 'the way it generates new opportunities through the combination and inflection of diverse elements and perspectives— an attitude of permanent dialogue': Butt, *Bach's Dialogue*, 35.

[9] Butt, *Bach's Dialogue*, 26.

[10] Butt, *Bach's Dialogue*, 35.

salvation, without the external apparatus of traditional sacramental practice',[11] something especially clear in the disciplined patterns of devotion and behaviour enjoined by Lutheran Pietism. Butt approaches the Bach Passions with these factors in mind. In the process of performance, he suggests, for example, that Jesus could well have been construed as something akin to a ruler authorized from below by his followers. The music given to the individuals who surround him—who sing arias and the dialogues, and who occupy *our* time—presents nothing less than the temporal construction of subjectivities. Music, he reminds us, 'can not only represent a sense of consciousness . . . it can also demonstrate how subjectivity can be developed and altered over time'.[12] More theologically, the music in effect invites us to share in these individuals' developing experience so that our own emotions and commitments can be transformed, in line with the Lutheran commitment to 'the responsibility placed on the individual believer to achieve union with Christ for ultimate salvation'.[13]

Especially telling is the way in which Butt relates this to broader, cosmological vistas. In early modernity, the 'inward turn' of the human self is concomitant with a loss of confidence in the wider order of things, in the cosmos being our intended 'home'.[14] Butt, following Charles Taylor and others, makes much of the conceptual shift to be found in many cultural fields: from a stress on living according to a pre-existing order external to the self, in relation to which we discover our position and vocation, towards a stress on the order that we construct or is internally discovered within our minds. Given the breakdown of pre-modern assumptions about universal 'resemblances' between the particulars of creation, a comprehensive interconnectedness of all things, together with the need for humans, inasmuch as they are conceived as distinct from their physical environment, to maintain a sense of coherence in an increasingly uncertain natural world, we find the realm of the 'artificial'—what we make—increasingly distanced from the cosmic, 'given' order. Butt suggests that the burgeoning fascination with musical forms

---

[11] Butt, *Bach's Dialogue*, 38. Butt speaks of 'the early modern Protestant tendency to define oneself through a direct relationship with Christ through faith, and developing a sense of personhood through a sense of individual autonomy': Butt, *Bach's Dialogue*, 56. It has been argued that the Protestant stress on freeing oneself from (certain) inherited traditions paradoxically encouraged the notion of the self as possessing godlike status—riding above time and history, enclosed in its own privacy, and possessing the ability to read and interpret Scripture without the mediation of ecclesiastical authority. For a highly polemical version of this and related arguments, see Graham Ward, 'The Future of Protestantism: Postmodernity', in Alister E. McGrath and Darren C. Marks (eds), *The Blackwell Companion to Protestantism* (Oxford: Blackwell Publishing, 2006), 453–67.

[12] Butt, *Bach's Dialogue*, 93.

[13] Butt, *Bach's Dialogue*, 43. The language of achievement here is unfortunate, given Lutheranism's stress on *sola gratia*.

[14] See 'Wider Movements and Questions' (pp. 35–8) in this volume.

and structures we witness in the decades preceding Bach could be read 'as a *compensation* for the severing of any assumed continuity with natural order'.[15] Relevant also is Bach's exploration of remote keys as part of the relatively new tonal system, which involved substantial adjustments to the 'natural' harmonic series, something impossible with the older tuning of fixed-pitch instruments. It is as if, says Butt, music is answering to the need for a 'surrogate order'.[16]

In this respect, Bach appears to encompass both pre-modern and modern. On the one hand, Butt points to what was almost certainly Bach's own attitude to music and cosmic order—the ancient and well-rooted pre-modern outlook, held by many Lutherans of the time (albeit in some respects philosophically and theologically distinct from its medieval antecedents), that music is, or ought to be, a respectful engagement with a God-given order embedded in the physical world at large.[17] And the 'subject'—in this case the composer—must

---

[15] Butt, *Bach's Dialogue*, 39. Italics original.

[16] Butt, *Bach's Dialogue*, 39.

[17] See 'Music and Cosmos: Comparing Calvin and Luther' (pp. 27–35) in this volume. See also John Butt, *Music Education and the Art of Performance in the German Baroque* (Cambridge: Cambridge University Press, 1994), 39–41; Christoph Wolff, *Johann Sebastian Bach: The Learned Musician* (New York: W. W. Norton & Co., 2000), 1–11. There is a much-quoted saying attributed to Bach about the 'thorough bass' (a foundational bass line with accompanying chords, very common in baroque music), which relates this device to the God-given created order. In another place, Butt calls this a 'late flowering of the Pythagorean view of well-composed music as natural harmony' (Butt, 'Bach's Metaphysics of Music', 46–71, 54). See Johann Sebastian Bach, *J. S. Bach's Precepts and Principles for Playing the Thorough Bass or Accompanying in Four Parts*, trans. Pamela L. Poulin (Oxford: Clarendon Press, 1994), 10–11. Relevant also is the witness of Bach's supporter, J. A. Birnbaum. Defending Bach's music in response to a criticism that it leads us 'away from the natural to the artificial', and likely reflecting the views of the composer himself, Birnbaum appeals to 'the eternal rules of music' and speaks of polyphonous music as an exemplar of the unity and diversity pervading the cosmos (Butt, 'Bach's Metaphysics of Music', 55–9). Wolff, *The Learned Musician*, 5–6. (The Birnbaum document suggests, however, that nature was sometimes *lacking* beauty, something that does not seem to trouble Wolff.) In 1747, Bach joined a learned group, the Corresponding Society of the Musical Sciences, one of whose members could write: 'God is a harmonic being. All harmony originates from his wise order and organisation . . . Where there is no conformity, there is also no order, no beauty, and no perfection. For beauty and perfection consist in the conformity of diversity' (as quoted in Wolff, *The Learned Musician*, 466). During his last years, Bach wrote music that would seem to be highly consonant with the theories current in this circle, especially the notion of music as 'sounding mathematics'—e.g., the *Canonic Variations on 'Vom Himmel hoch da komm ich her'* and most famously, the *Art of Fugue* (Malcolm Boyd, *Bach* (Oxford: Oxford University Press, 2000), 205–6).

With all this in mind, some have tried to align Bach's vision closely with some of the rationalist cosmologies of the German Enlightenment. However, Laurence Dreyfus argues that this kind of proposal pays insufficient attention to the role of human agency in Bach's practice. See Laurence Dreyfus, *Bach and the Patterns of Invention* (Cambridge, MA: Harvard University Press, 1996), 26–7; ch. 8. We cannot enter the complexities of these issues here; I can only register that I find arguments that Bach would have leaned heavily on thinkers such as G. W. Leibniz and Christian Wolff speculative and unconvincing, however commonplace the ideas of harmony, unity, natural laws, and the like might have been in some of Bach's circles. Leisinger comments that 'no documentary evidence can be presented that Johann Sebastian Bach ever possessed or read any

understand his divinely ordained vocation against this background. He is the self-effacing servant, with a God-given obligation to be faithful to the materials he is given. On the other hand, Butt contends that Bach's sense of vocation and dedication to his task as a musician was of a virtually unprecedented intensity, and that 'However much Bach may have believed in the natural order to which harmony pointed, his music contains a level of constructedness that is unparalleled for its time',[18] suggesting a more modern accent on the immense and impressive possibilities of human making. Butt believes this is especially important for 'discerning issues of modernity in music'. He highlights the notion of 'artificiality': 'the idea that progress can be achieved by acknowledging the imperfections of nature and modifying the system at hand to improve things from a human perspective'.[19] He writes: 'Bach's Passions . . . bring to a head the tensions between truth and fiction, nature and artifice, a confrontation that very much complicates their relation to the norm of religious truth. It is precisely this tension that might render them so productive within debates about modernity.'[20]

There is an important distinction to be made here which, although not denied by Butt, seems nevertheless somewhat blurred. One can speak of bringing forth elaborate and unprecedented forms of order through developing or enhancing 'natural' order (i.e. the inherent properties of physical sounds)—thus 'improving' on it in this sense. Bach's music, and what we know of his self-perception, points in this direction, thus perhaps signalling a relatively new conception of the composer in his era. And, further, inasmuch as one believes that nature has in some sense been marred, then this calling might even be spoken of in redemptive terms—a form of 'improvement'. There is some evidence that Bach thought along these lines. But it is quite a distinct matter to suggest that the pre-eminent role of the artist is to construct order out of an essentially and fundamentally disordered world, to assume that nature's order is at its deepest levels basically unreliable, or (even stronger) to suppose that nature has no order other than the order we bring to it or forge from it.[21] Varieties of this outlook became much more common in the decades after Bach, and even more so in philosophies of creativity we find in the nineteenth

---

of Leibniz's or Wolff's treatises' (Ulrich Leisinger, 'Forms and Functions of the Choral Movements in J. S. Bach's *St Matthew Passion*', in Daniel R. Melamed (ed.), *Bach Studies 2* (Cambridge: Cambridge University Press, 1995), 70–84, 84). Dreyfus argues that Bach is better understood as a subtle *critic* of Enlightenment thought than a staunch supporter of it (see Dreyfus, *Bach and the Patterns of Invention*, ch. 8).

[18] Butt, *Bach's Dialogue*, 63.

[19] Butt, *Bach's Dialogue*, 15.

[20] Butt, *Bach's Dialogue*, 23.

[21] Richard Rorty captures something of this in words of characteristic bluntness: 'About two hundred years ago, the idea that truth was made rather than found began to take hold of the imagination of Europe': Richard Rorty, *Contingency, Irony, and Solidarity* (Cambridge: Cambridge University Press, 1989), 3.

and twentieth centuries.[22] Butt does not project such sensibilities onto Bach.[23] But he does lay a very heavy stress on Bach's inventive, constructive powers, and is especially keen to do so, since he sees this as a major thrust of the emerging modernity of the time—a fast-growing confidence that nature can be brought to new levels of splendour through human creativity and industriousness.[24]

Three points can be made in the light of this. The first is that it is as well to be wary of assuming that creativity, inventiveness, and the generation of novelty are in some manner basically foreign to a Christian understanding of humankind's place in the world. It is in fact fundamental to a biblically based anthropology that humans are called to work with, develop, and enhance materials given to hand and mind—and this includes taking string and metal, reed and pipe and fashioning meaningful patterns of sound. This may well involve the continual generation of new forms of organization to elicit ever richer sonic configurations: the invention of major and minor scales could be seen as an example. Undoubtedly, there are strands in the Christian tradition—not least within Lutheranism—that have underplayed or neglected this call to fashion new forms of abundant order,[25] but the broader Christian perspective needs to be kept in mind before we label it as something peculiarly modern.[26] Second, without wanting to minimize the significance of wider cultural movements that would destabilize humanity's embeddedness and trust in a wider non-human order, it is surely overstating the case to claim with Butt that 'the Bachian approach showed that nature is *as much* constituted through art—that is, as a human construction—as providing the model that art must faithfully depict'?[27] We do not have to appeal to Bach's own beliefs and commitments to question this;[28] we need only follow through on

---

[22] For a luminous discussion, see Roger Lundin, *Believing Again: Doubt and Faith in a Secular Age* (Grand Rapids, MI: Eerdmans, 2009), 35–60 and ch. 2, esp. 73–83.

[23] He raises the question of whether Bach may have 'approached' what Butt calls 'the more modern "horizontal" sense of the artificial, something that had the potential to substitute for a nature that was no longer necessarily reliable, running parallel to what remained of natural order': Butt, *Bach's Dialogue*, 64. Wisely, Butt does not adjudicate on this. And he rightly distances Bach from the early Enlightenment view, represented by Johann Adolph Scheibe, with its privileging of words over music, which insisted music should be clear, transparent, simple, and uncluttered, that music was most 'natural' when it showed least human artifice: Butt, *Bach's Dialogue*, 64. See also Dreyfus, *Bach and the Patterns of Invention*, 236–42.

[24] 'From the early nineteenth century to the present day, a hallmark of our modernity has been the manner in which metaphors of *construction* have gradually overcome those of *discovery* in our understanding of truth': Lundin, *Believing Again*, 9.

[25] Butt, *Bach's Dialogue*, 291–2.

[26] See Richard Bauckham's perceptive comments about the difference between 'improving' and 'enhancing' in Richard Bauckham, *Bible and Ecology: Rediscovering the Community of Creation* (London: Darton, Longman & Todd, 2010), 34–6.

[27] Butt, *Bach's Dialogue*, 34. My italics.

[28] The weakness of some well-meaning Christian theological treatments of Bach is their suggestion that if we can demonstrate Bach held to this or that theological belief, we have

some of Butt's observations of Bach's music. A comment near the end of the
book reads: 'the more exhaustively the potential of the musical material is
researched, *the more "real" it seems to become, as if disclosing more of the
ultimate nature of matter*'.[29] This is hard to interpret in anything other than a
'realist' sense, that the music in some manner discloses 'the way things really
are'. Or we can take the trajectory Butt skilfully appropriates from Laurence
Dreyfus, that Bach's elaboration of musical material is not governed chiefly by
an external, pre-given logic, but rather chiefly by the material itself.[30] Bach,
that is, seems far more intent on exploring the logic and potential of the music
in hand than adhering precisely to pre-existing, extra-musical schemes of
organization. This provokes a vision of the created world that in some respects
is highly consistent with an orthodox, trinitarian theology. Many have argued
that rather than assume theological schemes in which forms are given an
eternal status in God's mind, or where God initially creates ideas or forms and
then subsequently creates the world, or where matter is created first and then
shaped into forms, it would be more true to the biblical affirmation of the
goodness and integrity of the world to affirm that it is created directly out of
nothing, such that it possesses its own appropriate forms, forms that God
honours and enables to flourish as intrinsic to its own nature.[31] Something
similar could be said of the attitude of a musician to the integrities of sound.

At a deeper level, without some belief in the value and inherent good order
of the physical world as *prior gift*, 'there before us',[32] then for all its efficacy,
modernity's constructive drive will all too easily lead to tyranny, something to
which the contemporary tale of ecological devastation poignantly testifies.
What is needed here, arguably, is a biblically rooted perspective, which insists
that the cosmos is not the product of an arbitrary will but the contingent
artefact of a benevolent God, whose own covenant love has overflowed to
fashion an 'other' that can share in and be upheld by this same love, an
environment with that human creatures are intended to engage and in which
they are intended to flourish through felicitous and respectful interaction. In
this scenario, the relations that modernity has often typically envisaged

---

thereby demonstrated that his music must express/reflect/display these theological commitments. Matters cannot be this simple.

[29] Butt, *Bach's Dialogue*, 291. My italics. Importantly, he says later: 'this could also be
interpreted as the imperative to make the most of what has been received, the Christian's
acknowledgement of his God-given talents and the intention to bring them to the most fruitful
issue, without wastage': Butt, *Bach's Dialogue*, 291.

[30] See Dreyfus, *Bach and the Patterns of Invention*, ch. 5.

[31] The point is put succinctly in Colin E. Gunton, *The Triune Creator: A Historical and
Systematic Study* (Edinburgh: Edinburgh University Press, 1998), 77–9.

[32] Roger Lundin, *There Before Us: Religion, Literature, and Culture from Emerson to Wendell
Berry* (Grand Rapids, MI: Eerdmans, 2007).

between humans and the natural world, artist and physical environment, composer and sound, are strikingly recalibrated.

I am not suggesting that Bach was in the business, or thought of himself as being in the business, of simply 'depicting' nature, passively observing it as one would an inert object and then merely translating its order in sound. His intense and astonishing inventiveness has stunned countless musicians since, and justifiably so. And to repeat—there is nothing intrinsically or necessarily 'modern' as opposed to 'Christian' about this feature of Bach's work. What we are suggesting—and this is the third point—is that we need not be compelled to imagine that this 'constructive' dimension of Bach's music has, by necessity, to work against what would seem to be (and was believed to be) an honouring of the integrities of musical sound.

In other words, perhaps we need to ask whether the key divergence between modernity and the biblical tradition we should be attending to in this connection—whatever might be said of the Lutheranism of Bach's day—is the former's pernicious tendency *to assume that discovery and inventiveness are inherently opposed to one another*, that the relation between 'nature' and 'artifice' are to be regarded in zero-sum terms: the greater the human artifice the less the respect for 'given' order, and vice versa. It is just this, I suggest, that Bach's music can serve to challenge—with its remarkable interweaving of coherence ('disclosing the ultimate nature of matter') and inventiveness ('constructedness'). Insofar as it does exhibit some such interwovenness, it is thoroughly consonant with a vision of humankind's embeddedness in the natural order of the kind we find in, for example, the opening chapters of Genesis. (To be fair, Butt mentions in passing that 'compensatory, autonomous' elements in Bach's music need not be seen as 'contradictory' to a sense of God's prevenient ordering,[33] but the point needs to be pressed much further.) Moreover, this outlook is not diminished, but greatly strengthened by Butt's acute comments about something he sees as implicit in Bach's work—a vision of the composer as the imitator of 'the *author* of nature', not simply the 'imitator of nature';[34] perhaps better put—the composer participating in and thus reflecting God's own active investment in the world. Again, this is not a uniquely modern notion, but, carefully qualified, is consonant with a large corpus of biblically rooted Christian literature, pre-modern as well as modern.

Of course, Bach's music cannot be used to prove or demonstrate the truth or otherwise of a theology of human artistry. But it may well serve to perform in sound something of the shape or configuration of such a theology and show something of its fruitfulness. And, at the very least, considered as a straddling of pre-modern and modern outlooks, this music can provoke us to question

---

[33] Butt, *Bach's Dialogue*, 40.   [34] Butt, *Bach's Dialogue*, 64–5.

the all-too-common supposition of modernity that 'creativity', the fashioning of new things, is *intrinsically* at odds with the calling to honour the integrity of the world's order.[35]

ORDER AND OPENNESS

In what is perhaps the most theologically evocative chapter of his book, Butt explores something that has captivated many devotees of Bach: the way in which his musical strategies involve not merely the reinforcement of a pre-existing certainty, message, or text, but what Butt calls a transformative 'dialectic'. The music exhibits a subtle interplay of the predictable and the unpredictable, in which breathtaking expanses of music are fashioned from relatively simple musical ideas (motifs, themes, etc.) in ways that are utterly convincing and yet delectably unanticipated. The music is heard as vibrant with contingency, destabilizing all determinisms, while at the same time as magnificently ordered: it 'perhaps gives us a feeling of change within a soundworld that is still wedded to the sense of a broader, consistent reality. This is music that welcomes—even creates—belief, even if it cannot on its own determine what sort of belief this should be.'[36]

As we have noted, Bach would have held to the grounding of music in invariable cosmic order, and in composition, the obligation to be faithful to this order. But as we also noted, his musical forms are generally not like rigid templates or moulds into which notes are poured, an organic unfolding of an inexorable predetermined logic, but seem to emerge from the qualities and character of the musical material being treated, and in ways that are hard to foresee.[37] 'This is a music that seems supremely wedded to a world of

---

[35] I have always thought one of the most striking features of Bach's Obituary is the way it can speak of the composer's 'ingenious and unusual ideas' and of his extraordinary grasp of the 'hidden secrets of harmony' without even a hint that the two have to be at odds. Hans T. David, Arthur Mendel, and Christoph Wolff (eds), *The New Bach Reader: A Life of Johann Sebastian Bach in Letters and Documents* (New York: W. W. Norton & Co., 1998), 305.

[36] Butt, *Bach's Dialogue*, 250.

[37] Butt, *Bach's Dialogue*, 243–6. Butt is surely right to warn against the danger of interpreting Bach according to later Romantic 'organicist' notions: Butt, *Bach's Dialogue*, 245–6. Bettina Varwig's discussion of Bach and musical form is highly instructive here also: Bettina Varwig, 'One More Time: J. S. Bach and Seventeenth-Century Traditions of Rhetoric', *Eighteenth-Century Music* 5, 2 (2008): 179–208. She speaks of 'an ingrained image of Bach the composer in general, as supremely rational and in control of the overall architecture of his creations. When such control is apparently absent, the threat of irrationality looms large' (191). Varwig views Bach's procedures as undoubtedly rational, yet 'this rationality need not be tied to the evidence of abstractable "forms" as orderly sequences of As and Bs; on the contrary, the score-notated representation of a compositional process that involves numerous procedures of variation and amplification can appear quite asymmetrical and bewildering in its variety and rate of change,

certainty and interconnectedness, yet its results, for many listeners at least, seem to be utterly unexpected and transformative.'[38] For Butt, it is one of the keys to Bach's enduring appeal that his music enacts a particular dynamic, a 'balance of rationality and particularity', a 'curious sense of order and subversion'.[39]

This may well bring to mind a (modern) sense of the individual composer, acutely attentive to the effects of his music on his listeners, and thus keen not simply to repeat formulae of the past. (This is undoubtedly part of what appealed to the Romantics about Bach.) This dimension of openness instantiates the composer's freedom vis-à-vis his inherited traditions: 'If Bach's music seems to presuppose inherited musical rules as part of a closed, God-given system, this is somehow combined with the awareness that the potentials within that system are technically infinite, that any particular choice is essentially contingent.'[40]

But there are other deeper perspectives that very naturally open up here. Perhaps most obviously, there are resonances with the way we might imagine the relation of Creator to creation. Butt himself tellingly comments that this music, with its interplay of regularity and contingency, evokes 'a creative figure far more nuanced than the self-satisfied God who can sit back once the best possible of all machines has been set in temporal motion'.[41] It is hardly a stretch to correlate the absence of determinism (either mechanistic or organic) with theological accounts of the created order that take *both* God's ordering *and* contingent interaction with the world seriously—in which, for example, the world's 'contingent order'[42] is being 'perfected' by

---

alongside an aural experience of a convincing overall trajectory'. She continues: 'It is...the kaleidoscopic display of continually reformulated, ever-changing phrase segments and their myriad fragmentations and expansions that seems to govern the design of the movement, in which the instantaneous creation and fulfilment (or subversion) of expectations determine a trajectory that generates and resolves localized and large-scale tensions without necessarily being devised or heard against a pre-formulated template' (191). Varwig proceeds to demonstrate this by means of a meticulous analysis of aspects of the Third Brandenburg Concerto (BWV1048), relating her findings to a notion of rhetoric associated with Erasmus of Rotterdam.

[38] Butt, *Bach's Dialogue*, 35.

[39] Butt, *Bach's Dialogue*, 246, 247. Understandably, Butt alludes here to Theodor Adorno, who 'noted that Bach was the first composer to crystallize the concept of the rationally constituted musical work, reconciled with the voice of humanity at precisely the historical moment when this latter was being stifled by the newly inaugurated rationalizing trend': Butt, *Bach's Dialogue*, 246. See Theodor W. Adorno, 'Bach Defended Against His Devotees', in Theodor W. Adorno (ed.), *Prisms* (Cambridge, MA: Spearman, 1981), 133–46. See also Simon Jarvis, *Adorno: A Critical Introduction* (Cambridge: Polity, 1998), 133–4.

[40] Butt, *Bach's Dialogue*, 242–3.

[41] Butt, *Bach's Dialogue*, 243. Butt here has G. W. Leibniz (1646–1715) in mind.

[42] Thomas F. Torrance, *Divine and Contingent Order* (Oxford: Oxford University Press, 1981).

the particularizing, proliferating ministry of the Holy Spirit, who effects faithful but unpredictable improvisations on a harmony already achieved in Jesus Christ.[43]

Butt makes some stimulating observations about the 'boundlessness' of musical process in Bach. Even at his most mathematical, Bach is anything but mathematically 'closed'. For example, although we find ample evidence in the *Goldberg Variations* of mathematical sequences and symmetries, we find these interlaced with striking and surprising irregularity.[44] Writing of a crucial point in these variations, Butt comments: 'rather than coming full circle with the canon at the octave, the canons "overshoot" with a further canon, now at the ninth. We have a sense of recurrence that could go on ad infinitum, but it is one in which things are somehow different at each recurrence.'[45] After extensive treatments of arias and choruses from the Bach's Passions, he writes that 'Bach's pursuit of the idea that each invention should imply a piece of unified substance brings consequences that could not have been predicted, so that *what seems to be an enclosed world of predetermined connections can in fact imply an infinitude of possibilities.*'[46] In another place:

> . . . there is something utterly radical in the way that Bach's uncompromising exploration of musical possibility opens up potentials that seem to multiply as soon as the music begins. By the joining up of the links in a seemingly closed universe of musical mechanism, a sense of infinity seems unwittingly to be evoked.[47]

While acknowledging that a degree of theological caution is required here, we might say that insofar as this does provoke a metaphysical vision, it is one quite congruent with regarding the world as the contingent creation of the triune God of Jesus Christ, whose creativity—and ours—is the outworking and reflection of his own differentiated inexhaustibility.

---

[43] I am not entirely convinced by Butt's intriguing discussion of Bach in relation to nominalism: Butt, *Bach's Dialogue*, 244–6. The argument seems to be that nominalism's elevation of the particular over the universal, resisting the predeterminations of any supposedly prior system, is evident in Bach's music, especially in its non-organic character. But it is not clear that Bach's music exhibits nominalism inasmuch as nominalism implies an *arbitrary* deity of naked choice and will; it could just as easily—more easily, perhaps—be associated with a God whose freedom is, to be sure, not driven by an external necessity, but by his own internal being as trinitarian love; a God whose creation of the world and subsequent interaction with it is from beginning to end an outworking of this non-coercive benevolence, displaying (accordingly) both consistency and 'openness'.

[44] Peter F. Williams, *Bach: The Goldberg Variations* (Cambridge: Cambridge University Press, 2001), 46.

[45] Butt, *Bach's Dialogue*, 109. Writing of a chorus in the St John Passion, 'Lasset uns den nich zerteilen', Butt remarks: 'One could imagine that, had [Bach] chosen, he could have spun the piece out yet further, building more on the implications of the various kinks and paradoxes in the seemingly stable fugal material': Butt, *Bach's Dialogue*, 262.

[46] Butt, *Bach's Dialogue*, 280. My italics.

[47] Butt, *Bach's Dialogue*, 292.

Once again, we must stress that pointing to these features of Bach's music does not conclusively demonstrate the truth or falsity of this or that theology or theological cosmology (though it undoubtedly evokes some cosmologies more readily than others). But it may well serve to question and perhaps destabilize some pernicious theological conceptions beloved of modernity. As Butt himself puts it, 'Bach's contribution is to offer us the sense of an order that lies *just out of the reach of fully modern sensibilities*, one that sets up some keen expectations of fulfillment but which somehow seems to retain a sense of openness and unexpectedness.'[48]

What is puzzling is that Butt does not draw attention to the fact that this dynamic of order and contingency is so integral to mainstream Christian theologies of creation, stretching back to the early Church.[49] This relates to a wider feature of Butt's argument that is apparent in a number of places. In one passage he points to the way Christian listeners will naturally draw theological significance from Bach's works; but, he continues, in this music 'something *richer* in its potential meanings and implications emerges, something very different from most of the music of the premodern world. Bach was creating something that had the potential to adhere to many more contexts and cultural expectations than much previous music.'[50] Here we simply venture a comment: it is one thing to argue that Bach produces music that transcends the specific concerns and emphases of his time (and the music which preceded his own), but another to suggest that when Bach's music speaks to and resonates with hearers and listeners in cultures other than his, something is happening that is discontinuous with, or far beyond, classical Christian faith, and is thereby 'richer'. I will return to this point towards the end of the chapter.

TIME AND ETERNITY

According to Butt, the overlapping of modern and pre-modern also marks Bach's treatment of time.[51] In Bach's Passion music there is a 'dynamic', 'progressive', directional temporality interlaced with the more ancient, stable, cyclical temporality typical of a pre-modern sensibility (although Butt is careful to point out that Bach's is not yet the progressivist time of the nineteenth-century Germanic musical tradition with its large-scale tensions

---

[48] Butt, *Bach's Dialogue*, 292. My italics.
[49] See e.g. the discussion in David Bentley Hart, *The Beauty of the Infinite: The Aesthetics of Christian Truth* (Grand Rapids, MI: Eerdmans, 2003), 275–88.
[50] Butt, *Bach's Dialogue*, 294. My italics.
[51] Butt, *Bach's Dialogue*, ch. 2.

and resolutions). Directional ('linear') temporality, according to Butt, is built into the Christian faith, together with the more cyclical time distinctive of liturgy and the physical world at large.

Butt believes that Bach's Passions move us beyond what would have been standard pre-modern views of time and history in his day, i.e. that sacred and secular history, natural and human time form a relatively undifferentiated, seamless, and stable whole. Especially in the St Matthew Passion, we are given numerous discontinuities, unpredictable novelty, and a strong sense of the irreducible distinction between present and past. Nor is Bach captive to a one-dimensional, profane, linear time—the clock-time of nascent modernity. Rather, he generates a subtle combination of different temporal patterns, different paces, and timescales. Yet this differentiation and variety is normally held within a temporal stability, combined with a 'progressive' momentum. Speaking of sections of the Mass in B Minor, Butt writes: 'Bach has given us a sense of symmetrical, circular time simultaneously with a linear or progressive quality. The Bachian sense of time demands progress within stability, a dynamic approach to cyclic time that evokes something of the energy of a spiral.'[52]

It is here that Butt's concerns overlap extensively with those of Karol Berger, whose book *Bach's Cycle, Mozart's Arrow* is in effect a study of different perceptions of time in modernity, as exemplified in music. To his study we now turn.

Berger on Bach, Time, and Eternity

Berger is bold. Undaunted by postmodern qualms about metanarratives, he declares: 'the main job of art before it became fully modern in the late eighteenth century was to give sensuous embodiment to the eternal—cosmic or divine—order and truth. Since that time, by contrast, the tendency has been to use art to proclaim human autonomy; for the moderns, for us, art is mainly a tool of self-affirmation.'[53] Within this grand sweep, he delineates a more localized trajectory running from Bach to Wolfgang Amadeus Mozart (1756–91), in which we can detect a shift from a preference for 'circular' time to that of 'linear' time, consonant with a metaphysical and theological shift from a perspective in which the world's time is understood to be held within God's all-embracing eternity to one in which time effectively excludes, even abolishes, any such primary eternity. There is linearity and goal-directed temporality in Bach, certainly, but it is subordinated to 'timeless stasis'.[54] Berger reads Bach as a 'late representative of the premodern ways of shaping

---

[52] Butt, *Bach's Dialogue*, 110.
[53] Berger, *Bach's Cycle*, 42.   [54] Berger, *Bach's Cycle*, 12.

musical time' and Mozart as an early representative of a 'fully developed modern approach to musical temporality'.[55]

As far as Bach is concerned (our main focus here), Berger's thesis is supported by, among other things, a close reading of the opening chorus of the St Matthew Passion. Written for a Good Friday Vespers service in 1727, this vast work opens with a giant movement, described by Christoph Wolff as 'a funeral march for the multitude of believers who ascend to Mount Zion and the holy city of Jerusalem'.[56] One choir sings the part of the Daughter Zion, the other the words of the Faithful. The Daughter Zion calls out to the Faithful (i.e. believers) to witness the sacrifice of Christ; the Faithful respond with short and puzzled questions. A third group of sopranists (and we shall assume they were a group for the moment), the singers of the heavenly Jerusalem, sings a chorale, a metrical paraphrase of the 'Agnus Dei'. Berger sees the chorus as a 'varied da capo' form, in which a return of the opening text with its music is adapted so as to enable a return to the tonic (or home key). But this particular varied da capo has a highly unusual ending: what would normally be extended in a series of phrases Bach condenses into a single phrase, creating a 'synthesizing culmination'.[57] With this compression there is 'no sense of imbalance, no sense that the end does not match the expansive beginning, no sense of something missing'.[58] Berger takes this as evidence of Bach's efforts to neutralize or circularize time, 'to abolish the succession of past, present, and future' in favour of the 'simultaneity of the present'.[59] Indeed, Berger contends that in both his instrumental and vocal music, Bach shows relatively little interest in 'linear time', the temporal ordering of musical events.[60]

Berger proceeds to give this a dense theological reading. In the case of the Passion's opening chorus, the temporal circularity is designed to facilitate a particular stance or attentive attitude on the part of the listener. The two choirs are not active protagonists in the events but reflective observers, 'contemplators'. As such, they occupy a distinct temporal level. In fact, considered as a whole, the Passion exhibits three such levels—there is the time narrated by the Evangelist (the time of the narrated events themselves), the time of the Evangelist's narrating, and the time of those who contemplate the narration, whose 'time' is in effect a neutralizing of time. Berger wants us to see the basic, determinative temporality as that of contemplation; this provides the perceptual matrix of the work. Certainly, the narrated story must be present (this is obviously the centre of the listener's attention) and

---

[55] Berger, *Bach's Cycle*, 10.
[56] Wolff, *The Learned Musician*, 302.   [57] Berger, *Bach's Cycle*, 59.
[58] Berger, *Bach's Cycle*, 59.   [59] Berger, *Bach's Cycle*, 59.
[60] Berger cites Dreyfus in this connection, who demonstrates that the ordering in time of events is normally far less important to Bach than the need to show the multiple possibilities that open up through transforming often very simple musical material: Dreyfus, *Bach and the Patterns of Invention*.

so must the time of the narrator, but 'Structurally or ontologically...the frame is more important'.[61] The two temporalities of story and storytelling are 'nested' within the temporality of contemplation, which is to say, within 'timeless eternity'.[62]

Berger holds that the story's personages and the contemplators, although undoubtedly distinct, nevertheless both belong to the 'world' being represented by the Passion. In most (if not all) of the Matthew Passion, those who play the role of contemplators *want to feel what it was like to be there. The temporal distance between them and the personages of the story cannot be obliterated, but in imagination they can bridge it.*[63] In turn, they are teaching *us* to feel the same, teaching us how to be participants. 'Zion and the rest'—the contemplators—'are there to tell us what to do, feel, and think.'[64] Through them we are now being summoned to identify with the personages of the story—*we* are to be 'there'—in order that the story's truth may be internalized in the present. Research has shown that Picander, Bach's librettist, was strongly influenced by the Lutheran sermon tradition, which laid a considerable stress on the goal of inward change, the transformation of the individual's heart.[65] We recall that not only was this setting of the Passion part of a preaching service (Vespers), with a sermon coming between each half, it was *itself* regarded as a form of preaching, through which the Gospel could take root in the hearer. These events happened *propter nos* and *pro nobis*.[66] The listeners are thus being enjoined 'to do the impossible and enter the world of the story as participants'.[67] Hence Bach's 'thwarting of time';[68] he must make it possible for the audience, through an imaginative act, to close the distance between that past and our present: 'time has to be rendered impotent, its flow either stopped or bent into a circle'.[69]

Berger's theological construal of the Passion is widened to assimilate a further perspective. Bach attempts to neutralize time because of the way in which Christ is conceived in the theological tradition. The life of Jesus as a historical figure is understood by the New Testament writers as enclosed within eternity—he is the enfleshment of the eternal Logos. And classical orthodoxy invites us to see the history of humanity as displaying a similar structure—human history's linear temporality is bounded by a beginning and

---

[61] Berger, *Bach's Cycle*, 107.   [62] Berger, *Bach's Cycle*, 107.

[63] Berger, *Bach's Cycle*, 117. My italics. This seems to be the only way of explaining chorales such as no. 17: 'I will stand here with you'; or Aria no. 20 in the context of Gethsemane—'I want to keep watch beside my Jesus'.

[64] Berger, *Bach's Cycle*, 110.

[65] Elke Axmacher, *'Aus Liebe will mein Heyland sterben': Untersuchungen zum Wandel des Passionsverständnisses im frühen 18. Jahrhundert* (Neuhausen-Stuttgart: Hänssler-Verlag, 1984).

[66] See Robin A. Leaver, *J. S. Bach as Preacher: His Passions and Music in Worship* (St Louis: Concordia Publishing, 1984) and Andreas Loewe, '"God's Capellmeister": The Proclamation of Scripture in the Music of J. S. Bach', *Pacifica* 24 (June 2011): 141–71, esp. 160–71.

[67] Berger, *Bach's Cycle*, 114.   [68] Berger, *Bach's Cycle*, 117.

[69] Berger, *Bach's Cycle*, 117.

end, 'beyond' which lies 'God's infinite time', namely eternity. Bach, like his contemporaries, is acutely aware of the ravages of irreversible time running towards death, time devouring all that we value, robbing us of all that is good. 'In man's time all is vanity because sooner or later everything passes into oblivion. Our only hope of permanence is the promise that we may be translated into God's time.'[70]

The vista is thus one in which this world's irreversible time is embedded, enfolded in what Berger calls 'the hierarchically more fundamental eternity of God'.[71] In this connection, Berger cites the opening declaration of Cantata 106: 'Gottes Zeit ist die allerbeste Zeit' ('God's time is the very best time'). It is a preference for 'God's time', i.e. eternity, which more than anything else accounts for Bach's fondness for cyclic structures and his comparative indifference (in many of his pieces at least) to the temporal arrangement of musical events. It also stands behind Bach's privileging of harmony: 'music's sounding harmony reflects the intelligible harmony of God's creation'.[72] The cosmically embedded principles of harmony are permanent and unchanging (even if in the music they are played out in time): 'the exploration of musical harmony is one way to contemplate what truly endures'.[73]

Bach's musical articulation of time and eternity Berger interprets as emblematic of an essentially 'Christian' view of reality. And just as Bach characterizes the pre-modern, Christian outlook ('[Bach] aspired to capture the traditional Christian worldview'[74]), so Mozart's music represents the modern. The Salzburg virtuoso reveals a musical world where temporal linearity is 'emancipated' from eternity and assumes the leading role; temporal order and succession become critically important. His is the age when a profound belief in human autonomy comes into its own. Freed from the obligations of eternal divine law, humans begin to regard themselves as masters of their own destiny, and the future lies open to the potentially limitless capacities of human achievement and progress.

It is when Berger contrasts 'Christian' with 'modern' outlooks that his assumptions about the outlines of purportedly standard Christian teaching on time and eternity are thrown into relief. A few sample quotations from this and related sections will have to suffice here. Christians, we are told, 'take the existence of the supernatural realm for granted';[75] 'humanity's participation in two different orders of reality, natural and supernatural, is precisely what the Christian worldview proclaims'.[76] 'In thinking about their individual existence, Christians above all desire salvation in the afterlife, and in the meantime they wish to do good in this life.'[77] The Christian God determines 'the bliss

---

[70] Berger, *Bach's Cycle*, 120. [71] Berger, *Bach's Cycle*, 119.
[72] Berger, *Bach's Cycle*, 127. [73] Berger, *Bach's Cycle*, 127.
[74] Berger, *Bach's Cycle*, 176. [75] Berger, *Bach's Cycle*, 158.
[76] Berger, *Bach's Cycle*, 143. [77] Berger, *Bach's Cycle*, 158.

each individual saved soul will enjoy in heaven';[78] 'the desired end is eternal
rest and peace in God's heaven'.[79] 'Of course, a Christian [like the modern]
wants to be happy . . . but he most desires eternal bliss hereafter.'[80] In connection with Immanuel Kant, Berger claims that 'unlike the otherworldly goal of
Augustine, [Kant's goal] neither postulates the eventual escape from time into
eternity nor privileges rest over change . . . The end of history is not the state
of passive, atemporal contemplation of divine perfection but rather a state of
active, open-ended development.'[81] Consistent with these assertions, Berger
writes that 'Christianity's greatest contribution to politics was the recognition
that politics did not matter all that much . . . Jesus . . . advised leaving politics
to Caesar, since politics do not affect human salvation.'[82] The following
compresses the assumed overarching metaphysics *in nuce*:

> Like the universe of Plato, the universe of Christians is split into two—the
> temporal, mutable here and now, this world in which we humans are born,
> dwell, and die, and the atemporal, immutable, transcendent beyond of
> God. But these two realms do not simply exist side by side. Rather, this world
> is enveloped in the transcendent one, is dependent on it, and owes its existence
> to it.[83]

We are, it seems, being presented with a characterization of mainstream
Christian thought in which 'supernature' is distinguished from 'nature', eternity conceived as radically disconnected with and ontologically superior to
time, and the Christian life perceived as heading towards a release from time
into the other-worldly 'beyond of God' (rendering politics in this life irrelevant), the ultimate goal being the soul's blissful, 'passive, atemporal contemplation of divine perfection'.

The contrast with Butt is obvious. Butt interprets Bach as holding together
elements of both modern and pre-modern outlooks. He discerns a directional
temporality signalling an emerging modernity, but this is intertwined with the
more stable cyclical temporality of premodernity. Butt sees a Christian approach to time as capable of embracing both types. For Berger, Bach represents an essentially pre-modern understanding of time, which he equates with
the Christian outlook. Timeless eternity is ontologically privileged over time,
and in due course this gives way to the far more linear, goal-directed temporality of modernity, an early exemplification of which we see in Mozart.

How are we to negotiate and evaluate these claims? Clearly, matters
are complicated by the fact that these scholars press us to work on many
fronts: musico-theoretical, musicological, historico-cultural, as well as theological. Here, in the first instance, and attending mainly to Berger, we confine

---

[78] Berger, *Bach's Cycle*, 163.   [79] Berger, *Bach's Cycle*, 166.
[80] Berger, *Bach's Cycle*, 159.   [81] Berger, *Bach's Cycle*, 169–70.
[82] Berger, *Bach's Cycle*, 160.   [83] Berger, *Bach's Cycle*, 118.

ourselves to theological comments on the time–eternity relation, setting them along with some observations on Bach's theological milieu. Then, reintroducing Butt's work, we turn to some of the relevant musical texts.

Berger's Time and Eternity

Without a doubt, there have been prominent currents in the Christian tradition that do manifest elements of the vision Berger ascribes to the Church (including a fair amount of popular Christian belief and culture). But it is a vision that is unquestionably divergent in critical respects from the testimony of the New Testament.[84] This is so even if we endorse Berger's account of broad changes in the development of modernity with regard to perceptions of time and history: the intense privileging of time over eternity; the way in which 'modernity emancipates human time from the enveloping divine eternity';[85] modernity's secularization of Christianity's grand narrative; and so forth. Especially useful for us in clarifying issues of time and eternity is the work of New Testament scholar Richard Bauckham, not only because of his conceptual lucidity but because he presses us to sense what is arguably the prevailing logic and thrust of diverse and complex scriptural texts.[86]

The differences between Berger's assumptions about time and eternity and the various strands of New Testament theology Bauckham highlights are marked. First, Bauckham brings to a head what he believes is a central commitment to the primordial goodness and full reality of time, where time is regarded as a dimension intrinsic to the created order (including human life) and from the beginning wholly willed by God as such. Bauckham argues that Platonism's devaluation of time—in which what is truly real (eternally enduring, timeless, and immutable being) is set in radical contrast to what is

---

[84] Part of the trouble here may be Berger's adoption of Augustine as his central, representative Christian theologian. Assuming for the moment that he interprets Augustine aright (and that is an open question), many would argue that even though Augustine may be said to represent mainstream Christian thought on many matters, when it comes to his treatment of time and eternity, for all his astonishing perception and insight, questions need to be asked about whether he is sufficiently rooted in the Christologically shaped ontology mandated by the biblical texts. See Jeremy S. Begbie, *Theology, Music and Time* (Cambridge: Cambridge University Press, 2000), 75–85.

[85] Berger, *Bach's Cycle*, 167.

[86] Here I draw mainly on the following: Richard Bauckham, 'Time and Eternity', in Richard Bauckham (ed.), *God Will be All in All: The Eschatology of Jürgen Moltmann* (Edinburgh: T & T Clark, 1999), 155–226; Richard Bauckham, *The Theology of the Book of Revelation* (Cambridge: Cambridge University Press, 1993); Richard Bauckham and Trevor A. Hart, *Hope Against Hope: Christian Eschatology at the Turn of the Millennium* (Grand Rapids, MI: Eerdmans, 1999); and his essay written with Trevor Hart, 'The Shape of Time', in Marcel Sarot and David Fergusson (eds), *The Future as God's Gift: Explorations in Christian Eschatology* (Edinburgh: T & T Clark, 2000), 41–72.

temporary, time-laden, and changeable—is beset by a 'failure to distinguish successiveness, in which all created things become what they are, and transience, in which all things pass away'.[87] Biblically speaking, transience is not itself evil, though its negating power—the fact that because of transience, all things come to nothing—has been exploited by human evil. This distinction between temporal successiveness and transience seems to elude Berger.

Consonant with this, second, is Scripture's witness to a direct involvement and interaction of God's eternity with created time, which involve time-embedded purposeful trajectories towards the consummation of all things.[88] This is grounded in the Creator's faithfulness to the created world and his promise for its eschatological renewal,[89] a commitment that has been concretely enacted and sealed in the history of Jesus Christ. Bauckham speaks of three constant features of human experience of time: successiveness, transience, and the openness of the future to the new, and claims that all three are engaged in Christ:

> In his incarnate life he becomes who he is in his human identity in the successiveness of time, which is essential to all creaturely becoming and identity. In his death, he is subject both to the transience which brings all things to nothing and to the human evil that exploits this negating power of time. In his resurrection, he is the promise of a new future which takes successiveness into eternity and redeems the transience from the past.[90]

Critical here is that eternity and time are not to be understood as abstract conditions or dimensions, univocally applicable to any given reality, but as conceivable only in accordance with the realities of which they are predicated; that is, they can only be properly explicated with respect to the eternity of the triune God and the temporality of this God's created cosmos, which in turn means only in relation to Jesus Christ, who embodies the climactic and decisive interaction of God's eternity and created reality. Berger certainly seems aware of the centrality of the incarnation for Christian faith, but fails to recognize fully its soteriological import, its place in the saving sweep of God's redeeming purposes for all things, the way in which, together with the resurrection of Jesus, it vindicates creation, proleptically prefiguring a final re-creation. In Berger's account, I suggest, eternity is being conceived a priori, in abstraction from the incarnation and is thus evacuated of its personal, covenantal, and world-committed character.

---

[87] Bauckham and Hart, 'The Shape of Time', 46.

[88] See his very concise essay, Richard Bauckham, 'Reading Scripture as a Coherent Story', in Ellen F. Davis and Richard B. Hays (eds), *The Art of Reading Scripture* (Grand Rapids, MI: Eerdmans, 2003), 38–53.

[89] See, for example, Bauckham's comments on the new creation in Bauckham, *The Theology of the Book of Revelation*, 51–3.

[90] Bauckham and Hart, 'The Shape of Time', 47.

Third, we are pressed towards envisaging the final consummation as involving the taking up of time into eternity. The new creation, the eschatological fulfilment of all things, does not entail the extension of this world's time, but rather 'the recovery and transformation of the whole diachronic extent of this world's time. All times will be gathered into eternity...In this way the whole creation, in its whole diachronic extent, will be redeemed from transience.'[91] Accordingly, 'transient time is essential to the kind of goodness [creation] has',[92] and its darker side, the consequent loss of all that is good, is countered in the eschaton's redemptive restoration. To share fully in redeemed temporality through Christ is to be delivered not only from the sin that takes advantage of transience but from transience itself. Immensely demanding as this may be to conceptualize, it is at root only the drawing out of a logic that takes seriously creation's primordial temporality as part of its inherent goodness: the universe was made not *in tempore* but *cum tempore*.

In this outlook, plainly, belief in God's promised future cannot be used to justify a withdrawal from our responsibilities vis-à-vis worldly power and its potential victims. Quite the opposite.

> Knowing that all generations have a future in God's new creation, we practise solidarity with their sufferings, their achievements and their hopes, telling their stories as still relevant parts of the grand narrative of God's love for the world.[93]

Further, the promised future is to be considered eschatologically new, in the sense that it cannot be generated by or arise from the immanent potentialities of this temporal world. It is a 'radically new future that takes the temporal beyond time...the radically new future which can only be the gift of the transcendent God'.[94] Berger is unable to accommodate such an outlook, for his ontology of eternity seems to be essentially inert, precluding the possibility of fresh forms of temporality being generated *by* eternity *out of* created temporality.

---

[91] Bauckham, 'Time and Eternity', 183. 'The end of history will happen to all history. In the resurrection all the dead of all history will rise to judgement and life in the new creation.' Bauckham and Hart, *Hope Against Hope*, 39.

[92] Bauckham, 'Time and Eternity', 183.

[93] Bauckham and Hart, *Hope Against Hope*, 40.

[94] Bauckham and Hart, 'The Shape of Time', 47. The same circle of ideas appears in Bauckham's exposition of the book of Revelation: 'Creation is not confined for ever to its own immanent possibilities. It is open to the fresh creative possibilities of the Creator...[The Creator] can give *new* life—eschatologically new life raised for ever beyond the threat of death. Whereas mortal life, cut off from its source, ends in death, God can give new life which is so united to his own eternal life that it can share his own eternity': Bauckham, *The Theology of the Book of Revelation*, 48–9. He goes on to explain that this applies not just to humans but to the entire created order: creation is given 'a quite new form of existence, taken beyond all threat of evil and destruction, indwelt by his own glory, participating in his own eternity' (49).

Presuming for the moment that Bauckham is in accord with the content of the New Testament's testimony, the disparity between this testimony and Berger's vision is acute and far-reaching. Of course, it might be objected that this is unduly heavy-handed on Berger, given that he is a musicologist, not a theologian. But he is nevertheless advancing a remarkably confident thesis about a shift from pre-modern to modern, where pre-modern is aligned with 'Christian' and assumed to embrace a grand, all-encompassing theology of time and eternity with a quite definite profile. It is reasonable to ask whether this profile accords with one that takes its chief bearings from Christianity's originating and normative texts.

A more telling response to our comments would be that Berger's focused interest is in Bach (at least in the first part of his book), and that whatever we say about Berger in relation to biblical texts or mainline theological tradition, the question remains: has he identified the theological shape of Bach's outlook faithfully? To what extent is Berger's interpretive frame with respect to time and eternity anachronistic with respect to the composer? The question is quite legitimate, and can be asked (a) with attention to Bach's own 'theological world'—taking into account the textual evidence of his ecclesiastical and liturgical milieu (and even of his own beliefs inasmuch as they can be determined); and (b) with attention to the musical techniques and strategies that might be considered relevant to the evocation of time and eternity, especially as they appear in his settings of sacred texts.

Bach's Theological World

When it comes to the precise conceptions of time and eternity that would have informed Bach's creative work, firm and final conclusions are hard to draw. His age was, after all, one of rapid change, and his ecclesial tradition marked by theological debates of immense complexity, strongly shaped by a variety of shifts in the social and practical construction of time.[95] And the relevant sources concerning Bach himself are relatively scant. Nonetheless, some things can be fairly safely assumed. It is generally agreed that Bach's theological outlook was shaped more than anything else by the Lutheranism of his day, and in his case a Lutheranism consonant with Nicene orthodoxy, neither strictly Pietist (though Pietist sentiments are undoubtedly present in Bach's output)[96] nor driven by the particular polemics of the stricter seventeenth- and eighteenth-century Lutheran theologians. Bach himself appears to have

---

[95] For a careful treatment of conceptions of time present in Bach's cultural environment, see Bettina Varwig, 'Metaphors of Time and Modernity in Bach', *Journal of Musicology* 29, 2 (2012): 154–90, esp. 156–75.

[96] Butt, *Bach's Dialogue*, 57–60.

been devout (although not exceptionally so for his time and place) and was certainly a serious student of the Bible.[97]

As far as eschatology is concerned, it is unlikely that Bach and his librettists would have envisaged a return of Christ within their own lifetime, but their milieu was one in which a sense of the brevity of life, coupled with a belief in the judgement of each person after death and the importance of living with that judgement ever in mind, was widely presumed. Some have noted a marked tendency to allow this to narrow the theological significance of the span of history between the present and the end of history, so that the faith and repentance of the individual in the present becomes paramount. In many of Bach's cantatas, for example, we find a pronounced sense of the transience of our lives, the fleetingness of this world's pleasures, and the foolishness of putting one's trust in them. We find a certain internalization of eschatology, in which biblical end-times metaphors are 'bent backwards' to confront us now with the need for a change of heart.[98] These are matters discussed at length by Butt.[99] The eternal beckons us at every moment, the crisis of faith is ever present. There is something to be said, then, for the view that Bach displays what Frank Kermode has seen as a modern reworking of the ancient expect-ation of an end-times crisis into a sense of a repeated judgement in the present moment, an 'eternal transition, perpetual crisis'.[100] At the same time, for the Christian, death can also be welcomed, since it will mark the end of sufferings and tribulations, and the beginning of a new life; it is a deliverance 'out of the Egypt of this world' (Cantata 70). Bach can set texts that are somewhat startling in the way they warmly address death as a friend—'With joy I anticipate my death: | Ah! If only it had taken place already!' (Cantata 82)[101] All this evokes an outlook that leans strongly in the Berger direction: a devaluing of time, this world, and the significance of our earthly lives in favour of an atemporal and infinitely more excellent future life.

However, there are strong countervailing currents. And they all turn on Christology. Concerning the believer's final joyful destiny, in the texts Bach

---

[97] For discussions, see e.g. Chafe, *Analyzing Bach Cantatas*, ch. 1; Robin A. Leaver, *Music as Preaching: Bach, Passions and Music in Worship* (Oxford: Latimer House, 1983); Michael Marissen, *Lutheranism, Anti-Judaism, and Bach's St John Passion* (New York: Oxford University Press, 1998); Jaroslav J. Pelikan, *Bach Among the Theologians* (Philadelphia: Fortress Press, 1986); Loewe, '"God's Capellmeister"': 143–54. On Pietism in Bach's time, see Tanya Kevorkian, *Baroque Piety: Religion, Society, and Music in Leipzig, 1650–1750* (Aldershot: Ashgate, 2007), 2–3, 10–12, 206–9.

[98] See e.g. Cantatas 20 and 60.

[99] Butt, *Bach's Dialogue*, 114–18.

[100] Butt, *Bach's Dialogue*, 117–18. See Frank Kermode, *The Sense of an Ending* (Oxford: Oxford University Press, 2000), 101.

[101] For a detailed and very fine study of this cantata, with its multilayered image (highly popular at the time) of death as peaceful sleep, which attends to a variety of social, cultural, and musical determinants, see Bettina Varwig, 'Death and Life in J. S. Bach's Cantata Ich habe genung (BWV 82)', *Journal of the Royal Musical Association* 135, 2 (2010): 315–56.

sets we find a persistent stress on the centrality of Christ and the believer's faith-union with him.[102] 'Eternity' cannot be detached from eschatological encounter and communion with Christ. The focus is on a person, not a state. The final chorale from Cantata 70 encapsulates this sentiment well:

> Not for the world, not for heaven
> Does my soul desire and yearn;
> I desire Jesus and his light,
> He who has reconciled me with God,
> Who frees me from judgement;
> I will not let my Jesus go.

Eternal life is essentially the life that Christ imparts, God's own abundant life. And this can (and should) be grasped now: 'Yes, yes, I hold Jesus firmly, | Then I also enter into heaven, | Where God and his Lamb's guests | Are in crowns at the Wedding. | There I shall not part from you, my salvation' (Cantata 157). In Cantata 60, Jesus responds to the believer's fear with the words 'Blessed are the dead who die in the Lord, from now on [*von nun an*]'. 'Fear' later responds: 'Well, then! | If I am to be blessed from henceforth: | Then appear again, O Hope! | My body may rest in sleep without fear, | My spirit can catch a glimpse of the joy hereafter.' As Eric Chafe puts it, 'the final words of Jesus' promise, "von nun an", enable the believer to live in the hope of eternal life and even to experience a vision of that life in the present through the Spirit'.[103]

Bearing this Christological perspective in mind—in which eternity is embodied in Christ, and through faith in him, experienced now and in the future—a number of comments are in order. First, it would be anachronistic to presume that these and similar texts (or Bach himself) portray a radical diminishment of the value of this life. The life of the world to come is certainly regarded as of superior quality to this life. Here Berger is surely correct. But there is little to suggest we can read into this a belittlement of the intrinsic value of the concrete realities of this time-bound life. A proneness to downplay the theological import of the timespan between the present and the end in the interests of an ever-pressing final judgement is qualified by the themes of discipleship that pervade many of the cantatas, for instance.[104] Further, although we find an irrepressible assurance that a believer's physical distress will cease, this does not presuppose a devaluing of the body per se, either in

---

[102] Leaver, 'Eschatology, Theology and Music', 145–6.

[103] Chafe, *Analyzing Bach Cantatas*, 223. Chafe misunderstands those last words of 'Fear', rendering them '*the Spirit* can take a glance into that joyful state'. The context makes clear that *Der Geist* is not a reference to the Holy Spirit but the believer's 'spirit', here contrasted with the body. It is a theologically felicitous mistake, however, for it would be held in Bach's time that it is by the Spirit that an eschatological foretaste is possible now.

[104] See e.g. Cantatas 39 and 77; and the discussion in Calvin Stapert, *My Only Comfort: Death, Deliverance, and Discipleship in the Music of Bach* (Grand Rapids, MI: Eerdmans, 2000), pt. iii.

this life or in the life to come. Belief in the bodily resurrection of Christ was, after all, basic to the Bachian credo.[105]

Second, we should not be misled by those descriptions of the future life we find in, say, the cantatas, which call to mind a somewhat motionless (and individualized) state. While Bach would have held that the believer's immediate post-mortem state was one of 'rest', this would have been seen as occurring prior to the new creation. Constrained by the liturgical requirements of the church year, Bach is obliged to set texts that deal directly and unambiguously with the dynamic (and corporate) dimensions of Scripture's portrayal of the eschaton, which are themselves congruent with the logic of the bodily resurrection of Christ, and do little to encourage a sense of the abandonment or erasure of all time and motion. Cantata 140 is perhaps the most conspicuous example, which picks up biblical wedding feast imagery—the bridegroom, Christ, coming to receive his bride, the Church (alluding to Matthew 25)— and closes with a richly worded chorale evoking the joyful, doxological city of unceasing worship portrayed in Revelation 21 and 22.[106]

Third, turning to Bach's attitude to death, some of Bach's texts (especially the non-biblical ones) do appear to be compliant, perhaps even at times sentimental. But others exhibit a shuddering horror that might strike some today as bordering on the pathological. If there is a way of reconciling these, it will be along Christological lines. Alfred Dürr sees the Bachian outlook in terms of Luther's *simul iustus et peccator*—death is at one and the same time to be feared (sin brings the possibility of damnation after death) and welcomed (through Christ our righteousness, death is the gateway to glory).[107] Christ has borne the ultimate consequence of sin—death—and his victory over sin is confirmed on the third day. Death is not to be trivialized. But for Christians

[105] We should not be misled by the phrase that opens Cantata 106—'Gottes Zeit ist die allerbeste Zeit' ('God's time is the very best time'). Berger takes this as demonstrating Bach's preference for eternity over time: 'God's time' (eternity) 'is not just ontologically more important—prior in some sense, one without which there would be no time of the created world—but it is also better, "the very best", even': Berger, *Bach's Cycle*, 119–20. But this is surely to misread the phrase. As the context shows, 'God's time' refers not to eternity but to God's timing—God's perfect will for things happening at the right time. The text continues: 'In him we live, move, and have our being, as long as he wills. | In him we die at the right time, when he wills.'

[106] For further examples of expressions of the fullness of life in the eschaton, see e.g. the texts of Cantata 70, with the significant line 'You shall flourish in Eden | To serve God for ever.'

[107] Alfred Dürr, '"Ich freue mich auf meinen Tod": Sterben und Tod in Bachs Kantaten aus musikwissenschaftlicher Sicht', *Jahrbuch des Staatlichen Instituts fur Musikforschung Preussischer Kulturbesitz* (1996), 41–51. It is worth bearing in mind that Bach himself knew death at close quarters, not least in his own family: both his parents died when he has 9, his first wife died when he was 35, and he outlived eleven of his own children. (I owe this reminder to Dr Stephen Crist.)

it is never to be treated without hope: those in Christ have nothing to fear, for they will be raised with him to life everlasting.[108]

Fourth, following through the New Testament trajectories on time and eternity we have opened up makes possible a rather different reading of the Matthew Passion than we find in Berger. For Berger, we recall, the 'contemplators' in the opening chorus who witness Christ's sacrifice stand in the same represented world as the persons in the events portrayed; there is a bridging of temporal distance between the world of the story and the contemplators' world. Likewise, for contemporary listeners, Bach wants to neutralize the time between past and present, so that the truth of what is portrayed may be internalized deeply within each of us. We, like them, are to consider ourselves *there*. So Bach deploys a variety of techniques to ensure that time renders 'insignificant its relentless flow from past to future', the aim being to frame and 'embed the time of the story within the timelessness of contemplation'.[109]

Berger's point about listeners needing to perceive themselves as 'being there' is surely to the point, as is his stress on rendering Christ present 'here' in the heart of the believer. But what Berger gives with one hand he takes away with the other. In his inclination to evacuate time of any ultimate theological worth, he seems to assume that the significance of the Passion story can be extracted from its temporal embeddedness in concrete happenings in the past, which *as such* constitute a promise for a comprehensive New Creation. This privileges a certain kind of contemplative posture on the listener's part, rather than one in which the believer can participate in the temporally extended redemption of created reality, enacted and embodied in Christ.

Interestingly, John Butt takes issue with Berger on just this point. Butt views the contemplators as belonging to *our* world, not to the world represented by the Passion setting.[110] From the Lutheran perspective, the function of the Passion is to help generate an experience in the present of Christ in our hearts. 'To see the two worlds [of personages in the story and contemplators] merely as one *representation* . . . would suggest that the listener is necessarily separate from the performance and thus, to some degree, passive.'[111]

This preserves more fully than Berger what Butt calls the 'separate represented world from the past'.[112] But does it go far enough? Bearing in mind

---

[108] See e.g. Cantatas 8, 27, 60, 72, 82, 95, 125, 156, 157, and 161. On Bach and death, see Richard J. Plantinga, 'The Integration of Music and Theology in the Vocal Compositions of J. S. Bach', in Jeremy S. Begbie and Steven R. Guthrie (eds), *Resonant Witness: Conversations Between Music and Theology* (Grand Rapids, MI: Eerdmans, 2011), 215–39; Leaver, 'Eschatology, Theology and Music'. For a detailed examination of Cantata 60, 'O eternity, you word of thunder', see Chafe, *Analyzing Bach Cantatas*, ch. 9; Robert E. A. Lee, 'Bach's Living Music of Death', *Dialog: A Journal of Theology* 24, 2 (1985): 102–6.

[109] Berger, *Bach's Cycle*, 117.

[110] Butt, *Bach's Dialogue*, 38.

[111] Butt, *Bach's Dialogue*, 38, n. 7.

[112] Butt, *Bach's Dialogue*, 38, n. 7.

what we have said via Bauckham about time and eternity, perhaps we might suggest something along the following lines. When it comes to the 'contemplative' sections of the St Matthew Passion, could we not regard them as urging us to see ourselves 'there', and to be inwardly transformed now, in order that we might view these events from the perspective of God's historically embedded purposes for humankind into which we are now being invited, and which will reach their ultimate fulfilment in the new creation? In this scenario, we are being granted—in union with Christ—a glimpse *from within time* of God's intentions for the entirety of creation's timespan, intentions into which God longs to draw us, temporally and concretely. Or, to put it differently, we are being invited to participate in eternity (through Christ the Son of the Father who lives in us through his Spirit) but *only as creatures*, which is to say, never in such a way that our temporality is effaced or dissolved away. We cannot, of course, prove this was the way Bach was imagining things, but there is nothing to preclude the possibility, and more than a little to encourage it.

Musical Witness

I have been concentrating on texts. What can we say about the way Bach's music might, or might not, share in these theological dynamics?

We return to what Butt says about Berger.[113] Butt concedes that in the course of the late eighteenth and nineteenth centuries, the temporal order of musical events became far more crucial than it ever was for Bach. While accepting Berger's thesis with regard to a long-term historical trajectory, and acknowledging that, for example, the opening chorus of the St John Passion is indeed strongly cyclical,[114] Butt is not convinced that all Bach's passion music can be accommodated within Berger's scheme. With regard to the Matthew Passion, while noting its symmetries, Butt claims that the sense of 'linear, passing time'[115] is in fact vivid and pronounced, much more so than in the John Passion. There is an 'overwhelming sense of change',[116] and a recognition of the uniqueness of its critical narrative events, many of which are portrayed as effecting subsequent change. Even in the more symmetry-laden John Passion, Bach balances 'repetitively ordered (or symmetrical) elements with a sense of musical direction'.[117]

---

[113] Butt, *Bach's Dialogue*, 109–11.

[114] In this respect, he contrasts the two Passions: Butt, *Bach's Dialogue*, 97–111. Butt believes that the John Passion 'tends to promote a "classical" sense of time as something rooted in eternity, emphasizing the eternal consistency of Christ's divinity and the sense of all the events as foreordained': Butt, *Bach's Dialogue*, 99.

[115] Butt, *Bach's Dialogue*, 106.

[116] Butt, *Bach's Dialogue*, 107.

[117] Butt, *Bach's Dialogue*, 109.

The Matthew Passion's opening chorus, 'Komm, ihr Töchter' is far more directional than Berger allows, says Butt: it reaches an open-ended conclusion, and includes interruptions, asymmetries, and unexpected, unique events.[118] Butt argues that both the Passions exhibit a musical incompleteness that reaches out to an eventual fulfilment: 'Bach's music both sets up a sense of immanent crisis, on numerous levels, historical and actual, objective and personal, but also a sense of potential resolution.'[119] The 'entire Matthew Passion', he asserts, 'lacks tonal closure...the work somehow craves completion beyond its own span'.[120] As we have noted already, unlike Berger, Butt wants to see Bach as standing 'on the cusp of musical modernity',[121] *combining* repetitive, symmetrical components and directionality (albeit to different degrees in different pieces), thus mingling pre-modern and modern sensibilities.

I find these observations very persuasive, and they support a far more subtle theological scenario than that suggested by Berger, one certainly more congruent with viewing the happenings portrayed in, say, the Matthew Passion, as the expression of a purposeful, time-implicated interaction of God's eternity with human history. The kinds of features Butt highlights—consistency interlaced with directionality, unique interruptions that issue in fruitful change, an irreducible open-endedness that resists tidy closure—are hardly unfamiliar to a well-trained scholar of the Passion texts, nor are they foreign to a vision of history in which the world is seen as being drawn towards its fulfilment by the faithful God of Israel, the God of Jesus Christ crucified and risen, a fulfilment that this world cannot generate out of its own immanent resources.

Could this music's 'open-endedness', however, provoke us to say rather more? If what has been embodied in the history of Jesus Christ and our participation in him are themselves an anticipation of the eschaton, are there not characteristics of Bach's music that might be heard as evocations of that stupendous future? The question is at least worth posing. We recall our earlier comments on novelty and change. Envisaging the taking-up of created time into God's eternity may well indeed stretch the human imagination to breaking point, but, as we noted, it is not clear that we are required to exclude the possibility of change in the eschaton altogether. Presumably, this will not be a change from imperfect to perfect but from one form of perfection to another. David Bentley Hart writes: 'Christian eschatology promises only more and greater harmony, whose developments, embellishments, and movement never end and never "return" to a state more original than music.'[122] Or, in Anthony Thiselton's words, 'To pass *from glory to glory* would not be an eternal *fortissimo*, but a crescendo of wonder

[118] Butt, *Bach's Dialogue*, 66–7, 101–3.
[119] Butt, *Bach's Dialogue*, 117.   [120] Butt, *Bach's Dialogue*, 100.
[121] Butt, *Bach's Dialogue*, 109.   [122] Hart, *The Beauty of the Infinite*, 284.

and praise.'[123] It is notable that both these two theologians resort to musical metaphors. If we are to speak (however guardedly) of temporality in the new creation, will it not be of a sort that entails addition without loss, expansion without diminution, yet is also utterly consistent, never arbitrary, always resisting static completeness? And it is just this kind of dynamic of abundance that scholars such as Butt are drawing attention to in much of Bach's music.[124] In the Mass in B Minor, for example, when Bach evokes the life of the world to come ('Et expecto resurrectionem mortuorum'), he does so by throwing us into an irrepressible dance—the corrupt body is liberated at last. Furthermore, contrary to images of the new creation that portray it as an ecology of bland singularity, when Bach concludes his immense Mass with 'Dona Nobis Pacem', we are offered a 'peace' replete with abundant musical lines, multiply superimposed and overlapping, tumbling over each other as the counterpoint expands. Though spatially and temporally structured, it is a space that is gloriously uncontainable—a multidimensional and ever-widening shalom. We might add: such an opulent vision makes considerably more sense if we are prepared to forgo a nameless, nondescript, unitarian eternity and allow differentiation to characterize the divine life: arguably, only a trinitarian eternity makes sense of Bach.

THE CONVERSATION CONTINUES

Thus far, we have attempted to examine some of the main theological dimensions of Bach's output as they are presented in two readings of his music, readings which explicitly set Bach in relation to the emergence of modernity. It is greatly to their credit that Butt and Berger are both prepared to plunge into theological territory as musicologists—if this does represent a new climate in Bach studies, it is surely to be welcomed. We have tried to allow both writers to be heard fairly, while also offering some critical comments, especially in relation to Berger. I wonder, however, if the conversation requires to be pressed a stage further, in a way that allows the testimony of Bach to raise rather more disturbing questions. A remark by the philosopher Andrew Bowie in relation to literary theory might be apt here: 'what sometimes seems to be

---

[123] Anthony C. Thiselton, *The Hermeneutics of Doctrine* (Grand Rapids, MI: Eerdmans, 2007), 578.

[124] See also Peter F. Williams, *The Goldberg Variations* (Cambridge: Cambridge Univeristy Press, 2001), 45–6. The dynamic includes constraint and contingency in contrast, interplay, and mutual enhancement. Indeed, much of Bach's music sounds improvised. This was one of the things about Bach that so intrigued the nineteenth-century composer and virtuoso Franz Liszt (1811–86)—who himself transcribed and arranged many of Bach's works—and which captivates many jazz musicians. (It is no surprise that Bach was a renowned improviser.)

missing . . . is a sense that theories might learn from the texts which they are used to interrogate'.[125]

Rebounding Questions

Both our authors conduct their discussions firmly within the orientations and parameters set by modernity. They do so, however, in different ways. Theologically, Berger's reading of Bach is dependent on a very particular account of the metaphysics of eternity and time, which in turn shapes his understanding of what he regards as central to Christianity. Although he sees this outlook as 'pre-modern', it has in fact received massive elaboration within modernity in various guises. Indeed, a sizeable body of writing would argue that it is especially distinctive of European Enlightenment and post-Enlightenment thought to fall prey repeatedly to radical forms of disjunction and dichotomy between time and eternity (however conceived, whether 'secular' or 'sacred'), and that many of modernity's deepest and most intractable aporias stem from a failure to coordinate them adequately and fruitfully.[126] One result has been a pervasive inability to come to terms with the depths and implications of the scriptural witness to the interaction of Creator and creature culminating in Jesus Christ. Bach's music, we have suggested, can serve to open up a rather different coordination of time and eternity, highly consistent, so our argument has been, with just that witness. As such, it constitutes a challenge not only to Berger's interpretation of Bach, but also to the kinds of tools he brings *to* that interpretation.

Butt's understanding of the Christian faith is far more nuanced and historically informed. He is also quite open about his commitment to what he believes are the more positive and fruitful features of modernity—a refreshing change in a climate that is all too keen to cast all things modern into outer darkness. But it is noteworthy that among those rudiments beloved of modernity he shows no signs of abandoning is a belief in the appropriateness of the marginalization or privatization of religion. He points to the tension between reason and revelation in the modern mindset and the tendency to confine matters religious to a zone of 'faith' largely disconnected from other aspects of life. But the appositeness of this is never questioned. Although quite prepared to take Bach's own faith commitments seriously for the purposes

---

[125] Andrew Bowie, *Philosophical Variations: Music as 'Philosophical Language'* (Malmö, Sweden: NSU Press, 2010), 71.

[126] See e.g. F. LeRon Shults, *Reforming the Doctrine of God* (Grand Rapids, MI: Eerdmans, 2005), esp. pt. i; Colin E. Gunton, *Yesterday and Today: A Study of Continuities in Christology* (London: Darton, Longman & Todd, 1983), ch. 6; Thomas F. Torrance, *Space, Time and Incarnation* (London: Oxford University Press, 1969); Thomas F. Torrance, *Space, Time, and Resurrection* (Grand Rapids, MI: Eerdmans, 1976).

of interpreting Bach's life and music in its period and culture, as a scholar it is clear Butt wishes to be bound largely to the restrictions enjoined by the modern project. In a telling passage he notes that he would tend to stress that concepts such as that of 'universal, transcendent, truth lying in art' and suchlike 'are themselves historically conditioned'. He continues: 'The value of [Bach's] music lies, I claim, not in any universal revelation it might offer (such a notion is perfectly understandable as a form of belief, *but not necessarily as scholarship*), but in the way it can imply a powerful dynamic relating to the modern condition.'[127] Suspicious of any attempt to 'universalize' Bach in a way that would ignore his embeddedness in particular social and cultural particularities, as if his music were expressive of a 'natural' state of humankind or the cosmos for example,[128] any inquiry into the 'universality' of Bach's music is to be strictly confined to the immanent, historical, and cultural sphere. Where does this leave the religious significance of Bach? While Butt recognizes that today the 'religious content [of Bach's Passions] seems to have become more important from a scholarly point of view (even if the scholars concerned do not share the type of religion they articulate), and it is arguably harder to separate them from considerations of the role and nature of religion in contemporary society',[129] he also suggests that in contemporary society we may be experiencing 'a weakening of the productive dynamic of modernity' and that Bach's music, which is able 'to transcend the specific dogma of [its] origins', might have a place in 'contributing to a specifically modern appropriation of religion', with its capacity to rework premodern legacies and thus relate Western civilization fruitfully to its past.[130]

It would seem, then, that the scholarly study of Bach in relation to modernity needs to assume the 'modern appropriation of religion', according to which claims to universality of any sort are to be treated as explicable entirely in sociocultural terms, and religious belief that turns on specific 'dogmas' is relevant to the private sector only, entirely distinct from that appropriate to rigorous scholarship. I am putting the matter more starkly than Butt (whose writing is consistently cautious and scrupulously qualified), but this does seem to be the logic of his position. Thankfully he is not under the illusion that he occupies some privileged high ground of academic 'neutrality'. He is too fine a scholar to believe in that chimera of modernity—a standpoint *within* history which is at the same time presumed to be located *outside* history. But aspects of the mindset(s) he identifies as characterizing modernity are nonetheless being treated as unquestionable, simply part of the givenness of things, and this includes some dominant academic attitudes towards the nature of religious belief. What is so fascinating and ironic is that, as we have seen, much of

---

[127] Butt, *Bach's Dialogue*, 293. My italics.   [128] Butt, *Bach's Dialogue*, 293–4.
[129] Butt, *Bach's Dialogue*, 294.   [130] Butt, *Bach's Dialogue*, 294.

the musical material he so perceptively interprets points towards a metaphysics that would sit very uneasily with, even subvert, such attitudes.

The question I am left with, then, is simply this: why should serious scholarship not consider the possibility that Bach's music might articulate a disturbing resistance to some of the metaphysical and, indeed, theological (or anti-theological) axes on which modernity and much modern scholarship have habitually turned?

4

The Nature of Music: Rameau, Rousseau, and 'Natural Theology'[1]

> Music theory for about the last 400 years has tried to ground itself in 'nature', in distinction to the supernatural and unnatural, believing that nature can somehow validate its truths; nature is the origin or ground that legitimises the theory. But what legitimises nature? What has been invested in nature that enables it to underwrite the enterprise of music theory?
>
> *Daniel Chua*[2]

The enterprise known as 'natural theology' has been at various times a conspicuous feature of the intellectual landscape of modernity. As most commonly understood today—broadly, as a form of theology that for various reasons wants to make its immediate and focused appeal (and sometimes its ultimate appeal) to criteria that are considered valid independently of 'special' revelation (epiphanies, sacred texts, religiously decisive historical events, and so forth)—it is often considered to have come into its own in modernity, though there are clear antecedents in previous eras. It is frequently traced to seventeenth- and eighteenth-century England, where various upheavals (scientific, social, political, and ecclesiastical) raised intellectual challenges to religious belief, which made recourse to universally accessible features of the physical world or to supposedly universal dimensions of human nature seem very attractive.[3]

---

[1] An earlier version of this chapter was delivered as a paper to the international conference 'Natural Theology Beyond Paley: Renewing the Vision for Natural Theology', 23–5 June 2008, Museum of Natural History, University of Oxford. I am very grateful for the comments I received there. My thanks also go to Dr Mareque Ireland for her scrutiny of some of the texts referred to in this chapter.

[2] Daniel K. L. Chua, 'Vincenzo Galilei, Modernity and the Division of Nature', in Suzannah Clark and Alexander Rehding (eds), *Music Theory and the Natural Order from the Renaissance to the Early Twentieth Century* (Cambridge: Cambridge University Press, 2001), 17–29, 17.

[3] For surveys, see Alister E. McGrath, *A Scientific Theology: Nature*, 3 vols, vol. i (Edinburgh: T & T Clark, 2001), 241–67.

In theological circles over the past decade or so, we have witnessed a flurry of writing and interest in natural theology.[4] Its reputation having been severely dented by those who have doubted its legitimacy (most notably Karl Barth), many have sought to revitalize the enterprise, and not least with respect to the arts. The business of making and enjoying the arts (including music) holds out attractive possibilities for natural theology, so it is said, especially in the apologetic arenas of late modernity, where the limits of narrowly intellectual arguments are readily apparent and the need to engage the affective and imaginative dimensions of 'sense-making' is acutely felt.[5]

The key term to explore in any claim to be doing natural theology is, of course, 'natural'. In this chapter I want to examine the ways in which music was drawn into debates that raged in the eighteenth century about what is to count as 'natural', debates that were critical to the intellectual and cultural landscape of Europe at the time. The aim is to explore some of the ways the concepts of 'nature' and 'naturalness' in modernity have been understood theologically, and thus some of the senses of 'natural theology'. I shall conclude with comments concerning the role that music might play in a theology that, chastened by these clarifications, could legitimately call itself 'natural'.

RAMEAU AND ROUSSEAU

Few disputes in the history of music are more enlightening than that between Jean-Philippe Rameau (1683–1764), the leading composer of the French Enlightenment, and the animated philosopher and writer Jean-Jacques Rousseau (1712–78). The issues between them were not always hammered out

---

[4] See e.g. Alister E. McGrath, *The Open Secret: A New Vision for Natural Theology* (Oxford: Blackwell Publishing, 2008); McGrath, *A Scientific Theology*, vol. i; Stanley Hauerwas, *With the Grain of the Universe: The Church's Witness and Natural Theology* (London: SCM Press, 2002); James Barr, *Biblical Faith and Natural Theology* (Oxford: Oxford University Press, 1994); James F. Sennett and Douglas R. Groothuis, *In Defense of Natural Theology: A Post-Humean Assessment* (Downers Grove, IL: InterVarsity Press, 2005); Russell Re Manning (ed.), *The Oxford Handbook of Natural Theology* (Oxford: Oxford University Press, 2013).

[5] See e.g. Anthony Monti, *A Natural Theology of the Arts: Imprint of the Spirit* (Aldershot: Ashgate, 2003). David Brown's recent hefty theological project includes, indeed to a large extent is constituted by, an expanded and transformed 'natural religion': David Brown, *God and Grace of Body: Sacrament in Ordinary* (Oxford: Oxford University Press, 2007), 9. He distinguishes this from 'natural theology as currently conceived' (*God and Grace of Body*, 9), by which he appears to mean certain expressions of analytic philosophy of religion. Brown is concerned with coming to terms theologically with large tracts of human experience he believes are redolent of God's presence but have been largely ignored by much traditional theology. This includes the arts— and, not least, music. See e.g. Brown, *God and Grace of Body*, 254. For comments on Monti and Brown, see Jeremy S. Begbie, 'Natural Theology and Music', in Russell Re Manning (ed.), *The Oxford Handbook of Natural Theology* (Oxford: Oxford University Press, 2013), 566–80.

directly with each other, and the controversy was one of a number of related quarrels at the time, involving Denis Diderot (1713–84) and Jean-Baptiste le Rond d'Alembert (1717–83) among others. But Rameau and Rousseau nonetheless throw into relief with great clarity two diametrically opposed approaches to the way we might account for music's power, approaches that continue to enjoy widespread support and discussion today.

An especially illuminating way of understanding the Rameau–Rousseau debate is to see it as turning on quite different understandings of the 'naturalness' of music, the way in which music is embedded in 'nature'. It took place during a period when European intellectual reflection on music was to a significant extent shaped by quite distinctive habits of thought, habits that we have already met in the preceding chapters.[6] To generalize very broadly: the theoretical world into which Rameau was born was marked by the virtual abandonment of the Pythagorean–Platonic theological cosmology and metaphysics that had sustained musical reflection for much of the medieval era, in favour of theories weighted heavily towards the anthropological.[7] Music is validated primarily in terms of human needs and aspirations, as an instrument of the human will. Where a cosmic outlook persists in music theory, through an appeal to the discoveries of natural science for example, the primary direction and motivation of interest is nonetheless human-centred, and explicit theological references, where present, generally play a relatively minor, insignificant role.

Along with this, there is the prevalence of what John Neubauer has called a 'verbal paradigm'.[8] Even if not tied directly to words (as in text-setting), music is frequently believed to operate in language-like ways—although quite how becomes a matter of considerable contention. In this climate, instrumental music finds itself on the defensive, without words to denote 'objects' clearly and reliably: the vast majority of writers on music in the eighteenth century see

[6] See 'Wider Movements and Questions' (pp. 35–8) and 'Subjectivity and Creativity' (pp. 43–50) in this volume.

[7] Daniel Chua goes as far as to speak of the 'vestiges of the old cosmology lingering in the early part of the [eighteenth] century', which were 'merely anachronistic murmurs to be silenced as superstition gave way to empiricism'. Daniel K. L. Chua, *Absolute Music and the Construction of Meaning* (Cambridge: Cambridge University Press, 1999), 80.

[8] John Neubauer, *The Emancipation of Music from Language: Departure from Mimesis in Eighteenth-Century Aesthetics* (New Haven: Yale University Press, 1986), ch. 2. 'The verbal paradigm is central to eighteenth-century conceptions of music as a semiotic form': Downing A. Thomas, *Music and the Origins of Language: Theories from the French Enlightenment* (Cambridge: Cambridge University Press, 1995), 174; see ch. 1 *passim*. See also Andrew Bowie, *Music, Philosophy, and Modernity* (Cambridge: Cambridge University Press, 2007), 51–4. This should not be taken as implying that medieval composers and theorists had no concern with the relation between texts/words and music—as if, with the Renaissance, there was a simple shift from the cosmological to the verbal. On this, see Leo Treitler, 'Medieval Music and Language', in Leo Treitler (ed.), *With Voice and Pen: Coming to Know Medieval Song and How It Was Made* (Oxford: Oxford University Press, 2003), 435–56.

vocal music as superior to instrumental music. Of a piece with this is a tendency, at least in the first two-thirds of the eighteenth century, to conceive musical 'meaning' in representative–referential terms—that is, in ways akin to the manner in which representative language is presumed to function, through a direct correspondence between musical and extra-musical phenomena. The key extra-musical phenomena here are the passions or affects. It is the human passions that constitute music's content. By corresponding to particular passions, music excites these passions in the hearer or listener. Hence the growth in this period of schemes designed to show the links between particular affective states and certain melodic figures, rhythmic gestures, harmonic progressions, and so forth. In due course, the links between music and what would later be called the emotions were understandably drawn into the purview of the material sciences. Impressed by the increasingly wide reach of the mathematicization of physics and, in due course, the growth of medical enquiry, a considerable number of theorists (though by no means all) held that music's power can and should be explained in just these terms (according to some, primarily, even exclusively): the sound of music is to be investigated by Newtonian physics, its affective impact by experimentally driven physiology.

Rameau and the 'Natural'

With these broad habits of thought in mind, we can turn to Rameau, who, according to one writer, 'epitomises the intellectual aspirations of the eighteenth-century Enlightenment'.[9] Although he was to change his position on some issues, his *Treatise on Harmony* of 1722, despite its anomalies and empirical inaccuracies (exposed in his day as well as ours), came to stand as one of the foundation stones of modern music theory.[10] Like most of his contemporaries, Rameau was convinced that the main purpose of music was to provoke emotion: 'The aim [of music] is to please and excite in us the various passions.'[11] But this required explication, not only to account for the

---

[9] Joel Lester, 'Rameau and Eighteenth-Century Harmonic Theory', in Thomas Christensen (ed.), *The Cambridge History of Western Music Theory* (Cambridge, MA: Cambridge University Press, 2006), 753–77, 759.

[10] *Traité de l'harmonie réduite à ses principes naturels* (Paris, 1722): Jean-Philippe Rameau, *Treatise on Harmony*, trans. Philip Gossett (New York: Dover Publications, 1971). For discussions of Rameau's music theory, see Thomas, *Music and the Origins of Language*, 91–7; Thomas Christensen, *Rameau and Musical Thought in the Enlightenment* (Cambridge: Cambridge University Press, 1993); Cuthbert Girdlestone, *Jean-Philippe Rameau: His Life and Work* (New York, NY: Dover Publications, 1969), ch. 14. 'There is hardly an idea in later eighteenth-century, nineteenth-century, or much twentieth-century harmonic theory that does not have its origin in Rameau's works': Lester, 'Rameau and Eighteenth-Century Harmonic Theory', 157.

[11] From *Génération harmonique* (1737), p. 30, in Jean-Philippe Rameau, *The Complete Theoretical Writings of Jean-Philippe Rameau*, ed. Erwin R. Jacobi, 6 vols, vol. iii (Middleton,

harmonic organization of the music of his day, but also to promote good compositional practice and performance.

Rameau was especially inspired by seventeenth-century science and keen to present his theory in ways that would gain approval among his scientific contemporaries. Likened to both Descartes and Newton in his lifetime, he sought to clarify and unify the accepted rules of harmonic theory within a single, unified, empirically grounded, and rationally coherent framework—a project that extended over some forty years and gained widespread recognition. What especially caught the attention of the *philosophes* of his day was his apparent ability to confirm their conviction that 'nature was governed by a small number of quantifiable and interconnected mechanistic principles that could be discovered through careful analysis and calculation'.[12] Not only could his theory elucidate musical experience (the making and enjoyment of music), it could engage one of the crucial concerns of the time: what is the 'natural principle' that undergirds each art and science? As far as music is concerned, in his mature work Rameau locates this principle in the 'sounding body' (*corps sonore*), in the harmony produced by the vibrations of a string, a column of air, or a vocal cord. The *corps sonore* generates not only a principal resonance but a series of overtones, and from the resulting proportions and ratios of these multiple vibrations, Rameau seeks to demonstrate the harmonic syntax of the music of his time, and thereby the secrets of its affective energy. Among other things, he sought to show that the consonant triad, deriving directly from the harmonic series, is basic to all consonances, that a dissonant seventh chord is basic to all dissonances, and that most chord progressions are reducible to a dissonant seventh chord resolving on to a consonant triad.[13] He also held that the movement from one chord to another is to be understood in terms of the succession of chord roots (the 'fundamental bass' (*basse fondamentale*)).

For Rameau, then, the emotional power of music (as we would say today) is grounded in a phenomenon of the natural world, namely harmony—the ratios and proportions of differently pitched notes—and in harmony alone. And he went on to claim that musical harmony could account for proportional relations not only in music but also in the physical world at large: musical principles were applicable to all the sciences. Needless to say, on this account, instrumental music is firmly validated and comes into its own. Music does not need words and texts to be meaningful, for its powers derive from the qualities and capacities of sounds themselves. Thus, despite his eventual fame as France's foremost operatic composer, Rameau accorded a relatively low

---

WN: American Institute of Musicology, 1967), 29, as quoted and translated in Christensen, *Rameau and Musical Thought*, 237.

[12] Christensen, *Rameau and Musical Thought*, 6.

[13] For a clear exposition of his harmonic theory, see Lester, 'Rameau and Eighteenth-Century Harmonic Theory'.

value to words when combined with music: it is principally the musical sounds that are responsible for the emotional vigour of an opera.

Rameau's method entailed observing a musical practice and its effects, framing hypotheses through careful analysis to account for these observations, and synthesizing a foundational principle (the resonance of the 'sounding body').[14] In this way, Rameau was combining the traditions of *musica theorica* with those of *musica practica*, the theoretical and the practical.[15] We should not forget that Rameau was a down-to-earth practising musician, a superlative composer as well as renowned teacher: his theoretical endeavours were driven in large part by a need to account for, and lend support to, his day-to-day musical experience.

What can we say about the vision of 'nature' and the 'natural' that underwrites this fastidious musician's theory? In what kind of 'nature' is music's 'natural principle' grounded? The dominant sense, it would seem, is of nature as the realm of physical phenomena together with the laws that govern them, the objects of empirical investigation conducted according to the methods of the disciplines of eighteenth-century science, especially physics and mathematics. Music's expressiveness finds its derivation in configurations of the physical world so understood. In reviewing the *Treatise*, his friend Louis-Bertrand Castel remarked that 'nature gives us the same system that M. Rameau discovered in numbers'.[16] Nature is thus being conceived and theorized without reference to the metaphysical. To be sure, Rameau was not an atheist, materialist, or ontological naturalist.[17] He engaged in metaphysical speculation in his later years, including theological speculation,[18] and in his last published piece of writing he could even claim that the *corps sonore* was 'une image vivante de quelques attributs de la Divinité'.[19] But in his central and influential musical writings, theology plays no substantial part—he did not, for instance, revert to any of the classic medieval theological cosmologies that embedded the mathematics of music directly in the will and being of God. Rameau—at least at the time of his controversy with Rousseau—was interested in mathematics only insofar as it could account for the human,

---

[14] Christensen, *Rameau and Musical Thought*, 39.

[15] Broadly speaking, *musica theorica* focused on the nature of musical materials, such as the mathematics of intervals, the proportions inherent in consonances, while *musica practica* was concerned with the actual execution of music, music as composed, sung, and played. 'Rameau's most consequential intellectual accomplishment lay in the *rapprochement* he was able to effect between these two traditions': Christensen, *Rameau and Musical Thought*, 31.

[16] As quoted in Christensen, *Rameau and Musical Thought*, 133.

[17] 'Ontological naturalism' I take to be the view that nothing exists beyond the space–time continuum amenable to examination by the natural sciences.

[18] Christensen, *Rameau and Musical Thought*, ch. 10.

[19] *Lettre de M. Rameau aux philosophes*, p. 2041, in Jean-Philippe Rameau, *The Complete Theoretical Writings of Jean-Philippe Rameau*, ed. Erwin R. Jacobi, 6 vols, vol. vi (Middleton, WN: American Institute of Musicology, 1967), 510.

sensory experience of physical phenomena. Musicians should attempt to be 'true to nature', certainly, but not for nature's sake (or for God's sake), but for the sake of effective emotional expression. In effect, Rameau practises a 'methodological naturalism' in which the terminus of enquiry is not number, or invisible principles, or God—still less magic, angels, celestial spheres—but rather the experimentally verifiable phenomena of sound as experienced (emotionally) in music.[20]

Having said this, along with his avowed concern to honour nature in this primary, 'scientific' sense, the picture is more subtle than we might imagine. First, when it came to Rameau's own 'rational' theorizing, a variety of influences seems to be at work affecting his conception of 'nature': as Christensen has shown, Cartesianism, Neoplatonism, materialism, experimental physics, Newton's theory of gravity, John Locke's 'sensationalist' theory of knowledge, as well as pantheistic and occasionalist beliefs all had an impact on him at various times.[21] A considerable range of factors seem to be shaping the rationality that in turn shapes Rameau's conception of nature.

Second, although undoubtedly wanting to show that the basic principles of music can be discovered by scientific investigation, Rameau also wants to give a substantial place to music as sensed, as experienced. He believed that humans have what he came to call an 'instinct' (*un instinct*)—the 'ear' (*l'oreille*)—for music. This seems to denote an active yet non-reflective, non-rational faculty, which although not yielding knowledge enables an immediate apprehension of music's expressive power (and thus an inchoate intuition of its basic principles).[22] This faculty operates unconsciously, and is a faculty of the senses, not (as with reason) of the mind. It is, Rameau says, a 'gift of nature'.[23] The 'principle of nature', the *corps sonore*, is the cause of the instinct; the instinct verifies or confirms the principle of which it is the effect. It is thus a manifestation of nature internal to the human being. Speaking of his theoretical work, Rameau writes 'I had to prove the Instinct by its Principle and this

---

[20] 'Methodological naturalism' I take to entail the systematic exclusion, in the process of rational enquiry, of anything that cannot be examined according to the empirical methods of the natural sciences. This leaves open the possibility of idealism, theism, and so forth, and stands in contrast to what I take to be 'ontological naturalism' (see n. 17), which counts as real only those phenomena amenable to investigation by the natural sciences.

[21] Christensen, *Rameau and Musical Thought*, *passim*.

[22] See his *Observations sur notre instinct pour la musique in 1754* translated in full in Jean-Jacques Rousseau, *Essay on the Origin of Languages and Writings Related to Music*, ed. and trans. John T. Scott (Hanover, NH: University Press of New England, 1998), 175–97. I am indebted in what follows to the thorough treatment of this 'instinct' to be found in David E. Cohen, 'The "Gift of Nature": Musical "Instinct" and Musical Cognition in Rameau', in Suzannah Clark and Alexander Rehding (eds), *Music Theory and the Natural Order from the Renaissance to the Early Twentieth Century* (Cambridge: Cambridge University Press, 2001), 68–92.

[23] Rameau, *Observations sur notre instinct*, 175.

Principle by the same Instinct. They are, both of them, the work of Nature.'[24] Thus 'nature' *includes* this internal human instinct. As David Cohen explains,

> The selfsame Nature that operates objectively in the *corps sonore* as a physical phenomenon also appears *within* the human subject as the faculty correlative to that phenomenon, by which we may initially and provisionally enjoy the fruits of that first and more fundamental gift, even before, and as the necessary preliminary to, the full possession of that gift by Reason.[25]

According to Christensen, Rameau's stress on the testimony of concrete encounter with music, his insistence (which grew as the years passed) on taking the acoustical experience of music seriously, stands in some tension with the demands of his theoretical systematization.[26] Sometimes Rameau can speak as if rational and mathematical verification is all-determinative—the rhetorical flavour in the preface to the *Treatise*, for example, is highly Cartesian, and in his day Rameau could be criticized for trying to shoehorn data into ill-fitting, preconceived theories. (Contemporary commentators will point to numerous incongruities in Rameau's theory, where empirical observation grates against the theoretical grid.[27]) Pulling in the other direction, however, is a very strong stress on the need to heed the ear's testimony: 'We may judge music only through our hearing; and reason has no authority unless it is in agreement with the ear.'[28] More generally, Christensen goes as far as to say: 'For all of Rameau's emphasis on reason, over and over again we find him ceding to experience, even when this forces him . . . to loosen the tight theoretical systems that he labored so intently to construct.'[29]

Third, as Cohen observes, far from being merely an inert substance, 'nature' in Rameau's writings is frequently personified, as if 'she' had good intentions and thoughtful concerns for the flourishing of humanity. Nature 'gives' us both the *corps sonore* and the instinct to perceive it and respond to it.[30] This readily evokes, of course, a quasi-religious or even divine dimension to nature

---

[24] Rameau, *Observations sur notre instinct*, 177.

[25] Cohen, 'The "Gift of Nature"', 91.

[26] Part of the background here is the way he combines a kind of Cartesian rationalism, with its return to first principles, with an increasingly popular eighteenth-century empiricism that appeared to be amply embodied in the methods of Newtonian science.

[27] See Nicholas Cook, 'Epistemologies of Music Theory', in Thomas Christensen (ed.), *The Cambridge History of Western Music Theory* (Cambridge, MA: Cambridge University Press, 2006), 78–105, 85–91; Lester, 'Rameau and Eighteenth-Century Harmonic Theory', 772–4.

[28] Rameau, *Treatise on Harmony*, 139. Speaking of Rameau's late work, Christensen comments: 'It was not any attribute of numbers by which the ratios of music enjoy their ontological status. Rather, it is that these ratios originate as a fundamental *sensory* experience of a natural phenomenon; they can be described by numbers, certainly, but cannot be ascribed to them': Christensen, *Rameau and Musical Thought*, 297. The italics are his.

[29] Christensen, *Rameau and Musical Thought*, 34.

[30] Cohen, 'The "Gift of Nature"', 90–2.

which was not, at this stage of intellectual history at least, seen as being wholly incompatible with the 'nature' of 'scientific' enquiry.

All this indicates that Rameau's working idea of 'nature' was rather less clear-cut than it might at first seem.

Rousseau and the 'Natural'

Given his stature and the breadth of his intellectual aspirations, it is hardly surprising to find Rameau provoking both widespread attention and sustained opposition. His most celebrated opponent was his junior by almost thirty years, Jean-Jacques Rousseau, better known today outside the musical sphere, perhaps, but who was in fact a passionate music-lover, serious instrumentalist, and noteworthy composer. Only recently has it become clear to many that his extensive writings on music are integral to his philosophical work.[31]

Rousseau was quick to grasp the importance of Rameau's *Treatise*, which he knew well. In fact, the two shared much in common, in particular a belief in seeking the underlying logic of harmonic movement, and they even agreed on some of the basic elements of that logic. But a series of exchanges in the 1750s and 1760s exposed sharp differences between them that were never resolved.[32] We can begin with Rousseau's broadside, the fiercely polemical *Lettre sur la musique française* (1753), with its savage denunciation of French music.[33] Here Rousseau homes in on what was to be the centre of his music philosophy: the 'unity of melody' (*unité de mélodie*).[34] Melody above all holds the key to

[31] The most exhaustive treatment I have found of Rousseau on music is Robert Wokler, *Rousseau on Society, Politics, Music, and Language: An Historical Interpretation of his Early Writings* (New York: Garland Publishing, 1987), esp. ch. 4. But see also Thomas, *Music and the Origins of Language*, ch. 4; Julia Simon, 'Rousseau and Aesthetic Modernity: Music's Power of Redemption', *Eighteenth-Century Music* 2, 1 (2005): 41–56; Colm Kiernan, 'Rousseau and Music in the French Enlightenment', *French Studies* 26 (1972): 156–65; Michael O'Dea, *Jean-Jacques Rousseau: Music, Illusion and Desire* (Basingstoke: Macmillan, 1995), ch. 2; John T. Scott, 'The Harmony Between Rousseau's Musical Theory and His Philosophy', *Journal of the History of Ideas* 59, 2 (1998): 297–308; Guy Dammann, 'The Morality of Musical Imitation in Jean-Jacques Rousseau', doctrinal dissertation (King's College, 2006).

[32] For accounts of the debate, see Wokler, *Rousseau on Society*; Cynthia Verba, *Music and the French Enlightenment: Reconstruction of a Dialogue, 1750–1764* (Oxford: Clarendon Press, 1993), chs 1–3; Thomas, *Music and the Origins of Language*, ch. 4; Melissa A. Butler, 'The Quarrel Between Rousseau and Rameau', *Studies on Voltaire and the Eighteenth Century* 08 (2004): 183–91; John T. Scott, 'Introduction', in Jean-Jacques Rousseau, *Essay on the Origin of Languages and Writings Related to Music*, ed. and trans. John T. Scott (Hanover, NH: University Press of New England, 1998), pp. xiii–xlii; Catherine Kintzler, 'Rameau et Rousseau: Le Choc de deux esthétiques', preface in Jean-Jacques Rousseau, *Écrits sur la musique* ([Paris:] Éditions Stock, 1979), pp. ix–liv.

[33] Rousseau, *Essay*, 141–74.

[34] See Jacqueline Waeber, 'Jean-Jacques Rousseau's "unité de mélodie"', *Journal of the American Musicological Society* 62, 1 (Spring 2009): 79–143.

music's emotional expressivity, says Rousseau. Melody finds its source and grounding in language, and it is from melody that the 'principal character of a National Music must be derived'.[35] From this perspective, Rousseau lauds Italian music for its melodic power, grounded in the lively expressiveness of its language. But the French tongue, he insists, is intrinsically unmelodious and unsingable, a point he drives home by unleashing a ferocious critique of a monologue from *Armide*, an opera by the celebrated Jean-Baptiste Lully (1632–87). His letter winds up:

> I believe I have shown that there is neither meter nor melody in French Music, because the language is not susceptible to them; that French song is but a continual barking, unbearable to any ear not prepared for it; that its harmony is crude, expressionless, and uniquely feels its Schoolboy padding; that French arias are not at all arias; that the French recitative is not at all recitative. From which I conclude that the French do not at all have a Music and cannot have any; or that if they ever have any, it will be so much the worse for them.[36]

As we would expect, this invective provoked snarling responses (Rousseau was even banned from attending the Paris Opéra). A more constructive account of music in relation to language emerged in his *Essai sur l'origine des langues* (probably dating from the early 1750s), part of whose purpose was to react to Rameau.[37] Music would seem to belong to the core of the argument of the *Essai*.[38] The argument pivots around the affective character of vocalization; for Rousseau 'vocal sounds . . . are the privileged signs of passion'.[39] He contrasts seeing and hearing:

> . . . when it is a question of moving the heart and enflaming the passions . . . [t]he successive impression of discourse, striking with repeated blows, gives you a very different emotion from the presence of the object itself, which you have seen completely with a single glance. Assume that someone is in a painful situation

---

[35] Rousseau, *Essay*, 144.

[36] Rousseau, *Essay*, 174. Rousseau was a major disputant in the so-called 'Querelle des Bouffons' (1752–4), provoked by the staging of Pergolesi's *La serva padrona* in Paris, which concerned the relative value of French and Italian music: Charles B. Paul, 'Music and Ideology: Rameau, Rousseau, and 1789', *Journal of the History of Ideas* 32, 3 (1970): 395–410.

[37] Rousseau, *Essay*, 289–332.

[38] *Pace* Jacques Derrida. Downing Thomas opposes Derrida's influential interpretation of Rousseau in *De le grammatologie*, at least to the extent that for Thomas, 'music is at the heart of the *Essai*, both because . . . the *Essai* is conceived—at least in part—as a response to Rameau, and because music explicitly remains present throughout the text as central to Rousseau's conception of language itself'. But he continues: 'Derrida's reading of Rousseau nevertheless remains a powerful and convincing one in that he insists on treating the *Essai* as part of larger philosophical and aesthetic concerns, not as a "badly digested" fragment of the second *Discours* or as a minor and thus peripheral digression on music': Thomas, *Music and the Origins of Language*, 89. See Jacques Derrida, *Of Grammatology*, trans. Gayatri Chakravorty Spivak (London: The John Hopkins University Press, 1997), ch. 3.

[39] Thomas, *Music and the Origins of Language*, 101.

which you know perfectly well: you will not easily be moved to cry in seeing the afflicted person, but give him time to tell you everything he feels, and soon you will burst into tears.[40]

Rousseau invites us to see both language and music as originating in pre-societal times, in a kind of melodic speech that directly reflected the accents and inflections of human emotion. They arose not because of basic physical needs (as many of Rousseau's contemporaries thought) but because of the passions unique to humans and essential to sociality—such as love, hatred, pity, anger. Our emergence from a solitary and merely physical existence to that of social and moral agency is marked by the appearance of these communicative, social passions. 'As soon as one man was recognised by another as a sentient, thinking being and similar to himself, the desire or the need to communicate his feelings and thoughts made him seek the means for doing so.'[41] And it is the *voice* that fulfils just this role, the *melodic* voice: 'A language that has only articulations and voices... has only half its riches; it conveys ideas, it is true, but in order to convey feelings, images, it still needs a rhythm and sounds, that is, a melody.'[42]

We should not miss the social and political thrust of Rousseau's argument. This primitive song-speech arose through articulating sentiments that are other-oriented, socially directed, through recognizing other sentient beings like ourselves and acknowledging them as human, something intrinsic to a just society. 'One feels that music concerns us more than painting because it makes one person closer to another (*rapproche plus l'homme de l'homme*) and always gives us some idea of those who are as we are.'[43] Or again, 'As soon as vocal signs strike your ear, they herald a being similar to yourself; they are, so to speak, the organs of the soul and if they depict solitude they tell you that you are not alone.'[44] Downing Thomas remarks that 'For Rousseau, vocal sounds are not so much expressions of ideas as they are moments of identification and social bonding... music is both an original and originating element in the social fabric.'[45] John Scott explains the link with Rousseau's political philosophy as it came to fruition in *The Social Contract*:

---

[40] Rousseau, *Essay*, 291.

[41] Rousseau, *Essay*, 289–90.

[42] Rousseau, *Essay*, 318. Or again: 'in order to move a young heart, to repulse an unjust aggressor, nature dictates accents, cries, complaints. The most ancient words are invented in this way, and this is why the first languages were tuneful and passionate': Rousseau, *Essay*, 294.

[43] *Essai sur l'origine des langues*, 421, as quoted and translated in Tracy B. Strong, 'Music, the Passions, and Political Freedom in Rousseau', in Christie McDonald and Stanley Hoffmann (eds), *Rousseau and Freedom* (Cambridge: Cambridge University Press, 2010), 92–109, 102.

[44] *Essai sur l'origine des langues*, 421, as quoted and translated in Strong, 'Music, the Passions, and Political Freedom', 100.

[45] Thomas, *Music and the Origins of Language*, 105, 121. 'Through melody, the listener re-experiences the emotional link to other beings which was once the intersubjective force that brought dispersed individuals into society; and at the same time, she/he re-encounters the

A melodic language binds the community through the unmediated expression of shared passion. The image of the unanimous expression of a common will based upon shared passions recalls the legitimate political community of the *Social Contract* and suggests that Rousseau's 'general will' should be conceived less as the combined articulation of rational interests than as a unison of voices, as in the singing of a national anthem, a unison based on the affective cultural foundation of common customs, opinions, and mores.[46]

Rousseau's vision of music is thus an imitative 'language of the passions' (*langage des passions*)—through its primordial link with vocality. But this glorious melodic language was not to last. Rousseau unfolds a lengthy narrative of decline in which music and language go their separate ways. In time, language loses its musicality—moving from accent to articulation, emotion to thought, speech-rhythm to syntax, eloquence to logic: language 'becomes more precise and less passionate; it substitutes ideas for feelings, it no longer speaks to the heart but to reason'.[47] And music loses its roots in the immediacy of the passionate voice, relying on stimulating physical pleasure to strengthen its moral impact. Rousseau believed that the barbarian invasions of the Roman Empire from the North replaced feeling-language with the language of need, turning musical melody into a harsh and flat succession of sounds. Especially desultory was the emergence of musical harmony in the Middle Ages, leading to an infatuation with harmony and harmonic science typical of the 'Northern' nations. Rousseau concludes the sorry tale:

> This is how singing gradually became an art entirely separated from the speech from which it takes its origin; how the harmonics of sound have caused vocal inflections to be forgotten; and how, finally, limited to the purely physical effect of the combination of vibrations, music found itself deprived of the moral effects that it used to produce when it was doubly the voice of nature.[48]

cultural order that defines the terms of the social bond': Thomas, *Music and the Origins of Language*, 128.

[46] Scott, 'Introduction', p. xxxiii. See also C. N. Dugan and Tracy Strong, 'Music, Politics, Theatre and Representation in Rousseau', in Patrick Riley (ed.), *The Cambridge Companion to Rousseau* (Cambridge: Cambridge University Press, 2001), 329–64. Music was for Rousseau 'an indispensable component of socialisation and the advent of culture . . . Melody expresses the passions through the imitation of vocal inflections and accents; and these accents are closely tied . . . to the constitution of the human being as a participant in cultural structures and exchanges which ultimately revolve, Rousseau claims, around the emotions that first determined them': Thomas, *Music and the Origins of Language*, 123; see the whole section 121–42. Matthew Voorhees argues that approaching Rousseau's political thought in the light of his views on music enables us to delineate different conceptions of freedom in his work; see Matthew Voorhees, 'Melodic Communities: Music and Freedom in Rousseau's Political Thought', *History of Political Thought* 32, 4 (2011): 617–44.

[47] Rousseau, *Essay*, 296. 'Écouter la voix de la nature ne signifie donc plus analyser les phénomènes sonores, il s'agit de consulter son cœur': Kintzler, 'Rameau et Rousseau', 19.

[48] Rousseau, *Essay*, 331.

Contemporary music (and language), then, is the upshot of a long history of deterioration. The tone of Rousseau's *Essai* is pathos-ridden; Julia Simon describes it as 'elegiac', a 'lament for an immediacy, fulfillment, plenitude and, ultimately, a satisfaction that is lacking in the present', expressing a 'plaintive relation to the past'.[49] Nonetheless, he does seem to leave open the possibility that music of an appropriate type can play a transformative role through its socializing power, healing to some extent the ruptures he believed threatened eighteenth-century cultural life. All music will carry at least some trace of its vocally passionate origins; indeed, the very fact of music witnesses to our deep-rooted sociality.[50] As Tracy Strong summarizes it: '*The actuality of the experience of music is testimony to the existence, or the possibility of the existence of a truly human social bond.*'[51]

All this can be usefully set alongside Rousseau's anthropology in other writings. Rousseau famously declared that his entire output rests on the 'great principle that nature made man happy and good, and that society depraves him and makes him miserable'.[52] He located 'natural goodness' in an original 'pure state of nature', in which humans were free from dependence on each other and transparent to each other. In this state, humans lead essentially solitary and self-sufficient lives. In due course, other-directed passions emerged, as natural self-love (*amour de soi*) turned into other-directed *amour-propre*, the most basic passion being pity. It is in this condition, it seems, we are to trace the emergence of music and language. Rousseau believed that these other-directed passions took a harmful turn when they became prideful and competitive, and the 'other' was diminished. Humans have now lost their freedom and independence, becoming dependent on each other. According to John Scott, for Rousseau, 'Personal dependence remains the essential problem of developed humans and the obstacle to our freedom and happiness.'[53] The tale of music Rousseau charts is symptomatic of this loss of social transparency and freedom engendered by the loss of our 'natural goodness'.

---

[49] Simon, 'Rousseau and Aesthetic Modernity': 46.

[50] 'Rousseau does not leave us with hopeless pessimism or with an empty utopia. He leaves us with a tentative, "maybe sometime, someplace"': Stuart A. MacNiven, 'Politics, Language and Music in the Unity of Rousseau's System', *Studies on Voltaire and the Eighteenth Century* 08 (2004): 166–74, 174. See Thomas, *Music and the Origins of Language*, 122–5; Simon, 'Rousseau and Aesthetic Modernity'; Julia Simon, 'Music and the Performance of Community in Rousseau', *Studies on Voltaire and the Eighteenth Century* 8 (2004): 192–200.

[51] Strong, 'Music, the Passions, and Political Freedom', 100. Italics original.

[52] Jean-Jacques Rousseau, 'Rousseau, Judge of Jean-Jacques: Dialogues', in Jean-Jacques Rousseau, *The Collected Writings of Rousseau*, ed. Roger D. Masters and Christopher Kelly, vol. i (London: University Press of New England, 1990), 213.

[53] John T. Scott, 'Politics as the Imitation of the Divine in Rousseau's *Social Contract*', *Polity* 26, 3 (1994): 473–501, 479.

What, then, did Rousseau make of Rameau, as far as music is concerned? Bluntly, he thinks Rameau dehumanizes music. So bewitched is the celebrated composer with the rational element of harmony that he loses sight of the passionate element of vocal melody.[54] A voice, after all, cannot sing harmony. Harmony is an 'extra', a material refinement; its beauties are conventional and to an untutored ear mere noise. Harmony is 'anything but founded on Nature... it is established merely on analogues and conformities that an inventive man could overturn tomorrow by others more natural'.[55]

> ...the pleasure of Harmony is merely a pleasure of pure sensation, and the enjoyment of the senses is always short—satiety and boredom follow close behind; but the pleasure of Melody and of Song is a pleasure of interest and of feeling which speaks to the heart, and which the Artist can always sustain and renew by dint of genius.[56]

In Rameau's scheme, melody's emotional potency is dependent on harmony; indeed, 'It belongs to Harmony alone to stir the passions; Melody derives its force only from that source, from which it directly emanates.'[57] There is nothing in nature (in its 'scientific' sense) akin to a melody, Rameau observes, whereas harmony is built into every vibrating body in the universe. Harmony is earthed in the *natura naturata*. What could possibly be more *natural* than that?[58] To which Rousseau responds: nature has no passion since it has no voice. Harmony is *un*natural, for its techniques are determined by rational laws and mathematical calculation. Harmony may have its place, but on its own it can never get us beyond the merely material. The enjoyment we gain from harmony considered on its own works purely at the level of physical sensation, not emotional expression. The bare physicality of Rameau's *corps*

---

[54] For Rousseau, 'ce n'est pas la nature des sons qui fonde la vertu expressive de la musique, c'est la ligne mélodique d'un discours, infléchie selon la variété des sentiments qu'il exprime': Kintzler, 'Rameau et Rousseau', 33–4.

[55] From 'Harmony', in the *Dictionnaire de musique*: Rousseau, *Essay*, 409.

[56] From 'unité de mélodie', in the *Dictionnaire de musique*: Rousseau, *Essay*, 477. Confusingly (for our purposes), in at least one place Rousseau speaks of 'natural' music as the kind of music 'limited to the physics of Sounds alone', which is attractive merely because of the physical pleasantness of its sounds, whereas 'imitative' music excites human emotions: Rousseau, *Essay*, 439.

[57] Preface to *Observations sur notre instinct pour la musique* (1754), p. vi, in Rameau, *The Complete Theoretical Writings*, iii. 260, as translated in Rousseau, *Essay*, 175.

[58] 'As long as melody alone is considered as the principal moving force of music's effects there will not be great progress in this art': Rameau insists. 'It is therefore only directly from the harmony, mother of this melody, that the different effects we experience in music arise': Jean-Philippe Rameau, 'Erreurs sur la musique dans l'Encyclopedie', in Erwin R. Jacobi (ed.), *The Complete Theoretical Writings of Jean-Philippe Rameau*, 6 vols, vol. v (Middleton, WN: American Institute of Musicology, 1969), 309–30, 44, as quoted and translated in Scott, 'The Harmony': 295.

sonore is empty of humanity; to insist that the power of music revolves around it is redolent of the kind of rationalism and materialism we need to resist, with all its sorry political and cultural ramifications.[59]

So Rousseau has little time for the notion of a 'universal' music. Passions may be universal but because of diverse physical contexts, different cultures produce different kinds of music. Music is inevitably shaped by temperament, diet, climate, historical contingencies; this is why music can vary so radically across different cultural groupings. If it is true, as some report, that certain melodies cure a tarantula bite (one of the more colourful topics Rousseau enjoys discussing), that is because the particular melody is appropriate to the sufferer's culture; not because of any immediate physical effect.[60]

Standing back, then, what vision of the 'natural' shapes Rousseau, this impassioned *philosophe*, as he is drawn into arguing about music? In the first place, Rousseau's is clearly a strongly *anthropological* vision.[61] Music must be earthed in human 'nature' before anything else, specifically in humankind's socializing affects. He has scant interest in rooting music in the constitution of the physical world at large. The elements of the material world are emotionally inert and impotent, whereas the human melodic voice is affectively charged, and that is what matters when accounting for music's expressivity. Second, his focus is on an anthropology of *origins*, on a condition prior to the corruptions of moral evil, when emotionally toned vocalizations played a pivotal role in establishing and maintaining social cohesion. We should underline that for Rousseau, music was not part of the 'state of Nature', the essentially asocial condition of human independence prior to the arrival of sociality. Music is emphatically not natural in this sense. Music (with language) finds its source in other-directed sentiments, in the drive to socialize. This drive is not intrinsically corrupt or misdirected, but it is nonetheless (as we might say today) 'artificial' or 'conventional', and as such, stands at one remove from the primary original condition.[62] The contrast between the natural individual and artificial sociality is crucial for Rousseau's whole case. Although music is grounded in a universal human nature (considered prior to

---

[59] On the relation between his music theory and his wider thought, see Scott, 'The Harmony'.

[60] Rousseau, *Essay*, 324.

[61] Guy Dammann comments: 'in the context of the *Querelle* and its continuations, the conception of nature at each pole is radically different: Rameau's conception is, broadly speaking, that of a natural scientist; Rousseau's, again broadly speaking, that of the anthropologist': Dammann, 'The Morality of Musical Imitation', 141.

[62] Rousseau writes: 'although the organ of speech is natural to man, speech itself is nonetheless not natural to him': Jean-Jacques Rousseau, 'Discourse on the Origin and Foundation of Inequality among Men (Second Discourse)', in Roger D. Masters and Christopher Kelly (eds), *The Collected Writings of Rousseau*, vol. iii (London: University Press of New England, 1992), 1–95, 82.

evil), in passions that are common to all, it is also being understood as socially and culturally formed.[63]

Third, although Rousseau was not a theologian, and theology does not play any explicit part in his arguments about music, he was no atheist, advocating a form of deism with a strong accent on religious toleration.[64] And the human nature in which Rousseau wants to situate music is certainly not being conceived without specific theological commitments. By the end of his *Second Discourse* he asserts that he has shown that 'man is naturally good' and that in this way he has 'justified' nature,[65] and makes it quite clear that he sees the laws of nature at large as the manifestation of Providence and that political life finds its proper grounding here. John Scott lucidly explains the momentum of Rousseau's thought, somewhat boldly using the term 'natural theology':

> Rousseau attempts to remedy the problem of personal dependence by making politics an imitation of the divine. He would make citizens dependent not on men, but on the laws: laws that imitate the immutable laws of nature. The citizen's dependence on the laws of the State must be as complete as natural man's dependence on the laws of nature, and the laws of nature are, for Rousseau, ultimately reflections of divine providence. Our original condition as well-ordered beings in a well-ordered whole provides a formal model for the remaking of our existence. For Rousseau, this well-ordered whole is not merely the 'nature' of the sceptical philosophers but a reflection of providence, and his natural theology thus provides a coherent foundation for his political thought.[66]

'Natural goodness' in Rousseau, then, is not to be taken in any straightforwardly moral way, but rather in what he calls a 'physical' sense, meaning something akin to 'properly ordered': 'For Rousseau, by (physical) nature we are a good or ordered part of a good or ordered nature.'[67] And this in turn is

---

[63] Lionel Gossman argues that Rameau and Rousseau 'represent two completely different ways of understanding the world and exemplify a conflict that is found at this time in many other areas of thought; . . . [the debate between them is] of the deepest significance both for the student of Rousseau and for the student of the eighteenth century': Lionel Gossman, 'Time and History in Rousseau', *Studies on Voltaire and the Eighteenth Century* 30 (1964): 311–49, 319, 320. He goes on to locate the key divergence in their respective perceptions of time: Rameau sets music in the context of a timeless rational order embracing the entire cosmos; Rousseau's vision is historically embedded and irreducibly time-laden. Although they clearly are different in this respect, I am inclined to see the pivotal difference in that Rameau's centre of gravity is in *nature* (in the 'scientific' sense), Rousseau's in *culture*.

[64] On Rousseau and religion, see Ronald Grimsley, *Rousseau and the Religious Quest* (Oxford: Clarendon Press, 1968); Victor Gourevitch, 'The Religious Thought', in Patrick Riley (ed.), *The Cambridge Companion to Rousseau* (Cambridge: Cambridge University Press, 2001), 193–246; Mark Hulliung, 'Rousseau, Voltaire, and the Revenge of Pascal', in Patrick Riley (ed.), *The Cambridge Companion to Rousseau* (Cambridge: Cambridge University Press, 2001), 57–77.

[65] Rousseau, 'Second Discourse', 74.

[66] Scott, 'Politics as the Imitation of the Divine': 474.

[67] Scott, 'Politics as the Imitation of the Divine': 477.

sustained by Providence. In his *Letter to Voltaire*,[68] he quite explicitly sets his vision of humanity within the physical world in a theological setting, arguing that we should learn to trust what he calls 'the ordinary course of things'.[69] Providence operates through the universal laws of nature.[70]

The similarities and critical differences between our two protagonists with regard to the music–nature relation should by now be evident. In accounting for the affective potency of music, both Rameau and Rousseau appeal to 'naturalness'. The concept of 'naturalness' was an enormously important matter for the leading eighteenth-century philosophers (of whatever brand), in a culture eager to secure a reliable ontology that could give sense and shape to scientific and cultural life. However, Rameau's orientation is primarily to the physical world at large, including the human body, to the physics and mathematics of sound as empirically demonstrable by the natural sciences, as well as to the human body (music's physiological effects), and (secondarily) to its perception by human instinct. To trace music's affective powers to its supposed mimicry of primitive human vocal inflections, as with Rousseau, can only be profoundly *un*natural in Rameau's eyes. Rousseau's approach to music, on the other hand, is oriented primarily to nature in a human–cultural sense, seeing music as emerging in a primordial human situation in which the vocalization of emotion is intrinsic to sociality. Music is first and foremost a human, culturally shaped invention, and fans out into many types, depending on the contingencies of surroundings and circumstance. To become embroiled in physics and mathematics simply misses the point; indeed, to do so is highly *un*natural.

WHAT IS NATURAL ABOUT NATURAL THEOLOGY?

What has all this to do with natural theology? In short: a great deal, because the debate pushes to the surface a cluster of substantial issues surrounding the status of 'the natural' which can hardly be avoided in any theological explor-ation of modernity and its legacies, and in turn, in any contemporary advocacy of natural theology, artistic or otherwise. First, and perhaps most obviously, it throws into relief a tension whose negotiation (practical or theoretical) has determined the shape of many of the most prominent binaries of modernity: that between nature and culture, discovery and construction, receptivity and creativity, rootedness in 'the given' and orientation to the 'new'.

---

[68] Rousseau, 'Letter to Voltaire, II'. See also Gourevitch, 'The Religious Thought', 203.
[69] Rousseau, 'Letter to Voltaire, II', 112.
[70] 'Accordingly, Rousseau depersonalizes even God by denying Him omnipotence and subordinating Him to impersonal necessity': Gourevitch, 'The Religious Thought', 203.

No less pointedly, second, we are reminded of what has become a recurring refrain in theological and philosophical treatments of modernity, that construals of 'nature' or 'the natural' are just that—construals. Employing these terms as if they were unambiguous vehicles of transparent description is demonstrably naïve, for not only do they relate to highly polysemous and polyvalent concepts, but their meaning is inevitably conditioned by social and cultural commitments and agendas, desires, and projects.[71] Alan Torrance observes: 'A beaver builds a dam and it is natural, human beings build a dam and it is vigorously protested as being unnatural—although human beings are being encouraged to eat vast amounts of natural fibre precisely because they are "natural beings".'[72] In this environment, theological interpretations of nature/the natural cannot be dismissed simply on the grounds that they *are* interpretations, as if that fact alone rendered them unserviceable or invalid. (And this is so despite the fact that it is a mark of modernity that conceptions of nature become increasingly a-theological, functionally atheist.) Further, a notion of nature that may seem to enjoy independence of metaphysical commitments, or which is presented as such, may on closer inspection reveal just the opposite.

That leads us to a third benefit of attending to the Rameau–Rousseau debate: when a 'natural theology' is being advanced, we will be pressed to be more theologically scrupulous about just what might be on offer. To what extent is the semantic field of 'natural' theologically conditioned and to what extent is it determined and presumed a priori, in advance of theological considerations? The pressure on Christian theology enjoined by the New Testament would seem to impel us towards a Christological focus here: one that takes seriously the Pauline affirmations of Christ as the one in whom, through whom, and for whom all things were created, and through whom all things have been reconciled (e.g. Colossians 1:15–20). This would necessitate setting 'nature' and its cognates in a hermeneutical context in which the being of the creature, human or otherwise, is interpreted according to what has

---

[71] For discussion, see Charles Taliaferro and Jil Evans (eds), *Turning Images in Philosophy, Science, and Religion: A New Book of Nature* (Oxford: Oxford University Press, 2011); L. L. Neil Evernden, *The Social Creation of Nature* (Baltimore: Johns Hopkins University Press, 1992); McGrath, *A Scientific Theology*, vol. i, ch. 3; C. S. Lewis, *Studies in Words*, 2nd edn. (Cambridge: Cambridge University Press, 1967), 24–74; Kate Soper, *What is Nature? Culture, Politics and the Non-Human* (Oxford: Blackwell Publishing, 1995); John Torrance, *The Concept of Nature* (Oxford: Clarendon Press, 1992); Steven Vogel, *Against Nature: The Concept of Nature in Critical Theory* (Albany, NY: State University of New York Press, 1996); John S. Habgood, *The Concept of Nature* (London: Darton, Longman & Todd, 2002); Bruno Latour, *Politics of Nature: How to Bring the Sciences into Democracy* (Cambridge, MA: Harvard University Press, 2004); Timothy Morton, *Ecology Without Nature: Rethinking Environmental Aesthetics* (Cambridge, MA: Harvard University Press, 2007).

[72] Alan J. Torrance, 'Response by Alan J. Torrance', in Hilary D. Regan and Alan J. Torrance (eds), *Christ and Context: The Confrontation Between Gospel and Culture* (Edinburgh: T & T Clark, 1993), 192–200, 196.

already been enacted in Christ, rather than one in which this enactment presupposes a prior act of creation deemed to be logically antecedent to, and determinative of, it.[73]

Nature/the Natural in Christ

To elucidate this further, it is worth marking out four broad senses of 'natural' as employed by those who use the expression 'natural theology', and with respect to each, indicating where an approach of the sort I have just advocated might lead us. (These are by no means the only ones.) First, 'natural' frequently has the sense of pertaining to *the physical world, understood as that concrete reality amenable to investigation by the physical and biological sciences* (the 'nature' which forms the chief grounding of Rameau's music theory). In this case, a Christological hermeneutic would entail centring on the Son through whom all things were made, who became physical flesh for our sakes, and was raised as an anticipation of the ultimate re-creation of all things. A perspective begins to open up consonant with this, in which nature is regarded as issuing from covenant love, fashioned freely out of nothing, wholly contingent upon the Creator yet ontologically distinct, and oriented to a final consummation prefigured in the raising of Christ from the dead. Second, 'natural' can have the sense of pertaining to *the quintessentially human* (the prime validating ground of music for Rousseau)—in which case a Christological hermeneutic directs us to a quite specific human person (not a generalized condition or semi-mythical state), and through this person to the intended eschatological destiny of humankind. On this view, what is 'naturally' human cannot be conceived in abstraction from what has been instantiated in Jesus of Nazareth, incarnate, crucified, and risen. The primordial human is none other than the New Adam, who lives out and embodies the eternally grounded divine intention for humans. Third, 'natural' can have the sense of pertaining to *those constructive activities designated by the term 'culture'* (crucial for Rousseau's conception of music); in other words, what humans do with their environment, what they 'make' of it. In this case, a Christological hermeneutic will conceive these activities initially in the light of the vocation given to humans as God's image-bearers: this finds its concrete realization in Christ, the one in whom creation finds its definitive, human voice and representative, and with whom, by the Spirit, we are invited into

---

[73] See the trenchant comments in Torrance, 'Response by Alan J. Torrance'. Torrance criticizes the notion of a Christology formed 'in the framework of nature' (he is responding to a paper by Jürgen Moltmann) for presupposing a foundational interpretation of nature that constrains Christology, instead of heeding the New Testament affirmation that Christ is subject to nothing, and is himself to be ultimately determinative of all readings of nature.

strenuous engagement with our environment, to extend and elaborate creation's praise, in anticipation of that transfiguration of all things that has already been embodied in him.

To these three we may add a fourth sense, implicit in the Rameau–Rousseau debate but not mentioned so far, namely 'natural' as pertaining to *properly functioning human reason*. In this case, a Christological hermeneutic orients us first of all to the reshaping of human rationality, embodied primordially in Christ and now enabled in us by the Spirit through the 'reschematizing' of our minds (Romans 12:2). Implied in this is that the ability to recognize and affirm theological truth, the transformation of our epistemological capacities, the 'conversion of the imagination'[74] required for the recognition of 'naturalness', is intrinsic to the dynamic of reconciliation. That is to say, the redemptive momentum in Christ includes, through the Spirit, the gift of being enabled to apprehend that momentum *as* redemption, and, indeed, requires such a gift, for on what grounds are we to assume that we possess in ourselves a fully reliable epistemological capacity, that some zone or mode of human reasoning is wholly immune to the distortions and deformations of human sin?[75] It is thus from this perspective (and not from one presumed to be superior a priori) that we are led to suspect the much-cherished belief in a universal rational faculty, tradition-free, independent of the contingencies of time, space, and culture, impervious to corruption, and thereby capable of laying down in advance unalterable criteria for authentic knowledge of, and speech about, God.[76]

We do not, of course, have the space here to defend adequately the kind of stance we are developing against the objections that might well be lodged against it, especially by those who want to find a place for the arts in a natural theology. But we can at least address one likely source of unease. To be so

[74] See Richard B. Hays, *The Conversion of the Imagination: Paul as Interpreter of Israel's Scripture* (Grand Rapids, MI: Eerdmans, 2005).

[75] The question is pressed by, among many others, Alan Torrance; see '*Auditus Fidei*: Where and How Does God Speak? Faith, Reason, and the Question of Criteria', in Paul J. Griffiths and Reinhard Hütter (eds), *Reason and the Reasons of Faith* (London: T & T Clark, 2005), 27–52. This is not, of course, to allege that all human reasoning outside the true Church is necessarily distorted and false—this would be yet another theologically unwarranted a priori move. It is rather to say that all human reasoning is *prone* to the distorting effects of sinful bias; no quarter of our minds can claim diplomatic immunity from prosecution.

[76] Among the huge corpus of literature on the chimera of a context-free reason or rationality, and on the related notion of reason qua reason as *necessarily* or inherently liberating, see e.g. Alasdair C. MacIntyre, *Whose Justice? Which Rationality?* (Notre Dame, IN: University of Notre Dame Press, 1988); Ernest Gellner, *Reason and Culture: The Historic Role of Rationality and Rationalism* (Oxford: Blackwell Publishing, 1992); Raymond Murphy, *Rationality and Nature: A Sociological Inquiry into a Changing Relationship* (Boulder, CO: Westview Press, 1994); Roy A. Clouser, *The Myth of Religious Neutrality: An Essay on the Hidden Role of Religious Belief in Theories*, rev. edn. (Notre Dame, IN: University of Notre Dame Press, 2005); Alister E. McGrath, *A Scientific Theology: Reality*, 3 vols, vol. ii (Edinburgh: T & T Clark, 2001).

insistently theological, it will be said, greatly risks compromising the integrity of the arts. Surely we must *first* respect the ('natural'!) particularities of artistic making and reception, give due space to the witness of music and painting, dance and drama, film and sculpture in their own right, and only *then* consider the obligations of a New Testament-oriented theology, with its Christological and pneumatological commitments. Downloading such immense and heavy metaphysical apparatus before we have allowed the arts their own say, before we have respected the reality of the arts on their own ground, can only lead to distortion.

This kind of plea is widespread in many quarters today, and its force certainly needs to be felt, lest we fall into some kind of crude theological instrumentalism. Theologians have an uncanny knack of sucking the life out of the arts in their zeal for orthodoxy—the examples are legion, and have understandably caused the Church much embarrassment. At the same time, it is not immediately obvious how the arts will *necessarily* be best served by assuming from the outset that a respect for 'reality' is best gained, if not from a neutral epistemic vantage point, then one more determinative than that provided by God's redemption of created reality in Jesus Christ. If we adopt an alternative—and by implication superior—viewpoint for reading the arts 'on their own ground', by what criteria have we deemed it worthy of such a status? On what ground have we come to the conviction that such a perspective will provide the required prolegomena for a theology that attempts to come to terms truthfully with the arts (or for that matter, with anything else)?[77]

Does this mean as a matter of principle that we renounce all proposals for 'natural theology'?[78] By no means. For it is precisely *because* of the orientation and criteria to which the New Testament directs us, centred on the transformative reconciliation of all things in the person of Christ, that this would be an unwarranted move. In particular, we need to hear very clearly what would seem to be the central passion of many contemporary advocates of natural theology, evident also in numerous biblical texts: namely, to bear witness 'to the nongodforsakenness of the world even under the conditions of sin',[79] to testify to the active presence of God where God is not overtly acknowledged *as* active and present, perhaps even where the very conception

---

[77] I am not yet persuaded that David Brown's project (see n. 5) has faced up to this kind of question sufficiently. See Jeremy S. Begbie, 'Openness and Specificity: A Conversation with David Brown on Theology and Classical Music', in Robert C. MacSwain and Taylor Worley (eds), *Theology, Aesthetics, and Culture: Responses to the Work of David Brown* (Oxford: Oxford University Press, 2012), 145–56.

[78] For a very useful survey of different types of natural theology, and—in my view—wise and judicious conclusions, see David Fergusson, 'Types of Natural Theology', in F. LeRon Shults (ed.), *The Evolution of Rationality: Interdisciplinary Essays in Honor of J. Wentzel van Huyssteen* (Grand Rapids, MI: Eerdmans, 2006), 380–93.

[79] Hauerwas, *With the Grain of the Universe*, 20.

of a god is repudiated and denied. If the God of Jesus Christ and the Holy Spirit is indeed the Creator who is active to redeem the totality of the space–time continuum, it is hard to see how we could do otherwise. Whether we call such an endeavour natural theology, or, as I would prefer, one responsibility within a larger Christian theology of creation, is open to debate.[80] But Eberhard Jüngel is surely justified in calling for a '*more* natural theology': one that moves outward from Christ as Creator and Reconciler of all things, and is thus more fully oriented towards 'nature' than many traditional forms of natural theology. Such an enterprise will lead us

> Deeper into [creation's] needs and difficulties (*aporiai*), but also deeper into its hidden glories! Deeper . . . into compassionate solidarity with those who cry *de profundis* . . . But even deeper into the joy of the unanswered mystery of the fact that we are actually here and are not rather nothing. Deeper into the joy of being able to see the one and only light of life reflecting in the manifold lights of creation and thus, in its light, being able to see with astonishment creation's own peculiar light.[81]

MUSIC'S 'NATURAL' WITNESS

For the remainder of this chapter, bearing in mind the theological orientations we have just outlined, we return to music and ask: how might music play a part in a theology that seeks to bear witness to the non-godforsakenness of creation even under the conditions of sin? I cite just four brief examples of a response to

---

[80] Alister McGrath is one who argues for a contemporary retrieval of 'natural theology'. 'A legitimate Christian natural theology', he writes, 'interprets nature in a Christian manner— namely, as God's creation': McGrath, *A Scientific Theology*, i. 295. I am less than convinced that retaining the term 'natural theology' here is wise, in that it will too easily trawl with it (or smuggle in) some of the more questionable characteristics of Enlightenment apologetics: in particular, ontological and epistemological conventions concerning 'nature'/'natural' that lack sufficient theological control. Colin Gunton contrasts natural theology with a 'theology of nature', the latter designating 'an account of what things naturally are, by virtue of their createdness': Colin E. Gunton, *A Brief Theology of Revelation: The 1993 Warfield Lectures* (Edinburgh: T & T Clark, 1995), 56; or, put differently, an interpretation of nature in the light of the self-revelation of God in Jesus Christ: Jürgen Moltmann, *God in Creation: An Ecological Doctrine of Creation* (London: SCM Press, 1985), 53–60. The failure to make some such basic distinction has propagated immense confusion in current debates about natural theology, resulting in, for example, the common (but mistaken) assumption that those who mount objections to natural theology (such as Karl Barth) will of necessity be working with a weak theology of God's activity in creation at large.

[81] Eberhard Jüngel, *Christ, Justice and Peace: Toward a Theology of the State in Dialogue with the Barmen Declaration*, trans. D. Bruce Hamill and Alan J. Torrance (Edinburgh: T & T Clark, 1992), 28–9.

that question, some of which relate to material found elsewhere in this book; they correspond to the four senses of 'nature'/'natural' I highlighted earlier.

Music and Cosmos

First, there is music's potential to bear witness to the character of the physical cosmos as the creation of the triune God of Jesus Christ. We might take our initial cue from Rameau's stress on the material embeddedness of musical sound, but we can set this against a far wider, theological canvas by rehearsing and expanding some of the observations we made in Chapter 3 concerning the music of J. S. Bach. David Bentley Hart has written that 'Bach's is the ultimate Christian music; it reflects as no other human artefact ever has or could the Christian vision of creation'.[82] There is more than a streak of hyperbole there, but the thrust of the sentiment cannot be dismissed. Of special importance is something that Laurence Dreyfus contends was central to Bach's art, namely 'invention' (*inventio*).[83] Many young pianists' first introduction to Bach will be one of his two-part inventions.[84] The composer tells us these were designed to serve as models for 'good inventions' and 'developing the same satisfactorily'. With its ancestry in classical rhetoric, in Bach's time *inventio* was widely used as a metaphor for the basic musical idea or unit that formed the subject matter of a piece. Not only this, it denoted the method whereby this idea could be discovered. The key for Bach was to find *generative* material, an idea that was capable of being developed in a variety of ways, for 'by crafting a workable idea, one unlocks the door to a complete musical work'.[85] The method of finding an invention was thus inseparable from thinking about how it might be developed—*elaboratio*. Hence Bach's concern to show us models of good inventions *and* of their development. It seems that most of Bach's contemporaries viewed *elaboratio* as among the duller elements of composing. Bach appears to have thought in terms of extensive elaboration from the start, even when choosing the initial material: 'One might even be tempted to say that in Bach's works both invention and elaboration are marked by an almost equally intense mental activity...In no other composer of the period does one find such a fanatical zeal directed so often toward what others considered the least interesting parts of a

---

[82] David Bentley Hart, *The Beauty of the Infinite: The Aesthetics of Christian Truth* (Grand Rapids, MI: Eerdmans, 2003), 283.

[83] Laurence Dreyfus, *Bach and the Patterns of Invention* (Cambridge, MA: Harvard University Press, 1996).

[84] J. S. Bach, 'Inventions and Sinfonias', *Aufrichtige Anleitung* (BWV 772–801).

[85] Dreyfus, *Bach and the Patterns of Invention*, 2.

composition.'[86] Bach seems to have had an almost superhuman eye for how relatively simple sets of notes would combine, cohere, and behave in different groupings.[87] Indeed, Christoph Wolff claims that the principle of elaboration 'determines like nothing else Bach's art and personal style'.[88]

In this light, certain key features typical of the musical fabric of a vast number of Bach's pieces can be highlighted—features we have touched upon in Chapter 3.[89] First, the elaboration is governed not chiefly by an external, pregiven logic, but first and foremost by the musical material itself. Dreyfus's research has shown that, whatever the precise order in which Bach composed a piece, the texture of the music suggests it is misleading to envision him starting with a fixed, precise, and unalterable 'form' (akin to a Powerpoint template) and then proceeding to fill it with music; rather, we would be better understanding him searching for inventions with rich potential, and accordingly finding an appropriate form.[90] Wolff speaks of Bach engaging in 'imaginative research into the harmonic implications of [his] chosen subject-matter'.[91] If we allow this aspect of his music to provoke a vision of creation as the Christian God's handiwork, it is one in which creation is not, so to speak, a surface that hides a more fundamental, prior group of forms, meanings, or truths, but one in which creation is fashioned directly out of nothing such that it is endowed with its own integral, appropriate forms, forms that God honours and enables to flourish as intrinsic to matter itself.[92] Second, in this music we are given to hear irreducible difference as intrinsic to unity. Bach's skill in deriving so much music from such tiny musical units means that he can offer intense experiences of complexity and unity interwoven. Even the resolutions in his music rarely neutralize its richness: the reconciliation at the end of the 'Dona Nobis Pacem' at the close of his Mass in B Minor does not compromise any of that piece's immeasurable diversity. Indeed, Bach is adept

---

[86] Dreyfus, *Bach and the Patterns of Invention*, 22: see the whole section 4–25.

[87] 'When [J. S. Bach] listened to a rich and many-voiced fugue, he could soon say, after the first entries of the subjects, what contrapuntal devices it would be possible to apply, and which of them the composer by rights ought to apply, and on such occasions, when I was standing next to him, and he had voiced his surmises to me, he would joyfully nudge me when his expectations were fulfilled': C. P. E. Bach (J. S. Bach's son), as cited in Hans T. David, Arthur Mendel, and Christoph Wolff (eds), *The New Bach Reader: A Life of Johann Sebastian Bach in Letters and Documents* (New York, NY: W. W. Norton & Co., 1998), 396.

[88] Christoph Wolff, *Johann Sebastian Bach: The Learned Musician* (New York: W. W. Norton & Co., 2000), 469.

[89] See 'Musical Witness' (pp. 67–9) in this volume. I am indebted in this section to Hart, *The Beauty of the Infinite*, 281–4.

[90] According to Dreyfus, this is why genre was far more important than large-scale form for Bach and why so many of Bach's pieces modify and even disrupt traditional forms; 'form was seen . . . as an occasional feature of a genre, and not the general theoretical category subsuming the genres that it later became': Dreyfus, *Bach and the Patterns of Invention*, 28.

[91] Wolff, *The Learned Musician*, 468.

[92] I am not, of course, suggesting that Bach was creating out of nothing; the point is about 'working with the grain of the universe', regarding form as intrinsic to matter.

at helping us perceive rich complexity *in* the apparently simple (for example, in the reprise at the end of the *Goldberg Variations*). The diverse particulars of creation, we might say, are not an elaboration of some more profound, more real, uniform simplicity, any more than the threefoldness of the Creator is the expression of a more basic singularity (as in modalism). In Hart's words, 'The "theme" of creation is the gift of the whole.'[93] And, we might add, the diverse unity of the whole participates in, and thus witnesses to, the differentiated unity of the Creator. Third, we are given the possibility of hearing the simultaneous presence of radical contingency and radical consistency. With almost any piece of Bach—although perhaps most of all in the solo instrumental works—the music will sound astonishingly free of necessity. Not only does Bach constantly adapt and reshape the forms and styles he inherits; even within the constraints he sets for himself, there is a remarkable contingency— Peter Williams even uses the word 'caprice' for this aspect of the *Goldberg Variations*.[94] So with the created order, we would do well to avoid the suggestion of closed harmonies and identical repetition, and speak rather of the particularizing, proliferating ministry of the Holy Spirit, effecting faithful but contingent improvisations on the harmony achieved in Jesus Christ.

Music and the Human

Second, there is music's potential to bear witness to *what is fundamentally human*. Christologically conceived, the *telos* of human living is the communally constituted humanity enabled by the Spirit through participating in the humanity of Jesus Christ. In this connection, we can point to just one particularly significant feature of music, concerning its socially cohesive power (a dimension that was critical for Rousseau, as we have seen).

It has long been known that rhythmic music possesses striking capacities to engender and sustain community. In recent years, biomusicologists and others have focused much attention on the phenomena of 'entrainment': the synchronization of one rhythmic process with another.[95] Spontaneously, we tap our feet, sway, bob our heads to music; and even more so when we are with

---

[93] Hart, *The Beauty of the Infinite*, 282.

[94] Peter F. Williams, *Bach: The Goldberg Variations* (Cambridge: Cambridge University Press, 2001), 46.

[95] See e.g. Martin Clayton, 'What is Entrainment? Definition and Applications in Musical Research', *Empirical Musicology Review* 7, 1–2 (2012): 49–56; Martin Clayton, Rebecca Sager, and Udo Will, 'In Time with the Music: The Concept of Entrainment and its Significance for Ethnomusicology', *ESEM CounterPoint* 1 (2004): 3–75; Henkjan Honing, 'Without It No Music: Beat Induction as a Fundamental Musical Trait', *Annals of the New York Academy of the Sciences* 1252, 1 (2012): 85–91; Adena Schachner, Timothy F. Brady, Irene M Pepperberg, and Marc D. Hauser 'Spontaneous Motor Entrainment to Music in Multiple Vocal Mimicking Species', *Current Biology* 19, 10 (30 April 2009): 831–6.

others who do the same. 'In every culture, there is some form of music with a periodic pulse that affords temporal coordination between performers and elicits synchronized motor responses from listeners.'[96] Visual, auditory, and motor cues work together to generate a potent and mutually reinforcing mix. And, given rhythm's strong connections with affect, this is one of the quickest ways in which emotion is spread and shared. We only need think of the chanting of a protest march, or mass synchronized movement at a rock concert.[97]

Some argue that entrainment was critical in the evolution of our capacity for communal culture, especially in situations of social uncertainty: for rhythmic synchronization makes it possible to experience the world in another's time. But this capacity of music goes with another, which complements it: what Ian Cross calls music's 'floating intentionality', its semantic indeterminacy.[98] A given piece of music is susceptible to a large (though not unlimited) range of interpretations; it under-specifies; generally, it does not and cannot denote with consistency and specificity. This flexibility allows the participant or hearer considerable space to develop his or her own 'reading' and application of the musical sounds. Putting these two together: music can grant an extraordinary sense of embodied togetherness (among other things, through entrainment processes), while at the same time allowing for—even encouraging—particularity and uniqueness (by virtue of its floating intentionality). Many other factors are involved here, of course, but recognizing that these two operate together in most corporate musical experience can be highly instructive. For example, in some contemporary 'alternative worship' experiments in the United Kingdom and the United States, wordless yet highly rhythmic music from various dance cultures are extensively used, and can engender an intense sense of solidarity, while at the same time allowing for widely diverse responses and stances among participants—something that would seem appropriate for those wary of being enlisted prematurely to adhere to specific beliefs, doctrines, or goals. Of course, one would want at some stage a higher degree of specificity in worship; nonetheless, music of this sort in this context may be witnessing to and perhaps serving to embody something of the differentiated and liberating unity promised in Christ and granted through his Body, the Church, by the Spirit.

---

[96] Aniruddh D. Patel, *Music, Language, and the Brain* (Oxford: Oxford University Press, 2008), 402; C. Drake and D. Bertrand, 'The Quest for Universals in Temporal Processing in Music', *Annals of the New York Academy of the Sciences* 930 (2001): 17–27.

[97] Apropos Rousseau, it is interesting to note evidence that would indicate that 'entrainment evolved as a by-product of selection for vocal mimicry': Schachner et al., 'Spontaneous Motor Entrainment': 831.

[98] Ian Cross, 'The Evolutionary Basis of Meaning in Music: Some Neurological and Neuroscientific Implications', in Frank Clifford Rose (ed.), *The Neurology of Music* (London: Imperial College Press, 2010), 1–15, 9–11.

Music and Culture

Third, there is music's potential to bear witness to the dynamics of felicitous cultural activity. We cite two examples, focusing on the dynamics of the relation between human agency and the 'givenness' of the material of musical sound.

For the first example we simply recall a section of Chapter 3, when we discussed the way in which Bach's output, considered in its time, can provoke us to imagine a mutually enhancing interplay (rather than a mutually exclusive struggle) between inventive productivity on the one hand and respectful honouring of the integrities of musical sound on the other.[99]

For a second example, we consider a case where music offers a kind of *via negativa*, in that it displays the fruitlessness of the common oscillation in modernity between an extreme passivity on the part of cultural agents on the one hand and an extreme constructiveness on the other, and the need for a theology that undercuts the assumptions on which such a polarity typically depends. For this I revisit *Theology, Music and Time*, where I turned the spotlight on the encounter in the early 1950s between two leading composers of the twentieth century, the Frenchman Pierre Boulez (b. 1925) and the American John Cage (1912–92).[100]

Boulez and Cage came to represent two radically opposed streams of post-war music: Boulez the arch-priest of strict musical organization, Cage of chance, where everything and anything seems to be able to count as music. The two men came to take a keen interest in each other's work and engaged in a number of exchanges. Boulez came into prominence in the 1940s and 1950s as a practitioner of what came to be known as 'total serialism'—a compositional method involving the rigorous organization of music according to stringent mathematical patterns.[101] Adopting an essentially logico-deductive approach to composition,[102] he sought to conform every parameter of his music to strict algorithmic schemes—in effect a quest for 'total compositional control'.[103] Gerald Bennett comments: 'Boulez's composition represents one of the great adventures of music in this century: the restructuring of the language by imposing on it relations of absolute logical consistency.'[104] And

---

[99] See 'Subjectivity and Creativity' (pp. 43–50) in this volume.

[100] Jeremy S. Begbie, *Theology, Music and Time* (Cambridge: Cambridge University Press, 2000), 179–99.

[101] See Richard Taruskin, *The Oxford History of Western Music: Music in the Late Twentieth Century*, 5 vols, vol. v (Oxford: Oxford University Press, 2010), 27–38.

[102] See Edward Campbell, *Boulez, Music and Philosophy* (Cambridge: Cambridge University Press, 2010), ch. 5.

[103] Jonathan Goldman, *The Musical Language of Pierre Boulez: Writings and Compositions* (Cambridge: Cambridge University Press, 2011), 7.

[104] Gerald Bennett, 'The Early Works', in William Glock (ed.), *Pierre Boulez: A Symposium* (London: Eulenburg Books, 1986), 41–84, 84.

yet for the listener, the demands were enormous. Although the music was ruthlessly organized it was virtually impossible to hear it as such, even if one was aware of the formal principles supporting it. Eschewing any hint of repetition or 'return', the constant variation paradoxically rendered the music extraordinarily dull.[105] Boulez himself was fully aware of this; he later reminisced that there was 'a surfeit of order being equivalent to disorder'.[106] Even if it is granted that a piece of music does not have to yield all its meaning in perception, a modicum of perceptual intelligibility would appear to be necessary to apprehend it *as music*. The musical 'sense' of total serialism seemed to elude even the most informed listener, and was understandably attacked by some as little more than arrogant social elitism.[107]

The irony was intensified through Boulez's interaction with Cage: for his own music sounded disturbingly similar to that of the American prince of 'chance'. Cage was deeply attracted to chance procedures and was later to initiate something of a craze for 'openness' and 'indeterminacy' in which ideological and political factors were interlaced with musical and aesthetic drives. For Cage at this time, sounds were seen not merely as supportive and subservient to some structure and form but as significant in their own right. Composing was a matter not of making an expressive continuity but of letting individual sounds 'find their own expressiveness within a blank canvas of empty time'.[108] 'Where people had felt the necessity to stick sounds together to make a continuity, we . . . felt the opposite necessity to get rid of the glue so that sounds would be themselves.'[109] Cage's goal, then, was to let sounds be themselves, unimpeded by service to any abstraction, so that, as Paul Griffiths puts it, 'the work [is], in the Zen spirit, a vehicle not of thoughts but only events'.[110] Composition is about *accepting*, rather than *making*. Boulez later

---

[105] For a subtle discussion of repetition and variation in Boulez, see Campbell, *Boulez, Music and Philosophy*, ch. 8.

[106] Bennett, 'The Early Works', 57.

[107] 'In the bluntest terms . . . the paradox created by "total serialism" is this: once the algorithms governing a composition are known (or have been determined), it is possible to demonstrate the correctness of the score (that is, of its component notes) more decisively and objectively than is possible for any other kind of music; but in the act of listening to the composition, one has no way of knowing (and, no matter how many times one listens, one will never have a way of knowing) that the notes one is hearing are the right ones, or (more precisely) that they are not the wrong notes': Taruskin, *The Oxford History of Western Music*, v. 36.

[108] James Pritchett, *The Music of John Cage* (Cambridge: Cambridge University Press, 1993), 74.

[109] Reginald Smith Brindle, *The New Music: The Avant-Garde Since 1945* (Oxford: Oxford University Press, 1987), 126.

[110] Paul E. Griffiths, *Cage* (London: Oxford University Press, 1981), 27. Cage later spoke of the purpose of music as being 'to sober and quiet the mind, thus making one susceptible to divine influence': As quoted in Richard Fleming and William Duckworth, *John Cage at Seventy-Five* (Lewisburg, PA: Bucknell University Press, 1989), 23; he uses the same phrase earlier in the interview (21).

mocked: 'To claim to be creating a musical "environment" to which one need pay no attention until it becomes of greater interest is an excuse for total laziness: laziness of planning, laziness of thought, and even laziness in performance.'[111] 'It is the acceptance of a passive attitude towards what exists: it is an idea of surrender', which opens the way to manipulation and even fascism.[112] And yet—to press the irony again—even to an educated ear, at this stage of their development, Cage's music sounds almost identical to Boulez's.

Boulez, it would seem, exemplifies the arch-modernist view of the artist whose sovereign constructive intellect brings order and meaning to the sonic world. Admittedly this was a particular type of mastery, in that the intellectual system mattered more than a particular mind, but it is intellectual mastery nevertheless. The question inevitably arises: to what extent does Boulez's 'computerized passion'[113] do violence to the materials of sound? To what extent are the 'systems' that determine the music consonant with the properties and intrinsic interrelationships of sounds themselves?[114] In an important article on Boulez's early works, Gerald Bennett observes that increasingly during the 1940s, the material Boulez uses begins to resist his rigorous structuring. As ever more elaborate and higher levels of abstraction are attained, he tends to obscure his primary musical lines and forms, and new structures begin to direct the course of the music's development.[115] Bennett declares that 'A struggle of the highest drama—and of the greatest importance—is being enacted here.' Boulez loses control over the material through the imposition of ever stricter control. It is 'one of the most important confrontations in the music of our time—that of a composer determined to force material to obey his complex structural demands on the one hand, on the other the musical material itself, increasingly reluctant to submit gracefully to

---

[111] Pierre Boulez, *Conversations with Célestin Deliège* (London: Eulenburg Books, 1976), 84.

[112] Boulez, *Conversations with Célestin Deliège*, 85.

[113] Jameux's phrase: Dominique Jameux, *Pierre Boulez*, trans. Susan Bradshaw (London: Faber and Faber, 1991), 54.

[114] Boulez may speak of the composition of *Structure Ia* as 'purely automatic' (Boulez, *Conversations with Célestin Deliège*, 56) and the material as a kind of 'given' with a self-generated life of its own, but the 'material' of which he speaks, which is allowed to control aspects of the music, has in fact already been intellectually shaped in a highly intricate way.

[115] To counter this, in at least one piece Boulez inserts a kind of shadow of the (hidden) musical lines on the surface level of the music, but this shadow 'loses its structural function and becomes merely decorative . . . it is now only embellishment': Bennett, 'The Early Works', 77. 'Intricately delicate structure becomes shimmering surface, surface masquerades as structure. The two become indistinguishable, which means the ultimate abrogation and annulment of structure itself': Bennett, 'The Early Works', 84. Bennett likens this to a half-timbered house where the framework has been covered up by repeated restoration and the new owners have painted on timbers to resemble a timbered house: Bennett, 'The Early Works', 77.

these demands'.[116] Bennett concludes: 'the adventure of Boulez's music is *an examination of the very foundations of composition itself*'.[117]

It is not hard to correlate these remarks with a paradigmatically modern conception of humanity's relation to the non-human environment: through ever stricter control we lose control of our God-given home, with catastrophic results. Speaking in 1975 of the composition of *Structures*, Boulez remarks that he was aware of the '*contrast*, which to my mind is necessary to composition, between *the will to make something out of the material and what the material suggests to one*'.[118] Here we could well cite Ernst Kris's (undoubtedly exaggerated) claim that in artistic modernism, 'the artist does not "render" nature, nor does he "imitate" it, but he creates it anew. He controls the world through his work . . . The unconscious meaning . . . is *control at the price of destruction*.'[119] The phrase 'control at the price of destruction' recalls Boulez's phrase 'excess of order being equivalent to disorder', and could well stand as the motto over many of the results of modernity's disrespect for the integrity of the non-human realm, all too often fuelled by questionable theologies of divine and human freedom.

Initially, Cage's approach seems more promising. As he sees it, we must relinquish the desire to control, and 'let sounds be themselves rather than vehicles for man-made theories or expressions of human sentiments'.[120] This does not entail complete passivity, for one is still composing the individual sounds that become the material of the composition, but this composing is only to provide 'opportunities for experience'. Cage's interest is not in expressing, limiting, or shaping, still less in 'conveying a message'. 'Until that time', Cage tells us, 'my music had been based on the idea that you had to say something. The charts [of the music of the early 1950s] gave me the indication of the possibility of saying nothing.'[121] To be sure, here music may be freed from the imposition of mathematical schemes, but the cost is an evacuation (or near-evacuation) of the notion of music as constructive, and an implicit rejection (or near-rejection) of the idea that human shaping might be fruitful and enriching. Further, we might add, for all the evocations of 'let it be', Cage's stress is very much on the 'randomness' of the extra-human world, not on its inherent reliability.

In this case, then, an interaction—played out audibly in musical sounds as much as words—between two massively influential composers can serve to highlight much of what is involved in attempting to coordinate the role of

---

[116] Bennett, 'The Early Works', 41.

[117] Bennett, 'The Early Works', 84. My italics.

[118] Boulez, *Conversations with Célestin Deliège*, 56. My italics.

[119] As quoted in Caroline Case and Tessa Dalley, *The Handbook of Art Therapy* (London: Routledge, 1992), 117.

[120] John Cage, *Silence* (London: Calder and Boyars, 1973), 10.

[121] Griffiths, *Cage*, 24.

human cultural agents vis-à-vis the constraints in which they live and work. Arguably, the problematic we have observed in these two musicians has been affected by an ancient hesitancy in the West about the goodness and order of the world's matter, leading to a suspicion about whether the non-human physical world is an environment with which we can interact closely in a way that is both fruitful and engenders human flourishing. In modernity, two extremes typically result. The one is a denial of our rootedness in the material universe, the other a denial of any kind of active transcendence over it. Boulez tends to line up with the first, Cage with the second.

The links with the Rameau–Rousseau debate are not hard to see. Certainly, we have come a long way from the wranglings of the eighteenth century. In Cage, there is none of the confidence in natural science we find in Rameau, none of the latter's concern to root music in an empirically verifiable order. And Boulez's investment in mathematical systems could never have been endorsed by Rousseau. Nonetheless, the struggle to coordinate effectively the tension between the 'artificiality' of human agency and the materials of musical sound is just as intense.

With regard to the way this tension plays itself out in the debate between Rameau and Rousseau, the old adage about being right in what we affirm more than in what we deny seems apposite. Their positive intuitions are surely well placed. There is every reason to believe that music achieves its expressive effects *both* through its embeddedness in a physical sonic order *and* through the contingencies and intentionalities of individuals, society, and culture. In the contemporary musico-theoretical world, few would deny that the pendulum has swung strongly towards the latter pole. This can be well illustrated in the work of Nicholas Cook, for example, whose lively philosophical acumen and pointed rhetoric exposes the key issues with great clarity. In an article on 'Epistemologies of Music Theory', he speaks of the 'transition from a theological to a scientific epistemology that took place during the seventeenth and eighteenth centuries', and confirms what we have already noted about Rameau, that he found it hard to marry Cartesianism and empiricism, 'systematization' and 'veridical description'.[122] Cook comments: 'what Rameau lacks is . . . the concept of arbitrary signification that plays a central role in the general theory of signs developed by French thinkers during the eighteenth century' in which 'signs belong . . . not to nature but to artifice'.[123] Cook is not slow to point out the way in which many modern theorists have reacted against 'natural law' thinking in music theory (not least because of its association with racist ideology). Forgoing a 'naturalistic epistemology' (a naïve realism that presumes the possibility of secure knowledge of the way things are), he points to a thread in music theory he calls the 'performative turn',

---

[122] Cook, 'Epistemologies of Music Theory', 83, 85.
[123] Cook, 'Epistemologies of Music Theory', 88.

according to which 'the validity of any theory is underwritten not by its objective truth (a concept that has lost its apparent self-evidence even in the natural sciences), but by intersubjectivity'.[124] That is, music theory gets its cash value from its performative effect, from the interpretive or cultural work it does in particular social settings as it serves particular interests. Under this umbrella, Cook says he is happy to live with 'plural epistemologies', 'a multiplicity of models of truth or justifiability',[125] believing that in any case all music theory operates in this way. Thus speaks the voice of Rousseau, but now massively amplified and modulated through the critical voices of late/postmodernity, where human and cultural interests come to overwhelm the entire theoretical scenario. Granted, there is no denial that music's physical properties do entail and engage with universal configurations of the physical world (including our bodies), or that they play a key part in the import of music for those who enjoy it. What is denied is that this is significant or relevant from the point of view of music theory. Gone is the notion that this is something that might encourage us to widen our perceptions beyond the purely human–cultural sphere, or—and perhaps this is the critical point—that might generate gratitude that we live in a world where a fruitful interaction with our physical environment is actually a possibility. Cook, it seems, can only widen the gap between 'nature' and 'culture' that has occasioned so many problems, resorting to a pragmatic notion of performability, or 'intersubjectivity', which, ironically, is no less vulnerable to ideological distortion than the concept of natural law.

In any case, it is unlikely that the pendulum will stop swinging between the nature–culture poles as long as the larger issues about what constitutes 'nature' and humans' interaction with it are not addressed more directly, and, we would argue, addressed with a 'theological imaginary' that refuses the aporias that so easily generate the polarity in the first place. We have alluded to such an imaginary in a number of places already: of the artist, as physical and embodied, set in the midst of a God-given world vibrant with a dynamic order of its own, not simply 'there' to be left wholly as it is, or escaped, or violently abused but there as a gift from a God of uncontainable generosity, a gift for us to interact with vigorously, form, and (in the face of distortion) transform, and in this way fashion something that, in at least some manner, can be heard as anticipating by the Spirit the shalom previewed and promised in Jesus Christ.

Music and Renewed Reason

Fourth, there is music's potential to witness to the thought-forms appropriate to a theologically renewed rationality—to that 'reschematizing' of the mind

---

[124] Cook, 'Epistemologies of Music Theory', 98–9.
[125] Cook, 'Epistemologies of Music Theory', 102.

(Romans 12:2) made possible through sharing by the Spirit in the mind of Christ. There is no need to elaborate on this here, for Chapter 6 in this book is devoted to an example of this in action: the ways in which the perception of musical 'space' elicits patterns of thought that can serve both to question some of the distorting routines of modernity and to enable a deeper penetration of patterns of thinking appropriate to the New Testament. And elsewhere, I offer parallel and extended treatments of the phenomenon of time, in which music can not only uncover something of the theological wisdom of modernity but also re-form some of its more damaging pathologies.[126]

* * *

I have tried to show that the concerns that drive many projects of natural theology are by no means to be dismissed, but that, at their best, they are to be carried forward by maintaining a good deal of circumspection about how we are to conceive and imagine the status and shape of 'nature' and 'the natural', and that the world of music affords considerable possibilities in this respect— both as a vehicle of clarification and as a way of opening out a variety of fresh possibilities for the theologian. Whether the world of theology takes up and commends these possibilities in the years to come remains to be seen.

---

[126] Begbie, *Theology, Music and Time.*

5

Musical Apotheosis: Early German Romanticism

Ah, thus I close my eyes to all worldly strife—and withdraw quietly into the land of music, as unto a land of faith.

W. H. Wackenroder[1]

My question is whether such works as Beethoven's *Eroica*, or his late quartets, and Wagner's *Ring*, or *Tristan* may not offer understandings of modernity, which, while relying on discursive language to be approached in these terms at all, still articulate something which philosophy cannot.

Andrew Bowie[2]

...there are modes of thought other than those based on Greek, Cartesian, Kantian, Hegelian, etc. philosophy.

André LaCocque and Paul Ricoeur[3]

'An die Musik'
Du holde Kunst, in wieviel grauen Stunden,
Wo mich des Lebens wilder Kreis umstrickt,
Hast du mein Herz zu warmer Lieb entzunden,
Hast mich in eine bessre Welt entrückt!
Oft hat ein Seufzer, deiner Harf entflossen,
Ein süsser, heiliger Akkord von dir
Den Himmel bessrer Zeiten mir erschlossen,
Du holde Kunst, ich danke dir dafür!

---

[1] As quoted in Carl Dahlhaus, *The Idea of Absolute Music* (Chicago: University of Chicago Press, 1989), 90.

[2] Andrew Bowie, *Music, Philosophy, and Modernity* (Cambridge: Cambridge University Press, 2007), 136 (hereafter *MPM*).

[3] André LaCocque and Paul Ricoeur, *Thinking Biblically: Exegetical and Hermeneutical Studies*, trans. David Pellauer (Chicago: University of Chicago Press, 1998), p. xvi.

'On Music'
Beloved art, in how many a bleak hour,
When I am enmeshed in life's tumultuous round,
Have you kindled my heart to the warmth of love,
And borne me away to a better world!
Often a sigh, escaping from your harp,
A sweet, celestial chord
Has revealed to me a heaven of happier times.
Beloved art, for this I thank you!

Franz von Schober (1796–1882), set to music by Franz Schubert
(1797–1828)[4]

In 1810, a review of Beethoven's Fifth Symphony appeared in a leading musical weekly, the *Allgemeine musikalische Zeitung*. Its author, then a relatively unknown E. T. A. Hoffmann (1776–1822), would have had no inkling of its potential impact, but its unusual combination of rhetorical power, philosophical allusion, and technical analysis made it 'arguably the single most important and influential work of musical criticism ever written'.[5] Music's quasi-divine potency has rarely had such a compelling advocate. And it is in textless music that his passion is most fully focused:

> When we speak of music as an independent art, should we not always restrict our meaning to instrumental music, which, scorning every aid, every admixture of another art (the art of poetry) [*der Poesie*] gives pure expression to music's specific nature, recognizable in this form alone? It is the most romantic of all the arts—one might almost say, the only genuinely romantic one—for its sole subject is the infinite. The lyre of Orpheus opened the portals of Orcus—music discloses to man an unknown realm, a world that has nothing in common with the external sensual world that surrounds him, a world in which he leaves behind him all definite feelings to surrender himself to an inexpressible longing [*unaussprechlichen Sehnsucht*].[6]

For Hoffmann, all this comes to a head with Ludwig van Beethoven (1770–1827)—the daunting colossus who in so many ways came to determine the course of the leading conceptions of music in the nineteenth century. In Beethoven's symphonic output Hoffmann sees the very epitome of his own

---

[4] Translation © Richard Wigmore, *Schubert: The Complete Song Texts* (London: Gollancz, 1988), 44–5.

[5] Mark Evan Bonds, *Music as Thought: Listening to the Symphony in the Age of Beethoven* (Princeton: Princeton University Press, 2006), p. xiv. The original can be found in E. T. A. Hoffmann, 'Beethovens Symphonie, No. 5', *Allgemeine Musikalische Zeitung* 12, 40–1 (4 July and 11 July 1810): cols 630–42, 652–9. The review appears in translation as 'Review of Beethoven's Fifth Symphony', in E. T. A. Hoffmann, *E. T. A. Hoffmann's Musical Writings: Kreisleriana, The Poet and the Composer, Music Criticism*, ed. David Charlton, trans. Martyn Clarke (Cambridge: Cambridge University Press, 1989), 234–51.

[6] As quoted and translated in W. Oliver Strunk, *Source Readings in Music History: The Romantic Era*, 5 vols, vol. v (London: Faber & Faber, 1981), 35–6.

exalted view of instrumental music. Haydn's symphonies 'lead us through endless, green forest-glades, through a motley throng of happy people' and Mozart 'leads us into the realm of spirits'.[7] But Beethoven 'unveils before us the realm of the mighty and the immeasurable . . . destroying within us all feeling but the pain of infinite yearning (*Sehnsucht*)'.[8] He 'sets in motion the machinery of awe, of fear, of terror, of pain, and awakens that infinite yearning which is the essence of romanticism. Beethoven is a purely romantic, therefore truly musical, composer.'[9] The composer's C Minor Symphony, Hoffmann proclaims, 'irresistibly sweeps the listener into the wonderful spirit-realm of the infinite' (*das wundervolle Reich des Unendlichen*).[10]

This lofty and celebrated prose represents a dramatic transformation in the way music was capable of being heard and conceived in modernity, one which had been fomenting in the late eighteenth century and began to flower with the early German Romantics of the 1790s. Writers were beginning to invite audiences to hear—better, *listen to*—symphonic and instrumental works in an unprecedented way, such that they were no longer to be approached 'solely as a source of entertainment, but increasingly as a source of truth'.[11] Andrew Bowie sums up the shift of attitude:

> From being widely regarded as something to be used to accompany social and religious occasions, rather than be listened to and played for its own sake, music came to be regarded by some influential writers, philosophers and composers as the source of revelations that were inaccessible to any other form of human expression.[12]

And these 'revelations' are spoken of in conspicuously elevated terms: music is robed in the metaphysics of the infinite. Hoffmann is inviting his readers to perceive this music as a manifestation of a boundless sublime (a category with a significant prehistory in his day).[13] As Carl Dahlhaus puts it, for the

---

[7] Hoffmann, 'Review of Beethoven', 237.

[8] Hoffmann, 'Review of Beethoven', 237, 238.

[9] Hoffmann, 'Review of Beethoven', 238.

[10] Hoffmann, 'Review of Beethoven', 239. In a later piece, Hoffmann lauds music's harmony, which can be heard as 'the image and expression of that communion of spirits, of that bond with the eternal ideal which at once embraces and reigns over us'. E. T. A. Hoffmann, 'Old and New Church Music', in David Charlton (ed.), *E. T. A. Hoffmann's Musical Writings: Kreisleriana, The Poet and the Composer, Music Criticism*, trans. Martyn Clarke (Cambridge: Cambridge University Press, 1989), 351–76, 357–8.

[11] Bonds, *Music as Thought*, p. xv. The distinctive and valuable perspective Bonds brings to his field is his concentration on the *act of listening*, or perhaps more accurately, on the theories of listening propounded by influential philosophers, engendering what he calls 'the premises of perception' (p. xviii).

[12] Andrew Bowie, 'Romanticism and Music', in Nicholas Saul (ed.), *The Cambridge Companion to German Romanticism* (Cambridge: Cambridge University Press, 2006), 243–55, 243.

[13] Although the word 'sublime' appears only once in Hoffmann's review, the concept is central for him, and had been for some time linked to the symphony: Bonds, *Music as Thought*, 45–50.

Romantics, 'Music that is "dissolved" from verbal and functional constraints "sublimates" or "exalts" itself above the boundedness of the finite to an intimation of the infinite.'[14]

Contrast this with Immanuel Kant (1724–1804), writing only twenty years earlier,[15] who famously spoke of instrumental music as 'more enjoyment than culture'.[16] As a 'language of the affects',[17] music—textless music, that is—cannot convey concepts or determinate thoughts. Once its tones have faded, nothing is left for the listener to attend to; it cannot issue in serious reflection. It 'speaks through mere sensations without concepts . . . it merely plays with sensations'.[18] Although in other important respects Kant was to have a decisive influence on the Romantics, here Kant concurs with the dominant flow of eighteenth-century music theory, which held that instrumental music, though emotionally charged, is highly imprecise and indistinct, and thus decidedly inferior to vocal music, which carries the immeasurable advantage of being bound to words and concepts.

But for Hoffmann it is precisely instrumental music's *freedom* from words and concepts that makes it so supremely effective.[19] What was once the lowest form of music becomes the highest form of the arts, later to be encapsulated in the concept of 'absolute' music.[20] Wordless instrumental music represents music coming into its own, reaching its fullest, most authentic condition.

Later in the nineteenth century, the kind of claims Hoffmann and his ilk made about music were subject to extensive criticism, even scorn—among other things for their lack of theoretical rigour, their careless imprecision. And to this day, a strong current of music theory and musicology has regarded romanticism of most types, but especially German romanticism, as impeding any serious musical critique, with its predilection for inflated hyperbole and metaphysical excess.

From the perspective of classical Christianity, romanticism's soaring theological ambitions for music will for many look like an undisciplined flirtation with idolatry (or with pantheism), rendering it unworthy of any serious

---

[14] Dahlhaus, *The Idea of Absolute Music*, 60.

[15] Bonds, *Music as Thought*, 6–10.

[16] Immanuel Kant, *Critique of the Power of Judgment* (Cambridge: Cambridge University Press, 2000), 205.

[17] Kant, *Critique of the Power of Judgment*, 206.

[18] Kant, *Critique of the Power of Judgment*, 205, 206.

[19] We should note that Hoffmann, writing in 1814, is quite prepared to praise, say, Palestrina's sacred music (which sets texts): Hoffmann, 'Old and New Church Music', 357–63. There is no real contradiction here, however, for what gives Palestrina's music its infinite or spiritual power for Hoffmann is not its texts but the musical sounds; the music is certainly not the mere servant of words.

[20] On which, see, among many others, Daniel K. L. Chua, *Absolute Music and the Construction of Meaning* (Cambridge: Cambridge University Press, 1999); Dahlhaus, *The Idea of Absolute Music*; Sanna Pederson, 'Defining the Term "Absolute Music" Historically', *Music and Letters* 90, 2 (2009): 240–62.

intellectual attention. But such quick dismissals are, I think, out of place. And for two reasons in particular. First and foremost, the theorization of music in German romanticism, intertwining with the practical music-making of the time, brings to the surface with striking clarity some of the most profound and most critically important theological matters at stake in modernity, many of them overlapping with and intensifying issues we have already encountered in the preceding chapters. Second, the elevation of music that characterizes this stream of thought is by no means absent in our own time, influencing some current theological perceptions of music rather more than is often realized. In some so-called 'contemporary worship' circles, for example, the vocabulary used of music and the confidence invested in it can bear striking resemblances to some of the more vertiginous claims of the Romantics.[21] That does not automatically give us grounds for rejecting it, but it shows us that in venturing into this territory we will likely find some features of the landscape that are decidedly familiar, and it is as well to be aware of both their dangers and delights.

In this chapter, we examine the emergence of this high estimate of (instrumental) music, paying special attention to its theological undercurrents and ramifications. To keep the discussion within manageable limits, we shall restrict ourselves to a conversation with one of the foremost scholars of the field, Andrew Bowie, Professor of Philosophy and German, Royal Holloway, University of London, whose attention to music as a force integral to the development of modernity and its associated discourses and philosophies, especially with respect to the Romantics, has been seminal and pioneering.[22] Although Bowie's studies of German philosophy have been appropriated to some extent by theologians, his treatment of music has been left largely to one side—something I believe is highly regrettable.

Fortunately, we do not need to traverse here the quagmire of argument about the meaning of 'romanticism'. It is enough to say that our interest is primarily in what has come to be known as early German romanticism (*Frühromantik*).[23] In 1796 a group began to meet in Jena, whose members included such luminaries as Friedrich Schleiermacher (1768–1834), Ludwig Tieck (1773–1853), 'Novalis' (G. P. F. F. von Hardenberg) (1772–1801),

[21] Jeremy S. Begbie, *Resounding Truth: Christian Wisdom in the World of Music* (Grand Rapids, MI: Baker Books, 2007), 245–6.
[22] See Andrew Bowie, *Aesthetics and Subjectivity* (Manchester: Manchester University Press, 1990); Andrew Bowie, 'Music and the Rise of Aesthetics', in Jim Samson (ed.), *The Cambridge History of Nineteenth-Century Music* (Cambridge: Cambridge University Press, 2002), 29–54; Bowie, 'Romantic Philosophy and Religion'; Bowie, *MPM*; Andrew Bowie, *Philosophical Variations: Music as 'Philosophical Language'* (Malmö, Sweden: NSU Press, 2010); Andrew Bowie and Ulrich Tadday, *Musikphilosophie* (Munich: Edition Text + Kritik, 2007).
[23] For a useful introduction, see Frederick C. Beiser, *The Romantic Imperative: The Concept of Early German Romanticism* (Cambridge, MA: Harvard University Press, 2003). See also: Ricarda Schmidt, 'From Early to Late Romanticism', in Nicholas Saul (ed.), *The Cambridge Companion to German Romanticism* (Cambridge: Cambridge University Press, 2006).

Friedrich Schlegel (1772–1829), and his brother August Wilhelm Schlegel (1767–1845). With remarkable rapidity, their leading ideas, inchoate and unsystematic, often expressed in fragments, and inextricably bound up with the complex social and political passions of the time, became widely discussed far beyond their circle. Hoffmann's review is just one example of the kind of writing that could issue from the ensuing ferment.

And the ferment extended very widely. The American and French Revolutions, with their social and economic upheavals and disorienting ambivalences; the fresh discourses of the Enlightenment, Pietism, and *Sturm und Drang*; massive renegotiations of the role of the Church in society: all forced searching questions not only about the content of intellectual life but about the very way reality could be apprehended by human thought. The 'seismic transformation of European culture required new modes of understanding the world',[24] and for many, music seemed to hold out enormous promise, not least when wrestling with theological or quasi-theological themes. Thus music often finds itself integral to the struggles that characterize Romantic writing—struggles concerning such immensities as the relation of finite and infinite, relative and absolute, God and world.

Here we concentrate on Bowie's treatment of music in the early German Romantics, concentrating especially on his longest study, *Music, Philosophy, and Modernity*. The book extends far beyond early romanticism, well into the twentieth century, but it is clear that he believes these thinkers point up key challenges that have proved crucial far beyond their time, and deserve a wide hearing today. We outline Bowie's reading of these figures, occasionally supplementing his interpretation with other sources, before going on to press some specifically theological questions.

SOUNDING THE INFINITE

Bowie's perspective on the first Romantics assumes a reading of eighteenth-century thought we have already met, namely that for a large part of that century, the dominant paradigm at work among those who sought to provide a philosophical account of music's 'meaningfulness' was linguistic and representational (or 'mimetic');[25] that is, language was seen as the primary form of the articulation of the world's meaning, and meaningful language is regarded at its core as functioning through representing pre-existing, ready-made ideas,

---

[24] Azade Seyhan, 'What is Romanticism, and Where Did it Come From?', in Nicholas Saul (ed.), *The Cambridge Companion to German Romanticism* (Cambridge: Cambridge University Press, 2006), 2.

[25] See 'Rameau and Rousseau' (pp. 75–6) in this volume.

thoughts, or entities in the world.[26] Other candidates for meaningfulness must follow suit. Thus if music was to gain semantic respectability it would need to conform to this standard. Instrumental (textless) music becomes the fly in the ointment, for it was the 'empty sign', having no verbal language to give it specificity and stable reference. The most common way of dealing with this problematic was to link musical sounds directly to the passions: music can be seen as a 'language of the heart' or 'language of the passions' (we recall the Rameau–Rousseau debate). Even here the dynamic is still fundamentally linguistic—the implicit framework remains that of representative language. To say music is a language of the passions is to say that it represents/mirrors/ corresponds (and so forth) to pre-existent human emotions. Musical signs are seen as transparent to human feelings in a way analogous to the supposed transparency of language.

Vocal music thus enjoys a far higher prestige than instrumental music, for it has words to keep it semantically stable and reliable. Even in this case, however, music and language are not seen as inherently incongruent or oppositional, for when successful, they operate in essentially the same (representational) way. Insofar as music does 'make sense', this is because inherent to it is a language-like modus operandi. And, we should add, for this reason, verbal language is in principle an appropriate medium for speaking about, and making explicit, the meaning(s) of music.

The Travails of Language

In the closing decades of the eighteenth century, the weaknesses and fragility of this paradigm begin to be felt acutely by some writers, to the extent that, as Bowie puts it, '*it ceases to be clear what language is*'.[27] And, just as important, 'it is no longer clear what music is either'.[28] Many factors are implicated, not least the burgeoning of instrumental music in the symphonies and concertos of composers like Mozart and Haydn. But especially important is the abandoning of the notion that human language is simply God-given, and Kant's stress on the active, constructive role of the mind in cognition. Several thinkers

---

[26] Alan Torrance summarizes well a common variety of this outlook: 'it is assumed first that the meaning of a term is that to which it refers (be it physical or spiritual "object" or "truth") and second that individual thought is historically and ontologically presupposed by language. The worldview assumed by this suggests that there are "things" (self-defining referents) to which we first *refer* by pure thought and second *express* where this "expressing" is carried out by attaching terms to these mental acts of referring. Meaning is essentially describable, therefore, in terms of mental events and the *adequatio intellectus et rei*, in such a way that a given correspondence between reality or "*things*", on the one hand, and *thought*, on the other, is simple presupposed': Alan J. Torrance, *Persons in Communion: An Essay on Trinitarian Description and Human Participation* (Edinburgh: T & T Clark, 1996), 326–7.

[27] Bowie, *MPM*, 48. Italics original.   [28] Bowie, *MPM*, 48.

are led to question whether a philosophical account of language along straight-forward representationalist lines can do justice to the *human*-made character of language, and to the temporal, bodily, sensuous, and affective interaction with the world (and other persons) on which human language-use necessarily seems to rely. According to Bowie, J. G. Herder (1744–1803) stands out as a leading figure here—an immensely influential writer, with a strong inclination towards (as we might say today) 'interdisciplinarity'.[29] For Herder, *all* human expression and articulation to a large degree *constitutes* whatever it makes intelligible. Language is primarily constitutive of what we understand, rather than being primarily designative.[30] This involves both a conviction about the inability of representationalist assumptions to allow for the variety of language use, and a strong sense of the inherent relation of linguistic terms to each other.[31] Because Herder is not bewitched by the representational ideal, he can penetrate to 'deeper structures and relationships shared by language and music'.[32] Like others before him (such as Rousseau and J. G. Hamann), Herder regards music (or musicality) as fundamental to understanding the origins of language, for while it is eminently coherent and comprehensible it is not yet a language, and it reminds us of what is in fact basic to language. The first language was primarily affective and sensuous, rather than denotative and classifying; physical gestures and tones mattered more than naming and desig-nating, for human flourishing mattered more than representational accuracy.

Music's Regeneration

According to Bowie, the lines that begin to come into view with Herder are carried forward by a variety of thinkers, and to a significant extent consolidated by German Romantic philosophers. In this connection, Bowie wants to throw into relief the work of Schleiermacher, whose reflections on music he believes are 'remarkably prescient with regard to contemporary philosophy'.[33] Though a

---

[29] Bowie, *MPM*, 54–78. See Philip V. Bohlman, 'Herder's Nineteenth Century', *Nineteenth-Century Music Review* 7, 1 (2010): 3–21. Other key figures in this connection include J. J. Winckelmann (1717–68), with his notion of ideal beauty; K. P. Moritz (1756–93), who questioned the 'mimetic' character of the arts; and C. G. Körner (1756–1831), according to whom the artist is to 'represent the infinite in perceptible form'. See Bonds, *Music as Thought*, 14–20.

[30] Bowie, *MPM*, 54–5. See Charles Taylor, *Philosophical Arguments* (Cambridge, MA: Harvard University Press, 1995), ch. 5.

[31] Bowie, *MPM*, 62–7.

[32] Bowie, *MPM*, 67.

[33] Bowie, *MPM*, 153; see the whole section 152–65. See also Bowie, *Aesthetics and Subjectivity*, ch. 6. In recent years, Schleiermacher scholarship is inclined to see his work as closer to mainstream Protestant orthodoxy than has often been supposed; see e.g. Christine Helmer, 'Schleiermacher', in David Fergusson (ed.), *The Blackwell Companion to Nineteenth-Century Theology* (Oxford: Wiley-Blackwell, 2010), 31–57.

pianist and singer of only modest ability, music was immensely important to Schleiermacher.[34] Not only do musical analogies and metaphors abound in his writings; for him, 'it is precisely to the religious feeling that music is most closely related'.[35] Music has particular powers to open up and awaken that dimension of human experience that Schleiermacher identifies as distinctively religious. According to Philip Stoltzfus, it was Tieck's friend W. H. Wackenroder (1773–98), with his view of instrumental music as the supreme form of human expressiveness, who was the most decisive inspiration behind Schleiermacher's conception of music.[36] In any case, the portrayal of music's power in Schleiermacher's charming *Christmas Eve* dialogue of 1805 is thoroughly in keeping with the convictions of the *Frühromantiker*—the notion of music tapping into a level of reality sensed only through immediate self-consciousness ('true content is the great chords of our inner nature'[37]), the notion of music extending beyond the objectivizing of images and words ('. . . every fine feeling comes completely to the fore only when we have found the right musical expression for it. Not the spoken word, for this can never be anything but indirect—a plastic element, if I may put it that way—but a real, uncluttered tone'[38]), and the privileging of the universal over the contingent particular ('Nothing peculiar or accidental restrains either [singing or piety] . . . Never does music weep or laugh over particular circumstances, but always over life itself'[39]).

Central to Schleiermacher's theological project is the concept of immediacy; in particular, 'immediate self-consciousness', an awareness that is preconceptual, prelinguistic, and precognitive. In his mature thought the term which comes to dominate Schleiermacher's articulation of this immediate self-consciousness is 'feeling' (*Gefühl*), in particular his notion of 'the feeling of absolute dependence', the consciousness of being utterly dependent on God, or, expressed differently, being conscious-of-oneself-as-being-in-relation-to-God.[40] This is a sense of lack—or, as we might say today, the existential experience of contingency; our awareness that self and world are not self-caused

---

[34] For the most substantial treatment of music in Schleiermacher's life and thought, see Philip Edward Stoltzfus, *Theology as Performance: Music, Aesthetics, and God in Western Thought* (New York: T & T Clark, 2006), ch. 3. See also Gunter Scholtz, *Schleiermachers Musikphilosophie* (Göttingen: Vandenhoeck & Ruprecht, 1981); Albert L. Blackwell, 'The Role of Music in Schleiermacher's Writings', in Kurt-Victor Selge (ed.), *Internationaler Schleiermacher-Kongress 1984*, vol. i (Berlin: Walter de Gruyter, 1985), 439–48; Begbie, *Resounding Truth*, 141–52.

[35] Friedrich Schleiermacher, *Christmas Eve: Dialogue on the Incarnation*, trans. Terrence N. Tice (Richmond, VA: John Knox Press, 1967), 46.

[36] Stoltzfus, *Theology as Performance*, 60–5, 74–7. For an intriguing discussion of Hoffmann in relation to Schleiermacher, see Ian Bent, 'Plato–Beethoven: A Hermeneutics for Nineteenth-Century Music?', in Ian Bent (ed.), *Music Theory in the Age of Romanticism* (Cambridge: Cambridge University Press, 1996), 105–24.

[37] Schleiermacher, *Christmas Eve*, 47.

[38] Schleiermacher, *Christmas Eve*, 46.   [39] Schleiermacher, *Christmas Eve*, 47.

[40] Friedrich Schleiermacher, *The Christian Faith*, trans. J. S. Stewart (Edinburgh: T & T Clark, 1999), 12–18.

or self-grounded. The term 'God' in this context does not, of course, denote an identifiably discrete 'object' or 'entity' to which we relate, for this would be to succumb to the kind of subject–object schema, typical of a certain kind of Protestant Orthodoxy, that Schleiermacher and his colleagues are keen to avoid.[41]

Although not subversive of language, concepts, cognition, or representation, music's content is nonetheless inarticulable in such terms. Rather, it gives immediate access to the dimension of being-in-the-world that underlies, and makes possible, all linguistic, conceptual, cognitive, and representational activity.[42] However, the immediacy of *Gefühl* can be mediated through art, and especially through dance and music. With respect to the differentiated momentum of music, as Bowie observes, '"note and movement" play the role of language for feeling'.[43]

Bowie is especially intrigued by Schleiermacher's views of language as constructive, which in important ways develop ideas found in Herder.[44] For Schleiermacher, our primordial openness to the world is never purely passive, but always to some extent productive, and this productivity includes language—which is why representational theories of language are so misleading. Language never simply reproduces pre-existent meanings—it certainly cannot be understood along the lines of the external representation of a prior, inarticulate, internal state (a common misunderstanding of Schleiermacher's view). It is rather part of the way meaning is generated by subjects or agents-in-relation, and is intrinsically (not merely contingently or accidentally) bound up with thought. Bowie wants us to remember that *music* had a key role in helping Schleiermacher recognize the constitutive role of language in our experience, and the inadequacy of representational theories. This is why Schleiermacher was especially interested in the 'musical' aspects of language— the fact that, for instance, spoken language depends for its significance on tone of voice, rhythm, and so forth; these things are 'constitutive of *Poesie*'.[45] The musical dimensions of language remind us that language does much more than name or picture; 'the rhythmic and the musical are not contingent

---

[41] Stoltzfus, *Theology as Performance*, 103.

[42] 'Feeling' is not, therefore, to be confused with 'affect' as used by the eighteenth-century theorists in their music theory.

[43] Bowie, *MPM*, 162. Compare Schlegel, for whom music is 'to be regarded less as a representational art than as a philosophical language . . . Feeling and wishing often go far beyond mere thinking; *music as inspiration*, as the language of feeling . . . is the only universal language': Bowie, 'Music and the Rise of Aesthetics', 38. It is worth adding that Schleiermacher wants to preserve a certain distance between the status of musical experience and the feeling of absolute dependence: the feeling of absolute dependence is purely receptive, whereas in the making and hearing of music, there is both passivity (passive receptivity to *Gefühl*) and activity, or productivity: Stoltzfus, *Theology as Performance*, 98–9, 104.

[44] 'Foucault claims that serious attention to the consequences of the shift in language away from representation only emerges later in the nineteenth century with Nietzsche: this is evidently not the case': Bowie, *Aesthetics and Subjectivity*, 172.

[45] Bowie, *Aesthetics and Subjectivity*, 167.

additions to language'.[46] But in addition, we are made to reckon with the fact that music can nonetheless express meaning, and in distinctive (non-linguistic) ways: Schleiermacher's account of music can help us acknowledge both the possibilities *and* the limitations of language.

Not all early Romantic accounts of music were as measured and carefully nuanced as Schleiermacher's. But they are generally one in seeing language's inadequacy as music's opportunity. Wordless music, for so long regarded as inferior to texted music, now becomes exalted as the highest form, not only of music but of all the arts. Bowie cites J. N. Forkel's claim of 1778 that music 'begins ... where other languages can no longer reach',[47] and Willhelm Heinse: 'Instrumental music ... expresses such a particular spiritual life in man that it is untranslatable for every other language.'[48] Hoffmann's review of 1810 echoes the same sentiments, paraphrased by Bowie thus: 'What music expresses is the essence of Romanticism ... precisely because it cannot be said in words.'[49] Thus music—instrumental music in particular, with its *absence* of determinacy or mimesis, its *inability* to be specific—can excel.

Longing for Home

Can we say more about the shape of music's expressivity? In his Beethoven review, Hoffmann makes repeated reference to the momentum of yearning or longing,[50] declaring it be the 'essence of romanticism'.[51] Writing of the Fifth Symphony as a whole, he tells his readers: 'The heart of every sensitive listener ... is certain to be deeply stirred and held until the very last chord by *one* lasting feeling (*Gefühl*), that of nameless, haunted yearning (*Sehnsucht*).'[52]

As is well known, the *Sehnsucht* theme pervades Romantic writing, what Paul de Man speaks of as a 'persistently frustrated intent toward meaning'.[53] What is perhaps less well known is the role it could be thought to play in the internal momentum of philosophical thinking. For some, the relation between

---

[46] Bowie, *Aesthetics and Subjectivity*, 174.

[47] Bowie, *MPM*, 54.   [48] Bowie, *MPM*, 54.

[49] Bowie, 'Romanticism and Music', 245. In 1800, in his *Kalligone*, Herder explicitly affirms instrumental music as the supreme art, for it provides access to the realm where the subject–object distinction is overcome. 'What cannot be made visible to man—the world of the invisible—becomes communicable to him in its [music's] manner, and in its manner alone.' Through reverent contemplation (*Andacht*), the listener is able to enjoy a 'higher, free realm', 'pure and free above the earth'. As quoted in Bonds, *Music as Thought*, 25.

[50] Hoffmann, 'Review of Beethoven', 238, 244, 247, 250.

[51] Hoffmann, 'Review of Beethoven', 238.

[52] Translation adapted from Hoffmann, 'Review of Beethoven', 250. Italics original.

[53] Paul De Man and Wlad Godzich, *Blindness and Insight: Essays in the Rhetoric of Contemporary Criticism* (London: Methuen, 1983), 129.

subject and object, mind and world, knower and known could be articulated through a philosophical understanding of the Absolute. Yet for others, the Absolute was intrinsically unsayable, inaccessible to philosophical grasp, by its very nature transcending all subject–object distinctions. 'A Romantic position is … one which questions whether a definitive philosophical account can be given of the relationship between what is subjective and what is objective.'[54]

Bowie highlights Friedrich Schlegel as especially telling in this regard. Schlegel came to reject the notion that music is a representative language of emotion (what he calls the 'flat viewpoint of so-called naturalness'[55]). To understand his contribution more fully, we need to take a step back and note a distinction Bowie highlights between two senses of inadequacy or lack that are basic to human experience.[56] The first is the sense that we can never attain a cognitive grasp of any reality. According to Bowie, G. W. F. Hegel (1770–1831) urges what is at its heart a philosophical resolution of this problem. Philosophy, with its drive to systematic wholeness, must transcend all forms of immediacy, all forms of sensuous particularity; this is the only way in which modernity's deep-rooted crises concerning contingency, transience, and decay can be overcome. 'Hegel's strategy is to push awareness of the transience of the life-world to its extreme, in order to show how it is to be overcome in philosophy.'[57] Music is no match here. 'Whereas the meaning of the word … is sustained against fading away by the idealisation inherent in thought, the musical note is seen as attached to the transient contingency of feelings.'[58] Feeling (*Empfindung*) for Hegel is by its very nature indeterminate, and philosophy moves beyond indeterminacy and sensuous particularity, from tone to word and concept, from the immediate and specific material of the sounding note to ideas and thoughts, which transcend this immediacy and materiality: 'Meaning does not rely on specific sensuous material, because mind can employ any material that can take on form as a sign.'[59] For Hegel, then, music 'is a non-conceptual residue which philosophy will eventually eliminate by conceptually "mediating" it'.[60] But, says Bowie, we need to ask if this 'may not involve some kind of exclusion or repression of certain kinds of meaning'.[61]

The irony is that just at the time Hegel was saying these things, music (and writing about music) was influencing philosophers as well as being influenced by them, and, moreover, spawning philosophy of a markedly different flavour from Hegel's. This leads us to the second more deep-rooted sense of lack delineated by Bowie. Here we become aware that a purely cognitive relation to

---

[54] Bowie, 'Romantic Philosophy and Religion', 176.
[55] As quoted in Dahlhaus, *The Idea of Absolute Music*, 70.
[56] See Bowie, 'Romantic Philosophy and Religion', 187.
[57] Bowie, *MPM*, 127.   [58] Bowie, *MPM*, 131.
[59] Bowie, *MPM*, 131.   [60] Bowie, 'Music and the Rise of Aesthetics', 39.
[61] Bowie, *MPM*, 134.

the world is impossibly narrow and restrictive; here our sense of lack in the face of finitude is a sense that we are not 'at home', and this calls for a very different response to Hegel. So say the Romantics, and music leads the way. Franz Christian Horn, writing eight years before Hoffmann but in the same journal, insists that 'Music is ineffable . . . it is not susceptible to pure intellectual perception . . . as soon as it stoops to the servitude of intellectual comprehensibility, it ceases to be music and becomes in effect a parody of itself.'[62]

Schlegel is determined to resist such servitude. He finds himself deeply impressed *both* by humankind's pre-conceptual feeling, a pre-rational awareness of finitude, limitation, and transience, *and* by the way in which thought reaches beyond limitation through its awareness that it *is* limited.[63] There is here both a striving towards infinity, the unconditioned, 'an indeterminate, infinite drive which is not directed at a determinate object, but has an infinite goal',[64] as well as a reliance on conditioned structure, determinate form. Philosophy will therefore have something of this double character: on the one hand, it is motivated by 'the desire to attain something which can never be present, but which yet demands to be attained'.[65] (Novalis said that philosophy is 'really homesickness, *the drive to be at home everywhere*'.[66]) But on the other hand, this longing is not 'an indeterminate wish for something inaccessible, because it goes together with the understanding, the capacity for knowledge'.[67] Philosophy entails 'a freedom which can expand towards infinity' but 'which has to become limited for determinate thought to result at all'.[68]

Here music comes into its own. And Bowie stresses that it is musical *rhythm* that especially impresses Schlegel, for it is marked by the same twofoldness that should characterize philosophy. Rhythm involves *both* an expansive energy, an 'on-and-onness', a reaching for 'incomprehensible infinity' ('Music is most of all longing [*Sehnsucht*]'[69])—which on its own would result in merely an ecstatic anarchy of feelings—*and* structured repetition, forms of limitation, and determination. (In this light, Hoffmann's Beethoven review now begins to make more sense—his keenness that we sense the music's

---

[62] Peter Le Huray and James Day (eds), *Music and Aesthetics in the Eighteenth and Early-Nineteenth Centuries* (Cambridge: Cambridge University Press, 1981), 273. It is thus probably important to make some kind of distinction between romanticism and idealism (as in, say, Hegel); the latter's confidence in conceptual philosophical thought being far greater. See Bowie, 'Romantic Philosophy and Religion', 181–6; Bowie, 'Music and the Rise of Aesthetics', 42. The distinction is not always apparent in literature in this field, as evinced, for example, by Evan Bonds's catch-all term 'idealism' (which includes the Romantics). See Bonds, *Music as Thought*, 12–28.

[63] 'Feeling involves both limitation and its opposite, because the awareness of limitation *as* limitation cannot itself just be derived from limitation, even though it requires limitation to emerge': Bowie, *MPM*, 92.

[64] Bowie, *MPM*, 99.   [65] Bowie, *MPM*, 93.

[66] As quoted in Bowie, *MPM*, 140. His italics.

[67] Bowie, 'Romantic Philosophy and Religion', 187.   [68] Bowie, *MPM*, 94.

[69] As quoted in Bowie, 'Romanticism and Music', 247. 'What [music] alone can express is longing for the infinite and infinite melancholy.' As quoted in Bowie, *MPM*, 98.

infinite longing *and* his intense interest in its 'rational' structure.) For Schlegel, rhythm is being regarded as a fundamental mode of living-in-the-world, and it is not to be thought of as foreign or irrelevant to abstract thought—on the contrary, philosophy, properly understood, actually depends on it. Music, in other words, enables us to apprehend something of what it is to belong to the world, to recover that sense of immediacy with the world that the Romantics believed had been lost in their day.

We are, then, faced with a situation in which music is being drawn upon to re-form philosophy's own self-understanding and practice, and in the process give it far greater existential import. 'The Romantics' attention to music gives them . . . a new understanding of philosophy, not as a systematic answer to metaphysical questions, but as a search for ways of coming to terms with the modern experience of finitude.'[70] In this way, music is given a crucial responsibility in negotiating the alienations of modernity that contemporary philosophy was struggling with, but in the process, questioning and challenging the adequacy and comprehensiveness of the philosophical strategies customarily employed.

The Music of Nature

As we would expect—though this is not developed at length by Bowie in *Music, Philosophy, and Modernity*—for all its wariness of systematization, romanticism is characterized by an immense cosmic sweep. Schleiermacher can insist that the essence of religion 'is neither thinking nor action, but intuition and feeling. It wishes to intuit the universe, wishes devoutly to overhear the universe's own manifestations and actions, longs to be grasped and filled by the universe's immediate influences.'[71] Julia Lamm has recently contended that early German romanticism was characterized by a form of what she calls 'Neo-Spinozism' (after the philosopher Baruch Spinoza (1632–77)), which pressed beyond traditional notions of a personal God without falling into nihilism or atheism.[72] The 'infinite', a living force, surging in and through everything finite, is intrinsically uncontainable, overflowing

---

[70] Bowie, *MPM*, 137.

[71] Friedrich Schleiermacher, *On Religion: Speeches to Its Cultured Despisers* (Cambridge: Cambridge University Press, 1996), 102.

[72] Julia A. Lamm, 'Romanticism and Pantheism', in David Fergusson (ed.), *The Blackwell Companion to Nineteenth-Century Theology* (Oxford: Wiley-Blackwell, 2010), 165–86. Bowie himself argues that the Romantics were trying to find a way between a closed rationalist pantheism (associated by some with Spinoza), and the intensification of Kant in the subjectivism of J. G. Fichte (1762–1814): both were perceived as implicitly nihilist/atheist: Bowie, 'Romantic Philosophy and Religion', 177–81. How far Schleiermacher—by far the ablest theologian among the early Romantics—can be drawn into those categories is a matter for debate.

the finite—the 'excessiveness' of the prose of the likes of E. T. A. Hoffmann testifies to just this uncontainability—yet is not manifest except through the finite.[73] We are, says Lamm, being offered

> a philosophy of immanence that can be characterized as a dynamic coincidence of opposites...The true Romantic, or the truly religious person, maintains the tension between opposites, without losing either side, because she or he recognizes that all finite opposition is ontologically grounded in the unity or coincidence (not identification) of the infinite and finite.[74]

What is at play in the symphony, 'romantically' heard, is this dynamism of opposites, the life of this immaterial infinite active in and through finite materiality; the symphony is a manifestation of what Novalis calls the 'symphony of the universe' (*des Weltalls Symphonie*).[75] Critical for these writers, in Lamm's words, was 'the experience of the universe pressing in on them and expressing itself through them',[76] and supremely through creative productivity. The composer participates in the infinite productivity that swells and courses in and through all things. In 1814, Hoffmann writes:

> Our mysterious urge to identify the workings of this animating natural spirit [of the times], and to discover our essence, our other-worldly abode in it, which gives rise to the pursuit of knowledge, lay also behind the haunting sounds of music, which described with increasing richness and perfection the wonders of that distant realm. It is quite clear that in recent times instrumental music has risen to heights earlier composers did not dream of, just as in technical facility modern players clearly far surpass those of earlier times.[77]

---

[73] Writing of a piece of profuse, extravagant prose about music by Tieck, Carl Dahlhaus comments: 'it is just the arbitrariness, the unbounded imagination with which Tieck wounds prosaic logic, that turns this exegesis into a poetic text that lets the reader imagine what is granted the hearer of absolute music: an experience that overcomes him for an instant, but which cannot be held fast. The musical impression is as fleeting as it is compelling': Dahlhaus, *The Idea of Absolute Music*, 69.

[74] Lamm, 'Romanticism and Pantheism', 175–6.

[75] As quoted in Chua, *Absolute Music*, 172. Schelling can write: 'Music is...nothing other than the aurally perceived rhythm and harmony of the visible universe itself': F. W. J. Schelling, 'Philosophie der Kunst', in *Werke*, ed. Manfred Schröter (Munich: 1959), 142–55 (section 83), as quoted and translated in Le Huray and Day (eds), *Music and Aesthetics*, 280. For Schlegel, the 'sacred plays of art are only a remote imitation of the infinite play of the universe': Friedrich von Schlegel, *Dialogue on Poetry and Literary Aphorisms*, trans. Ernst Behler and Roman Struc (University Park, PA: Pennsylvania State University Press, 1968), 89. Compare Wackenroder, who can write of the effect of a symphony on Berglinger, his fictitious musician: 'a wonderful mixture of happiness and sadness in his heart, so that he was equally near to laughing and crying—a feeling that we meet so often on our way through life, and which no art is more able to express than music'. As quoted and translated in Bellamy Hosler, *Changing Aesthetic Views of Instrumental Music in 18th Century Germany* (Epping: Bowker, 1981), 195.

[76] Lamm, 'Romanticism and Pantheism', 177.

[77] Hoffmann, 'Old and New Church Music', 372.

In this outlook, according to Daniel Chua, instrumental music 'was given the double task of inscribing itself within the totality of the universe and of delineating the creative processes of the ego to affirm the subject's autonomy in the totality of the world, and so resolve the antagonism between subject and object'.[78]

One way of reading this is as a revival of the pre-modern Pythagorean tradition that had sustained music theory for so many centuries—something especially evident in F. W. J. Schelling (1775–1854), whose writings had a substantial impact on the early Romantics.[79] Embroiled in an intellectual climate keenly sensitive to modernity's disorientations, with humans orphaned amid a 'disenchanted' universe,[80] music is once again finding an integral place in a theologically charged vision of the cosmos. But the theology has been drastically reconfigured. Instrumental music 'sounds' the inaudible again, but the inaudible is not the harmony of the spheres or the ratios of heaven, but the infinite play of the world's immanent spirit, the infinite surge coursing through all things, coming to realization supremely in and through the creative productivity of the human subject. This was not so much a re-embedding of music in the cosmos as a remythologizing of the cosmos via music, in a culture where 'stars no longer sang, and scales no longer laddered the sky'.[81] To be sure, the early Romantics' conception of the non-human world mediated through music was deeply ambivalent, given their heightened sensitivity to nature's transience. The 'longing for home', after all, is bound up with a keen awareness of what we cannot control in the world around us, including the 'darker' aspects of nature.[82] Nonetheless, we are a long way from the common caricature of the Romantics as purveyors of an individualized expressivism, where music is characterized merely as the externalization of an

---

[78] Chua, *Absolute Music*, 169.

[79] For a helpful overview of Schelling on music, see Stoltzfus, *Theology as Performance*, 56–9. 'The Absolute, for Schelling, is grasped through the mediation of formal structures of music, which harmonize, reconcile, and bring to a totalizing "indifference point", within the intuition of the consciousness, the primordial gulf between finite and infinite, real and ideal, nature and morality, body and soul, and art and religion': Stoltzfus, *Theology as Performance*, 59.

[80] See the discussions of the theme of homelessness in nineteenth-century literature in Roger Lundin, *Believing Again: Doubt and Faith in a Secular Age* (Grand Rapids, MI: Eerdmans, 2009), 129–34, 274–6; also Steven Bouma-Prediger and Brian J. Walsh, *Beyond Homelessness: Christian Faith in a Culture of Displacement* (Grand Rapids, MI: Eerdmans, 2008).

[81] Chua, *Absolute Music*, 21. John Neubauer, *The Emancipation of Music from Language: Departure from Mimesis in Eighteenth-Century Aesthetics* (New Haven: Yale University Press, 1986), 193–210. On these developments, with particular reference to the 'work' concept, see John Butt, 'The Seventeenth-Century Musical "Work"', in Tim Carter and John Butt (eds), *The Cambridge History of Seventeenth-Century Music* (Cambridge: Cambridge University Press, 2005), 27–54, 46–7.

[82] Bowie highlights the ambiguous attitude to nature evident in Carl Maria von Weber's opera *Der Freischütz* (1821), and the Romantic idea of the 'uncanny' (*das Unheimliche*, lit. 'the unhomely'): Bowie, 'Romanticism and Music', 250.

individual's emotional interiority. Something much more far-reaching and world-embracing is being envisaged, on the grandest possible scale.[83]

Philosophy and Music

Bowie is less concerned with the details of the Romantics' theological cosmology, however, than he is with its import for philosophy. Basic to the Romantics' outlook is that there are some ways of being-in-the-world that resist verbal and conceptual analysis and articulation but which cannot thereby be discounted as meaningless. Accordingly, Bowie urges that we need an expansion and reconfiguration of philosophy in order to recognize and come to terms with such realities. This is the challenge of music, instrumental music in particular—hence Schlegel's remark that 'there is a certain tendency of all pure instrumental music towards philosophy'.[84] And instrumental music issues its challenge not as an idea or concept, but as something *practised*—made, performed, listened to. Music *shows* what cannot be said or conceptually thought.[85] Of course, music can become an object of philosophical conceptual thought and language, but—Bowie is contending—not before it has become a *mode* of thought, a vehicle of philosophy.

It is worth noting that such a vision of music was probably more likely to arise in a German context than in any other. The historian Leonard Kreiger, writing of styles of intellectual history, once distinguished between the 'German–Italian historicist' school (e.g. Dilthey, Cassirer) and its North American counterpart (e.g. Lovejoy, Boas). The latter tend to invest their interest in discrete ideas, 'components analysed out of the systems and combinations in which they were originally invested', whereas the former favour tracing culturally embedded patterns of thinking (even though determinate, discrete concepts will be involved).[86] Speaking of this European orientation, Michael Steinberg comments that it

> opens the door to the singular importance of music within German-speaking intellectual culture, or rather the reason why music was discursively enabled, so to

---

[83] We should not forget, however, the more worldly aspects of this: the aspirations to universality through music were inevitably linked to political aspirations—the belief that German music in particular could transcend its Germanness was almost bound to link up with a belief in a universal, indeed quasi-theological role for the German nation.

[84] Friedrich von Schlegel, *Kritische Schriften und Fragmente* (Paderborn: Schöningh, 1988), 155, as quoted and translated in Bowie, 'Music and the Rise of Aesthetics', 34.

[85] For the Romantics, 'it is not analysis but *initiation* into instrumental music that gives an intuition of God': Chua, *Absolute Music*, 175.

[86] Leonard Krieger, 'The Autonomy of Intellectual History', in Leonard Krieger and M. L. Brick (eds), *Ideas and Events: Professing History* (Chicago: University of Chicago Press, 1992), 159–77.

speak, to play so important a part within this intellectual style—the reason why the age of Hegel is also the age of Beethoven, the reason why, at this cultural moment, it makes sense to assert that the music is thinking. *Music, and specifically the kind of power and pulse associated with Beethoven, in fact carries the rhythmic, quasi-physical momentum of the current of moving ideas*, such as freedom; thus it seems to contain the same idea of freedom that Beethoven may occasionally formulate in words, along with countless others of his generation who produced many more words on the subject, and more coherently, than he did.[87]

This naturally provokes the question: prior to the Hoffmann review, what kind of music did the early Romantics of the 1790s and early 1800s have in mind as they lauded its infinite resonances? References to sounding music in their writings are in fact fairly scant. And as far as Hoffmann is concerned, the philosophical ideas he draws on were in circulation long before his encounter with Beethoven—according to Mark Evan Bonds, they were alive during the 1790s, before Beethoven had written any of his symphonies.[88] And the kind of music that would seem to embody most fully the Romantic philosophy of the unattainable idea and endless yearning, the simultaneous presence of form and of every form being transcended (or on the verge of being transcended), was not to appear until some considerable time *after* the early Romantic philosophy had waned—in the music of Schumann, Mendelssohn, and later, Wagner, Mahler, and others.[89] Does this mean that early Romantic musical philosophy was conceived in theoretical remoteness from sounding music, and wholly prior to it?

Matters are not so straightforward. There does seem to be a tendency in these writers to treat instrumental music as primarily a concept, to have it occupy an 'ideational, metaphysical space', as Kiene Brillenburg Wurth puts it,[90] but this should not suggest an isolated, theoretical space. The phenomenon of longing, for example, is arguably present in the decades before the Romantics, in 'sonata form' for example, which depends on a harmonic journey from a basic key 'away' to others before 'returning' to the home key, a journey that can be greatly extended and involved, generating a sense of yearning for closure and return, for 'home'. All this is basic to the first movements of the eighteenth-century symphonies of Mozart and Haydn. It is Bowie's contention—and this is central to his case—that the influence between music and philosophy can in fact run both ways, and that the case

---

[87] Michael P. Steinberg, 'Music as Thought', *Beethoven Forum* 14, 2 (2007): 182–6, 185. My italics.

[88] Bonds, *Music as Thought*, 11, and chs 1–3 *passim*.

[89] 'When the Schlegels, Novalis, Tieck, and Schelling were writing in Jena, Schumann was not even a sperm': Chua, *Absolute Music*, 178.

[90] Kiene Brillenburg Wurth, *Musically Sublime: Indeterminacy, Infinity, Irresolvability* (New York: Fordham University Press, 2009), 48.

of the early Romantics proves the point: music 'already articulates what conceptual thought as yet fails to articulate, and vice versa'.[91]

PROVOCATIONS

It will be clear by now that even in the more restrained of the early Romantic visionaries, listening to instrumental music is being given an unmistakably theological aura. The heavy leaning of the Romantics towards 'music religion' has been widely discussed.[92] It found what was perhaps its most florid expression in Ludwig Tieck: 'Flowing out of every tone is a tragic and divine enthusiasm which redeems every listener from the limitations of earthly existence.'[93] Or again: instrumental music 'is certainly the ultimate mystery of faith, the mystique, the completely revealed religion. I often feel as though it were still in the process of being created, and as though its masters ought not to compare themselves with any others.'[94] And the notion of the artist as high priest is well represented in the words of Schlegel:

> The priest as such exists only in the invisible world. In what guise is it possible for him to appear among men? His only purpose on earth will be to transform the finite into the infinite; hence he must be and continue to be, no matter what the name of his profession, an artist.[95]

Such quotes could be multiplied many times over. To his credit, Bowie has no intention of joining the cult. But he is nonetheless emphatic that music's stubborn irreducibility, even if overplayed by the early Romantic imagination, needs to be taken seriously. And he is in no doubt that the highly charged rhetoric of the movement, and its associated philosophy—fragmentary, hyperbolic, densely metaphorical, and unsystematic as it often is—cannot be lightly dismissed, for it signals challenges of immense significance for philosophy's engagement with the upheavals of modernity. In a review of *Music, Philosophy, and Modernity*, Lydia Goehr sums up what is at stake:

> To a significant extent, Bowie's book is well read as an attempt to demystify and thus to show the philosophical *truthfulness* or credibility of the hyperbole that has attended so many philosophical claims about music, without, however, the

---

[91] Bowie, *MPM*, 77.

[92] See e.g. Dahlhaus, *The Idea of Absolute Music*, ch. 6. On the notion of 'art religion', see Abigail Chantler, *E. T. A. Hoffmann's Musical Aesthetics* (Aldershot: Ashgate, 2006), ch. 1.

[93] As quoted in Edward A. Lippman, *A History of Western Musical Aesthetics* (Lincoln, NE: University of Nebraska Press, 1992), 207.

[94] As quoted in Dahlhaus, *The Idea of Absolute Music*, 89.

[95] Friedrich von Schlegel, *Philosophical Fragments*, trans. P. Firchow (Minneapolis: University of Minnesota Press, 1991), 95.

demystification leading to music's reduction to that which it self-evidently is not: namely, a conceptually-determinate language of *truth*.[96]

Central to this project is Bowie's questioning of the assumption that philosophy *already possesses* the necessary and adequate tools to come to terms with a phenomenon such as music: much depends on 'doing justice' to music, honouring the distinctiveness of musical practices.[97] Modern philosophers, Bowie believes, have generally supposed that music constitutes a problem which philosophy needs to solve by deploying the language and conceptual tools already at their disposal, including their exacting protocols of 'meaningfulness'. Romanticism provokes us to wonder if 'music might be able to say more about philosophy than philosophy can say about music'.[98]

Philosophy's need to learn from music is especially evident when faced with the profounder turmoils, antinomies, and aporias engendered by the course of modernity—the experience of loss and transience, or of the non-human world as destructive. For Bowie, musicians reacted to these phenomena in ways that not only demand serious attention in the corridors of philosophy departments, but that should compel philosophers to ask whether their favoured modes of language, conceptuality, communication, and criteria of meaningfulness might require revising.[99]

In all this, of pivotal importance is the relation between music and language, and the question of how music 'means': 'it is precisely the things which resist verbal articulation', Bowie contends, 'that ought to constitute an important focus of a philosophy which tries to engage with all dimensions of modern culture'.[100] Or again: 'Questioning of the idea of verbal language as representation of a ready-made world leads to a new sense that the uses to which words can be put do not adequately cover all that we need to express, and music is significant in extending what can be expressed.'[101] Bowie's particular bête noire in this regard is the application of some forms of Anglo-American analytic philosophy to the philosophy of music. Certain types of proposition are believed to convey reliable knowledge about pre-existent and observable objects, and these propositions are presumed to form the tools with which one can distinguish forms of language 'which reliably contact with the world' from those that do not. Clearly, music cannot be shoehorned into such schemes.[102]

---

[96] Lydia Goehr, 'Normativity Without Norms: Review Article of Andrew Bowie, *Music, Philosophy, and Modernity* (Cambridge: Cambridge University Press, 2007)', *European Journal of Philosophy* 17, 4 (December 2009): 597–607, 599. Italics original.

[97] Bowie, *MPM*, 43.

[98] Bowie, 'Music and the Rise of Aesthetics', 29.

[99] Bowie writes of a tension 'between philosophy as that which seeks to explain aspects of modernity, and philosophy as that which seeks to advert to new forms of world-disclosure which offer new semantic potential': Bowie, *MPM*, 137.

[100] Bowie, *MPM*, 397.   [101] Bowie, *MPM*, 385.

[102] 'Analytic philosophers of music tend to assume that an account of verbal meaning has been established, and that this is what allows them to attempt to determine the status of musical meaning': Bowie, *MPM*, 4.

By contrast, what Bowie calls the 'European traditions' (e.g. Vico, Herder, Kant, the Romantics) attend to the considerable multiplicity of ways in which language is actually employed in concrete situations, and the different ways in which the world is thereby disclosed and negotiated.[103] Although finding some post-structuralists 'melodramatic' when it comes to charting different eras of signification, he can nonetheless quote Samuel Wheeler with approval: 'If there are no magical, naturally referring words, then meaning is nothing deeper than uses of ordinary words in particular circumstances.'[104] The territory is, of course, familiar to students of Ludwig Wittgenstein (1889–1951) and those of his ilk, where language's employment of metaphors, non-propositional figures of speech, bodily gestures, and so on, and its inextricable embeddedness in social and cultural practices are all regarded as intrinsic to its meaningfulness.

The drawbacks of an 'analytic' approach, if adhered to as a kind of all-purpose solvent in the philosophy of language, are strikingly evident in relation to the much-discussed status of metalinguistic statements. And here Bowie makes some of his most interesting observations. The dilemma is well known. As long as one construes the relation between word and world (and thus meaning) in terms of a linkage between fixed items in the world and linguistically articulated meanings which are said to mirror or correspond to them in some manner, one cannot explain the relation between words and world in a way that avoids vicious circularity. For the 'explanation' of the word–world relation would always have to presuppose what is being explained; there is no escape from the relation—the notion of an 'external viewpoint on language is a mirage'.[105] But Bowie cites some notes from the early work of Wittgenstein, where the philosopher asks 'is *language* the *only* language?' Wittgenstein wonders whether there might be 'a means of expression with which I can talk *about* language',[106] and he suggests that music might fill this role. Bowie comments:

> Whereas science can talk about the world, it cannot talk about what enables it to talk about the world, namely the very fact that the world is intelligible to us at all. *The implication is therefore that music can 'talk' about language in a way verbal language cannot.*[107]

---

[103] Bowie is not uncritical of this European stream, however. For instance, he believes it leads to 'fetishizing "Philosophy" as some kind of source of superior insight', and in any case, he seems suspicious of making clean-cut distinctions between 'analytic' and 'continental' thought. See Bowie, *Philosophical Variations*, 21, 105–14. It should be stressed that Bowie's objections are more to the *analytic philosophy of music* than to analytic philosophy per se. I owe this important qualification to Bowie himself.

[104] Bowie, *Philosophical Variations*, 17. The quote is from Samuel C. Wheeler, *Deconstruction as Analytic Philosophy* (Stanford, CA: Stanford University Press, 2000), 63.

[105] Bowie, *MPM*, 270.

[106] Ludwig Wittgenstein, *Notebooks 1914–1916* (Oxford: Basil Blackwell, 1979), 52.

[107] Bowie, *MPM*, 41. Italics mine. Bowie greatly expands his reflections on Wittgenstein in Bowie, *MPM*, 261–88. On Wittgenstein and music, see Jerrold Levinson, 'Musical Thinking', *Journal of Music and Meaning* 1 (Fall 2003): sect. 2; Stoltzfus, *Theology as Performance*, ch. 5.

However one interprets Wittgenstein's comments, it is clear that Bowie is urging us to see music as constituting a quite particular mode of responding to the world, a way of relating to reality which has much to 'tell us' about that rich, inarticulate, semantic environment which underwrites the meaningfulness of any verbal language: 'the very ability to understand a verbal account of meaning of any kind itself relies on conditions which are themselves not verbal'.[108] This pushes us towards a substantial revision of the epistemological model Bowie believes underlies the analytical approach, that of the 'spectatorial subjective mind confronting an objective world'.[109] Rather, we come to know the world as meaningful through active, social, and physical involvement with it. Indeed, 'meaning has to do with pre-conceptual engagements with things, with embodied "being in the world", where one acts, feels, etc.'.[110] Accordingly, the notion of meaningfulness needs redescription: for Bowie 'any form of articulation that can disclose the world in ways which affect the conduct and understanding of life can be regarded as possessing meaning'.[111] Music is meaningful in that it is intelligible, coherent, and able to influence others—evidence that it 'can mean without necessarily meaning anything exhaustively representational, referential, or conceptual'.[112]

The conductor and pianist Daniel Barenboim caught something of this vision in a tribute to his friend Edward Said:

> Edward saw in music not just a combination of sounds, but he understood the fact that every musical masterpiece is, as it were, a conception of the world. And the difficulty lies in the fact that this conception of the world cannot be described in words—because were it possible to describe it in words, the music would be unnecessary. But he recognized that the fact that it is indescribable doesn't mean it has no meaning.[113]

We might want to quibble with the phrase 'conception of the world', but the basic point resonates well with Bowie.

---

[108] Bowie, *Philosophical Variations*, 22. Bowie draws substantially on Charles Taylor in this connection; Taylor writes of 'the way in which the representations we frame, and our entire ability to frame them, are underpinned by our ability to cope with the world in a host of ways: from our capacity as bodily beings to make our way around in our surroundings, picking up, using, avoiding, and leaning on things to our knowing as social beings how to relate to and interact with friends, strangers, lovers, children, and so on': Charles Taylor, 'Rorty and Philosophy', in Charles B. Guignon and David R. Hiley (eds), *Richard Rorty* (Cambridge: Cambridge University Press, 2003), 158–80, 159.

[109] Bowie, *MPM*, 8.

[110] Bowie, *MPM*, 378. This, of course, is widely supported in a large range of contemporary epistemology.

[111] Bowie, *MPM*, 6.

[112] Goehr, 'Normativity': 599. Goehr is here paraphrasing Bowie.

[113] Daniel Barenboim and Edward W. Said, *Parallels and Paradoxes: Explorations in Music and Society* (New York: Knopf Publishing Group, 2004), p. x.

Two further points are worth adding here. First, Bowie's case is character-ized by a resistance to reductionism on at least two fronts—and both signal significant philosophical courage. There is his resistance to the reductionism of 'scientism', and its closely related philosophical traditions. But there is also a resistance to reductionist theory of the sort that, having unmasked 'great works of music' as shoring up oppressive discourses of gender, class, and race, would believe its work to have been done, as if this were the most significant and valuable contribution theory could ever make. Bowie, some-times associated with the so-called 'new aestheticism',[114] asks: 'Was what an aesthetic approach saw in the best of Western and other culture *merely* an illusion from which we should now be liberated?'[115] Without opposing such unmasking in principle, he nevertheless asks: 'why should one bother to concern oneself with well-known products of Western culture, if it were not that they offer *more* than is apparent when their often quite evident failings with regard to contemporary social, ethical and other assumptions are ex-posed?'[116] His appropriation of the Romantics' music philosophy is one example of his working through the implications of that 'more'.

Second, Bowie's stress on music's irreducibility should not be taken as a plea for its isolation, as if it were wholly incommensurable with other forms of meaning-making.[117] Although music may provide a way of relating to the world that is not condensable to verbal and conceptual articulation, and although 'it is only in the active process of engagement with music that one can experience the open-ended challenge which it poses',[118] language and concepts may (and almost always do) affect the way we make and hear music, and the making and hearing of music may enrich our use of, and contribute to the formation of, language and conceptual thought.[119]

---

[114] See John J. Joughin and Simon Malpas (eds), *The New Aestheticism* (Manchester: Man-chester University Press, 2003) and Guy Dammann, 'Review of John J. Joughin and Simon Malpas (eds), *The New Aestheticism* (Manchester: Manchester University Press, 2003)', *Journal of Applied Philosophy* 22, 2 (2005): 199–203.

[115] Andrew Bowie, 'What Comes After Art?', in John J. Joughin and Simon Malpas (eds), *The New Aestheticism* (Manchester: Manchester University Press, 2003), 68–82, 70.

[116] Bowie, 'What Comes After Art?', 70. My italics. 'Contemporary aesthetic production may be more decentred, and the era of the great works may for that reason even belong to the past, but that is not a reason to underestimate what great works do that nothing else can. Perhaps, then, we are not reaching the end of the significance of great art from the Western traditions, but are instead only at a point where some of the academic world seems to have lost sight of just how significant that art may still be': Bowie, 'What Comes After Art?', 80.

[117] Stephen Halliwell argues that the Romantics' rejection of certain forms of representational theory in the arts does not entail a repudiation of the ancient concept of 'mimesis' (imitation) but rather a transformation of it, what he calls 'renegotiated or redefined mimeticism': Stephen Halliwell, *The Aesthetics of Mimesis: Ancient Texts and Modern Problems* (Princeton: Princeton University Press, 2002), 365.

[118] Bowie, *MPM*, 137.

[119] 'A verbal account cannot replace the experience of music itself, although a verbal account still affects how we hear music, and the music can, in turn, affect how we understand the verbal account': Bowie, *MPM*, 271.

METAPHYSICS AND THEOLOGY

Unlike many music theorists, Bowie is not one to flee the realm of metaphysics. But what kind of metaphysics underwrites his case?

He contrasts two broad types. 'Metaphysics₁' he describes (acknowledging his debt to Heidegger's story of metaphysics) as the attempt to 'map out the place of humankind in the universe by giving an account of the true nature of being', adding that 'Modernity is inaugurated by the move towards the idea that we ourselves, qua thinking subjects, are the foundation of that true account.'[120] And if the human thinking subject stands at the centre, nature is the 'object' to be studied and described. Through scientific enquiry—the natural sciences are generally valorized in this schema—nature is ever more deeply understood, and on this basis, ever more fully controlled. However, despite the spectacular success of the natural sciences, the development of modernity has exposed the contingency and 'fragility of the subject', our need for and attachment to things we cannot control, things that cannot be coerced by our wills. Faced with the resistance of the world to these needs and desires, metaphysics₁ is woefully deficient. 'Metaphysics₂' Bowie describes as the 'attempt to establish a *meaningful* place for humankind, both in the rest of a nature which we acknowledge to be a threat, and in a potentially equally threatening second nature'.[121] (By 'second nature', Bowie appears to have in mind the negative effects produced by our attempts to control nature, which reproduce nature's most threatening aspects.) Crucial to this is acknowledging the 'contradictory nature of modern experience',[122] the renunciation of the possibility of complete control, recognizing those things that resist the kind of discourse and conceptualization appropriate to the natural sciences, *but which can still be experienced as meaningful.*[123] And this is where we must listen to the early Romantics.

Bowie rightly debunks the misconception that the Romantics opposed science. It is rather the hegemony of a certain kind of scientific ambition that they contested, one that would 'demythologize' the universe, stripping it of all significance except that which can be accounted for by the natural sciences. 'The call for a "new mythology", which would link the theoretical notions of philosophy and science to sensuous experience, in the form of images and stories, is . . . crucial to Romantic thinking.'[124] Bowie is himself

---

[120] Bowie, *MPM*, 33.

[121] Bowie, *MPM*, 36. Italics original.

[122] Metaphysics₂ 'should not be regarded as seeking to conceal the contradictory nature of modern experience in the name of an illusory harmony'. Bowie continues: 'although the Romantics seek to create systematic coherence in their thinking, they do so on the basis of the feeling that ultimate coherence will elude them': Bowie, *MPM*, 103.

[123] Bowie, *MPM*, 36.

[124] Bowie, 'Romantic Philosophy and Religion', 186.

opposed to 'scientism', the vaulting pretensions of science to colonize every dimension of human life with a pre-stipulated form of explanation. But it turns out that he regards *theological* versions of metaphysics$_2$ (including theological forms of 'negative metaphysics') as quite unacceptable, indeed as regressive. The notion that the world's processes are upheld by some kind of deity is simply not an intellectually viable option today. Bowie's obviously heartfelt belief in the positive value of music in the current cultural context *presumes* the impossibility of subscribing to theological truth as a public commitment: 'music can be seen as one of the resources available for confronting the consequences of the death of God. This might sound rather melodramatic, but I don't think that it necessarily is.'[125]

Bowie, it seems, is committed not only to the rejection of creedal Christianity's metaphysics but also of the early Romantics' metaphysics of an infinite *Geist*, or anything akin to it. Ironically, then, even metaphysics$_2$ is 'demythologized'. We cannot here trace Bowie's exploration of musical metaphysics beyond Hegel, as expressed by Schopenhauer, for example. It is enough to observe that Bowie's position appears to be marked by an unmistakable pathos. It is tellingly evident in his discussion of emotion and music, the manner in which music relates us to things beyond our control.

> The very fact that music can have to do with 'things outside ourselves that we do not control', thus with experiences of transience, loss, and longing (as well, of course, as love, and joy) connects us with the world in ways which knowledge may not. The emotions attached to knowing that we will all die and that nothing will ultimately last can be merely paralysing, whereas the musical articulation of the ways in which the world is disclosed in the light of such emotions seems to take one somewhere else, *even if it does not redeem one from the facticity that it also evokes.*[126]

He continues:

> *The idea of such redemption is, of course, what modernity should have taught us to renounce.* Having done so, we then need to pay more attention to the resources in modernity for responding to the consequences of this renunciation.[127]

Music's place in the wake of this obligatory repudiation of redemption is bitter-sweet indeed: a temporary solace in a bleak landscape of 'facticity'. In the context of metaphysics$_2$, music can provide a 'secularized' form of 'transcendence',[128] a vehicle for us to feel temporarily 'at home', but in an age that is post-theological, and within a universe that is ultimately indifferent to every human need and aspiration. The refusal of the theological is especially jarring when we recall Bowie's avowed eagerness to come to terms with things not

---

[125] Bowie, *MPM*, 398–9.   [126] Bowie, *MPM*, 39. My italics.
[127] Bowie, *MPM*, 39. My italics.   [128] Bowie, *MPM*, 382.

wholly amenable to scientific explanation; not only jarring but ironic, given that the origin and ground of the dismissal is to be found just here, in his construal of what the science of modernity 'should have taught us'. To suggest that 'the order of things is justified by its being grounded in a divinity' is no less than a form of 'self-deception . . . The aim of rendering the universe meaningful is now contradicted by a science which has progressively undermined the special position of humankind, reducing the earth to the status of a minor cosmic contingency, and humankind to being a result of evolutionary mechanisms.'[129] Bowie is not commending scientism here (that is certainly not the driving force of his project)—only theological responses *to* scientism. Nonetheless, we should still question what would seem to be the assumption that religious faith entails the 'rejection of well-confirmed science'.[130]

Elsewhere a penetrating and acute critic of the more damaging pretensions of modernity, Bowie is reluctant to query the stark, fatalistic naturalism that has come to constitute one of modernity's more pervasive trajectories, and which has proved so problematic on so many fronts. Despite being intent on 'doing justice' to things, it is unfortunate that he does not consider in depth the intense treatments by Jewish and Christian faith traditions of the very intellectual–cultural movements he so ably expounds, nor the extraordinarily subtle accounts of language that they have generated (accounts which could do much to nuance and support his own deft critiques both of crude representative and apophatic philosophies of language), nor the sophisticated and sensitive exposures of scientism that have emerged from many theological quarters, on which he could so usefully draw. To be sure, the tone is far from the brazen 'heroic secularity' of some contemporary writers, but he is curiously content to fall back on the relatively parochial notion that religious belief is, to pick up a phrase from another writer, 'a curious residue coating the ruins of the Western tradition',[131] together with the popular (mis)conception of theology as something wholly beyond all public accountability:

> If the core aspects of theology lie outside the realm of explanation and legitimation by evidence and argument, *as the modern world has shown that they do*, both religion and art are excluded from the publicly warranted, evidence-based validity that is required of the sciences. The question is whether this is necessarily to be regarded as a problem.[132]

We are told firmly that religious convictions are to be kept strictly private: there is nothing wrong with religion 'giving meaning to individual lives' but it should be 'privatized'; 'religionists' should not bring their claims 'into the game of public justification'.[133] Needless to say, the Christian persuasions of

---

[129] Bowie, *MPM*, 36. [130] Bowie, *MPM*, 36.
[131] Roger Lundin, *Believing Again*, 118. [132] Bowie, *MPM*, 380. My italics.
[133] Bowie, *MPM*, 381. Roger Lundin remarks that 'To be a modern believer is to recognize that in the deepest personal sense, belief is optional': Lundin, *Believing Again*, 7.

some of the authors he draws on most strongly to support his reading of modernity (Charles Taylor, for example) are not considered.

RETRIEVAL AND ADVANCE

It may well be that part of the problem here is a narrow construal of theology, a familiarity with only a certain kind of rationalist theology of the sort that the early Romantics (rightly in my view) eschewed.[134] In any case, this is hardly the place for a full-scale critique of the early Romantics from a rather richer theological perspective, nor of Bowie's marginalization of theological realism. With limited space, something much more modest is appropriate, and I hope, more constructive.

To begin with: retrieval. Bowie's is clearly an exercise in retrieval—an attempt to persuade philosophers and others to explore and learn from the Romantics' engagement with music, not despite but *with* its hyperbolic overdrive and metaphorical surfeit, while yet presuming that the Romantics' quasi-theology cannot be endorsed in any straightforwardly realist or concrete sense as articulating 'the way things are'. If Bowie's case is itself a form of retrieval, the question arising for the theologian is: what can be retrieved from Bowie's retrieval? Are there currents in his reading of the early Romantics that theology needs to hear, for the sake of illuminating, elucidating, and responding to the challenges of modernity? And, the tougher question: what happens to theology when these currents are taken seriously?

The methodological gauntlet Bowie throws down to philosophy clearly has its parallel in theology. The debates about musical meaning we have touched upon (and they are by no means over) make clear that music is persistently resistant to models that rely heavily or exclusively on narrow and distorted understandings of the way verbal language operates. The links between Bowie's conviction that 'music might be able to say more about philosophy than philosophy can say about music' and our concerns about theology in this book are not hard to see. That theology in modernity has found it exceedingly hard to come to terms with music is due in no small part to its reliance on philosophical strictures that massively constrain what is to count as meaningful. There are countless examples, but a case in point is that vein in Protestant thinking that is reluctant to acknowledge that music might do its *own* kind of God-glorifying work without having to be tied directly and immediately to texts.[135] If music-making and music-hearing involve thought processes that can mediate aspects of the world otherwise closed or opaque,

---

[134] I owe this observation to Nick Adams.

[135] See 'Returning to Geneva' (p. 38) in this volume.

then we will need to concede the possibility of there being times when 'music might be able to say more about theology than theology can say about music'. So, for example, 'hearing' a culture through music *may* disclose more that is especially theologically relevant, and disclose it far more accurately, than standard philosophy- or science-based commentary. The early Romantics' exploration of 'homelessness' and their sense of its sonic embodiment in the structured yet forward-driving character of music, even before 'romantic' music proper was written, is a field ripe for treatment by theologically attuned cultural historians of the late eighteenth and nineteenth centuries. So often this phenomenon is narrated exclusively through the disciplines of literature and philosophy, but if Bowie is correct, music was deeply entangled with verbal discourse on this theme in ways that implicate theological concerns at every turn and invite full and serious exploration.

The critical pressure-point for the theologian here, I would suggest, concerns the doctrine of creation. Can one operate with a theology sufficiently variegated to do justice to the myriad ways in which humans, as social and embodied agents, enter into fruitful relations with each other and their physical environment? Arising out of this is the related issue of the embeddedness of language in time, body, sense, and affect, and on language's inextricable connections with society and culture. All these are biblically rooted emphases and commonly articulated in current theology, but it is hard to find contemporary theologians reflecting on how music as a pre-conceptual and prelinguistic practice is eminently well suited to help us recover a sense of the importance of what Michael Polanyi calls the 'tacit dimension'[136] pervading all language use (a major concern of the early Romantics). Further, there is surprisingly little thought given in theology to just how language might *relate* to highly developed non-verbal systems of articulation such as music, and what we might learn about the nature of the theological enterprise from these relations.[137]

In addition, there is the possibility that the making and hearing of music can, within an enterprise oriented to the scriptural testimony to the God of Jesus Christ, enrich theology more directly: by serving to embody aspects of the Gospel and our apprehension of it that may well escape other means through which these realities come to be perceived. And if this is so, it may well generate fresh forms of language and conceptuality for the theologian, which in some cases can elicit the dynamics of the Gospel more faithfully than some of the well-tried, default languages and conceptual schemes typical of modernity.

Having said all this, we recall that Bowie firmly closes off the possibility of theology affording anything normative beyond the privacy of the individual;

---

[136] Michael Polanyi, *The Tacit Dimension* (New York: Doubleday, 1966).
[137] This is the major focus of Chs 7 and 8.

modernity has ordered public religious truth-claims off the scholarly playing field, and there can be no going back on this. In this context, the theologian will inevitably ask: what would a refusal of such severe strictures entail? One could, of course, engage at length in a direct critique of the assumptions that underwrite them. Another strategy, however—one which would doubtless be strenuously resisted by Bowie—would be to engage in critique but with a view to asking: might there be aspects of his convictions about music's place in modernity (and late modernity) that could be more fruitfully advanced if brought within a theological ambit? To this end, I offer reflections on three themes.

Normativity

The first concerns the matter of normative commitments. There is a huge emphasis in Bowie on the physical, socially and culturally mediated character of all our commerce with the world. Normativity is always humanly constituted; it never comes 'neat'. Bowie is dedicated to doing justice to what he calls the 'normativity of everyday life': we are able to understand certain 'forms of exchange and communication' which, although we rely on them constantly, we cannot prove or establish while at the same time employing them. Even science assumes that which it cannot demonstrate.[138] In a review of *Music, Philosophy, and Modernity*, Lydia Goehr argues that this refusal of externally imposed norms is crucial for Bowie: 'from philosophy's perspective, it is sufficient to establish the socially-constituted normative character of [a social practice such as music] without however determining or prescribing specific norms'.[139] Music is a pre- or non-representational social practice and functions in a given social group according to accepted rules regarded as normative, but music cannot be tied to any particular norms that might be prescribed by the philosopher from outside musical practice. Philosophy cannot be in the business of fixing things in advance; it cannot impose an a priori theory about how music is to mean, or stipulate any specific norms of meaning. And of a piece with this rejection of 'top-down' philosophy is his denial of any theory that would try to ground music in the 'natural' non-human order—i.e. that would pretend this or that music was more faithful to the natural order than another.[140] For this would suggest that music can jump out of its social and cultural skin to attain some kind of 'universal' status—an impossibility.

---

[138] Bowie, *MPM*, 37.   [139] Goehr, 'Normativity': 599.

[140] Bowie declares: 'Such ideas have been discredited by musicological, historical, and anthropological research, which shows that there are no transcultural aspects of music which can be said to be more "natural" than others': Bowie, *MPM*, 39.

However, there is another side to all this. Goehr argues that the 'music' for which Bowie wants to allow room in philosophy may be less free of philosophical shaping than he would like to think. She writes:

> [Bowie] can only tell us what philosophy is conveyed by music itself by using already philosophical terms, even if his point is that music conveys philosophy in its own musical terms. He then uses the philosophical terms that he has introduced to capture the philosophy that is conveyed by music to challenge other philosophical terms that have been traditionally applied to music. This suggests that, in a view in which music is appealed to as a measure to assess the philosophy that is meant to account for music, the 'music' appealed to is already as much a philosophical idea as it is a musical phenomenon.[141]

Goehr points out that extended and close consideration of musical practice— music as made and heard in particular contexts, or specific pieces of music— plays very little role in Bowie's argument (to be fair, something Bowie openly admits), leaving us with far more about the history of the *philosophy of* music than the history of music.[142] Paradoxically, therefore, there is more than a whiff of the notion that philosophy stands above the contingencies of history and circumstance (including the contingencies of modernity, presumably).

According to Goehr, then, although disavowing top-down philosophy, in practice Bowie allows philosophy considerable normative weight, and thus a substantial degree of 'objectivity'.[143] All this, of course, provokes the question: 'How . . . does philosophy, being itself historically conditioned, produce objective statements about the historical world?' Goehr continues: 'The answer depends on what is preserved of traditional philosophical conceptions of objectivity.'[144] Bowie 'wants quite explicitly to retain something objective and realist in his account and thus cannot give up the ghost of representation altogether'.[145] Indeed, 'Objectivity is one of Bowie's deepest concerns.'[146] His style is anything but ironic, his tone frequently urging, persuading. He is capable of making sweeping assertions about the nature of the physical world as a whole: most pointedly, he simply assumes without question that it is ultimately meaningless, directionless, and doomed to extinction. And he clearly believes music enables a fruitful, if temporary, means of being at home in the world, coping with a universe that eludes our full control.

The tension is hardly one unfamiliar to theologians of modernity. The root issue concerns whether or not human life is part of and embedded in realities that are not simply 'there' in a brute, neutral sense, but, as the Christian tradition affirms, created by God 'out of nothing', for the purpose of felicitous, covenantal relationship, and towards which humans are called to exercise a

---

[141] Goehr, 'Normativity': 601. [142] Goehr, 'Normativity': 602.
[143] Goehr, 'Normativity': 602–3. [144] Goehr, 'Normativity': 602.
[145] Goehr, 'Normativity': 604. [146] Goehr, 'Normativity': 602.

degree of respect and active responsibility, in part for the flourishing of humankind. Everything depends, to put it at its mildest, on whether the world we inhabit possesses any value other than the value we grant it or fashion from it.[147]

Especially relevant here is the Jewish and biblical stress on both the liberty of the created world in its contingent yet ordered otherness (against the Romantic tendency to blur the Creator–creature distinction), and God's covenantal, irrevocable dynamic commitment to all created things—human and non-human. In this setting, respecting 'objectivity' does not entail a grudging obedience to abstract norms, but rather acknowledging the prior context of our embodied, concrete relatedness to the gifted world we inhabit, in the midst of which, so the tradition maintains, God has made his purposes known. The marked emphasis in the early Romantics, taken up by Bowie, on the active, physical, bodily, social, and cultural mediation of all our commerce with the world can be strongly affirmed, but to do so does not logically exclude the possibility of the reality of norms (or normative states of affairs) that precede and exceed human artifice (whether in the created world or the mind of God), nor in principle exclude the possibility of access to such norms. Such exclusions are only possible if certain metaphysical commitments are set up unalterably in advance.

Bound up with this is epistemology. Goehr is not the only reviewer to ask whether Bowie's complaints about certain kinds of philosophy and associated theories of representation have been overplayed.[148] Though endorsing Bowie's refusal of 'naïve realism' (or representationalism), Goehr rightly points out that 'there remain *reflective* realist and representational theorists in our midst—Arthur Danto being one of them—who are sympathetic to more embodied understandings of how philosophy represents the world'.[149] There are in fact numerous writers of a similar temperament,[150] and the most insightful of them make much of what some philosophers have come to call

---

[147] Bowie himself is not, it should be noted, claiming that all value is fashioned or imposed; his account of Heidegger and Adorno show him to be rather subtler on this matter: Bowie, *MPM*, chs. 8 and 9.

[148] See Guy Dammann, 'Review of Andrew Bowie, *Music, Philosophy, and Modernity* (Cambridge: Cambridge University Press, 2007)', *British Journal of Aesthetics* 48, 4 (2008): 459–61.

[149] Goehr, 'Normativity': 604. Her italics.

[150] e.g. Michael Polanyi, *Personal Knowledge: Towards a Post-Critical Philosophy* (New York: Harper & Row, 1964); Roy Bhaskar, *A Realist Theory of Science* (London: Verso, 2008); Taylor, 'Rorty and Philosophy'; Taylor, *Philosophical Arguments*, ch. 1. See also José López and Garry Potter, *After Postmodernism: An Introduction to Critical Realism* (London: Athlone, 2001). In one place Bowie declares he is neither a realist nor an anti-realist but regards the realism/anti-realism debate as probably 'pointless': Bowie, *Philosophical Variations*, 108. Concerning the same passage, I am puzzled by the way Bowie appears to align 'critical realism' very closely with 'scientism'.

the 'background': the embodied, pre-conceptual 'semi- or utterly inarticulate understandings that make sense of our explicit thinking and reactions'.[151]

Finitude

Second, some comments on human finitude. Bowie is acute to modernity's excessive confidence in humanity's power to probe, comprehend, and thus *control* the material world. The early Romantics, he believes, were motivated in large part by an opposition to subject–object schemes that would render the ideal truth-seeking posture of humans as that of disengaged subject observing an object such as to gain true knowledge of it, and then control it. And Bowie is clearly sympathetic to the Romantics in this respect.

To attempt to attain ever greater, and potentially unlimited, control over the world is, of course, an attempt to achieve a godlike status. It involves the propensity to assume we can in some manner abstract ourselves from temporal and spatial contingencies, and attain a timeless, spaceless, quasi-infinite perspective from which we can perceive the totality of things with transparent clarity, and in the light of this govern whatever it is we survey. In many ways, Bowie's project can be seen as an attempt to put philosophy in its place in the wake of such hubris, to question all vaulting pretensions towards an infinite vantage point—music being his key instrument. It has been the perennial temptation for theology, needless to say, to claim to provide just this stance, the timeless overview. As Bowie would doubtless quickly point out, this is the ultimate hubristic move—it has demonstrably led to some of the worst oppressions human history has ever known.

A wiser way forward would begin by not only admitting but celebrating that humans are finite through and through, and that this always belonged to the divine intention. All knowledge is spatially and temporally located, limited. But what, then, of theological claims? The Christian faith ventures to claim that *within* this finite world, a calling, an invitation has been issued to engage in an interaction with the physical world and with others that does not entail our extraction from finitude and particularity. Generating and sustaining this is a fellowship or communion with the God who issues that call, a fellowship that does not negate our constrained, embodied humanness but, supremely through the Son who became (finite) flesh, brings it to its

---

[151] Charles Taylor's engagements with Richard Rorty are especially instructive in this regard. See e.g. Taylor, 'Rorty and Philosophy', 159. Taylor holds that: 'all exercises of reflective, conceptual thought have the content they have only as situated in a context of background understanding that underlies and is generated in everyday coping': Taylor, 'Rorty and Philosophy', 166.

full fruition. Theology's discourse is not therefore grounded in a humanly engineered attempt to transcend the limits of finitude, nor does it relate to a blind private belief system, clung to with no warrant or justification in the face of life's darker threats, but is rather to be seen as a form of sharing, by grace, in that divine knowledge made possible and available through Jesus Christ. Such knowledge ('embodied trust' might be a better term) draws upon all our faculties, and is always partial, always 'on the way'—not all is now given, the New Testament insists. And yet precisely as initiated by Christ and the Spirit, such knowledge and its language is nonetheless capable of being trustworthy, worthy of trust. Here Schlegel's notion of philosophy as structured yearning, a reaching-out beyond every determinate thought, so powerfully enacted in music, can be appropriated for theology, but with the crucial qualifier that the activity of the New Testament's infinite *Geist* is tied inextricably to what has been achieved in the concrete historical particularity of the human Jesus, and is now in the process of enabling our particularity to flourish in his image.

Hope

And yet, we might ask, what of the darker side of things that so haunts the Romantics (as well as Bowie)? This leads to a third set of comments. For Bowie, humans must learn to live courageously without delusion. On the macro-scale our situation is bleak indeed: modernity has told us that humans are a 'minor cosmic contingency' inhabiting a physical world that in many respects is deeply hostile to human existence: there are many things we cannot and will never understand or control. We recall that 'metaphysics$_2$' is the 'attempt to establish a meaningful place for humankind, both in the rest of a nature which we acknowledge to be a threat, and in a potentially equally threatening second nature' (the desultory effects of trying to control nature). Bowie is hostile to any hint of sentimentality, and eager to rescue the Romantics from the caricature of them as nature worshippers. He reflects that

> The Romantic association of music with the 'longing' occasioned by the suspension of human existence between finitude and a sense of what is beyond finitude . . . already suggested how modernity needed new ways of dealing with the irreconcilable. The essential tension that underlies many philosophical responses to music after the Romantics can . . . be seen to have to do with whether, as Nietzsche and Adorno sometimes claim, music offers a deceptive illusion of reconciliation, or whether it can offer a kind of reconciliation which does not conjure away real problems.[152]

---

[152] Bowie, *MPM*, 408–9.

Although clearly impressed by the early Romantics' ability to hold together a sense of the 'facticity' of loss and transience with an overarching drive towards some form of reconciliation (with music as key to that integration), Bowie's spurning not only of a Christian metaphysics but also its modified form in the early Romantics means that the resulting estimation of music's possibilities is in fact fairly meagre. For there is no agency beyond that of humans caught in their ambivalent state, no ontology that could ever render music anything more than provisional succour in a decidedly chilly cosmos.

The suspicion that Christianity is inherently sentimental has been repeatedly rehearsed in modern discourse. Bowie will quickly point out that those who profess this faith have frequently shown themselves adept at 'conjuring away real problems'. Quite so. Much depends, therefore, on whether the central 'turn' of the New Testament can be kept in view: the three days of Easter, in which the 'facticities' of loss, transience, and death were engaged concretely and directly—not philosophically or conceptually—and with a liberating finality. In the last resort, if theology is to be saved from the kind of oppressive presumption that Bowie rightly fears for any theoretical discipline, this will happen only insofar as it is rooted in these very particular occurrences, earthed in a facticity deeper than loss and transience, which put to death all humanly generated lurches at infinity and with it that fearful dread that our apparently inexorable journey towards futility might indeed be just that: futile.

To come at this from another angle, while on a superficial level the Romantic concept of *Sehnsucht* may seem to display something of the teleological dynamic of hope, by its very nature it is shot through with a thick and weighty pathos, and one that arguably opens it to the charge of sentimentality (insofar as sentimentality entails emotional indulgence, the cultivation and nurturing of pain–pleasure states for their own sake with no desire for, or confidence in, resolution[153]). The pathos is well brought out by Kiene Brillenburg Wurth in her recent book *Musically Sublime*. She proposes that *Sehnsucht*, instrumental music, and the sublime are 'intersecting concepts' for the early German Romantics.[154] She contrasts the 'legitimate' sublime—as represented, for example, in Kant—with that exhibited in the Romantics' *Sehnsucht*. In the earlier Kantian tradition, the experience of the sublime is an awareness of being overwhelmed by something uncontainable, beyond our grasp. In Kant this is either mainly 'mathematical'—when we are overwhelmed by size and are confronted with the limits of our sense perception (such as we might experience under a starry sky or when suddenly faced with a mountain

---

[153] Jeremy S. Begbie, 'Beauty, Sentimentality and the Arts', in Daniel J. Treier, Mark Husbands, and Roger Lundin (eds), *The Beauty of God: Theology and the Arts* (Downers Grove, IL: InterVarsity Press, 2007), 45–69.

[154] Brillenburg Wurth, *Musically Sublime*, 47.

massif), or 'dynamical'—when we are overwhelmed by a power that makes us acutely aware of our own finitude and physical vulnerability (such as we might feel in a raging storm). In Kant, according to Wurth, we find a 'plotlike structure';[155] the subject turns inward to realize the immense scope of his or her own reason: 'the law of reason that whatever frightens or overwhelms the subject cannot *but* be transcended by reason functions as an affective buffer and even a guarantee for a happy ending'.[156] In other words, there is a move *from* the overwhelming experience *to* a sense of release, from crisis to resolution. In the early Romantics, however, the experience of the sublime does not attain a transcendence of the crisis. *Sehnsucht* is '[b]ent on preventing its own realization',[157] writes Wurth. It 'performs a simultaneity of pain and pleasure insofar as it hovers in between a forward- and backward-moving tendency. Pulling back as it almost realizes itself, *Sehnsucht* constitutes a limit-experience that interlaces pleasure with pain, tension with respite, and never quite evolves beyond being on its way, beyond its own lack.'[158] Particularly intense here is a sense that the 'object' of desire never exists 'outside the rhythm of desire'.[159] The joy is *in* and *with* the lack of any determinate object—hence the Romantic fascination with childhood longings, the incompleteness of youth, the expectancy of sunrise; and hence also the early Romantic valorization of instrumental music, with its undecidability, its refusal to settle on an object beyond its own sounds. *Sehnsucht* belongs to what Jean Paul Richter called 'the twilight realm of holy anticipation'.[160]

I am not recommending a return to the Kantian sublime—which is fraught with problems. But I am suggesting that if the theme of longing is to be incorporated in the dynamic of hope and in a way that eschews sentimentality, and if music is to be appealed to in the process, it will only be through recovering something of the category of promise, a trajectory set in motion within time, engaging the worst of history, geared towards a quite concrete *telos*—in Christian terms, a future already enacted in Christ, and brought into the present through the Spirit, the presence of whom generates a very particular kind of 'holy anticipation'. The *Sehnsucht* of the Spirit is manifest in the groaning of the world towards that re-creation already achieved and embodied in the risen Christ. On that divine longing every other longing depends.

---

[155] Brillenburg Wurth, *Musically Sublime*, 49.
[156] Brillenburg Wurth, *Musically Sublime*, 5.
[157] Brillenburg Wurth, *Musically Sublime*, 47.
[158] Brillenburg Wurth, *Musically Sublime*, 17.
[159] Brillenburg Wurth, *Musically Sublime*, 50.
[160] From *Preparatory School for Aesthetics*; as quoted in Brillenburg Wurth, *Musically Sublime*, 58.

6

Room of One's Own?
Music, Space, and Freedom[1]

> Too often...we have simply assumed that two elements operate in a zero-sum relationship to one another, without asking ourselves whether they might be better understood as bearing a 'musical' character.
>
> *David Cunningham*[2]

> Three tones sound. In each of them space encounters us and we encounter space. None of them is in a place; or better, they are all in the same place, namely everywhere... [S]imultaneously sounding tones do not run together into a mixed tone. No difference of places keeps them apart; yet they remain audible as different tones... [T]he tones connected in the triad sound *through one another*... or let us say that they interpenetrate one another...
>
> *Victor Zuckerkandl*[3]

Few passions characterize modernity more clearly and potently than the quest for freedom. So central has it become to the identity and lifeblood of European and American culture over the past few hundred years, that the story of modernity simply cannot be told without it. And as a myriad of studies have amply shown, the manner in which freedom is conceived today is inextricably intertwined with modernity's ambivalent posture with regard to the Christian God.

[1] I am particularly grateful for conversations on this theme with Imogen Adkins, whose important doctoral work on the spatiality of music will, I hope, soon be published; and for the perceptive comments of Elizabeth Eichling. The first part of my title echoes that of a famous essay of 1929 by Virginia Woolf, widely regarded as pivotal for feminist literary criticism: Virginia Woolf, *A Room of One's Own* (Norwalk, CT: The Easton Press, 2003).
[2] David S. Cunningham, *These Three are One: The Practice of Trinitarian Theology* (Oxford: Blackwell Publishing, 1998), 65–79.
[3] Victor Zuckerkandl, *Sound and Symbol: Music and the External World* (London: Routledge & Kegan Paul, 1956), 297, 298, 299.

In this chapter, I will approach the theme of freedom by means of addressing what is widely regarded as a pervasive tendency in the way it has been treated in modern and late modern thinking. What will strike the reader as unusual is that my response to it will be largely musical: I will draw on an aural phenomenon that is basic to most of our experiences of musical sound. My proposal is that many theologies that have grappled with the manifold issues surrounding freedom have been hampered by particular ways of imagining the 'space' in which freedom is believed to be realized, and that what would seem to be a relatively insignificant feature of musical perception can yield remarkable resources for exposing, engaging, and alleviating the obstacles and complications that these habits of mind have generated. This is, in other words, an exercise in music therapy for theologians.

One of Ludwig Wittgenstein's most celebrated aphorisms runs thus: 'A *picture* held us captive. And we could not get outside it, for it lay in our language and language seemed to repeat it to us inexorably.'[4] Wittgenstein has in view his own early representative approach to language, according to which meaningful language consists of propositions composed of names and logical connectives, and the use of such language is essentially a matter of naming or picturing facts. He came to realize that such an account was severely inadequate. But the quotation is eminently applicable to the way theology has too often been pursued—inadvertently captive to habits of thought that are embedded and reiterated in our verbal language, but which distort rather than deepen our perception of the realities we engage. And Wittgenstein's term 'picture' here is especially apt. For although in this chapter we are not concerned with visual images in particular, we are concerned with modes of thought that take their shape chiefly from the ways in which visual perception operates.[5] Some of these, I want to show, have confined theology in ways that are unnecessary as well as damaging, not least when it comes to theologizing about freedom. Insofar as the captivity is dependent upon the visual character of our conceptualizing, attempts to free ourselves by substituting one form of visualization for another will hardly help; what is needed (to 'get outside') are fresh modes and models of thought that permit the realities in question to

---

[4] Ludwig Wittgenstein, *Philosophical Investigations* (Oxford: Blackwell Publishing, 1953), ¶48e (115).

[5] I shall leave aside the question—important as it is—of whether there can be any such thing as a *purely* visual argument. On this, see Steven W. Patterson, '"A Picture Held us Captive": The Later Wittgenstein on Visual Argumentation', *Cogency* 2, 2 (Spring 2010): 105–34. Alistair McFadyen writes impressively about the dependence of modern accounts of sin and freedom on the conceptuality of physical spatiality: Alistair I. McFadyen, 'Sins of Praise: The Assault on God's Freedom', in Colin E. Gunton (ed.), *God and Freedom: Essays in Historical and Systematic Theology* (Edinburgh: T & T Clark, 1995), 32–56. In this chapter, I am indebted to McFadyen's article. However, my argument is that the spatial models that need questioning are not merely 'physical', but *visually* oriented. That there may be *other* ways of conceiving space is not considered by McFadyen.

declare themselves more fully and clearly. The perception of musical sounds holds considerable potential in this regard.[6] Indeed, the sheer effectiveness of music in this regard makes its relative absence in most contemporary theology puzzling as well as regrettable.[7]

ZERO-SUM THEOLOGY

We begin with the obvious. Distinct objects in our visual field occupy bounded locations, discrete zones, such that they cannot overlap without their integrity being threatened. We cannot see a patch of red and a patch of yellow in the same space *as* red and yellow. We see either red *or* yellow; or (if the colours are allowed to merge) we see a mixture of the two—orange. This, we should stress, is not an observation with the interests of physical science uppermost—that is, about objects inhabiting a three-dimensional, physical world; the point is about the phenomena of visual perception, about the way things appear to us.

The spatiality here is one of juxtaposition and mutual exclusion: different entities can be next to each other but cannot be in the same place at the same time. This is the space according to which we can distinguish 'somewhere' from 'elsewhere'; things take up bounded places within it—space becomes, in effect, the aggregate of places. It is the space by virtue of which we can measure

---

[6] With regard to Wittgenstein's saying, Gordon Baker writes: 'The cure is to encourage surrender of the dogmatic claims "Things *must/cannot* be thus and so" by exhibiting other intelligible ways of seeing things (other *possibilities*), that is, by showing that we can take off the spectacles through which we now see whatever we look at . . . To the extent that philosophical problems take the form of the conflict between "But this isn't how it is!" and "yet this is how it *must* be!" . . . they will obviously be dissolved away once the inclination to say "must" has been neutralized by seeing another possibility': Gordon Baker, '*Philosophical Investigations* Section 122: Neglected Aspects', in Robert L. Arrington and Hans-Johann Glock (eds), *Wittgenstein's Philosophical Investigations: Text and Context* (London: Routledge, 1991), 35–68, 48–9. Even here, we should note, there is a marked dependence on the discourse of sight.

[7] Jürgen Moltmann makes some revealing remarks in an autobiographical sketch: 'Every comprehensive theology takes us beyond the category of time into the categories of space, place, expanse, and limit. We then arrive at spaces of time and space-times in our existence in the world. Developing in this direction, I found numerous theological studies on the concept of God and time, but almost none that addressed the theological concept of God and space. As we know from modern physics, time and space are complementary, but they are not symmetrical for us humans. You can experience different times at the same place, but you cannot exist at the same time in different places. In space we exist beside each other simultaneously. In time, however, we exist after one another successively': Jürgen Moltmann, 'God in the World—The World in God: Perichoresis in Trinity and Eschatology', in Richard Bauckham and Carl Mosser (eds), *The Gospel of John and Christian Theology* (Grand Rapids, MI: Eerdmans, 2008), 369–81, 371. What is perplexing is that, to my knowledge at least, when he does write about space theologically, trinitarian space included, Moltmann does not draw upon music, even though so many of his inclinations move in this direction. See for example his reflections in *God in Creation: An Ecological Doctrine of Creation* (London: SCM Press, 1985), sect. vi; see also 13–17.

intervals between things; it is divisible. It also carries with it the possibility of differing magnitude—objects can be larger than and smaller than others, and if one object enters the bounded area occupied by another, its increased area necessitates the other's decrease. The order or structure of this space will be conceived in terms of the relation of parts to one another against the background of a spatial whole. Further, we might add, this is the spatial experience not only of the eye, but also of touch, and which gives rise to geometrical measurement.[8]

Needless to say, the space of visual perception is often taken to be indicative of bona fide space, space as it 'really is'. It is certainly congruent with some of the leading philosophical and scientific conceptions of space in intellectual and scientific history. One of the most influential, with a long (and varied) history, conceives space as a type of receptacle or container, with objects or events located 'inside' it, in their appropriate places. But whatever its specific formulation, conceiving space according to the patterns of visual experience is habitual for most of us, so much so we probably never stop to wonder if other options are even available.

If left unchecked, however, this conceptual habit spawns considerable problems, not least in the popular imagination, as even a glance at the history of theology quickly shows. And this is perhaps nowhere clearer than in the modern theological imagination of freedom.[9]

How Can God and The World Be Free Together?

As long as we remain wedded to 'pictures' of distinct quasi-material objects in bounded domains, difficulties are almost bound to arise when we come to ask how an infinitely free God can be both external and internal to the world's space—'transcendent' and 'immanent', to use the traditional terminology—difficulties that arguably obfuscate the testimony of Scripture. God's 'thereness' and 'hereness' will tend to be understood against the background of a 'hyperspace', discrete portions of which both God and the world inhabit. It is not hard to see how this can encourage and support a philosophy of univocity—ontological and linguistic—in which God and the created world are regarded as belonging to the same genus. Repeated protests in recent

---

[8] Here I am drawing on Zuckerkandl, *Sound and Symbol*, esp. 275–6, 282–5, 293–4.

[9] In a contribution to a recent series of essays on transcendence, David Wood writes: 'the spatiality of our understanding of transcendence is rarely as crude as imagining "another place" (or another time) where transcendence happens. *But we should never underestimate the power of the most vulgar models*': David Wood, 'Topologies of Transcendence', in John D. Caputo and Michael J. Scanlon (eds), *Transcendence and Beyond: A Postmodern Inquiry* (Bloomington, IN: Indiana University Press, 2007), 169–203, 171. My italics.

theology against the notion that 'being' can be predicated univocally of both God and the world, such that God is conceived as 'a being' of the same order as other 'beings' (albeit an infinitely greater one), begin to make rather more sense.[10]

Accordingly, because in this kind of scheme the spaces that God and the world occupy cannot overlap or interpenetrate without threatening the other's integrity, there will be a propensity to regard transcendence and immanence as competing options. Kathryn Tanner speaks (critically) of 'contrastive transcendence', a transcendence defined negatively in terms of what God is not, such that God is envisaged as essentially disengaged from the world; God's freedom is thus fundamentally freedom *from* all that is not God.[11] By the same token, divine immanence will be understood as the polar opposite of transcendence, denoting an involvement with the world that borders on imprisonment. Evidently, conceiving or speaking of a God who is *both* ontologically other than the world and yet actively engaged with it becomes deeply problematic.[12]

Even if we find a way of negotiating or living with these obstacles such that the transcendent God is held to be involved 'in' the world in some sense, it is

---

[10] See 'A Tale of Origins' (pp. 5–6) in this volume.

[11] Kathryn Tanner, *God and Creation in Christian Theology: Tyranny or Empowerment?* (Oxford: Blackwell Publishing, 1988), ch. 2. Over thirty years ago, Colin Gunton argued cogently that many of our difficulties with the concept of transcendence arise through the domination of visual patterns of perception: Colin E. Gunton, 'Transcendence, Metaphor and the Knowability of God', *Journal of Theological Studies* 31, 2 (1980): 501–16.

[12] Some have pointed to a tension in the work of René Descartes (1596–1650) between a notion of God as cause and sustainer of the world, and the idea that 'true extension' can only be understood in terms of the measurable space of the physical world. Since God does not have extension in this sense, Descartes finds it hard to elucidate the nature of God's causal agency 'in' the world. See William C. Placher, *The Domestication of Transcendence: How Modern Thinking about God Went Wrong* (Louisville, KY: Westminster John Knox Press, 1996), 131–2; F. LeRon Shults, *Reforming the Doctrine of God* (Grand Rapids, MI: Eerdmans, 2005), 18–22. It is well known that Isaac Newton struggled hard to find an appropriate 'place' for God's causality within the created world. He posited an absolute space and time, extending infinitely and immutably in all directions (Isaac Newton, *The Principia: Mathematical Principles of Natural Philosophy*, trans. I. Bernard Cohen and Anne Miller Whitman (Berkeley and Los Angeles: University of California Press, 1999), 6), and could speak of absolute space as the 'sensorium' of God, that by virtue of which God is truly present to everything. Newton denied he was a pantheist, but Placher comments that 'given a geometrical understanding of space and univocal meanings for terms like "present" and "existence", he was hard put to explain why his thought would not lead in that direction': Placher, *The Domestication of Transcendence*, 141. On this, see the illuminating article by Geoffrey Gorham, 'Early Scientific Images of God: Descartes, Hobbes, and Newton', in Charles Taliaferro and Jil Evans (eds), *Turning Images in Philosophy, Science, and Religion: A New Book of Nature* (Oxford: Oxford University Press, 2011), 25–45. T. F. Torrance interprets Newton in the context of theories of space as receptacle, with God conceived as the infinite container of all things. This effectively rules out any particular acts of God within the container: God 'can no more become incarnate than a box can become one of the several objects it contains': Thomas F. Torrance, *Space, Time and Incarnation* (London: Oxford University Press, 1969), 39.

no less challenging to conceive how this God can be active within the world's space without undermining its integrity. The more of God, the less the world is able to realize its true being—or so it would seem—for the two cannot occupy the same 'place'. The notion of intermittent salvific divine intervention might be appealing here: God does *some* things but not *all* things; God is active in some places but not in all places. This, however, only intensifies the danger of imagining that God's action necessarily violates the world's freedom, like a burglar breaking into a house. The ease with which we slip into 'God-of-the-gaps' patterns of thinking illustrates well the power of visual–spatial models— that which we cannot explain through the cause and effect 'internal' to the world we attribute to the 'external' agency of God, the *deus ex machina*. Tanner captures well the effect on construals of divine agency when a con-trastive transcendence holds sway:

> Divinity characterized in terms of a direct contrast with certain sorts of being or with the world of non-divine being as a whole is brought down to the level of the world and beings within it in virtue of that opposition: God becomes one being among others within a single order. Such talk suggests that God exists alongside the non-divine, that God is limited by what is opposed to it [*sic*], that God is as finite as the non-divine beings with which it [*sic*] is directly contrasted. A cosmology influenced by such suggestions will characterize a divine agency in terms appropriate for a finite one. Like that of a finite agent, God's influence will be of a limited sort: it may not extend to everything, it may presuppose what it does not produce, it may require the intervening agencies of others.[13]

The other option easily suggested by the visual–spatial conceptuality is the opposite extreme—a merger of God and world such that Creator and creature are to some degree ontologically identified or synthesized, a metaphysical move that has taken numerous forms in modernity. Although there can be no denying their immense attractiveness, and the sophistication with which they are often presented, such schemes are obviously vulnerable to the charge that both God and creature will lose their distinctive integrity, and thereby their freedom.[14]

Intertwined with these developments are particular conceptions of infinity. Relevant here is the distinction between 'mathematical' and 'metaphysical' infinity: in the former case, infinity is understood according to the indefinite

---

[13] Tanner, *God and Creation*, 45–6.

[14] The kind of questions we are putting to models of 'contrastive transcendence' are obviously pertinent, though in different ways, to theological schemes such as 'panentheism' with its particular dependence on the preposition 'in' (all things are 'in' God). Critical issues concerning what is to be invested ontologically in the language of containment here can hardly be avoided. For discussion, see Chan Ho Park, 'Transcendence and Spatiality of the Triune Creator' (doctrinal dissertation, Fuller Theological Seminary, published by Peter Lang, 2005), esp. 52–61. Similar questions have understandably been asked of Jürgen Moltmann's highly spatial notion of divine creation as withdrawal (*zimzum*); see Park, 'Transcendence and Spatiality', 108–25.

extension of a series, in the latter, as intensive and qualitative. According to LeRon Shults, in the seventeenth and eighteenth centuries the latter was eclipsed through an over-employment of the categories of extension and quantity, deployed in creaturely senses. God's infinity was typically construed in terms of infinite extension (in accordance with the pattern of the extension of finite things) and thus negatively: God is infinite in that God is without limit.[15] Thus God becomes 'a being that is simply extensively greater than creatures...'. Such a being becomes 'caught in the dialectic of "more" or "less", in the tension between transcendence and immanence—either far from or close to other beings.'[16] Here, in other words, divine and human space, and their relation, are being conceived in creaturely, visual–spatial terms, as entailing the mutual exclusion of places and the articulation of difference and distinction through juxtaposition.

How Can God and Humankind Be Free Together?[17]

Very much the same considerations apply to the way we correlate divine and human freedom. Divine and human agency become ontologically comparable (agency is predicated of God and humans univocally) and compete for the same space, operating in inverse proportion. For God to be in my space means that I will be either displaced or diminished in some manner. The more God's power is affirmed, the more human agency is rendered inconsequential. The more of God, the less of us (and vice versa). The linking of human agency with

---

[15] Shults, *Reforming the Doctrine of God*, esp. 22–6, 98. Some will point to precursors of this in medieval thought. So, for example, Conor Cunningham argues that Duns Scotus bequeathed a notion of infinity as essentially quantitative: Conor Cunningham, *A Genealogy of Nihilism: Philosophies of Nothing and the Difference of Theology* (London: Routledge, 2002), 28–32. He quotes Anne Davenport's assessment—although the infinite 'cannot be reached by finite steps, it belongs conceptually to the same univocal "measure" of excellence to which the finite belongs': Cunningham, *A Geneaology of Nihilism*, 30; the quote is from Anne Ashley Davenport, *Measure of a Different Greatness: The Intensive Infinite, 1250–1650* (Leiden: Brill, 1999), 280.

[16] Shults, F. LeRon, *Reforming the Doctrine of God*, 98. Karl Barth writes: 'We assign [God] the highest place in the world; and in so doing we place him fundamentally on one line with ourselves and with things': Karl Barth, *The Epistle to the Romans* (Oxford: Oxford University Press, 1968). Walter Lowe comments: 'So entrenched is the tendency Barth postulates that even the term "infinite" leads us to imagine a (limitless) extension of the finite ... To draw a term from the postmodern thinker Emmanuel Levinas, the qualifier "infinite" does not assure exemption from the hegemony of "the Same"': Walter Lowe, 'Postmodern Theology', in J. B. Webster, Kathryn Tanner, and Iain R. Torrance (eds), *The Oxford Handbook of Systematic Theology* (Oxford: Oxford University Press, 2007), 617–33, 618.

[17] In this chapter, I am not considering at any length the relation of human freedom to creation at large, where, regrettably, freedom is too often pitted against its polar opposite, determinism. For especially penetrating discussions, see Robert W. Jenson, *Systematic Theology: The Works of God*, 2 vols, vol. ii (New York: Oxford University Press, 1999), 22–3; Peter Van Inwagen, *An Essay on Free Will* (Oxford: Clarendon Press, 1983).

the modern doctrine of autonomy[18] spawns the view that anything that is not in its entirety the agent's undetermined act is, just to that extent, a denial of the agent's freedom. It is little wonder that some of the most virulent currents of modern atheism trade heavily on the belief that worshipping God entails a self-abnegation that insults, indeed robs us of our dignity. 'To enrich God,' declared Ludwig Feuerbach, 'man must become poor; that God may be all, man must be nothing.'[19] We must move into the space once occupied by this fictional deity and recover our diminished or 'displaced' dignity. In drawing out the lines of thought here, David Bentley Hart is characteristically forthright:

> ... what we habitually understand democratic liberty to be—what we take, that is, as our most exalted model of freedom—is merely the unobstructed power of choice. The consequence of this, manifestly, is that we moderns tend to elevate what should at best be regarded as the moral life's minimal condition to the status of its highest expression, and in the process reduce the very concept of freedom to one of purely libertarian or voluntarist spontaneity. We have come to believe ... that the will necessarily becomes more free the more it is emancipated from whatever constraints it suffers.[20]

Armed with such assumptions—that freedom is at its base level being freed *from* the other, that all restrictions are arbitrary and extrinsic and as such a threat to our freedom, that freedom is, in effect, no more than 'the ability to do otherwise'—it is almost impossible not to regard belief in an infinite deity as inherently inimical to human flourishing. Indeed, some would contend that it belongs to the very core of modernity that freedom not only can be, but must be, defined without any reference to God.

Understandably, theologians have been quick to distinguish an authentic Christian vision of freedom from such scenarios. But they have been rather less swift in exposing the 'zero-sum' schemes[21] that have so often fuelled the debates about freedom *within* the Christian tradition. The issue is not only *whether* God is or is not invoked in speaking of freedom but *what kind* of God is invoked, and what kind of relations this God is assumed to establish with humans and the world at large.[22] Even if we hold to some sort of convergence

[18] J. B. Schneewind, *The Invention of Autonomy: A History of Modern Moral Philosophy* (Cambridge: Cambridge University Press, 1988).

[19] Ludwig Feuerbach, *The Essence of Christianity*, trans. George Eliot (New York: Harper & Row, 1957), 26.

[20] David Bentley Hart, *In the Aftermath: Provocations and Laments* (Grand Rapids, MI: Eerdmans, 2009), 77.

[21] See David B. Burrell, *Freedom and Creation in Three Traditions* (Notre Dame, IN: University of Notre Dame Press, 1993), 2.

[22] There is a sizeable body of opinion that would link modern 'libertarian' theories of freedom to early modern 'voluntarism' of one sort or another, in which the dominating scenario is that of the sovereignty and total autonomy of the will (divine and/or human). The connections may not be simple or directly causal, but they are almost certainly there. The consequences for a voluntarist doctrine of God include a pointed stress on divine inscrutability together with

of divine and human agency, it is repeatedly suggested by implication that each must be allowed its own exclusive portion of the available space. We only need think of some of the historic struggles over doctrines of salvation: if freedom is understood as being essentially about absolute self-determination, a polarity typically arises between, on the one hand, a conception of God's unmerited saving grace as an untrammelled, unrestricted divine causality at work in the world (at its worst, turning God into a tyrant), and on the other, a notion of human 'decision' envisaged as an entirely unprompted, self-generated response to God (an expression of 'my personal space') such that divine agency becomes effectively dispensable.

Between these two extremes lie numerous attempts to divide things up so that both agencies have at least something of their own to contribute to the soteriological package. We are thus pressed rather too easily towards a 'contractual' rather than a 'covenantal' soteriology. A covenant, theologically speaking, is an unconditional pledge not dependent on the worth of the other party or parties; a contract is an agreement dependent on the fulfilment of certain conditions. A contract tacitly implies a finite, creaturely space shared by two agents, in which both agree—in effect—to occupy different zones ('if you do this much, I'll do that'). As Alan Torrance, Douglas Campbell, and others have shown, contractual soteriology can drastically misrepresent Scripture's witness to the character of divine grace: God's love becomes conditional upon the fulfilment of certain prior actions, the imperatives of obedience become logically prior to the indicatives of grace, and human agents are presumed to have it within themselves to effect at least the first stage of their own repentant faith in God (as if standing outside their own space, seeing clearly the problem between them and God, and then taking the first step towards reconciliation).[23] William Placher makes some pertinent comments

---

acute problems in conceiving divine purposes as anything other than arbitrary. As far as human freedom is concerned, the issues are well summarized by David Burrel in 'Can We be Free Without a Creator?', in L. Gregory Jones, Reinhard Hütter, and C. Rosalee Velloso da Silva (eds), *God, Truth, and Witness: Engaging Stanley Hauerwas* (Grand Rapids, MI: Brazos Press, 2005), 35–52. Classical schemes in which the purpose or end of human life is always in view remind us that even 'freedom to choose' only makes sense in the light of a teleology, 'the goal-directedness of human development' (42). Modernity typically defines freedom without reference to God, and thus (commonly) without reference to an ultimate *telos*, apart, that is, from 'the power to choose'. God quite naturally becomes conceived as the infinite being who curbs, inhibits, or even suppresses human 'freedom'. With 'the unique relation that both distinguishes creator from creatures and unites them' being forgotten, 'many contemporary accounts of freedom inevitably regard the creator as another operator in the scene, and so a rival to created agency'. Burrell continues: 'the resultant "creator" can no longer be the God whom Jews, Christians, and Muslims worship, but can only be "the biggest thing around"' (45).

[23] See Alan J. Torrance, 'The Theological Grounds for Advocating Forgiveness and Reconciliation in the Sociopolitical Realm', in Daniel Philpott (ed.), *The Politics of Past Evil: Religion, Reconciliation, and the Dilemmas of Transitional Justice* (Notre Dame, IN: University of Notre Dame Press, 2006), 45–85; Douglas A. Campbell, *The Quest for Paul's Gospel: A Suggested*

about those who have attempted to give due place to human integrity as against a divine 'grace' that has in effect become conceived as an overpowering, even deterministic force. Having surveyed a number of theologians of the seventeenth century, he comments:

> Lutheran synergists, Catholic Molinists, Arminians, and covenant theologians— the differences are important, but the similarities are quite striking. All thought of God and human beings as operating in some sense on the same level, so that, if human beings were to do something toward their salvation, then one had to reduce the divine contribution.[24]

In this light, it is no surprise that much modern theology has warmed readily to 'kenotic' (self-emptying) models of the God–human relation, where God in some manner 'limits' himself so as not to suppress or diminish human agency.[25] Sarah Coakley sums up the conception of freedom she believes lies behind some of these schemes. There is, she says, a

> 'space' granted to humans by God to exercise freedom—for good or ill . . . the 'freedom' thus exercised by humans must be of the 'incompatibilist' sort, that is, the type supposedly free from conditioning control by another. The visual picture here . . . is of a (very big) divine figure backing out of the scene, or restraining his influence, in order that other (little) figures may exercise completely independent thinking and acting.[26]

Coakley notes the gendered connotations of the doctrine of God at work here: that of 'a normative "masculine" self who gains independence by setting himself apart from that which gave him life and indeed continues to sustain him'.[27]

Strategy (London: T & T Clark, 2005), ch. 8; Douglas A. Campbell, *The Deliverance of God: A Rereading of Justification in Paul* (Grand Rapids, MI: Eerdmans, 2009), esp. 15–35; James B. Torrance, 'Covenant and Contract: A Study of the Theological Background of Worship in Seventeenth-Century Scotland', *Scottish Journal of Theology* 23 (1970): 51–76.

[24] Placher, *The Domestication of Transcendence*, 162–3. Placher also observes how those on the other side, keen to champion the 'sovereignty' of divine grace (Jansenists, Lutheran Pietists, Puritans), were paradoxically prone to domesticating it in practice, preoccupied as they were with the question of assurance: Placher, *The Domestication of Transcendence*, ch. 6. We are, of course, touching on massively complex and contested territory with a fraught history in relations between Protestants and Roman Catholics. For a subtle account of many of the issues at stake, concerned with showing that 'grace and free will do not need to come into a conflictual competition in the mystery of the *initium fidei*', see Reinhard Hütter, 'St Thomas on Grace and Free Will in the *Initium Fidei*: The Surpassing Augustinian Synthesis', *Nova et Vetera* 5, 3 (2007): 521–54.

[25] For a recent account and defence, see David W. Brown, *Divine Humanity: Kenosis Explored and Defended* (London: SCM Press, 2011).

[26] Sarah Coakley, 'Kenosis: Theological Meanings and Gender Connotations', in John C. Polkinghorne (ed.), *The Work of Love: Creation as Kenosis* (Grand Rapids, MI: Eerdmans, 2001), 205.

[27] Coakley, 'Kenosis', 205. See also Sarah Coakley, 'Feminism', in Philip L. Quinn and Charles Taliaferro (eds), *A Companion to Philosophy of Religion* (Oxford: Blackwell, 1997), 601–6.

The only other viable option—on these kinds of presuppositions—is some form of synthesis: a dissolution of the divine into the human or vice versa, where, needless to say, the integrity of each is endangered.

Similar remarks could be made about the pervasiveness of visual–spatial construals of interpersonal freedom. The huge damage done to theology by the dominance of libertarian philosophies—where freedom becomes a matter of obtaining and moving into a vacant place of one's own, unconstrained and unconditioned as far as possible by other persons, and maximizing the extent of that space as much as is practically possible—is a theme amply rehearsed in a wide range of current literature.[28]

Two In One Space

These tangled problematics find concentrated expression in Christology, and understandably so. Classical Christianity has held that in Jesus Christ we are given the utterly free movement of God towards us and a wholly free movement of a human being towards God. How can this be? In the visually conceived world, the ancient orthodoxy of the Church according to the Council of Chalcedon of 451 CE, that Christ is both human and divine (without confusion or change, separation or division), is notoriously hard to articulate or conceive in a way that does justice to the New Testament's irreducibly awkward witness to the co-presence of both in this one historical person. The critical danger, again, is in assuming that deity and humanity are ontologically comparable categories, instances of the same genus jostling for the same space—in this case the three-dimensional, physical space of Jesus of Nazareth. Typically we find the two 'natures' are either thought to exist in some kind of precarious equilibrium—like a tightrope walker with a double-weighted bar, poised far above heresy; or else some sort of compromise must be negotiated through attenuation of one of the natures—it is claimed, for example, that in the incarnation the eternal Son underwent some type of pulling back, non-exercise, or even abandonment of his divine powers or attributes (as in some nineteenth- and twentieth-century 'kenotic' Christologies), or that the humanity of Jesus had to be a curtailed version of the authentic article in order to

---

[28] Among the finest treatments are those found in Richard Bauckham, *God and the Crisis of Freedom: Biblical and Contemporary Perspectives* (Louisville, KY: Westminster John Knox Press, 2002), and Colin E. Gunton (ed.), *God and Freedom: Essays in Historical and Systematic Theology* (Edinburgh: T & T Clark, 1995). Roger Lundin's comments on Heidegger's concept of the modern 'age of the world picture' are telling: 'In the realm of the *world picture*, we can do little more than cultivate a mutual toleration of our incommensurable perspectives': Roger Lundin, *Believing Again: Doubt and Faith in a Secular Age* (Grand Rapids, MI: Eerdmans, 2009), 179. Italics are Lundin's.

cope with a potentially overpowering divine presence.[29] These options, of course, threaten to weaken or even undermine salvation: for how can *God* redeem *humanity* if neither retain their fullness?

Essays on Chalcedon by Richard Norris and Sarah Coakley have suggested that the debates on either side of the Council (and in some modern Christologies) can give the impression that 'deity' and 'humanity' are two entities on the same ontological level, 'differing items of the *same* order', 'competing for the same space'.[30] This shows that spatial problems of this type are by no means unique to our era. But they have undoubtedly been exacerbated in modernity through a proneness to think in the visual–spatial terms we have been describing. Whatever one's final assessment of modern kenotic Christologies, for example, it is hard to deny that unguarded use of the terminology of 'retraction', 'setting aside', 'self-limitation', and so forth will tend to encourage the projection of inappropriate aspects of visualizable, creaturely space into theological ontology, generating unnecessary and damaging antinomies. Significantly, Coakley comments that such Christologies tend to be vitiated by the assumption that divinity and humanity are categories that 'can be collapsed into one flat package' and then (not surprisingly) considered incompatible. Writing in connection with Kathryn Tanner's work, she says that 'Christology that intends to be "orthodox" radically loses its way if it starts

---

[29] The irony is that the New Testament passage from which such Christologies ultimately derive—Philippians 2:5–11—most probably does not carry any of these connotations, even if we do maintain (as I believe we should) that Paul is here affirming a conception of the 'pre-existence' of Christ. For a clear discussion, see Gordon D. Fee, 'Exploring Kenotic Christology: The Self-Emptying of God', in C. Stephen Evans (ed.), *Exploring Kenotic Christology* (Oxford: Oxford University Press, 2006), 25–44.

[30] Sarah Coakley, 'What Does Chalcedon Solve and What Does it Not? Some Reflections on the Status and Meaning of the Chalcedonian "Definition"', in Stephen T. Davis, Gerald O'Collins, and Daniel Kendall (eds), *The Incarnation: An Interdisciplinary Symposium on the Incarnation of the Son of God* (Oxford: Oxford University Press, 2002), 143–63, 147. See Richard Norris, 'Chalcedon Revisited: A Historical and Theological Reflection', in Bradley Nassif (ed.), *New Perspectives on Historical Theology: Essays in Memory of John Meyendorff* (Grand Rapids, MI: Eerdmans, 1996), 140–58. Norris believes that in the debates surrounding Chalcedon the two natures came to be conceived in 'reified' or concretized terms as differing items of the same ontological order, what he calls 'interchangeable contraries', forgetting that '*there is no overarching category in which both [Creator and creature] can be classified*' (156; his italics). He thinks that Chalcedon itself is more reticent: there, the question posed is not 'how to fit two logical contraries together into one, as its ancient and modern interpreters have all but uniformly supposed, but how to dispense with a binary logic in figuring the relation between God and creatures': Norris, 'Chalcedon Revisited', 158. Coakley takes Norris to task for what she sees as his Lindbeckian thesis about Chalcedon as merely 'regulatory', his neo-Kantian epistemological assumptions, and his inconsistency in assuming that ontological statement is present in Chalcedon even as he is denying it: Coakley, 'What Does Chalcedon Solve and What Does it Not?', 149–52. But she believes Norris is right in (among other things) holding that 'to gloss the human and divine "natures" as inherently two of the same kind, and/or in "contradiction" with one another, is not implied by the text of the [Chalcedonian] "Definition" per se' (148). She goes on to say, however, that neither can this interpretation be entirely ruled out! (148).

from the assumption that the humanity and divinity of Christ are like two vying (but potentially well-matched?) contestants striving to inhabit the same space'.[31]

Few have explored the consequences of receptacle or container notions of space and time more fully than the Scottish Reformed theologian T. F. Torrance.[32] With considerable acuity he notes the way we are encouraged to imagine the relation between God and created space—and thus between the incarnate Christ and the Father—in creaturely spatial terms. He attacks both finite and infinite versions of receptacle philosophies.[33] In the case of the finite version, the incarnation is imagined as the Son of God's complete entry into a finite container, with an implied abandonment of heaven. Crudely, the Son must be either 'up there' with the Father or 'down here' with us; he cannot be in both 'places' at the same time. For Torrance, the Lutheran objection to the Calvinists' insistence that the eternal Son is *both* in heaven upholding the universe *and* living on earth as Jesus of Nazareth—namely, that this implies that part of the Son was still 'outside' Jesus of Nazareth (the so-called 'Calvinist extra' (*extra Calvinisticum*))—illustrates the point well. Torrance is thus wary of Lutheran theologies that speak of the total self-emptying of the infinite Son into a finite body-receptacle, and of Christologies that posit a communication of the property of ubiquity (omnipresence) to Christ's humanity in order to render it capable of receiving the divine fullness. Such systems are bound to compromise one or other of the natures.[34] He is equally suspicious of the notion of space as infinite receptacle, and especially of portraying God himself in such terms, for this would make the incarnation impossible to affirm (how could God be both container and contents?), and opens the door to Arianism and/or deism.[35]

---

[31] Sarah Coakley, 'Does Kenosis Rest on a Mistake? Three Kenotic Models in Patristic Exegesis', in C. Stephen Evans (ed.), *Exploring Kenotic Christology: The Self-Emptying of God* (Oxford: Oxford University Press, 2006), 246–64, 261, 262. She continues: 'We are not trying to squeeze together, or coalesce, two sets of features which (annoyingly?) present us with logical opposites; rather, we are attempting to conceive of a unique intersection precisely *of* opposites, in which the divine—that which is *in se* unimaginably greater and indeed creator and sustainer of the human—is "united", *hypostatically*, with that "human", forming one concrete subject': Coakley, 'Does Kenosis Rest on a Mistake?', 262. Italics are Coakley's. The term 'opposites' is perhaps unfortunate here, given Coakley's commitments to non-competitive understandings of the God–world relation.

[32] Torrance, *Space, Time and Incarnation*; Thomas F. Torrance, *Space, Time, and Resurrection* (Grand Rapids, MI: Eerdmans, 1976). For exceptionally clear discussions of Torrance on these matters, see Paul D. Molnar, *Incarnation and Resurrection: Toward a Contemporary Understanding* (Grand Rapids, MI: Eerdmans, 2007), 90–6; Paul D. Molnar, *Thomas F. Torrance: Theologian of the Trinity* (Farnham: Ashgate, 2009), 124–35.

[33] Torrance, *Space, Time and Incarnation*, 62–3.

[34] Torrance, *Space, Time and Incarnation*, 30–6.

[35] Torrance, *Space, Time and Incarnation*, 39, 63.

Three in One Space

It is a common criticism of Chalcedon that its affirmations are insufficiently trinitarian. Certainly, it is no surprise to find the various aporias we have pointed up reaching acute expression in conceptual struggles concerning the trinitarian 'space' of God, the very fount of all freedom. There have, of course, been a multitude of renderings of the Trinity in visual art, many of which bear commanding and effective witness to God's triunity. That is not at issue here. However, if we are to think oneness and threeness together in a manner appropriate to the New Testament but at the same time in a way that is not attentive to the dangers of being overdetermined by visual thought-patterning, we are likely to be led into complications parallel to those we have just observed in Christology. For, to ask the obvious, how can three occupy the same (visualizable) space and be perceptible *as three*? Modern theology's struggles in this respect are hardly unprecedented, but are certainly highly conspicuous to any student of trinitarian doctrine of the past two or three hundred years, and a good case could be mounted for claiming that they have been exacerbated by the inclinations of thought and language we have been highlighting. Strenuous attempts to maintain threeness typically result in some form of precarious equilibrium: the divine persons are strongly affirmed in both their particularity and their undivided unity, but left there in lifeless tension. Repeated appeals to 'mystery' in this context sound decidedly thin and unsatisfying, especially when compared to the fulsome and dynamic interpenetrative interplay of Son and Father attested in, say, John's Gospel. And not surprisingly, there have been various forms of compromise on offer— theologies that veer towards heavily 'socialized' (near-tritheistic) trinitarianism on the one hand, or varieties of modalism on the other (distinction *ad extra*, undifferentiated oneness *ad intra*).

* * *

In none of what I have said am I assuming straightforward, direct causal links between particular doctrines and visual patterns of thought and language. Things are far more complex and intricate. Visual conceptualization may well be one factor at work in the way freedom has been imagined in modernity, but there are undoubtedly many more.[36] My proposal is fairly modest, but I hope not thereby insignificant: that in modernity, an unwarranted reliance on

---

[36] Even the perceived role and capacity of 'the visual' in modernity has undergone substantial changes. For an intriguing treatment of early modernity in this regard, see Stuart Clark, *Vanities of the Eye: Vision in Early Modern European Culture* (Oxford: Oxford University Press, 2007). Clark argues that the relation between what we see and what we know 'was particularly unsettled in late Renaissance Europe. In one context after another, vision came to be characterized by uncertainty and unreliability, such that access to visual reality could no longer be normally guaranteed. It is as though European intellectuals lost their optical nerve': Clark, *Vanities of the Eye*, 2.

conceptual frameworks that favour spatial visualization and its associated language have likely aggravated, and in some places perhaps generated, a range of problems that have repeatedly frustrated and distorted Christian theology in its attempt to explicate the New Testament's rendering of the character of freedom, divine and human.

If we move from the visible to the audible, however, a rather different world unfolds.

SOUND SPACE

I play a note on a piano. The tone I hear fills the whole of my aural field, my heard space. It does not occupy a bounded location. It 'saturates our hearing'.[37] It is 'everywhere' in that space; there is nothing 'outside' it, no spatial zone where the sound is not. I then play a second higher tone along with the first. This second sound fills the entirety of the *same* (heard) space; yet I hear it as distinct, irreducibly different. In this aural environment, two different entities, it would seem, can be in the same space at the same time. And they are not each in a place that we can describe as 'here' rather than 'there'. Each seems to be 'everywhere'.

Appeals to physics here—that sound waves, considered as physically locatable phenomena, do occupy measurable places in space—are understandable, but beside the point. The focus of our interest is in sound as a perceptual experience, and, arising from that, as a determinant in shaping thought and language. We are not concerned with the three-dimensional space in which musical instruments, singers, and sound waves are situated, but rather with sonic space *as heard*, the kind of space we are given to hear as we perceive musical tones.[38]

Sounds as 'Secondary Objects' and 'Pure Events'

What kind of existence do these sounds (as heard) have? Clearly, sounds are not ordinary three-dimensional objects like dogs and trees, nor ordinary events like dogs barking or trees swaying. Yet are they not objects and events of *some* sort? Roger Scruton has recently argued that sounds are best regarded

---

[37] Roger Scruton, *The Aesthetics of Music* (Oxford: Clarendon Press, 1997), 13.

[38] It is also worth underlining that in this essay we are not considering the spatial representation of music or musical form (as in a score or diagram); on this understanding of musical 'space', see Mark Evan Bonds, 'The Spatial Representation of Musical Form', *Journal of Musicology* 27, 3 (2010): 265–303.

as 'secondary objects' and 'pure events'.[39] Concentrating on the 'intentional objects'[40] of audition—what we hear when we identify something *as* 'a sound'—he contends that 'Sounds are *"audibilia"*, which is to say that their essence resides in "the way they sound".'[41] They are secondary in that their existence, nature, and qualities depend on the way they are perceived; at the same time, they are not properties or qualities, but objects with qualities, analogous to smells.[42] When we call a sound rough or pleasant, we are attributing a quality to the sound, not to the object that produced it, nor to the physical changes the object undergoes: we can identify and describe the sound without referring to its physical source. If I describe the intentional object of my sight, the description will be (in part at least) a description of the physical object. The remark 'I see a red car' both describes my perception and (to some extent) describes the car across the street. But to describe a sound as soft says nothing about the object that produced the sound: 'The auditory field, unlike the visual field, does not depict its cause.'[43]

According to Scruton, having acknowledged sounds as secondary objects, we can go on to speak of sounds as 'pure events'—they are happenings, but do not happen *to* particular, identifiable entities.[44] When a building collapses, the event happens to the building but the sound the building makes as it disintegrates is not an event in the building's life or a change in which the building shares; it is an event in itself, a 'pure event'.[45] On this account, then, sounds can be detached from the source that produces them, and the physical disturbances they entail. It is not necessary to refer to the source or cause of a sound in order to identify and describe it, and organizing sounds so that we can make sense of them does not necessarily entail any knowledge of what

[39] Scruton, *The Aesthetics of Music*, 6–13; Roger Scruton, *Understanding Music: Philosophy and Interpretation* (London: Continuum, 2009); Roger Scruton, 'Sounds As Secondary Objects and Pure Events', in Matthew Nudds and Casey O'Callaghan (eds), *Sounds and Perception: New Philosophical Essays* (Oxford: Oxford University Press, 2009), 50–68.

[40] Intentionality concerns the directedness of the mind in perception, its 'aboutness': 'intentional objects' are objects of one's 'mental acts' (thinking, judging, etc.). See T. Crane, 'Intentionalism', in Brian P. McLaughlin, Ansgar Beckermann, and Sven Walter (eds), *The Oxford Handbook of Philosophy of Mind* (Oxford: Clarendon Press, 2009), 474–93.

[41] Scruton, 'Sounds as Secondary Objects', 57.

[42] A distinction is commonly made between 'primary qualities'—properties of objects that are possessed by an object independent of any observer (such as, size, solidity, shape, and so on); and 'secondary qualities'—properties that provoke sensations in the observer (such as taste, smell, and so forth: secondary qualities concern the way things *appear* to us).

[43] Scruton, *Understanding Music*, 26.

[44] Scruton, *Understanding Music*, 61–2.

[45] Hence Scruton's rejection of 'physicalist' accounts of sound: viz. those that understand sounds as identical with the events that generate them (see e.g. Casey O'Callaghan, *Sounds: A Philosophical Theory* (Oxford: Oxford University Press, 2007); Robert Casati and Jerome Dokic, *La Philosophie du son* (Nîmes: Jacqueline Chambon, 1994)). See Scruton, *Understanding Music*, 20–3, and ch. 2 *passim*.

produced them. Sounds can be 'intrinsically ordered in our hearing, without reference to an order of physical objects and events'.[46]

Here an important distinction should be kept in mind between noises and (musical) tones. The conductor Sir Thomas Beecham is supposed to have quipped that 'The English people may not understand music, but they absolutely love the noise that it makes.'[47] Hearing sounds as music, Scruton argues, is qualitatively different from hearing noises. In the latter case, our inclination is usually to follow them through to their source. When I hear crashing from my daughter's bedroom upstairs, I want to know the object or event that has caused it. I could detach the noise from any thought about what created it (as with any sound) and consider it on its own—but it would be odd to do so. I am interested in the noise primarily because of what it can tell me about an object or event. I use the sound to orient me in visual space, to help me locate myself with respect to the tangible and measurable three-dimensional world. But this is not normally the case with musical tones: I am interested in these not because they tell me about their source (though they may do that), but because of what they can do by virtue of their intrinsic relations to each other, their own musical order (pitch, melody, harmony, and rhythm). Indeed, recognizing music as such *depends* on our ability, at least to some extent, to detach sounds from their physical causes: the power of music relies on this ability. Musical sounds—as heard—are not subject to the three-dimensional order of visible, tangible, and measurable objects.[48]

---

[46] Scruton, 'Sounds as Secondary Objects', 28.

[47] Derek Watson (ed.), *The Wordsworth Dictionary of Musical Quotations* (Ware: Wordsworth Editions, 1994), 331.

[48] Scruton, *Understanding Music*, 30. Scruton alludes to the 'octave illusion' presented by Diana Deutsch: two different successions of tones are played simultaneously, one into each ear through headphones. What is 'heard' by the listener in each ear is not what is actually played into each ear. 'The auditory *Gestalt* is not merely incongruent with the physical events that produce it. It is organized according to principles that are intrinsic to the world of sounds': Scruton, *Understanding Music*, 27; Diana Deutsch, 'An Auditory Illusion', *Nature* 251 (1974): 307–9; Diana Deutsch, 'The Octave Illusion Revisited Again', *Journal of Experimental Psychology: Human Perception and Performance* 30, 2 (2004): 355–64.

Andy Hamilton has challenged Scruton's 'acousmatic' thesis—namely that 'to hear sounds as music involves divorcing them from the worldly source or cause of their production': Andy Hamilton, 'The Sound of Music', in Matthew Nudds and Casey O'Callaghan (eds), *Sounds and Perception: New Philosophical Essays* (Oxford: Oxford University Press, 2009), 146–82. Hamilton says Scruton 'wrongly denies that the non-acousmatic aspect is genuinely musical': Hamilton, 'The Sound of Music', 160. He contends that listening to music always involves, at least to some extent, a combination of acousmatic and non-acousmatic experience, and *both* are genuinely musical. Our awareness of a particular instrument at a concert, or a player's movements, or the physical impact of a sound through our body, may in fact be critical to the total musical enjoyment: '"real-life" causality is a genuinely musical part of musical experience'. He adds: 'For "genuinely musical" here, one could substitute "genuinely aesthetic"': Hamilton, 'The Sound of Music', 172. At issue here, of course, is what is to count as intrinsic to bona fide 'musical experience' or to authentic 'musical listening'—Scruton's understanding of these is arguably too restrictive and somewhat idealized. For our purposes, we simply note that hearing/listening to

The Space of Sounds

What kind of 'space' is this, then? 'The essential feature of a spatial dimension', according to Scruton, 'is that it contains places, which can be *occupied* by things, and between which things can move.'[49] A tone cannot 'move' from one pitch to another without changing its character. The pitch spectrum is not a dimension analogous to the dimensions of physical space:

> ... there is no clear orientation of sounds in auditory space: no way of assigning faces, ends, boundaries, and so on to them, so as to introduce those topological features which help us to make sense of the idea of 'occupying' a place ... the acousmatic experience offers a world of objects which are ordered only *apparently*, and not in fact.[50]

Scruton concedes that musicians regularly use spatial language—notes 'move up and down' and so forth. Musical perception is *necessarily* metaphorical: we hear tones *as* rising, falling, and so on; we hear *in* the tones a spatial order.[51] And all language that results from such hearing is no less metaphorical. But, he insists, we should avoid investing these metaphors with inappropriate content.

Are matters quite so clear-cut? One question worth considering, for example, is whether or not musical space enables the perception of aspects of the physical world's space that are opaque to visual–spatial models. Is the only kind of existent spatial order that which we can visualize? Moreover, acknowledging that the spatiality of musical perception does not correspond to the spatial order of three-dimensional objects, and that the language we use of musical–auditory space will indeed entail metaphor, this does not in any sense rule out the truth-disclosing potential of the spatial language and concepts generated by the distinctive spatiality of musical experience. There is after all no a priori reason to believe that all our spatial language and concepts must have their truth-bearing capacity assessed entirely according to the extent they measure up to what we have already decided from our visual experience is to be deemed 'essential' space (space 'in fact'). In any case, the type of spatial language and conceptuality especially critical for our purposes

---

music necessarily *involves* the capacity to abstract sounds (tones) from their sources and causes, and to hear them as related to each other in meaningful internally related configurations, even if we allow that other acousmatic experience may be (and usually is) relevant to hearing the sounds *as music*. Without this capacity, there could be no musical experience. Whether or not our ability to abstract from 'real-life causality' can ever be complete, and whether or not such a total perceptual disengagement would even be desirable, is quite another matter. In any case, this chapter is not concerned with musical perception in its wider, physical contexts, only with one, albeit crucial, dimension of it.

[49] Scruton, *The Aesthetics of Music*, 14. Scruton asserts bluntly: 'the distinction between place and occupant is ... fundamental to the concept of space': Scruton, *The Aesthetics of Music*, 47.

[50] Scruton, *The Aesthetics of Music*, 14.

[51] Scruton, *The Aesthetics of Music*, ch. 3.

is not that of 'up' and 'down' and so on, but the type we employ to make distinctions between objects that exist simultaneously or concurrently but which we nevertheless recognize as distinct.

Interpenetration

Bolder and rather more penetrating in this regard is the remarkable work of the Austrian musicologist Victor Zuckerkandl (1896–1965).[52] He describes the space manifest in musical tones as a space of 'interpenetration'. When one tone is heard along with a different tone, it does not drive the first away, nor is it in a different place, nor does it merge with the first to create a new tone. Both are heard as full and distinct. They do not occupy discrete places. The space we hear is not an aggregate of places: 'somewhere' cannot be distinguished from 'elsewhere'. We cannot measure heard tones geometrically or point to boundaries to distinguish them. There is no spatial magnitude of elements—one tone cannot take up 'more space' than the other. There is no possibility of 'the more of the first tone, the less of the other' (presuming one does not drown out the other through greater loudness). Spatial order here is not the relation of spatial parts to one another against the backdrop of a spatial whole, since we are not encountering the space of juxtaposition and mutual exclusion; the distinction between parts and whole is irrelevant in this context. The tones can 'sound through' one another, interpenetrate. They can be *in* one another, while being heard *as* two distinct tones.[53]

'Coming From' and 'Coming Towards'

Zuckerkandl also writes of sonic space as 'coming from', 'coming towards'. A colour I see is the property of a physical object; it is 'with' the object, 'out

---

[52] Zuckerkandl, *Sound and Symbol*; Victor Zuckerkandl, *The Sense of Music* (Princeton: Princeton University Press, 1971); Victor Zuckerkandl, *Man the Musician* (Princeton: Princeton University Press, 1973). Shepherd and Wicke are the only music scholars I have found to appreciate the importance of Zuckerkandl's work for our understanding of the experience of sound, time, and space: John Shepherd and Peter Wicke, *Music and Cultural Theory* (Cambridge: Polity Press, 1997), 122–3, 129–36, 141, 150–2, 154, 159, 160.

[53] Zuckerkandl, *Sound and Symbol*, chs 14, 15, and 16. It might be objected: visual art can suggest this very powerfully. The reply: it can indeed *suggest* it, or evoke it—as in the impressive 'polyphonic' art of Paul Klee (1879–1940), which does seem to radiate a sense of the overlaying of diverse colours. See Hajo Düchting, *Paul Klee: Painting Music* (Munich: Prestel, 1997), 65–79; Andrew Kagan, *Paul Klee: Art and Music* (Ithaca, NY: Cornell University Press, 1983). But the fact remains that in this case we do not perceive distinct colours in the same place; we perceive difference only by comparing 'edged' units of colour. This is not in any way to downplay Klee's artistry, only to highlight the divergence between two types of perception.

there'. But, as we have noted (via Scruton), a perceived tone is not 'with' the thing that produced it. It has detached itself from the physical object, and as such it is impinging upon me, always coming towards me. Its happening (as 'pure event', in Scruton's sense) *is* its coming towards me. Here, says Zuck-erkandl, I am experiencing space not simply in the form of an inert vessel or container through which a sound travels, but space in the form of 'coming towards'—a living space, in other words: 'Space that has become alive as a result of sound! Hence not sound that has come alive in space . . . but space that becomes an occurrence through tone.'[54] Or, we might say: space as an intrinsic dimension of tone. This is why a single tone is not dull in the same way that, say, staring at a blank sheet of white paper is. In the latter case, we get bored because there is 'nothing there'. But 'It would never occur to [a person] to say that he hears *nothing* when he hears only one tone';[55] rather, he hears a sound coming towards him. It is this quality that gives sound a depth—not the visual depth generated by physical distance, but the dynamic depth of 'coming towards me', 'coming from': 'depth in auditory space is only another expres-sion for this "coming from . . ." that we sense in every tone'.[56]

Resonant Order

If the language of 'coming from'–'coming towards' may be somewhat obscure, more readily accessible is Zuckerkandl's account of musical–spatial order. In the interpenetration of sounds in our heard space, as we have seen, the integrity of each heard sound is not effaced but, in principle at least, preserved. In the case of musical tones in particular, another momentum is often at work, such that the integrity of each sound is not only preserved, but enriched.

If I hear a truck outside, the wind blowing through the trees, and a baby crying all at the same time—the sounds may well interpenetrate, creating a differentiated aural space, but we would hardly claim an auditory *order* was present.[57] The noises bear no internal relation to each other; they just happen

---

[54] Zuckerkandl, *Sound and Symbol*, 277.   [55] Zuckerkandl, *Sound and Symbol*, 283.
[56] Zuckerkandl, *Sound and Symbol*, 289.
[57] This kind of everyday experience is nonetheless a testimony to the interpenetrative capacities of simultaneously heard sounds in contrast to visual perception. This is brought out well by John Hull in his book *Touching the Rock*, when he reflects on the experience of losing his sight. Deprived of sight, he asks:

> What is the world of sound? I have been spending some time out of doors trying to respond to the special nature of the acoustic world . . . The tangible world sets up only as many points of reality as can be touched by my body, and this seems to be restricted to one problem at a time. I can explore the splinters on the park bench with the tip of my finger but I cannot, at the same time, concentrate upon exploring the pebbles with my big toe . . . The world revealed by sound is so different . . . On Holy Saturday I sat in Cannon Hill Park while the children were playing . . . The footsteps came from both sides. They met, mingled,

Figure 6.1. Sympathetic resonance

to be together in the one aural space. But in the case of a three-note major triad, the three tones are perceptibly related, not just to me as the hearer but internally to one another. They are mutually *resonant*; they 'set each other off', enhancing, 'enlarging' each other as particular and distinct. Thus we perceive an ordered chord, not three noises.

This order arises because of the way regularly constituted vibrating bodies, such as strings, participate in a phenomenon known as the harmonic series—a series of distinct frequencies present in the vibrating body. Certain strings will resonate strongly with some (but by no means all) other strings. If I play middle C on a piano, and open up the string an octave above by silently depressing the appropriate key, the upper C string will vibrate (very quietly) even though it has not been struck (Figure. 6.1). This is because the upper C is the second harmonic (or first overtone) of the 'fundamental' lower C.[58] The upper C has been provoked to sound through 'sympathetic resonance'.

This is clearly not a case of mutual diminution: rather, the *more* the lower string sounds, the *more* the upper string sounds. The tones we hear are not in competition, nor do they simply allow each other room. The lower sound establishes the upper, frees it to be itself, enhances it, without compromising its own integrity. Moreover, when certain other strings are opened up along-side both these strings—for instance, to make an extended major chord—we will hear those other strings coming to life.

A chord of this sort therefore opens up a distinctive kind of spatial order we may call 'resonant order', in which tones are heard to relate intrinsically to one another in such a way as to generate and reinforce each other. This ordered space is responsible for the dynamism we are used to intuiting in most of the music of Western culture—because of the internal relatedness of tones to one

---

separated again. From the next bench, there was the rustle of a newspaper and the murmur of conversation . . . I heard the steady, deep roar of the through traffic, the buses and the trucks . . . [The acoustic world] stays the same whichever way I turn my head. This is not true of the [visually] perceptible world. It changes as I turn my head. New things come into view. The view looking that way is quite different from the view looking this way. It is not like that with sound . . . This is a world which I cannot shut out, which goes on all around me, and which gets on with its own life . . . Acoustic space is a world of revelation. (John Hull, *Touching the Rock: An Experience of Blindness* (London: SPCK, 1990), 61–4).

[58] This will not work if the upper note is, say, a D♭, for D♭ is only very distantly related to C harmonically.

another through the harmonic series, even single chords will have certain 'attractions' towards, and 'gravitational pulls' from, other tones and chords. The playing-out of music in time is a playing-out of this tonal order.[59]

This musical space we have been describing—an interpenetrating, coming from–coming towards, resonantly ordered space—makes possible something we will only meet in music: that of radically different words being audible simultaneously while at the same time being pleasurable and intelligible. In Act II of Giuseppe Verdi's *Otello*, for example, there is a famous quartet when what happens in the Shakespeare play on separate occasions is brought together.[60] Four voices sing simultaneously, yet of different things, in one texture. If merely spoken this would be near-impossible to understand, let alone enjoy. But when the simultaneous words are taken into the spatial order of musical tones, the effect is comprehensible and captivating. Zuckerkandl speaks of this as generating a 'supermeaning, the meaning of a whole'.[61] Another example: in U2's song 'The Fly', the lower voice sings of trying to hang on to love like a fly climbing up a wall, while at the same time the upper voice (called 'gospel' voice) sings in falsetto of love coming down from above. Two very different sets of words are concurrently sung and both given new meaning—and thus a 'supermeaning'—in and through their sonic simultaneity.[62]

Music, then, is capable of evoking a space for the hearer that is, so to speak, 'edgeless', an inherently expansive space that has no close parallel in the world of the eye.[63] The experience is well described by Maurice Merleau-Ponty:

> When, in the concert hall, I open my eyes, visible space seems to me cramped compared to that other space through which, a moment ago, the music was being unfolded, and even if I keep my eyes open while the piece is being played, I have the impression that the music is not really contained within this circumscribed and unimpressive space.[64]

---

[59] For an illuminating exposition of the tonal order of Western music, see e.g. Brian Hyer, 'Tonality' on *Oxford Music Online* [website]: <http://www.oxfordmusiconline.com>, accessed 9 November 2010.

[60] James A. Hepokoski, 'Verdi's Composition of *Otello*: The Act II Quartet', in Carolyn Abbate and Roger Parker (eds), *Analyzing Opera: Verdi and Wagner* (Berkeley and Los Angeles: University of California Press, 1989), 125–49.

[61] Zuckerkandl, *Sound and Symbol*, 332.

[62] U2, 'The Fly', on *Achtung Baby* [CD] (Island, 1991), track 7.

[63] It may well be argued that in the case of visual perception and the visually perceivable world there is a parallel—that of resonances between colours. However, as far as *interpenetration* and *coming from and coming towards* are concerned, it is hard to see a visual parallel to these aspects of sound-as-perceived.

[64] Maurice Merleau-Ponty, *Phenomenology of Perception* (New York: Humanities Press, 1962), 257–8.

SOUND DOCTRINE

We are proposing, then, that the space of musical tones is a space of inter-penetration, of coming from–coming towards, and of resonant order. Clearly, this resists being construed in terms of receptacle spatiality; this space is not a container, but rather the space *of*, space as an intrinsic dimension or condition of objects and events, space understood in accordance with that which 'has' space. With this in mind, we revisit the theological *loci* we highlighted earlier.

Transcendence and Immanence Transposed

To return to the Creator–creature relation—once we are freed from the supposition of an area of super-space in which God and the world are both situated, the ontological and conceptual machinery of contrastive transcend-ence will seem far less apposite, with its tendency to posit transcendence and immanence as polar opposites and then to elaborate various compromises and mediations between them. The way is opened up for far more biblically grounded accounts, congruent with God's covenantal commitment disclosed in his triune self-revelation. God's transcendence transcends a merely crea-turely understanding of transcendence—it transcends the contrasts by which finite beings are distinguished and differentiated, and cannot be conceived as a spatial relation in the visual–tangible–measurable sense. Rather, God stands in a *creative* (covenantally propelled) relation to created space. Because God is radically *for* the world we can speak of a 'dynamic transcendence': the transcendence of a God who creates all things out of nothing, sustains and redeems all things towards their eschatological fulfilment. This is a transcend-ence of the Giver, fundamentally oriented *to* and *for* the world's flourishing. God's triune being is a being-towards, known by the creature as a 'coming from' or 'coming towards'. Tanner observes that

> A non-competitive relation between creatures and God is possible, it seems, only if God is the fecund provider of *all* that the creature is in itself; the creature in its giftedness, in its goodness, does not compete with God's gift-fullness and good-ness because God is the giver of all that the creature is for the good. This relationship of total giver to total gift is possible, in turn, only if God and creatures are, so to speak, on different levels of being, and different planes of causa-lity . . . God does not give on the same plane of being and activity as creatures, as one among other givers and therefore God is not in potential competition (or co-operation) with them . . . God, from beyond this plane of created reality, brings about the *whole* plane of creaturely being and activity in its goodness.[65]

---

[65] Kathryn Tanner, *Jesus, Humanity and the Trinity: A Brief Systematic Theology* (Edinburgh: T&T Clark, 2000), 3, 4. Compare Henk Schoot: 'God is not transcendent in the sense that he

Divine immanence accordingly can be (re)conceived as a creative involvement with the world that is not confined to interventions in this or that particular zone or place. If God is not characterized fundamentally by contrast with this or that being, God may be directly and immediately involved with the entirety of the space–time continuum, albeit in diverse ways. Such an immanence does not merely *permit* transcendence, but *requires* it. Only a God who is non-identical with the creation—both in the sense that God creates all things out of nothing (not as an extension of his being), and in the sense that the God–world distinction transcends even the contrastive distinctions by which finite beings are distinguished—can be truly and savingly present *to* and *for* the world in its entirety, directly and immediately. Similarly, transcendence entails immanence—if divine transcendence is positively understood as the transcendence of the triune plenitude, the transcendence of divine covenantal commitment to fellowship, there can be no portion of created reality that lacks divine engagement. Musical conceptuality lends itself very naturally to perceiving and articulating these dynamics, for it sidesteps the pernicious notion of a prior, conditioning super-space and operates with an 'otherness' not driven by negation and opposition but by gracious fullness, and by the promotion and enhancement of the particularity of the other. All three features of musical tone-perception are seen to be relevant here. *Interpenetration*—we are freed from thinking in terms of the divine and created as mutually exclusive zones. *Coming from–coming towards—creatio ex nihilo* is the outcome of God's own triune 'space' in action (not a movement into (or out of!) a pre-existing space); God's sustenance and gracious approach towards us in Jesus Christ do not happen through some intervening 'gap' between God and creation (as some cosmologies suggest), but rather as a result of God's own 'space' towards the world, the space that *is* God-towards-us, God-for-us, God's own dynamic, triune depth, his eternal coming-forth-ness. *Resonant order*—God not only allows the created world 'room' but establishes it in its very otherness, augmenting it in its distinctive particularity through engaging intensely with it.

Accordingly, working from a centre in the triune God's self-disclosure entails refusing to imagine God's infinity simply in terms of the absence of limits, according to a prior model of infinitely extended (immaterial)

---

needs a difference to be the unique one he is. God is not different within a certain genus, on the basis of a common similarity . . . God is "outside" of any genus, and thus God is not different from creatures the way in which creatures mutually differ. God differs differently . . . Such an account undermines the opposition between transcendence and immanence, because God is not transcendent in such a way that he is simply "outside of" or "above" the world, and thus not transcendent in such a way that it would exclude his "descent" into the world': Henk J. M. Schoot, *Christ the 'Name' of God: Thomas Aquinas on Naming Christ* (Leuven: Peeters, 1993), 144–5. See also Karl Barth, *Church Dogmatics*, trans. Geoffrey W. Bromiley and Thomas F. Torrance, vol. iv/1 (Edinburgh: T & T Clark, 1958), 186–7.

substance (which is to posit God in relation to other things-in-places, namely 'beyond' them). God encompasses and permeates all things, carrying them to their goal. Some consider the work of Gregory of Nyssa (*c.335–c.394*) especially significant here,[66] insofar as he demonstrates the dangers of applying creaturely extensive terms to God and of supposing a univocity of being with regard to God and the world, and inasmuch as he offers a positive vision of infinity (which includes a kind of 'extension') arising from the trinitarian liveliness of the God who is unconditionally and actively committed to the created world. For Gregory,

> The God who is infinite and no being among beings is also the personal God of election and incarnation, the dynamic, living, and creative God he is, precisely because being is not a genus whereunder God as 'a being' might be subsumed, but is the act through which beings are given form by the God who is never without form and beauty.[67]

The transcendence of one tone or chord over another (say, of a fundamental over its first overtone) is the transcendence of irreducible difference, certainly, but a difference that brings life, abundance, fullness to the other tones. There is much to suggest that it is only within some such musical–conceptual context that the extensive language of quantity, measure, 'greater than', and so forth will find its proper place in discussions of divine infinity.[68]

None of this is to suggest that every dilemma and difficulty regarding the Creator–creation relation can be instantly or wholly resolved through engaging musical phenomena, but it is to say that some of the perceived problems will be shown up as pseudo-problems, some of them as far less intractable than initially thought, and many can be recast in forms that lead to far greater understanding.

Agency in Concord

Similar things can be said with regard to divine and human agency, and to inter-human agency. As with transcendence and immanence, there is little to be gained from attempting to secure some perilous equipoise between divine and human agency (as if both belonged to the same causal system), just as there would be little point in speaking of the sympathetic resonance of a tone

---

[66] Shults, *Reforming the Doctrine of God*, 101–2; David Bentley Hart, *The Beauty of the Infinite: The Aesthetics of Christian Truth* (Grand Rapids, MI: Eerdmans, 2003), 235–6.

[67] Hart, *The Beauty of the Infinite*, 235.

[68] It is important not to favour a qualitative *as opposed to* a quantitative understanding of infinity. Because God's being is a differentiated triune life we may properly employ the extensive language of quantity to God, which itself relies on the notion of 'place'. See Hart, *The Beauty of the Infinite*, 235.

with another as a phenomenon of 'balance'. Nor need we assume univocity of predication—as if God's agency and human agency had to be understood as basically of the same ontological category, occupying different zones in the same space, with the resulting tendency to set them in competitive opposition. Creaturely dependence on God cannot be understood in the terms appropriate to visually perceptible objects. Karl Rahner writes:

> The relation between God and creature is characterized, precisely in contrast to any causal independence otherwise met within the world, by the fact that self-possession and independence increase in direct, not in inverse proportion.[69]

Kathryn Tanner thus speaks of God's 'creative agency'[70]—God liberating human particularity through direct engagement such that we are enabled to live according to the liveliness intended for us, the specific form of our intended resonance of life with God. Saving faith is not thereby rendered void, nor need it be regarded as the act of some supposedly wholly unconstrained will, but rather as being enabled by God to participate, through the resonating agency of the Spirit, in God's own resonance. Such *is* human freedom.

We hardly need spell out the consequences of this for thinking through the Church's corporate freedom—where we are freed *by* the other *for* the other, and in this manner, find (against our expectations and self-willed desires) our God-intended resonant space. Freedom is never possession but always gift; not the result of individual choices but graciously bestowed. And we might add: this is by no means to exclude or belittle the agency of God in and through others in the Body of Christ who shape human agency and enhance our freedom: 'Other agents may *affect* human agency, but it is God who *effects* it, who constitutes its effectiveness.'[71]

Speaking more widely: constraints, far from being the enemy of freedom, are in fact its condition—notwithstanding the obvious but crucial fact that some constraints are radically dehumanizing. Theologically, this means that no adequate account of freedom can be given *except* by speaking of the loving constraints of the Creator for the creature, the constraints of our physical embeddedness and finitude, and the ecclesial constraints of the Body of Christ. Denial of constraint is a denial of our humanness.[72]

---

[69] Karl Rahner, *Encyclopedia of Theology: The Concise Sacramentum Mundi* (New York: Seabury Press, 1975), 598. In another place, Rahner speaks of the tendency in some quarters to presume that God can only 'become greater and more real by the devaluation and cancellation of the creature': Karl Rahner, *Theological Investigations*, vol. i (Baltimore: Helicon Press, 1961), 188.

[70] Tanner, *God and Creation*, ch. 2.

[71] John M. G. Barclay, 'Introduction', in John M. G. Barclay and Simon J. Gathercole (eds), *Divine and Human Agency in Paul and His Cultural Environment* (London: T & T Clark, 2006), 1–8, 7.

[72] For further discussion, see Jeremy S. Begbie, *Theology, Music and Time* (Cambridge: Cambridge University Press, 2000), 198–245. 'Nothing could be more misleading than the

Is this not the kind of environment in which we should set the classic debates about 'free response' in relation to divine grace? In his introduction to a collection of essays on divine and human agency in the writings of the Apostle Paul, John Barclay notes the need to 'unthink' some of our presuppositions.[73] With Paul's writings in mind, he asks:

> Is it helpful to frame [divine and human agency] in terms of chronological anteriority, or is the placement of one agency 'within' the other a better metaphor? It appears that human agency is the *necessary expression* of the life of the Spirit, and certainly not its antithesis; the two are not mutually exclusive as if in some zero-sum calculation...

He continues:

> ... everything depends on how one conceives the 'human agent' reconstituted in Christ. Although in one sense we may speak properly of a 'dual agency', in non-exclusive relation, this would be inadequately expressed as the co-operation or conjunction of two-agents, or as the relationship of gift and response, if it is thereby forgotten that the 'response' continues to be activated by grace, and the believers' agency *embedded within* that of the Spirit.[74]

We recall the distinction between covenant and contract. Whereas a contract is an arrangement whereby conditions are fulfilled by two parties in order to secure certain ends such that each party occupies his or her own active 'space', a covenant (whether bilateral or unilateral) is driven by an unconditional commitment that goes not just halfway, so to speak, but 'all the way' to engage and 'embrace' the space of the other. Reconciliation, the New Testament's *katallagē*, finds its concentrated depth in the incarnate Son's journey into that far country of our entrapment, wholly identifying, *as* the eternal Son, with our predicament. This is the enfleshment of God in the midst of our dissonance; a reaching-forth of the triune God, that is not satisfied with some midpoint but spans and encompasses the *total* divine–human 'space' such that, through Christ's dying and rising, a radically new divine–human resonance can be

---

popular philosophy that freedom is constituted by the absence of limits. There is, to be sure, a truth which it intends to recognize, which is that the "potency" of freedom requires "possibility" as its object... Where the popular philosophy becomes so misleading is in its suggestion that we can maximize freedom by multiplying the number of possibilities open to us. For if possibilities are to be meaningful for free choice, they must be well-defined by structures of limit': Oliver O'Donovan, *Resurrection and Moral Order: An Outline for Evangelical Ethics* (Leicester: Inter-Varsity Press, 1994), 107. Understanding authentic freedom 'requires not only belief that we possess an actual nature, which must flourish to be free, but a belief in the transcendent Good towards which that nature is oriented... We are free not because we can choose, but only when we have chosen well': Hart, *In the Aftermath*, 79.

[73] Barclay, 'Introduction', 4.

[74] John M. G. Barclay, '"By the Grace of God I Am What I Am": Grace and Agency in Philo and Paul', in John M. G. Barclay and Simon J. Gathercole (eds), *Divine and Human Agency in Paul and His Cultural Environment* (London: T & T Clark, 2006), 140–58, 156. Italics are his.

established, so that we, 'embedded' in the Spirit's agency, might be retuned to the one he knows and calls 'Abba'.

This notion of the resonant interpenetration of agencies can, of course, be extended to interpersonal agency. Paul's vision of the Church in 1 Corinthians 12 as both one and many—to cite just one pertinent text—is not that of a mosaic of bounded places in which the whole is simply the sum of the parts, still less an aggregation of interest groups self-protected against the encroachment of others, nor—the chronic tendency of many Western churches—a homogenous mass in which all diversity has been effectively wiped out in the name of 'oneness', but a diverse body of mutually resonating members, in which, through an excentric dynamic set in motion by the Spirit, particularity is established, sustained, and enabled to flourish just *as* persons are united in fellowship.[75]

Christological Counterpoint

All of this bears very obviously on Christology. Indeed, it is precisely a failure to think out of a centre in the Christological redemption of the space–time order that accounts for so many endemic hindrances in this field.[76] With musical conceptuality, our proneness to regard divine and human agency in Christ as inherently opposed will be less likely to take hold, nor the somewhat questionable Christologies proposed as solutions. We will be more capable of conceiving the person of Christ not as the Son entering a finite receptacle but as the co-presence of God's space and the space of the creation: the Son sharing created space while yet remaining the Father's eternal Son and thus primordially inhabiting God's eternal trinitarian space. We will begin to be

---

[75] In his prison writings, Dietrich Bonhoeffer employs the model of polyphony with regard to the relation between our love for God and our other, earthly affections; he also uses it to speak of the divine and human in Christ, alluding to Chalcedon. These thoughts are not developed systematically, but there can be little doubt that he is intuitively sensing the theologically possibilities of drawing on the 'interpenetrating' and mutually animating character of multivoiced music: Dietrich Bonhoeffer, *Letters and Papers from Prison* (London: SCM Press, 1972), 302–3. For discussion, see Jeremy S. Begbie, *Resounding Truth: Christian Wisdom in the World of Music* (Grand Rapids, MI: Baker Books, 2007), 160–2. A case could be made to the effect that Bonhoeffer had realized some of the potentially distorting consequences of visual–spatial thought patterns (such as those entailed in the notion of the *deus ex machina*). See the comments by Lundin in *Believing Again*, 206–10.

[76] See the illuminating account of 'double agency' in the work of Karl Barth in George Hunsinger, *How to Read Karl Barth: The Shape of His Theology* (New York: Oxford University Press, 1991), ch. 7. Against the charge that Barth's conception of divine sovereignty and human responsibility is incoherent (with its concern to hold asymmetry, intimacy, and integrity together), Hunsinger highlights the Christological configuration of Barth's mind on the matter: 'Barth's account of fellowship in particular and of divine and human agency in general cannot possibly be understood unless it is seen that this conception falls within the terms of the Chalcedonian pattern': Hunsinger, *How to Read Karl Barth*, 185.

more alert to the dangers of regarding the relation between the incarnate Son and the Father according to the determinants of visual–tangible–measurable space (the earthly Christ 'here' in our space, and the Father 'there' in God's space), more inclined to preserve the kind of 'in-one-anotherness' of Son and Father evoked in John's Gospel.[77] We will also perhaps be less inclined to think in terms of maintaining an uneasy equilibrium, or negotiating some kind of give-and-take compromise between the divine Son and the humanity he assumes, and more disposed to think in terms of the interpenetrating resonance of God's agency and human agency, the latter achieving its freedom by being embedded in the freedom of the former.[78]

Pressing this a little further: the 'divine nature' could well be explicated in terms of the incarnate Son in full reciprocal resonance with his Father, enabled through the agency of the Spirit and now interpenetrating our space so as to be made accessible and available to us. Likewise with respect to Christ's 'human nature': in the incarnate Son our assumed humanity has been liberated by the Spirit to resonate with the Father, our privilege being to participate by the Spirit in this perfectly resonant response to the Father already made on our behalf. In these ways—answering the common complaint that Chalcedon lacks trinitarian vigour—an enriched Chalcedonian imagination is released, one which can arguably follow through the New Testament's Christological and trinitarian momentum more fully and faithfully.

Trinitarian Soundings

We have journeyed into trinitarian territory. And this is hardly surprising, since the doctrines of transcendence and immanence, divine and human agency, and Christology all presuppose God's trinitarian 'space' as their implicit grammar.

It is almost routine in current theology to argue that the theological dilemmas and quandaries concerning freedom we have identified have arisen through a lack of attention to God's triunity; less common are analyses of patterns of thinking that have generated or exacerbated the problems in the first place, or proposals for more effective alternatives. What could be more appropriate than to conceptualize and articulate God's triunity in terms suggested by hearing a three-note chord—that is, as a resonance of life-in-three; the three reciprocally interpenetrating, without exclusion yet without merger, irreducibly distinct yet together constituting the one divine space; the

---

[77] I owe the phrase 'in-one-anotherness' to my former colleague, Richard Bauckham.

[78] For an illuminating discussion along these lines (which draws on Zuckerkandl) see Colin E. Gunton, *Yesterday and Today: A Study of Continuities in Christology* (London: Darton, Longman & Todd, 1983), ch. 6, esp. 111–19.

life of each a 'coming forth' and 'going towards' the others; each animating, establishing, and enhancing the others in their particularity?[79] It is hard to read Zuckerkandl's account of listening to a three-note chord without also hearing harmonies of trinitarian doctrine:

> Three tones sound. In each of them space encounters us and we encounter space. None of them is in a place; or better, they are all in the same place, namely everywhere . . . [S]imultaneously sounding tones do not run together into a mixed tone. No difference of places keeps them apart; yet they remain audible as different tones . . . [T]he tones connected in the triad sound *through one another* . . . or let us say that they interpenetrate one another . . .[80]

CONCLUSION

In this chapter, I have pursued one main line of argument in an effort to demonstrate the fruitfulness of drawing on the conceptuality and language of musical perception for reconfiguring the way we commonly theologize human freedom. Clearly, many caveats are in order. For example, in the case of the mutual resonance of two strings, we are speaking of two objects belonging to the same ontological class, something obviously not applicable to the

---

[79] Clearly, applying spatial language to God's immanent life requires considerable caution. For very good reasons, much of the Christian tradition has insisted on affirming the non-spatiality (and non-temporality) of God. However, I am inclined to side with Murray Rae's recent and highly nuanced treatment of the issue. Rae is fully aware of the dangers of conceptual moves that result in a projection of the creaturely spatiality into the divine (for example, arguing that if 'Jesus exists in creaturely space . . . there must be some kind of analogy of creaturely spaciousness that belongs to the being of God himself'). But he nevertheless proposes (with Barth, but against John Webster and Ian Mackenzie) that we may legitimately speak of God possessing his own space, on the basis of 'the differentiation of the persons of the Trinity, revealed in the economy as belonging to the being of God himself': Murray Rae, 'The Spatiality of God', in Myk Habets and Phillip Tolliday (eds), *Trinitarian Theology After Barth* (Eugene, OR: Wipf & Stock, 2011), 70–86, 78. God's antecedent, trinitarian differentiation is the ontological condition of God's differentiation from creation, and a condition of all differentiation between creaturely entities. 'Space' is being conceived here pre-eminently out of a centre in God's own space, not according to a notion of 'space' imported from elsewhere. In this chapter, my methodological intention is similar: I have no wish to let music provide an a priori conception of space to which a theology of freedom is then expected to conform. Rather, music can offer a mode of clarification and correction to a theology that seeks to be primarily oriented and conformed to the self-disclosure of God's own trinitarian 'space'.

[80] Zuckerkandl, *Sound and Symbol*, 297, 298, 299. If this essay were expanded further, of course, we could explore much more fully the ways in which dynamic multi-voiced music (such as a fugue) might help us develop aspects of trinitarian theology. See Jenson, *Systematic Theology*, ii. 236; Jonathan P. Case, 'The Music of the Spheres: Music and the Divine Life in George Steiner and Robert W. Jenson (Part II: Intersections)', *Crucible* [online journal] 3, 2 (September 2011): <http://www.ea.org.au/Crucible/Issues/Past-Issues/Vol-3-No-2-September-2011.aspx>, accessed 17 June 2012.

Creator–creature relation. Further, we need to be wary of an indiscriminate reduction of all relations to the same type or level—an undoubted danger amid the current vogue for 'relationality' evident in some theological quarters.[81] The intra-trinitarian relations, the relation of human and divine in the hypostatic union, the relation between Christ and the Church, between persons in the Church—all these need to be carefully differentiated. The trinitarian *perichoresis* cannot be mapped onto concrete human relations without substantial caution.[82] Nor can the infinite freedom of the triune God be compared to humans' finite freedom without considerable qualification.[83] Also, due attention needs to be given to the asymmetry of the God–human relation, the precedence and priority of God, not least because of the peril of sliding back into treating divine and human agency as two agents on the same level. And, of course, in this chapter we have said little about sin, evil, and the cross—the related theme of dissonance would require extensive discussion if this chapter were to be expanded. Further still, vibrating strings are clearly not persons or

[81] For discussion of these matters, see John C. Polkinghorne (ed.), *The Trinity and an Entangled World: Relationality in Physical Science and Theology* (Grand Rapids, MI: Eerdmans, 2010).

[82] For strong exhortations to caution regarding *perichoresis*, see Oliver Crisp, 'Problems with Perichoresis', *Tyndale Bulletin* 56 (2005): 118–40; Randall E. Otto and E. Randall, 'The Use and Abuse of Perichoresis in Recent Theology', *Scottish Journal of Theology* 54, 3 (2001): 366–84. On the hazards of applying trinitarian relations to the Church, see Mark Husbands, 'The Trinity Is Not Our Social Program: Volf, Gregory and Barth', in Daniel J. Treier and David Lauber (eds), *Trinitarian Theology for the Church: Scripture, Community, Worship* (Downers Grove, IL: InterVarsity Press, 2009), 120–41.

In recent years, some have voiced strong concerns about the language of 'participation' or 'sharing' (*koinonia*) used of our redeemed relation to the triune God, fearing (among other things) that it will lead to a compromising of the Creator–creature distinction, the priority of God's covenantal action, and the necessity of the cross. See e.g. John Webster, 'The Church and the Perfection of God', in Mark Husbands and Daniel J. Treier (eds), *The Community of the Word: Toward an Evangelical Ecclesiology* (Downers Grove, IL: InterVarsity Press, 2005), 75–95, 80–7; Bruce L. McCormack, 'What's at Stake in Current Debates Over Justification?', in Mark Husbands and Daniel J. Treier (eds), *Justification: What's at Stake in the Current Debates* (Downers Grove, IL: InterVarsity Press, 2004), 81–117. Properly qualified, however, I see no compelling reason to abandon the language of participation as an appropriate way of conveying at least one dimension of the meaning of *koinonia*. And musical interpenetration, along with generative or sympathetic resonance (where one sounding body is definitely primary), may have much to offer in offsetting the anxieties expressed about the concept. We saw earlier the importance of understanding human agency not in terms of a self-generated and self-sustained response to an extrinsic divine action, but as being drawn into the trinitarian initiative of grace, enacted in the Son and now available to us through the agency of the Spirit. Our response, accordingly, is a sharing in Christ's response on our behalf, in the power of the Spirit, and in such a way that its distinctiveness, its particularity, is not effaced but brought to fulfilment. For a recent and highly nuanced treatment of these and related themes, see J. Canlis, *Calvin's Ladder: A Spiritual Theology of Ascent and Ascension* (Grand Rapids, MI: Eerdmans, 2010).

[83] See e.g. Bauckham, *God and the Crisis of Freedom*, 198–209; and the illuminating essay by Brian Hebblethwaite, 'Finite and Infinite Freedom in Farrer and von Balthasar', in F. Michael McLain and W. Mark Richardson (eds), *Human and Divine Agency: Anglican, Catholic, and Lutheran Perspectives* (Lanham, MD: University Press of America, 1999), 83–96.

agents—even if perceiving them may serve to release us from thinking or speaking of God's agency as a form of impersonal efficient causation, or of grace as sub-personal substance, or of divine personhood as separable from divine action.

It is also worth bearing in mind that for the purposes of our argument we have been abstracting an experience of musical sound from what is always in practice a constellation of experiences, multi-sensual and multimedia, involving far more than hearing and far more than the musical sounds themselves; music is always experienced along with sights and smells, memories and hopes, passions and politics. And, of course, we have been abstracting 'thinking about' music from its concrete enactment. Any sequel would need to consider the implications for the way the Church, for example, actually uses music in its worship and witness.

Notwithstanding all this, however, the central contention of this chapter still, I believe, stands: namely, that musical perception can yield quite distinctive and hugely fruitful resources for reshaping the way we commonly think about and articulate human freedom, resources that directly address and sometimes significantly alleviate numerous dilemmas that have profoundly shaped both modernity's and modern theology's construction of freedom, both within and outside the Church. Attending to the phenomenology of musical perception can not only assist us in circumventing many of these difficulties, it can also massively deepen and extend our apprehension of freedom in the process. This is not, of course, to suggest or imply that engagement with music resolves every theological predicament relating to freedom. Still less is it to imply that inasmuch as music could contribute to theology it would reduce or defuse what ought to remain a mystery; quite the opposite—at its best, by eliciting more fully the dynamics of, say, the realization of our freedom as we participate in the infinite freedom of God, engagement with music can render that mystery all the more resistant to reductionist strategies that rob those dynamics of their true depth, power, and wonder.

Before closing, two additional points are worth making. First, at the risk of underlining the obvious, spatial thought and language are unavoidable in theology.[84] Despite a distinct move away from spatiality in some theological quarters in recent times—a strong attraction to narrative and drama is especially noticeable, for example—spatial concepts and discourse are inescapable, and not least because they pervade Scripture. The question is not *whether* we employ spatial modes of thinking and speaking, but *what we are investing in them*, what we imagine is being delivered by them and through them.

---

[84] 'It is simply impossible for me to form a spatial conception of Heaven and Hell . . . But the imagination can function only spatially; without space the imagination is like a child who wants to build a palace and has no blocks': Czesław Miłosz, *To Begin Where I Am: Selected Essays*, ed. Bogdana Carpenter and Madeline G. Levine (New York: Farrar, Straus and Giroux, 2001), 320.

Engaging with music may mean we come to hear far *less* in our spatial language and thought—and it may also mean we hear far *more*.

Second, some will suspect my argument is designed to provide further fuel for that habitual denigration of all things visual that is thought to belong to the lifeblood of Protestantism. Or, on a wider front, some might imagine a whole-sale support for a line of argument that has emerged in a sizeable quantity of writing in recent years, which points to a widespread and damaging dominance of visuality in Western culture at large, indeed a hegemony that has led, some claim, to various forms of alienation, control, and normalization ('ocularcentr-ism', or what Marie-José Mondzain has called 'optocracy'[85]).

It would certainly be fascinating to explore this literature on visuality (vis-à-vis Protestantism and beyond) alongside the kind of contrast between visual and musical–sonic perception I have just elaborated. But for the moment, three comments will need to suffice. First, to assume that a comprehensive opposition to all things visual lies at the core of Protestantism is unsupport-able; the intense visual sensibility of the Protestant tradition has by now been well established, and the issues surrounding its suspicion of images are far more varied, multi-levelled, and nuanced than is often supposed.[86] Second, my purpose has not been to exalt one sense at the expense of another (that would be yet another misguided zero-sum game), but rather to show that an over-reliance on or overdetermination by one sensory mode may well encourage, perhaps even engender, certain habits of thought and language that theology could well do without. Third, I am inclined to think that in the years to come theology is going to have to develop a rather more rich and subtle approach to the relation between different sensory modes, media, and art forms than has

---

[85] Marie-José Mondzain, *Image, Icon, Economy: The Byzantine Origins of the Contemporary Imaginary* (Stanford, CA: Stanford University Press, 2005), 162. See e.g. Martin Jay, *Downcast Eyes: The Denigration of Vision in Twentieth-Century French Thought* (Berkeley, CA: University of California Press, 1994); David Michael Kleinberg-Levin, *Modernity and the Hegemony of Vision* (Berkeley, CA: University of California Press, 1993); David Michael Kleinberg-Levin, *The Philosopher's Gaze: Modernity in the Shadows of Enlightenment* (Berkeley, CA: University of California Press, 1999); Alain Corbin, *Time, Desire, and Horror: Towards a History of the Senses* (Cambridge: Polity Press, 1995); Walter J. Ong, *Ramus, Method, and the Decay of Dialogue: From the Art of Discourse to the Art of Reason* (Cambridge, MA: Harvard University Press, 1983); Chris Jenks, 'The Centrality of the Eye in Western Culture: An Introduction', *Visual Culture* (London: Routledge, 1995), 1–25; Robert Paul Doede and Paul Edward Hughes, 'Wounded Vision and the Optics of Hope', in Miroslav Volf and William H. Katerberg (eds), *The Future of Hope: Christian Tradition amid Modernity and Postmodernity* (Grand Rapids, MI: Eerdmans, 2004), 170–99. From a somewhat extreme theological perspective, see Jacques Ellul, *The Humili-ation of the Word* (Grand Rapids, MI: Eerdmans, 1985); far more measured are the perceptive comments of Roger Lundin in *Believing Again*, 193–210.

[86] See e.g. William A. Dyrness, *Reformed Theology and Visual Culture: The Protestant Imagination from Calvin to Edwards* (Cambridge: Cambridge University Press, 2004); David Morgan, *Protestants and Pictures: Religion, Visual Culture and the Age of American Mass Production* (New York: Oxford University Press, 1999); Christopher R. Joby, *Calvinism and the Arts: A Re-assessment* (Leuven, MA: Peeters, 2007).

been noticeable to date. In a perceptive essay, Ben Quash comments on Hans Urs von Balthasar's stress on the 'polyphonic' texture of Scripture:

> All [its] genres are valuable. Each has its own surplus of meaning to contribute to the others. Each genre will have particular strengths at opening up and exploring particular aspects of reality. Each will have a particular range and depth of penetration. Thus the theologian who has the ability to command a wide set of genres will find his or her capacity to conceptualize, to interpret, and to partici-pate in the life of the Christian community and the wider world, enriched in consequence.[87]

Much the same could be said of different modes of sense perception, and associated art forms. Of course, to suggest a priori that all art forms or sensory modes must be accorded equal weight and value in theology would be disin-genuous. We cannot decide this sort of thing in advance. In response to the frequent calls today for a 'recovery' of the visual (or perhaps the aural) in churches, it is worth asking: 'Why? On what theological grounds?' In any case, the senses invariably operate by implicating each other in highly complex ways, and many art forms are experienced along with other art forms and perceived with different senses simultaneously. (Most of the images that bombard a teenager today come with sound, for example, despite all that is said about ours being a 'visual' culture.) The challenge, then, is not to set this or that sense (or art form) on a pedestal, but to cultivate an alertness to the distinctive theological capacities and limitations of each, with a view to each making its own particular contribution to the enrichment of Christian life and thought, alert to the ways they can and do interact with each other.

Having said all this, it seems appropriate that we end by returning to the main thread of the chapter, and quote a delicious evocation of the powers of musical sound. Mozart bubbles over with enthusiasm to the Emperor Joseph II about his new opera, *The Marriage of Figaro*:

MOZART: . . . I have a scene in the second act—it starts as a duet, just a man and wife quarrelling. Suddenly the wife's scheming little maid comes in unexpectedly—a very funny situation. Duet turns into trio. Then the hus-band's equally screaming valet comes in. Trio turns into quartet. Then a stupid old gardener—quartet becomes quintet, and so on. On and on, sextet, septet, octet! How long do you think I can sustain that?

JOSEPH: I have no idea.

MOZART: Guess! Guess, Majesty. Imagine the longest time such a thing could last, then double it.

---

[87] Ben Quash, 'Real Enactment: The Role of Drama in the Theology of Hans Urs von Balthasar', in Trevor A. Hart and Steven R. Guthrie (eds), *Faithful Performances: Enacting Christian Tradition* (Aldershot: Ashgate, 2007), 13–32, 28.

JOSEPH: Well, six or seven minutes! maybe eight!

MOZART: Twenty, sire! How about twenty? Twenty minutes of continuous music. No recitatives.

VON SWIETEN: Mozart—

MOZART: [ignoring him] Sire, only opera can do this. In a play, if more than one person speaks at the same time, it's just noise. No one can understand a word. But with music, with music you can have twenty individuals all talking at once, and it's not noise—it's a perfect harmony.[88]

---

[88] Peter Shaffer, 'Amadeus' on the *Daily Script* website: <http://www.dailyscript.com/scripts/amadeus.html>, accessed 14 August 2012.

7

Music and God-Talk (1): Mapping the Field

Unvorstellbarer Gott!
Unaussprechlicher, vieldeutiger Gedanke!
Läßt du diese Auslegung zu?
Darf Aron, mein Mund, dieses Bild machen?
So habe ich mir ein Bild gemacht, falsch,
wie ein Bild nur sein kann!
So bin ich geschlagen!
So war alles Wahnsinn, was ich
gedacht habe,
und kann und darf nicht gesagt werden
O Wort, du Wort, das mir fehlt!

Unrepresentable God!
Inexpressible, many-sided idea,
will you let it be so explained?
Shall Aaron, my mouth, fashion this image?
Then I have fashioned an image too, false,
as an image must be.
Thus am I defeated!
Thus, all was but madness that
I believed before,
and can and must not be given voice.
O word, thou word, that I lack![1]

'O word, thou word, that I lack!' Moses' searing cry at the close of the second act of Arnold Schoenberg's unfinished opera *Moses und Aron* exposes one of the most deeply explored torments of modernity, recurring in a multitude of forms—the impossibility of uttering, and with it the potentially fatal risk of attempting to utter that which by its nature seems to resist all utterance. 'Unvorstellbarer Gott!' Unrepresentable God! Moses spurns any suggestion that the invisible, unimaginable God could be mediated in or through the particularities of the finite world. Unlike Aaron, for whom things must find

---

[1] The close of Act II of Schoenberg's *Moses und Aron*. Translation adapted from K. H. Wörner, *Schoenberg's Moses and Aaron* (London: Faber & Faber, 1963), 194–5.

concrete expression, not only in visible objects but also in words ('can you | Worship what you dare not even represent?'), Moses suspects that even words may be idolatrous images of the 'un-imagable'. So he has no option but to shatter the Tablets of the Law. 'Without Aaron, God's purpose cannot be accomplished; through Aaron it is perverted. That is the tragic paradox of the drama.'[2] Moses' final exclamation and desperate silence take on added force when we recall that Schoenberg, about to return formally to Judaism from Lutheranism, began composing his opera in Berlin in 1930, amid the rise of what was surely modernity's most bestial abuse of language, involving horrific perversions of theological speech, brazenly representing the unrepresentable without qualm or caution.

But entwined with this monumental theological struggle, the opera also offers a study in the apparently irresolvable tension between words and musical sounds, 'the impossibility of finding an exhaustive accord between language and music'.[3] Aaron sings, and sings fluently and eloquently; but Moses speaks, or, rather, he expresses himself in *Sprechgesang*, a kind of halfway between singing and speaking. Aaron's fluency, attractive as it is, can only lead to loss. 'Words distort; eloquent words distort absolutely.'[4]

In Chapters 2–6, questions about language have never been far from the surface. Our main purpose has been to demonstrate some of the ways music (and discourse about music) can contribute to the theological narration of modernity, and, where appropriate, help resolve some of the entanglements and aporias that have habitually arisen in such narrations. Implicit in virtually everything we have discussed are issues concerning the nature and scope of language, and most acutely, language concerning God and God's relation to the world. In Chapters 7 and 8, this will be our focus. How can attention to music help us penetrate and illuminate modernity's investment in theological speech and writing, and perhaps even help us address some of the intractable difficulties that have rendered such language so problematic for so many?

We approach the field from a specific angle, focusing on that stubborn yet strangely fertile tension between music and word so potently rendered in *Moses und Aron*. Our concern is to ask what theology can learn from the relation between music and speech/writing as it has been played out in various ways in practice and as it has been theorized, especially in the modern context. The long-range interest here is thus with an aspect of what might broadly be called theology's 'inter-disciplinarity': to what extent can theology, which of necessity deploys language, engage with and profit from practices that are undeniably coherent, intelligible, and can affect other practices, but whose

---

[2] George Steiner, 'Schoenberg's *Moses und Aron*', in George Steiner, *George Steiner: A Reader* (London: Penguin, 1984), 234–45, 242.

[3] Steiner, 'Schoenberg's *Moses und Aron*', 238.

[4] Steiner, 'Schoenberg's *Moses und Aron*', 241.

modi operandi appear to be in many respects distinct from those on which spoken and written language depend?

In modernity, typically, two extremes rear their heads as theologians attempt to link language to cultural phenomena such as music. One is the notion that language can in some manner encapsulate or enclose reality (including divine reality). This typically results either in a posture of suspicion towards anything that seems to elude verbal seizure (exemplified in some forms of Protestantism), or in an attempt to construe non-verbal media as a species of language—in the case of music, to show that at a fundamental level music operates (or should operate) in language-like ways. Insofar as it is non-linguistic, it is assumed, music is meaningless. At the other extreme, we find the notion that spoken and written words are best relegated to the status of the peripheral or dispensable, and that the theologian should engage in a full-blooded and enthusiastic embrace of non-verbal media—such as music. The fact that theology has often found itself swinging between these poles—between a kind of hyper-Protestant verbalism on the one hand and a wordless aestheticism on the other—is due in large part, I believe, first, to the lack of an adequate account of what is involved in inter-media or multimedia relations, and second, to a failure to situate our conceptions of theological language (and ultimately all language) within a sufficiently dynamic, Christological, and trinitarian context. The yet deeper issue underlying both these weaknesses, I suggest, concerns what would commonly be called the doctrine of creation, the extent to which one can hold that *both* music and language are grounded in a shared, divinely bestowed order, even if in one that is highly complex and sometimes mysteriously opaque.

In this chapter, we address the first of these concerns. We critically examine some of the principal ways in which the music–language relation has been theorized in modernity, drawing especially on the work of Cambridge music theorist Nicholas Cook. In Chapter 8 we address the issue of theology's particular investment in language, and the grace-driven, Christological, and trinitarian setting of that investment. We then go on to consider the implications of our findings for the practical interaction of music and theological language, and conclude with some brief reflections on the wider matters of creation and ontology.

Language seems to be music's most persistent partner in modernity. And not only in modernity: as far as we know, music and language have always been closely intertwined, and far beyond those occasions when they have been directly conjoined (as when texts are set to music). 'Speaking about music is extraordinarily difficult; yet music is interwoven with few human activities as inseparably as language.'[5] Evolutionists are agreed that the emergence of

---

[5] Philip V. Bohlman, 'Ontologies of Music', in Nicholas Cook and Mark Everist (eds), *Rethinking Music* (Oxford: Oxford University Press, 1999), 17–34, 25.

music and language are closely related, even if there is much dispute about the process.[6] And in music theory it has often been held (and sometimes taken for granted) that some kind of analogous relation holds between them; certainly the music–language relation has determined much of the Western European musical tradition.[7] That many nineteenth-century writers felt able to discern and articulate narratives in instrumental symphonies is a case in point (the journey of a hero in Beethoven's Fifth Symphony, for example), as is the way in which many discussions of musical text-setting presume that music can (and must) 'fit' the words. To be sure, fierce arguments have raged over the relative superiority of music and language (something memorably portrayed in Richard Strauss's last opera, *Capriccio*), and some have insisted that music and language are radically discrete zones, that any connection between the two is entirely arbitrary. But it has been far more common to presume some kind of close kinship between the two.

What is rarely appreciated with anything like the force it deserves is that theological factors have been heavily implicated in these discussions and debates. Not surprisingly, this has been most obvious in the Church—especially in its worship, where words and music are regularly bound together. As we saw in Chapter 2, it was vital to Calvin that the words sung in worship should be audible and comprehensible, and take the semantic lead over music. But on wider fronts, strong theological or quasi-theological currents have often played a part in formulations of music's associations with language. In Chapter 5, we examined the early German Romantics' exaltation of wordless music to quasi-sacred status, something closely bound up with reactions to a perceived desacralization of nature in society and culture at large. It is therefore worth exploring our territory with well-tuned theological antennae: we will contend that Cook's account of music's interaction with other media can be of considerable help in exposing the strengths and weaknesses of various models of the music–language relation, but we also attempt to elicit the theological dimensions and resonances of his case, and (in Chapter 8)

---

[6] See e.g. Aniruddh D. Patel, *Music, Language, and the Brain* (Oxford: Oxford University Press, 2008), ch. 7; Ian Cross, 'The Evolutionary Basis of Meaning in Music: Some Neurological and Neuroscientific Implications', in Frank Clifford Rose (ed.), *The Neurology of Music* (London: Imperial College Press, 2010), 1–15; Ian Cross and Ghofur Eliot Woodruff, 'Music as a Communicative Medium', in Rudolf Botha and Chris Knight (eds), *The Prehistory of Language* (Oxford: Oxford University Press, 2009), 77–98; Ian Cross and Iain Morley, 'The Evolution of Music: Theories, Definitions and the Nature of the Evidence', in Susan Hallam, Ian Cross, and Michael H. Thaut (eds), *The Oxford Handbook of Music Psychology* (Oxford: Oxford University Press, 2009), 61–81; Barry Ross, 'Challenges Facing Theories of Music and Language Co-evolution', *Journal of the Musical Arts in Africa* 6, 1 (2009): 61–76.

[7] Don Hárran, prefacing his mammoth survey of word–tone relations in Western music from antiquity to the seventeenth century, goes as far as to say that 'the intimate relation between music and language acts as a motivating force for the development of Western musical culture': Don Hárran, *Word–Tone Relations in Musical Thought: From Antiquity to the Seventeenth Century* (Neuhausen-Stuttgart: American Institute of Musicology, 1986), 1.

appropriate his work in a context that gives priority to the character and responsibilities of Christian theological language.

MODELLING MULTIMEDIA

How, then, might we begin to understand the relation between the practices of music and language? Nicholas Cook's study, *Analysing Musical Multimedia*,[8] is one of the most sustained attempts to provide a framework for theorizing the way music relates to non-musical media (Cook's interest being mainly confined to words and moving images). The author is convinced that musical experience always entails multimedia experience, whether we admit it or not. Music is invariably perceived along with other media, and these inevitably affect the meaning(s) we discern in, or attach to the music. One of Cook's primary purposes is to bring this basic but oft-forgotten feature of music-perception into theoretical prominence.[9]

One of the reasons we are so often slow to admit the multimedia character of musical experience is because we lack the necessary conceptual resources, and it is this Cook attempts to alleviate. In the course of his discussion he delineates three models of multimedia, three ways of theorizing music's relation to other media. He calls these 'conformance', 'contest', and 'complementation'.

Direct Correspondence: Conformance

The model here is of a direct correspondence between one medium and another. A combination of music and text will be regarded as successful just to the extent that the media align, accord with each other. So, for example, the rhythm of the words 'God Save the King!' in Handel's anthem 'Zadok the Priest' are directly reproduced in the rhythm of the music. Cook makes an important distinction between 'dyadic' and 'unitary' conformance.[10] In the

---

[8] Nicholas Cook, *Analysing Musical Multimedia* (Oxford: Clarendon Press, 1998).

[9] The term 'medium' needs some clarifying here. In relation to the arts and discussions of multimedia combinations, among other things it can refer to (i) the material component or 'stuff' ('trace') employed (e.g. oil paint in a painting); (ii) an 'art form' with a particular history (e.g. poetry, music); (iii) a sensory mode (e.g. the auditory, the visual); (iv) a particular kind of cognitive processing. In practice, the term slips back and forth between these (and other) senses. Cook advocates a flexible, structural approach, speaking of different media as 'independent dimensions of variance'. We recognize ballet as multimedia because we can recognize a certain independence, 'a degree of autonomy as between music and dance' as they interact to create the aesthetic effect that is so distinctive of ballet: Cook, *Analysing Musical Multimedia*, 261–4. We follow Cook's understanding as our primary usage.

[10] Cook, *Analysing Musical Multimedia*, 101.

former, neither medium predominates, they simply form a pair; in unitary conformance, one medium takes the lead and the other is subordinate to it. In the case of the Handel example, it might be said, we have unitary conformance; the music's rhythm mimics the rhythm of the words as spoken. In this way, the music serves the text—indeed, the metaphor of servant or service is common among advocates of unitary conformance.

Unitary conformance, Cook observes, has been by far the most popular model for understanding inter-media relations. It is sometimes simply assumed, sometimes prescribed. And both versions can be found in the Church. Many textbook histories of Christian worship, for example, are in effect histories of liturgical words: they typically presume that meaning is carried primarily and determinatively in texts and spoken language, and that the other media will fall into line by default and thus can be, if not ignored, at least relegated to a subsidiary chapter or appendix. Music will at best magnify meaning already believed to be present 'in' the text. Early Christian treatments of rock music were often, in effect, analyses of lyrics—and many never got any further.[11] Much writing in the burgeoning field of theology and film silently supposes that music cannot be seriously implicated as a distinctive contributor to theological meaning—words and images enjoy by far the lion's share of the attention.

Others are keen to point out that music *cannot* be assumed to fall into line with words. And that is just the problem, they say. Just because music tends to take on a life of its own, the unitary conformance model needs to be recommended, prescribed. In setting texts the aim must be to minimize as far as possible any difference between the media, to play down anything that the music might be contributing of its own that does not have an immediately recognizable and explicit counterpart in the words. The words take primacy and the music must conform, and in so doing reproduce or, better, amplify the meaning(s) of the text. This recommendation has a long and venerable history. Antonio Salieri famously entitled his one-act opera of 1786 *Prima la musica, e poi le parole*—'First the Music, and Then the Words'. The joke of the title and libretto depends on the well-established assumption that in composing an opera, music is being added to a pre-existing text, not the other way around.[12]

Plato was one of the first to enunciate a version of this model: 'rhythm and the harmony of music should conform to language, not vice versa'.[13]

[11] A student recently commented to me how many Christian or theological books on U2 were about the lyrics alone; he struggled to find something written about the band's music.

[12] See the discussion in Peter Kivy, *Antithetical Arts: On the Ancient Quarrel Between Literature and Music* (Oxford: Clarendon Press, 2009), 3–7; also Armen T. Marsoobian, 'Saying, Singing, or Semiotics: "Prima la Musica e Poi le Parole" Revisited', *Journal of Aesthetics and Art Criticism* 54, 3 (1996): 269–77.

[13] Plato, *Republic*, trans. Robin Waterfield (Oxford: Oxford University Press, 1993), 98.

A formidable formulation in modernity can be found in the writings of composer César Cui (1835–1918), who believed in a direct conforming of music to text at every possible level, both lexical (as if 'hugging the contours of language'[14]) and semantic.[15] It is noteworthy that practically every theorist of church music who has addressed music–word relations recommends unitary conformance (of music to text) as the ideal. We have already seen it at work in Calvin.[16] It is often thought to be a peculiarly Protestant phenomenon, yet it can be found extensively in other traditions.[17]

Following Peter Stacey, Cook underlines some intriguing things about this model as it has been played out. First, the pre-eminence of one medium over another can flip in the opposite direction, but in a way that leaves the basic conceptual structure of the model intact. So those who note the shift in some music theory in the nineteenth century from the primacy of words to the primacy of music will typically assume the only way of conceptualizing this is in terms of unitary conformance—either music must conform to words or the other way around.[18] Second, according to Stacey, we find a steady move (culminating in the nineteenth century) from favouring conformity at the lexical level to recommending it at the semantic level; by the early 1900s, what primarily matters about language is its meaning (not its sound, shape, and so forth).[19] This makes the flip-over of primacy from language to music in Romantic texts much easier to understand: the argument about music and language now becomes a tussle about which is more *meaningful*. But perhaps most important, third, in musical history the theory rarely lines up with the practice. Stacey writes: 'on the one hand theorists invoked textual primacy, on the other composers' natural tendency to elaboration tended to obscure it'.[20] To have media alignment operating at every level is, as Cook puts it, 'vanishingly rare'.[21] Marked discrepancies between music and texts are nearly always present, even when conformance theory is being most strongly advocated. Handel's 'God Save the King' is certainly not an example of total

---

[14] I borrow the marvellous phrase from Daniel Chua's characterization of the sixteenth-century Florentine Camerata: Daniel K. L. Chua, *Absolute Music and the Construction of Meaning* (Cambridge: Cambridge University Press, 1999), 34.

[15] For a succinct account of Cui's theory, see Richard Taruskin, 'Stravinsky's "Rejoicing Discovery": In Defense of His Notorious Text-Setting', in E. Haimo and P. Johnson (eds), *Stravinsky Retrospectives* (Lincoln, NE: University of Nebraska Press, 1987), 162–99, 162–4.

[16] See 'The Primacy of Scripture' (p. 24) in this volume.

[17] The Roman Catholic Council of Trent (1545–63) is often cited in this regard. To be fair, however, the extent to which textual intelligibility was a major or central concern of the Council of Trent is a moot issue (see Craig A. Monson, 'The Council of Trent Revisited', *Journal of the American Musicological Society* 55, 1 (Spring 2002): 1–37).

[18] Cook, *Analysing Musical Multimedia*, 108.

[19] Cook, *Analysing Musical Multimedia*, 107–8.

[20] Peter F. Stacey, 'Towards the Analysis of the Relationship of Music and Text in Contemporary Composition', *Contemporary Music Review* 5, 1 (1989): 9–27, 13.

[21] Cook, *Analysing Musical Multimedia*, 106.

conformance—because there are numerous aspects of the music that do not obviously or immediately amplify these words.

That something odd is going on here is obvious when we recall the simple fact that no one goes to the opera primarily for the words: it is regarded as a *musical* form (it will be filed under 'music' in a library). Music must be doing more than magnifying the texts. Peter Kivy points up the underlying irony nicely: 'the aesthetics of text-setting in Western art music . . . embodied two apparently incompatible precepts; that music *is* the principle [*sic*] player, *and* that the text should (temporally speaking) come *first*'.[22] (And, we might add, not only temporally speaking, but semantically speaking as well.)

It is basic to Cook's case that 'media such as music, texts, and moving pictures do not simply communicate meaning but participate actively in its construction'.[23] And this leads Cook to make an important distinction between media that are 'consistent' and media that are 'coherent'.[24] In the model of conformance, the driving logic is that of total consistency. There is to be a direct accord between the media at every level, something well-nigh impossible. But media may be coherent with each other in that they elaborate *in different ways* some 'third' reality, an underlying content, idea, scene, emotion, or whatever. So we might say that the grief of the text of the opening song of Schubert's *Winterreise* is rendered by the music, but by employing distinctly musical methods—chord patterns, harmonic tensions and resolutions, falling phrases. The music is *appropriate* to the text but appropriate *in musical ways*. To speak of media as coherent allows for this kind of differential elaboration. This is in fact very common; as Cook contends, at some level at least, the different media are not going to correspond in obvious ways.

Disturbing Incongruity: Contest

And so to the second model. Here the constituent media are regarded as incommensurate and contradictory, such that they vie for the same territory: each attempts to 'deconstruct the other, and so create space for itself'.[25] For instance, in collaborating with Henry Purcell, John Dryden confessed that 'the Numbers of Poetry and Vocal Musick, are sometimes so contrary, that in many places I have been oblig'd to cramp my Verses, and make them rugged to the Reader, that they may be harmonious to the Hearer'.[26] Another example: in a context where words are expected to be heard and understood,

---

[22] Kivy, *Antithetical Arts*, 13.   [23] Cook, *Analysing Musical Multimedia*, 261.

[24] Cook, *Analysing Musical Multimedia*, 98–101.

[25] Cook, *Analysing Musical Multimedia*, 103.

[26] John Dryden, 'Preface to *King Arthur: Or, The British Worthy*', in Vinton A. Dearing (ed.), *The Works of John Dryden*, vol. xvi (Berkeley and Los Angeles: University of California Press, 1996), 3–8, 6.

the rhythm and metre of music in a song may work against the rhythm and metre of the words. Or again, music can trawl with it connotations wholly inappropriate to the text—some will find it a major challenge to sing 'God is our strength and refuge' to the theme tune of the film *The Dambusters* (though at the lexical level, the words seem to fit the melody effortlessly).

However, overt contest can be used to positive effect: Benjamin Britten's *War Requiem* is full of examples of musical devices subverting, destabilizing the more traditional meanings and associations of the Requiem Mass texts but in the interests of what is arguably a profound rendering of those texts in relation to the horrors of war.[27] Stravinsky's *Symphony of Psalms* provides many instances of the expected, spoken accents and rhythms of words being undermined by the music (serving Stravinsky's concern to 'depersonalize' the singing of the Psalms) and of overtly celebratory words being set to monochrome, subdued, and serene sequences of chords (apparently to evoke the self-effacing disposition of humility, which Stravinsky believed to be at the heart of authentic praise).[28]

In fact, Cook argues that contest—collision and contradiction—is unavoidable at some level, given an inevitable degree of incommensurability between different media. What is frequently treated as an 'essentialized contest between media—the war between music and words—can often . . . be seen more accurately as a contest between different levels of signification'.[29] In the Dryden example, the poet is complaining about contest at the lexical level only; most would agree that, considered as a whole, the resulting music–text combination is superb. Indeed, Cook wants to urge that contradiction (at *some* level) is essential to the semantic energy and interest of successful multimedia.

Before we can understand that properly, however, we need to turn to Cook's third model.

Peaceful Difference: Complementation

Here the differences between media are recognized (unlike the ideal of consistency), but contradiction is assumed to be a hindrance.[30] The media are

---

[27] Peter Evans, *The Music of Benjamin Britten* (London: Dent, 1979), 450–67; Philip Ernst Rupprecht, *Britten's Musical Language* (Cambridge: Cambridge University Press, 2001), 187–244. In a penetrating essay, Ellen Rosand writes of the way in which madness is depicted in opera through contest between words and music: Ellen Rosand, 'Operatic Madness: A Challenge to Convention', in Steven Paul Scher (ed.), *Music and Text: Critical Inquiries* (Cambridge: Cambridge University Press, 1992), 241–87.

[28] See Robin Holloway, 'Stravinsky's Self-Concealment', *Tempo* 108 (1974): 2–10.

[29] Cook, *Analysing Musical Multimedia*, 124.

[30] Here I should acknowledge my earlier misunderstanding of Cook, as in Jeremy S. Begbie, 'Unexplored Eloquencies: Music, Religion and Culture', in Sophia Marriage and Jolyon Mitchell (eds), *Mediating Religion* (Edinburgh: T & T Clark, 2003), 93–106, 101–4. Crucially, Cook's

typically seen as operating in discrete zones or spheres. Cook distinguishes between two kinds of complementation: 'contextualizing' and 'essentializing'. In the latter case, each medium is regarded as possessing its own particular properties and exercising a distinctive role by virtue of those properties. In the contextualizing version, the media are regarded as 'occupying the same terrain' but one medium fills the gaps left by the other: as when, for example, a text has 'music-shaped' openings, gaps that lend themselves to distinctively musical phenomena. In advertisements, where time is money, it is often left to the music to do quickly what would take much longer with images or words.

Cook shows a marked distaste for essentialist complementation, with its habit of ascribing fixed and exclusive properties and capacities to things. He sniffs the kind of thinking found in some accounts of normative gender relations: conflict is avoided by each medium being assigned a clear-cut role according to characteristics presumed to be inherent and invariant. With respect to words and music this is frequently expressed in terms of denotation and connotation: words denote while music connotes. In a hymn, for example, the words are said to designate objective referents while the music evokes diffuse associations, moods, emotional attitudes. As Cook points out, things are rarely as neat as this—words, for example, can connote compellingly. Denotation and connotation 'are not attributes of one medium or another, but functions which one medium or another may fulfil in any given context'.[31] Cook is thus happier with the notion of contextualizing complementation. Even here, however, he is not content. What Cook is so keen to avoid is perhaps best illustrated by the patterns one finds on some quilts, where different colours are arranged to sit alongside each other, peacefully and harmoniously, occupying their own space. For Cook, what is missing is the dynamic of *interaction* between media, media that are understood as being inevitably *incommensurate* in at least some respects.[32]

Standing Back

As we might expect, Cook wants to avoid siding with one model over the other two. Each is inadequate on its own. In any multimedia context, the dynamics of all three will be operative to some degree: we ought to take account of 'the

---

model of complementation does not allow for the kind of interaction (and incompatibility) that he sees as present in successful multimedia. He describes *contest* as the 'paradigmatic' model of multimedia (Cook, *Analysing Musical Multimedia*, 106, 128), not complementation (as I suggested).

[31] Cook, *Analysing Musical Multimedia*, 120.

[32] He believes complementation, where it does occur, 'constantly teeters on the edge of contest': Cook, *Analysing Musical Multimedia*, 120.

relative preponderance of conformance, complementation, and contest'.[33] But although Cook would probably resist the term, a 'super-model' of sorts does seem to emerge, closely bound up with deeply held and far-reaching convictions about the way meaning is realized through music.[34] We can risk a sketch of the main elements of this wider vision.

Most basic of all, first, Cook believes *the notion of 'music alone' is vacuous*— 'Pure music . . . is an aesthetician's (and music theorist's) fiction; the real thing unites itself promiscuously with any other media that are available'[35]—even though (as Cook has no trouble showing) many of the debates about how music 'means' are governed by the assumption that music *can* and *should* be considered on its own. He is resolutely set against what he calls 'the ideology of musical autonomy',[36] and what he sees as its inbuilt ethical thrust: modernity's concern to mark out a carefully guarded zone for music, to preserve its unique voice and structural integrity, to treat socially and culturally abstracted 'absolute music' as the ideal, and so forth.[37] In fact 'music never *is* alone'.[38] It is always perceived in a multimedia context (whatever the case may be when it is composed); musical culture is always 'irreducibly multimedia in nature'.[39] Meaning is thus not an attribute of a sound structure but 'the product of an interaction between sound structure and the circumstances of its reception'.[40] Properly speaking, musical sounds have the '*potential* for the construction or negotiation of meaning in specific contexts'.[41]

---

[33] Cook, *Analysing Musical Multimedia*, 106.

[34] One reviewer comments: '*Analysing Musical Multimedia* delivers not just a well-thought-out model for the analysis of cultural works composed of a variety of sound and visual media, but something close to a "grand unified theory" of musical signification': Andrew Dell'Antonio, 'Review of Nicholas Cook, *Analysing Musical Multimedia* (Oxford: OUP, 1998)', *Notes* 56, 3 (March 2000): 676–80, 676.

[35] Cook, *Analysing Musical Multimedia*, 92.

[36] Cook, *Analysing Musical Multimedia*, p. vi.

[37] This is by no means confined to 'classical' circles: 'When music videos were first introduced, rock die-hards saw them as intruding upon the authenticity of the musical experience and the authority of the musicians': Cook, *Analysing Musical Multimedia*, 128.

[38] Cook, *Analysing Musical Multimedia*, 265. His italics.

[39] Cook, *Analysing Musical Multimedia*, 23.

[40] Cook, *Analysing Musical Multimedia*, 23.

[41] Cook, *Analysing Musical Multimedia*, 23. His italics. In an article that has become something of a classic, Simon Frith writes of popular songs: '. . . *in analysing song words we must refer to performing conventions which are used to construct our sense of both their singers and ourselves, as listeners*. It's not just what they sing, but the way they sing it that determines what a singer means to us and how we are placed, as an audience, in relationship to them. Take, as an example, the way sexual identities are defined in pop songs. All pop singers, male and female, have to express emotion. Their task is to make public performance a private revelation. Singers can do this because the voice is an apparently transparent reflection of feeling: it is the sound of the voice, not the words sung, which suggests what a singer *really* means': Simon Frith, 'Why Do Songs Have Words?', in A. L. White (ed.), *Lost in Music: Culture Style and the Musical Event* (London: Routledge & Kegan Paul, 1987), 105–28, 97–8. Italics original. This comports well with a pervasive strand in semiotics, according to which 'texts'—a term that encompasses not only literary texts but any cultural product—are not to be regarded as closed, fixed,

Cook is not slow to point out that those who have most strongly insisted 'authentic' music is that which has stripped itself of all extra-musical attachments, especially language, are those who nevertheless seem to want to write vast quantities about it. We are reminded that it was just when what was later to be called 'absolute' music was first being valorized that the programme note was being invented.[42] Words driven out through the front entrance rushed in through the back door. Roger Scruton captures this kind of irony nicely:

> I am currently reading a mercifully short book by Vladimir Jankélévitch, *Music and the Ineffable*, in which the argument is stated on the first page—namely, that since music works through melodies, rhythms and harmonies and not through concepts, it contains no messages that can be translated into words. There follows 50,000 words devoted to the messages of music—often suggestive, poetic and atmospheric words, but words nevertheless, devoted to a subject that no words can capture.[43]

Second, as we hinted earlier, Cook's objection to much theoretical writing in the field is that it overlooks the *interaction* that inevitably occurs in multimedia perception: 'multimedia is to be understood as the perceived interaction of different media'.[44] All three of the models he examines fall short on this score. None really allows for the possibility that our engagement with one medium could substantially alter our engagement with the other, and thus none can do justice to the fact that in multimedia, *fresh* meaning may be

---

immanent structures, but open fields of meaning, inseparable from the contingencies of their making and reception. Every text is produced and received in relation to already existing texts, and is thus never 'alone'. A literary text—as with a musical text—is always read within a cultural or semiotic system, and the reader is always in the business of meaning-production by relating this text to a host of other texts, themselves embedded in other sign systems. 'Intertextuality' is unavoidable. For a lucid introduction to intertextuality, especially in relation to biblical studies, see Stefan Alkier, 'Intertextuality and the Semiotics of Biblical Texts', in Richard B. Hays, Stefan Alkier, and Leroy A. Huizenga (eds), *Reading the Bible Intertextually* (Waco, TX: Baylor University Press, 2009), 3–22.

[42] See Cook, *Analysing Musical Multimedia*, 266–7. 'Although the standard historical narrative states that music emancipated itself to become a language in its own right during Romanticism, this new musical language remained, nevertheless, inseparable from the language *about* music. Romantic music aesthetics and modern musicology are predicated not only on the difference between language and music, but also on the mediation of that difference': Berthold Hoeckner, *Programming the Absolute: Nineteenth-Century German Music and the Hermeneutics of the Moment* (Princeton: Princeton University Press, 2002), 3–4. Italics original.

[43] Roger Scruton, 'Effing the Ineffable', *Big Questions Online* [website] (2010): <http://www.rogerscruton.com/articles/1-politics-and-society/51-effing-the-ineffable.html>, accessed 27 July 2011. For a more sympathetic review of Jankélévitch, see Julian Johnson, 'Review of *Music and the Ineffable* by Vladimir Jankélévitch (Princeton University Press, 2003)', *Music and Letters* 85, 4 (2004): 643–7. Martha Nussbaum asks about Gustav Mahler: 'how can he continue to assert the "aboutness" of music while denying resolutely—if intermittently (since he keeps producing programs of his symphonies)—that it has any story or subject that we can describe?': Martha C. Nussbaum, *Upheavals of Thought: The Intelligence of Emotions* (Cambridge: Cambridge University Press, 2001), 255.

[44] Cook, *Analysing Musical Multimedia*, 135.

generated. In a combination of words and music, he insists, the music will be a co-generator of meaning. In hearing an MP3 of a folk-rock song, for example, we hear the lyrics through the music and the music through the lyrics, such that our reception of the meaning(s) of each can be modified and perhaps enriched substantially. There is an interplay, a mutual inter-animation of the media: we receive, so to speak, a joint production.[45]

Third, basic to Cook's argument is that multimedia interaction is *metaphorical* in character.[46] When words and music are combined, the respective attributes of the two media intersect to create an area of overlap (by virtue of similarity at some level) such that the remaining attributes of the one can 'become available' to the other. Just as in a linguistic metaphor, a whole cluster of associated connotations of one term becomes accessible to the other, so also in the case of music and words. In hearing a song, if a person's name appears in the lyrics, and at the same time a musical phrase is played or sung that evokes certain affective connotations, those connotations will likely be attached to the person named.

For this to happen there must be some readily perceivable similarity between the two media at some level—in the case of music and words, at the lexical level of metre or rhythm perhaps ('God Save the King'). But that congruity is only the start of the process. What makes the combination interesting and effective is the ascription of attributes of one medium to the other (on another level) that this similarity makes possible. Cook can thus speak of an 'enabling similarity', a similarity that facilitates the transfer of attributes from one medium to the other, such that the perceived significance of one is in some way changed—nuanced perhaps, widened, deepened. In this way, music does not simply reproduce an existing meaning 'in' the words with which it is combined, but makes possible the perception of fresh meanings.

Fourth, because of the way Cook understands this interaction, the categories of *similarity* and *difference* are still serviceable, but not if they are presumed to mark out a sliding scale along which a given music–text combination may

---

[45] 'A verbal account cannot replace the experience of music itself, although a verbal account still affects how we hear music, and the music can, in turn, affect how we understand the verbal account': Andrew Bowie, *Music, Philosophy, and Modernity* (Cambridge: Cambridge University Press, 2007), 271. In a recent article on rap music, Kyle Adams argues that the lack of analysis of music–text relations in rap is due to the assumption that the music is simply supporting the lyrics: Kyle Adams, 'Aspects of the Music/Text Relationship in Rap', *Music Theory Online* [online journal] 14, 2 (May 2008): <http://www.mtosmt.org/issues/mto.08.14.2/mto.08.14.2. adams.html>, accessed 28 November 2011. In 1985, Robert Walser observed that in rap, 'the music is not an accompaniment to textual delivery; rather, voice and instrumental tracks are placed in a more dynamic relationship in hip hop, as the rapper *interacts* with the rest of the music': Robert Walser, 'Rhythm, Rhyme, and Rhetoric in the Music of Public Enemy', *Ethnomusicology* 39 (1995): 193–217, 204, my italics. Adams comments: 'Since the music is composed prior to the lyrics, the meaning of the text is often secondary to the way in which it *interacts* with the underlying music': Adams, 'Aspects', my italics.

[46] Cook, *Analysing Musical Multimedia*, 66–74.

be placed.[47] Both similarity and difference are needed: 'it is only by virtue of what is "commensurable" ... that signification can be drawn out of heterogeneity, and only by virtue of the "divergence" of media that there is anything for the similarity to enable'.[48] Without similarity, we *couldn't* bring words and music together; without difference, we *wouldn't* bring them together. Not surprisingly, then, for Cook contest is in fact the 'paradigmatic' model insofar as it is the incongruity between media that is central to the generation of the new 'emergent' meaning.[49] In a similar vein, Julian Johnson can write:

> ...it's the *gap* between music and language that becomes a question for the philosophy of music, not the similarity. But the similarity ensures that this gap is not characterised by non-relation; instead, it makes for a highly-charged space, which sparks across the tension between like and not-like, between the assumption of linguistic manners and the myriad ways in which they are displaced, deformed, undercut, or ignored.[50]

Fifth, Cook is adamant that what holds for the music–word relation in text-setting holds also for all words *about* music—the vast plethora of language that surrounds it, from an academic paper on Palestrina to a blog on Adele. Music is always to some extent interacting with language. When we make music, we are inescapably affected by what we have heard said or written about this or other music. When we hear music, our perception is unavoidably shaped by the language that has been intertwined with it—in album liner texts, programme notes, magazines, discussion with friends. 'We use words to say what music cannot say, to say what we *mean* by music, what music means to us. And in the end, it is largely words that determine what music *does* mean to us.'[51] We should not be duped by the common plea to 'let music speak for itself'; it never does. It is thus no surprise to find that the key debates and models surrounding the music–language relation also characterize the debates and models surrounding musico-theoretical discourse.

PRESSING QUESTIONS

Cook, then, offers a sophisticated and multifaceted argument, the heart of which is that in multimedia combinations, media such as music and language

---

[47] Cook, *Analysing Musical Multimedia*, 107.

[48] Cook, *Analysing Musical Multimedia*, 81.

[49] Cook, *Analysing Musical Multimedia*, 128.

[50] Julian Johnson, 'Between Sound and Structure: Music as Self-Critique' (unpublished paper delivered at Music and Philosophy, a study day at King's College London on 20 February 2010).

[51] Nicholas Cook, *Music: A Very Short Introduction* (Oxford: Oxford University Press, 1998), p. vii.

generate fresh meaning through metaphorical interaction, each medium bringing different capacities to bear. Undoubtedly, his work provides much-needed correctives to a large amount of thinking and writing on word–music relations, in the Church and theological circles as much as anywhere else, with wide repercussions—as we shall see. Nonetheless, some caveats are worth registering.

Cook believes the assumption of primacy governs the majority of writing on multimedia relations: that in any instance of multimedia regarded as success-ful, one medium is regarded 'as the origin of meaning',[52] and is compared to the other medium (or media) according to a scale of similarity and difference, the recommendation normally being that similarity ought to be aimed for as far as possible (unitary conformance): one medium always is (and/or should be) the servant of the other.[53] So understood, Cook considers the assumption of primacy as unwarranted and potentially damaging, especially because it makes it impossible to allow for the emergence of 'new meaning'.[54] Among other things, it obscures the interactive dynamic and attribute transfer that he is so keen to highlight as essential to the process of meaning-generation.[55]

These anxieties are set against a very wide canvas: 'how we theorize multi-media', he writes, 'is not simply a technical matter: it reflects broad cultural and even philosophical orientations'.[56] Cook's bête noire is 'expression theory', according to which language simply represents or reproduces a meaning that already exists (rather than participating in the construction of meaning), a theory he sees as originating in 'Plato's pronouncements on the correct relationship between words and music'.[57] This he links, via the work of Joanna Hodge, to 'classical aesthetics' and a cluster of associated commitments—the representation through art of a prior, stable, prelinguistic 'originary meaning'; the 'picture' theory of meaning; absolute values, and so forth. These commitments pass themselves off as universal and 'natural', but they are in fact ideologically loaded. Indeed, hegemonic models of multimedia—such as unitary conformance—are redolent with hegemonic sociopolitical arrangements.

---

[52] Cook, *Analysing Musical Multimedia*, 115.

[53] According to Cook, in *conformance*, primacy (or unitary conformance) becomes *amplification*: a meaning already present in a medium is enhanced (without any entailment of difference); in *complementation*, primacy becomes *projection*: a meaning is extended into a new domain (but without contest); in *contest*, primacy is *dominance*—one medium struggles against, resists the other: Cook, *Analysing Musical Multimedia*, 112.

[54] Cook, *Analysing Musical Multimedia*, 115.

[55] In one place, he writes of 'a largely unconscious (and certainly uncritical) assumption' in discussions of music–image relationships that they 'are to be understood in terms of hegemony or hierarchy rather than interaction': Cook, *Analysing Musical Multimedia*, 107.

[56] Cook, *Analysing Musical Multimedia*, 116.

[57] Cook, *Analysing Musical Multimedia*, 116.

Likewise, essentialist suppositions about the purported intrinsic, stable properties of different media, and the privileged position given to some media over others, can be unmasked as driven by (questionable) social and cultural interests. Cook speaks of the 'ethics of autonomy'—the morally charged investment of theorists in preserving the integrity and structural unity of this or that art form, linked to a valorization of the unique skills of the creative genius whose sole and unique authorship must be protected.[58] As we might expect by now, he favours a highly constructivist approach to language theory and meaning, in which context and contingency are always in view, and according to which there can be no meaning other than that which humans themselves generate.

While I am sympathetic to Cook's antipathy to 'representative' theories of language and meaning (especially when, in their unnuanced forms, they are regarded as being comprehensive in scope[59]), and to some forms of 'essentializing', some critical points are in order. First, concerning primacy: even Cook does not exclude the possibility of primacy *and* interaction belonging together in multimedia combinations. It is surely quite possible to hold that a text, say, should take the semantic lead, that there should be a primary or guiding concern to be faithful to the semantic constraints and direction of a given text, while at the same time believing that music can interact with that text in our perception of it so as to enable a fuller and deeper engagement with the realities with which that text deals, and in this sense to provoke or elicit new and fresh meanings. To allow this need not *necessarily* involve us in presuming a picture-theory of language, or the textual enclosure of a single determinate meaning, or the intrinsic superiority of words over music in all respects, or hegemonic power schemes. An a priori capitulation to crude versions of unitary conformance is undoubtedly a danger, but arguably no more dangerous than the a priori rejection of the possibility of a primacy operating fruitfully in an instance of media interaction.

Of course, if we were to argue for such a possibility, we would need to show why we would want to recognize the primacy of this or that language use. And at a deeper level we would need to hold that some kind of stability of meaning could actually pertain to some language, that not all meaning is humanly generated—which would in turn push us towards some version of epistemological or linguistic 'realism'. All this would, of course, take us far outside Cook's philosophical comfort zone. But from a theological perspective, such

---

[58] Cook, *Analysing Musical Multimedia*, 127–8.

[59] Among the many rigorous and subtle discussions of these matters, see e.g. Anthony C. Thiselton, '"Behind" and "In Front Of" the Text', in Craig G. Bartholomew, Colin J. D. Greene, and Karl Möller (eds), *After Pentecost: Language and Biblical Interpretation* (Grand Rapids, MI: Zondervan, 2001), 97–120, esp. 102–6; Alan J. Torrance, *Persons in Communion: An Essay on Trinitarian Description and Human Participation* (Edinburgh: T & T Clark, 1996), 325–55.

moves are unavoidable, given the Christian faith's commitment to particular language forms that it regards as normative through divine engagement, and to a vision of language as integrally bound up with corporate, responsible interaction with the physical world we inhabit as our intended environment. We return to these issues in Chapter 8.

Second, I find Cook's resistance to 'essentializing' similarly overplayed, too enmeshed in the postmodern captivation with the instability of meaning(s). With respect to the complementation model, he is surely right to question 'separate spheres' thinking. Oversimple assertions such as 'music connotes while words denote' are surely to be avoided; music's range of functions is much wider, and the same goes for language. And there is every reason to distrust the notion that one can *first* neatly decide a medium's distinctive properties or capacities and *then* consider what happens when these are brought into play with other media. Media are constantly in interaction with each other and entangled in a wealth of variable contingencies.

Having conceded all this, however, it remains the case that distinct media can be considered with respect to features that do seem to mark them out *as* both similar and distinct in the majority of contexts. Many would claim that there are some strikingly pervasive similarities and differences between music and language, evident across a wide variety of settings. So on the one hand, while we may eschew the suggestion that music is a subset of spoken and written language, or a sort of verbal language in disguise, a substantial quantity of research indicates striking resemblances between the two media, especially with respect to structural characteristics (syntax and logic, for example) and processing mechanisms.[60] There are good grounds for speaking of at least some kind of analogous relation between the two, for saying that music displays features that can usefully be described as linguistic, and vice versa. And on the other hand, there is plenty to support the belief that language can perform some functions denied (or at least virtually denied) to music, and vice versa—in practically any context. It would appear that music does generally have connotative powers of an order lacking in language, and that its capacities for accurate and stable denotation are massively limited compared to those of language. Music's ability to combine simultaneously sounding tones (see 'Trinitarian Soundings' (pp. 169–70) in this volume.) is not one possessed by language.[61] For another example, we could turn to John Butt's fascinating

---

[60] See e.g. Fred Lerdahl and Ray Jackendoff, *A Generative Theory of Tonal Music* (Cambridge, MA: MIT Press, 1996); Patel, *Music, Language, and the Brain*; Aniruddh D. Patel, 'Music and the Brain: Three Links to Language', in Susan Hallam, Ian Cross, and Michael H. Thaut (eds), *The Oxford Handbook of Music Psychology* (Oxford: Oxford University Press, 2009), 208–16.

[61] '*Language lacks the place of simultaneity* . . . it is hard to imagine the equivalent of a phenomenon such as harmony (or counterpoint or polyphony) in natural language. This plane of simultaneity is one of the factors that makes music untranslatable': Kofi Agawu, 'The Challenge of Semiotics', in Nicholas Cook and Mark Everist (eds), *Rethinking Music* (Oxford: Oxford University Press, 1999), 138–60, 145, 146. Italics are his.

observations in the course of his study of J. S. Bach and modernity. It is traditionally thought, he notes, that subjectivity and consciousness cannot be represented.

> It may well be true that it is impossible to invent verbal descriptions of inner consciousness . . . But music can not only represent a sense of consciousness—one that we can choose to map with our own—it can also demonstrate how subjectivity can be developed and altered over time.

He continues:

> Music, of all the arts, can embody a specific aspect of modern subjectivity by means of a procedure (working in musical time) rather than reproducing any particular substance, disposition or pre-existing order.[62]

I am suggesting, then, that the organization of perceptible sound patterns in music lends it particular capabilities *just as* it participates in meaning construction in a multimedia mix, and (we might note) in ways that can be highly instructive theologically. None of this need be relinquished in the pressure to recognize the constitutive role of contingency, context, interaction with other media in all musical experience, and the different roles that music can play in different situations.

With these reflections in mind, we can now explore much more fully what theology's commitment to language might entail, especially with respect to how such a commitment might engage the irreducible witness of music.

---

[62] John Butt, *Bach's Dialogue with Modernity: Perspectives on the Passions* (Cambridge: Cambridge University Press, 2010), 93.

8

Music and God-Talk (2): Interaction in Action

> . . . nothing is more destructive of theology, of our attempts appropriately to speak of God, than *glibness*.
>
> *Nicholas Lash*[1]

'O Wort, du Wort, das mir fehlt!' ('O word, thou word, that I lack!') Those who dare to think and speak of the Christian God are those who know they cannot escape the struggle of Moses in Schoenberg's drama, but who nonetheless hold that the very lack that so inflames him has, through an unbidden initiative, an unanticipated advance, already been engaged, already addressed.

It is in this context that our enquiry is to be set. In Chapter 7, we explored some of the ways in which the ancient and sometimes turbulent marriage between music and word has been construed, especially in modernity, focusing on Nicholas Cook's extended treatment, which recommends a model in which there is a perceived metaphorical interaction between different media, each medium bringing particular capacities to bear. We asked some critical questions about the wider philosophical assumptions undergirding his approach, and this inevitably drove us in a theological direction. In this chapter, we develop this theological orientation more fully. Our guiding question is: how might an engagement with music, and discourse about music, contribute to the formation of theological language, and to a more faithful, enriching, and fruitful 'inhabiting' of theological language already in use? And, wrapped up with this: how might this contribution be realized in a way that does justice to the theologian's obligation to respect both the 'primacy' of particular language uses and the distinctive character of musical practices?

---

[1] Nicholas Lash, 'Reflections on Where We Have Come From', *Modern Theology* 26, 1 (2010): 45–52, 49.

WHAT KIND OF PRIMACY?

We said a fair amount about the concept of primacy in Chapter 7, especially in relation to the commonly heard plea to give pre-eminence to words over music in musical text-setting. Traditionally, theology—indeed, all Christian 'God-talk'—has been committed to the normative priority of specific patterns of speaking and writing. It is hard to deny that modernity has too often given rise to theologies marked by narrow and superficial understandings of this priority—here the sting of Cook's critique of widespread assumptions about language needs to be felt keenly.[2] The unfortunate tendency to imagine the theologian's work as reducible to the arrangement and manipulation of propositions, alleged to depict the things of God in a direct one-to-one correspondence, would be a case in point. Accounts of Scripture's authority that pay no attention to the diversity of its language use would be another. But however disastrously articulated and practised the Church's commitment to language has often been, it remains the case that intrinsic to the integrity of Christian faith is the claim that words are employed 'to hear God (Scripture), to ponder and pass on what [is] heard (theology and preaching), and to speak back to God (praise and prayer)'.[3] And implicit here is a commitment to the normative authority of certain instantiations of speech and writing—supremely the texts of canonical Scripture. It is further held that these commitments are validated at their deepest level not by human wishful thinking but by purposive divine action.

These, of course, are weighty and densely textured claims, and notoriously liable to destructive abuse (as the story of the Church painfully demonstrates). But if we are to consider how the deployment of theological language might be enriched by music (and by discourses about music) we can hardly ignore them, and must struggle to give at least some account of their grounding, rationale, and implications. Here I will need to be selective, and the lines of argument broad and bold; in this section, my purpose is merely to angle our discussion in certain directions.

Speaking and Writing *Sola Gratia*

Amid the wide variety of views about the status of God-talk, it is tempting to presume that the crucial dividing line lies between, on the one hand, those who aspire to the ideal of a perfectly adequate speech, and on the other, those who imagine the ideal is perfect silence—in short, between those who think we

---

[2] See 'Pressing Questions' (pp. 190–1) in this volume.
[3] Alan E. Lewis, *Between Cross and Resurrection: A Theology of Holy Saturday* (Grand Rapids, MI: Eerdmans, 2001), 20.

should say as much as possible and those who believe we should say as little as possible. I suggest that the more critical line—to express it rather crudely—lies between those who believe we have been left to ourselves and those who do not.[4] Classical Christianity has audaciously held that human language has been incorporated into the dynamic of divine grace, into the drama of God's reconciling self-communication, in such a way that it becomes irreplaceably intrinsic *to* that drama.[5] In other words, engagement with the finitude and potential frailties of words is integral to the fabric of God's redemptive action among humans. This finds its climactic *locus* in the incarnate life of Jesus Christ, in whom Israel's ancient speech, and in turn our own, has been decisively assumed and regenerated. Human word-use is thus to be regarded as inextricably part of the flesh assumed by the eternal Word. Speech, no less than any other dimension of our humanity, in this particular speaking person, the Word-made-Word-user, has been reforged and reshaped, purged and renewed. Through him, crucified and risen, and through the outpouring of the Holy Spirit on the community gathered in his name, fresh patterns of communally embedded speech have been set in motion. The most basic form of speech to emerge is that of prayer and ecclesial worship, and with this, the language of the Gospel, the *euangelion*, the language that directly testifies to what God has done in Jesus the Messiah. And the most basic inscription of the Church's language forms is its canonical texts: it is pre-eminently (though not exclusively) through engaging these that the revitalization of language integral

---

[4] 'The difference between Christianity and the gnostic spirit is . . . simple and straightforward: for the latter, apophaticism means that *we* have continuously to *make up* language in which to speak of God, since all speech fails as soon as it is used; for Christianity, apophaticism means that we are *given* language that is *immune* to our manipulating, that is "sacramental" in its density': Robert E. Jenson, '"The Father, He . . ."', in Alvin F. Kimel (ed.), *Speaking the Christian God: The Holy Trinity and the Challenge of Feminism* (Grand Rapids, MI: Eerdmans, 1992), 95–109, 109.

[5] For expositions of this, see e.g. Thomas F. Torrance, *The Ground and Grammar of Theology* (Charlottesville, VA: University Press of Virginia, 1980); Thomas F. Torrance, *Transformation and Convergence in the Frame of Knowledge: Explorations in the Interrelations of Scientific and Theological Enterprise* (Belfast: Christian Journals, 1984); Alan J. Torrance, '*Auditus Fidei*: Where and How Does God Speak? Faith, Reason, and the Question of Criteria', in Paul J. Griffiths and Reinhard Hütter (eds), *Reason and the Reasons of Faith* (London: T & T Clark, 2005), 27–52; Nicholas Wolterstorff, *Divine Discourse: Philosophical Reflections on the Claim that God Speaks* (Cambridge: Cambridge University Press, 1995); Kevin J. Vanhoozer, *Is There a Meaning in This Text? The Bible, the Reader, and the Morality of Literary Knowledge* (Leicester: Apollos, 1998); Kevin J. Vanhoozer, *Remythologizing Theology: Divine Action, Passion, and Authorship* (Cambridge: Cambridge University Press, 2010); Andrew Moore, *Realism and Christian Faith: God, Grammar, and Meaning* (Cambridge: Cambridge University Press, 2003). There are important differences between these writers but their common commitment to the 'intrinsicity' of human language to God's redemptive self-manifestation is not in doubt. For a similar, if more heavily philosophical, argument, see James K. A. Smith, *Speech and Theology: Language and the Logic of Incarnation* (London: Routledge, 2002), and for a wide-ranging treatment of the notion of divine drama and our linguistic participation in it, see Kevin J. Vanhoozer, *The Drama of Doctrine: A Canonical–Linguistic Approach to Christian Theology* (Louisville, KY: Westminster John Knox Press, 2005).

to the divine regeneration of the human race is to be effected. Scripture, we may say, not only tells the drama of redemption, nor is it merely the outcome of that drama; it is also a vehicle of redeeming divine discourse—as Kevin Vanhoozer expresses it, it is not 'a textual object, but . . . a field of divine communicative action'.[6]

Christians are thus those baptized into a worshipping and missional community of speaking and writing, one that, inasmuch as it is faithful to its primary texts through the Spirit, shares by grace in the language-renewing event of Jesus Christ.

What can be said about theology in this context? Theology—the thinking and rethinking that happens 'at the turn from hearing to speaking the gospel'[7]—by its very nature entails language, but, it would seem, of a particular kind and modality: at its root, it will be a participation in the reconfiguration of language that God's communicative action has made possible. Even in the case of the most elaborate and subtle formulations of doctrine and dogma, this dynamic of 'semantic participation'[8] provides the leading momentum. Inasmuch as any theological language can be deemed truthful, such truthfulness will not be a function of the capacity of language per se to mediate this or that reality, nor of scriptural texts considered in and of themselves, nor will it be due to some epistemic or linguistic powers of humankind presumed to be immune to distortion; rather, linguistic truthfulness is to be seen as enacted first in Christ and now made available to language hearers and users as they are incorporated together into Christ by the Spirit. Put differently, our fallen linguistic capacities have been assumed into the eternal communion of the Son with the Father: it is only by sharing in *this* 'correspondence' through the Spirit that language can recover its intended resonances, its truth-bearing potential.[9]

On such an account, then, language is not primarily 'a system through which we give meaning to the world'[10] but a *gifted* medium that enables a realization of meaning intended to promote communion (fellowship) with God, each other, and the world at large: '*the design plan for language*', writes Vanhoozer, is '*to serve as the medium of covenantal relations with God, with others, with the world*'.[11]

---

[6] Kevin J. Vanhoozer, 'Scripture and Tradition', in Kevin J. Vanhoozer (ed.), *The Cambridge Companion to Postmodern Theology* (Cambridge: Cambridge University Press, 2003), 149–69, 165.

[7] 'Theology is critical and possibly innovative interpretation at the turn from hearing to speaking the gospel': Robert W. Jenson, *Systematic Theology: The Triune God*, 2 vols, vol. i (New York: Oxford University Press, 1997), 16.

[8] Alan J. Torrance, *Persons in Communion: An Essay on Trinitarian Description and Human Participation* (Edinburgh: T & T Clark, 1996), 325–71.

[9] Moore, *Realism and Christian Faith*, 144.

[10] Thomas McLaughlin's phrase; as quoted in Nicholas Cook, *Analysing Musical Multimedia* (Oxford: Clarendon Press, 1998), 116.

[11] Vanhoozer, *Is There a Meaning in this Text?*, 206. Italics original.

Imposing as these reflections may appear—and I am expressing things in very broad terms—they are arguably only spelling out the consequences of the Church's Christological and trinitarian confession of *sola gratia*: by grace alone.[12] Alan Lewis portrays it thus:

> Here are beings of language, and hence of relationship, to whom God as Logos gives himself in personal love, and whom, in their own logos—their words and their reason—he empowers to hear, understand and speak to him in response. Just because the analogy moves 'from above', because the reality of 'word' has its ground in God himself, there is a relationship with and a participation in the divine made possible by human words. Through the mysterious, self-transcending power of language men and women may burst through the limits of factual communication and reach out for genuinely personal understanding and encounter with each other and with God.[13]

Clearly, a perspective is being opened up here from which not only the nature and character of theological language but of *all* language use would need to be (re-)conceived—as Andrew Moore, among others, has cogently argued.[14] Indeed, we can endorse wholeheartedly (and now with considerably greater strength) Cook's most pointed suspicions about certain varieties of language theory. For example, we are given *theological* reasons for eschewing the kind of representative or 'picture' theories that he rightly interprets as intertwined with the ills of modernity. In such accounts it is typically presumed that the meaning of a term is that to which it refers, and that language is temporally and ontologically dependent on thought, the mental processes of an individual. With this goes the conviction 'that there are "things" [self-defining

---

[12] See George Hunsinger, 'Postliberal Theology', in Kevin J. Vanhoozer (ed.), *The Cambridge Companion to Postmodern Theology* (Cambridge: Cambridge University Press, 2003), 42–57, 50–3.

[13] Alan E. Lewis, 'Ecclesia Ex Auditu: A Reformed View of the Church as the Community of the Word of God', *Scottish Journal of Theology* 35, 1 (1982): 13–31, 16. For those tempted to set the 'personal' against the 'verbal', Karl Barth's warning is apposite: 'The personalizing of the concept of the Word of God, which we cannot avoid when we remember that Jesus Christ is the Word of God, does not mean its deverbalizing. But it (naturally) means awareness of the fact that it is person rather than thing or object even if and in so far as it is word, word of Scripture and word of preaching': Karl Barth, *Church Dogmatics*, trans. Geoffrey W. Bromiley and Thomas F. Torrance, vol. i/1 (Edinburgh: T & T Clark, 1975), 138.

[14] In this section, I am indebted to Andrew Moore's fine and unjustly neglected book; Moore, *Realism and Christian Faith*. He observes that 'Attempts to argue for the meaningfulness of Christian language before considering its redemption—its being brought back from the abyss of unmeaning—are bound to be unsatisfactory because such arguments will negate the metaphysical commitments which are required if they are to be made successfully . . . it is only the resurrection and glorification of the incarnate word that enables us to see how—in virtue of God's goodness in creation—*any* language is sustained above the abyss of unmeaning': Moore, *Realism and Christian Faith*, 155. In a similar vein, James K. A. Smith writes: 'Not only is the Incarnation the condition of possibility for speech *about God* . . . it is the condition of possibility for speaking—or at least the condition of possibility for a proper understanding of language': Smith, *Speech and Theology*, 154–5. Italics original.

referents, such as physical objects, ideas, truths, spiritual entities or whatever] to which we first *refer* by pure thought and second *express*... by attaching terms to these mental acts of referring',[15] the correspondence between thought and thing/reality being simply assumed without question.[16] And it is further supposed that a word, written or uttered, will carry an identical meaning regardless of the situation, as if it possessed a fixed semantic content that is invariably present whenever the word is employed. This kind of outlook has met with a barrage of not only philosophical but also theological critique. Here it is enough to point out that much of the latter has centred on the highly dubious anthropology that commonly underwrites it: the disengaged knowing or speaking mind, usually that of an individual, positioned as against this or that reality in spectatorial detachment. This contrasts markedly with the perspective that a focus on the concrete history of Jesus Christ will more readily encourage: a biblically mandated stress on the concrete embeddedness of humans in the world; an active, sense-mediated engagement with the environment humans inhabit as physical creatures, in the midst of flesh-and-blood communities whose patterns of living ineluctably configure the use of all language. Accordingly, language becomes more a means of 'indwelling' the world than portraying, depicting, or naming it.[17]

Finitude, Corruption, and Meaning

In this environment, there is no need to play down the commonplace that theological language (as with any language) is both limited and prone to distortion. The danger of 'glibness' that Nicholas Lash raises in our opening quote can be taken with full seriousness. Indeed, it is only the concrete momentum of God's grace in Jesus Christ that fully exposes the finitude of language and its potential corruption.

Regarding finitude: God's accommodation to our speech and writing is part of the eternal Son's assumption of our temporally and spatially conditioned humanity; the creatureliness of language is not overridden or left behind. Language is confirmed *as* creaturely and it is *as* such that it has been appropriated by, and enabled to witness truthfully to, the divine. The other side of this is that just because theological language finds its ultimate legitimation in the God whose grace is not contained or bounded by finitude, it is always to remain open to (or be opened up by) that which far exceeds its grasp, even *as*

---

[15] Torrance, *Persons in Communion*, 326.

[16] Whether terms are believed to refer to 'external' objects or 'internal' thoughts and feelings, the essential structure is the same.

[17] The metaphor of indwelling is associated especially with the work of Michael Polanyi; see Tony Clark, *Divine Revelation and Human Practice: Responsive and Imaginative Participation* (Eugene, OR: Cascade Books, 2008), 94–8.

and *when* it affords truthful mediation—its expressible content is always outstripped by virtue of God's active transcendence over space and time.

Regarding corruption: God's language-redeeming action exposes the susceptibility of all language to radical deformation. The postmodernist properly seeks to unearth the destructive drive and baleful effects of modernity's ambitions to transcend finitude, to attain a quasi-infinite grasp of reality through linguistic prowess, and especially when a particular event of speech or writing is believed to enjoy the direct imprimatur of God. The lust for mastery and control has been habitual in the Church as much as anywhere else, something to which a catalogue of social and political catastrophes in the Church's life, past and present, bears witness. The utterance 'Thus says the Lord' (or its equivalent) has likely been responsible for more human death and misery than any other.

All of this presses us to recast our understanding of the so-called 'crisis of representation' that is said to haunt late modernity: the problem of the 'objective depiction of a stable other'.[18] As commonly expounded, the central question—all too familiar to first-year students of theology or religious studies—becomes something like: how can human language, with all its contingent, social, cultural, and political interests, successfully refer to, designate, or correspond to any stable reality beyond appearances? And in the case of language about God, the problematic is ratcheted up: how can humans with their finitely embedded language possibly secure linguistic access to an infinite reality ('God') presumed to transcend all social, cultural, and political particularities?

The very form of these questions, of course, in their theological versions, easily courts idolatry—by suggesting that God is, or ought to be conceived as, some variety of 'object' that can be compared (even if only by negation) to finite objects, and, by implication, an object at our disposal.[19] By contrast, the incarnate life of Christ reveals that the central predicament in play is not finitude vs infinity, nor the inherent shortcomings of language, but a moral disruption of the Creator–creature covenant rooted in a perverse yearning to usurp and displace God. The result is a divine–human alienation that compromises the communicative capacity of all language, whether used directly of God or not. It is this that is unmasked just *as* it is being answered in the human life of Jesus Christ. He is the one true 'representer', the authentic Logos of God who assumes human *logoi* to re-present humankind to the Father. In him, the

---

[18] Thomas R. Lindlof and Bryan C. Taylor, *Qualitative Communication Research Methods* (Thousand Oaks, CA: Sage Publications, 2002), 53. Andrew Moore is especially perceptive on this theme: Moore, *Realism and Christian Faith*, ch. 6.

[19] That is, the question can often encourage, or even assume, an ontology presumed to embrace both Creator and creation, such that God becomes a quasi-perceptible object akin to this-worldly objects, and one which must answer to the demands of being accessible to veridical knowledge and 'depiction' by means of a certain kind of language. (We have already spoken of this: e.g. 'How Can God and the World Be Free Together' (pp. 144–5) in this volume).

reconstitution of our language (its structure and its concrete use) becomes integrally part of a redirecting of human desires towards the praise of God, a re-turning which incorporates, on Good Friday, a decisive immersion in, and defeat of, the worst of humanity's idolatrous drives. And this is enacted precisely in order that God may be God and not an object at our disposal. Needless to say, all this is eschatologically charged: truthful speech is indeed possible, but it awaits the eschaton to be set in its richest environment, when its frailty and vulnerability to falsehood will be no more, when its authentic *telos—koinonia* in the Spirit—will at last be fully realized.[20]

Finally, it is perhaps worth underlining the obvious: that the question of language's ability to render any reality independent of the language user is closely related to the question of whether there can be any meaning beyond that which humans themselves generate and validate.[21] To return to Cook: he certainly knows that the ontological stakes are high in the vision he commends, yet he does not seem to feel the need to question the supposition that there can be no meaning, significance, or value (let alone purpose), except insofar as it is humanly produced. The matter of the 'meaningfulness' of language, however, can not ultimately be severed from the question of—for want of a better phrase—the meaning of meaning: is human life embedded in any concrete reality that possesses intrinsic significance and worth *prior* to human constructive interests, which is 'there before us'?[22] In short: are there things that do not depend on us for their importance? Theologically, we are pressed here towards a doctrine of creation, one in which the divine giftedness of a physical world whose constitution is intrinsically part of the purposes of the Creator is not compromised, and in which humans are regarded as embodied and social creatures created to interact fruitfully with this environment—not least through language. Lash helpfully clarifies what is at stake here: 'To say that the world makes sense is', he claims,

> to say *two* things. Firstly, it is to insist, against the darker and more anarchic 'constructivisms' of modern thought, that such sense as there is to things, such plot or order or intelligibility, is not simply placed there by the impudence of our imagination but is, more deeply, given and bestowed in the very fabric of things . . . secondly, to say the world *makes* sense is also to acknowledge . . . that

---

[20] 'The full meaning of "saviour"', writes Moore, 'is instantiated in Jesus and is the resultant of the semantic meaning of the word "saviour", the teleological meaning of God's bringing his promise to fulfilment in Christ, and the narrative meaning expressed by the Gospels' testimony to him': Moore, *Realism and Christian Faith*, 164.

[21] As Roger Lundin has put it, 'one of the central dilemmas of contemporary cultural life' is 'How are we to believe in anything, if we consider truth to be something that has been *created* entirely by our desire to believe rather than something that has been *discovered* through our capacity to learn and to receive?': Roger Lundin, *Believing Again: Doubt and Faith in a Secular Age* (Grand Rapids, MI: Eerdmans, 2009), 228. Italics original.

[22] Roger Lundin, *There Before Us: Religion, Literature, and Culture from Emerson to Wendell Berry* (Grand Rapids, MI: Eerdmans, 2007).

sense and meaning have a history, that they are products and processes, and that human beings (as the world's word-bearers) contribute enormously both to the making and enrichment of sense and also to its impoverishment and destruction.[23]

Our *making* sense, then, is only possible in the midst of a world that carries its own 'sense'. Inasmuch as language use plays a part in human flourishing, in embodied, social, and fruitful living in the world, it is because it has become a vehicle through which reality's sense (non-human and human) discloses itself and becomes accessible to us, something ultimately possible only through the grace-ful action of God.[24] It has been a major thread of the chapters in this book that this applies to music as well as to language; indeed, that the possibility of music contributing to an enhanced language use, theological or otherwise, depends on its being a means whereby we fruitfully 'indwell' (albeit pre-conceptually and prelinguistically) the world in which we, as physical and social creatures, are embedded.

MUSIC IN THE COMPANY OF
THEOLOGICAL LANGUAGE

To return to the main argument: we have been contending that theology is inescapably committed to a certain form of primacy with regard to language, not through its own choosing but by virtue of the nature of God's own self-presentation. In the light of this, it would be disappointing (to say the least) if, like the Pied Piper's children, theologians were suddenly to be so entranced by music that they forgot where and who they were, and dropped all sense of responsibility to word, speech, or normative text.

That being said, problems may just as easily lurk on the other side. For many would complain that theology has too often been bedevilled by a

---

[23] Nicholas Lash, 'Ministry of the Word or Comedy and Philology', *New Blackfriars* 68, 801 (January 1987): 472–83, 477–8.

[24] George Steiner rightly and famously asserts that 'any coherent account of the capacity of human speech to communicate meaning and feeling is, in the final analysis, underwritten by the assumption of God's presence': George Steiner, *Real Presences: Is There Anything in What We Say?* (London: Faber & Faber, 1989), 3. However, as long as he operates with what amounts to an extremely slender ontology of God, coupled with a vision of artistic making as 'counter-creation', it is debatable whether he can offer a satisfactory riposte to the corrosiveness of the deconstructionist challenge (let alone a satisfactory account of human creativity). See Moore, *Realism and Christian Faith*, 148–51; Jeremy S. Begbie, *Theology, Music and Time* (Cambridge: Cambridge University Press, 2000), 235–41; Brian L. Horne, 'Art: A Trinitarian Imperative?', in Christoph Schwöbel (ed.), *Trinitarian Theology Today* (Edinburgh: T & T Clark, 1995), 80–91; Jonathan P. Case, 'The Music of the Spheres: Music and the Divine Life in George Steiner and Robert W. Jenson (Part II: Intersections)', *Crucible* [online journal] 3, 2 (September 2011): <http://www.ea.org.au/Crucible/Issues/Past-Issues/Vol-3-No-2-September-2011.aspx>, accessed 17 June 2012.

valorization of language that of necessity generates a shrunken view of—among other things—music. Can we do justice to both?

In this section, our central question can be expressed as follows: bearing in mind our findings so far, can we give an account of how an involvement with music, and discourse about music, might contribute constructively to the formation of theological language, and how it might lead to a more faithful and fruitful 'indwelling' of existing theological language—thus enabling a more profound perception of the realities theological language renders, and with that, an expansion and enriched use of its terms? And is this possible without diminishing the capacities of either music or language?

In this section, I will do no more than suggest the possible shape of such an account, drawing on the material earlier in this chapter and in Chapter 7. Our core concern is not with text-setting (as in a sacred oratorio, for example) but with what music might bring to language that is not immediately or directly associated with music. And we will have in mind *doctrinal* language in particular. On this we can take our initial cue from Kevin Vanhoozer, who describes doctrine as '*direction* for the fitting participation of individuals and communities in the drama of redemption'.[25] Doctrine provides such 'direction' in two senses. It directs our attention to the meaning and significance of the trinitarian theo-drama, and as such might be described as 'the conceptual clarification of the Christian Gospel which is set forth in Holy Scripture and confessed in the life and practices of the church'.[26] But it is also to be understood as action-oriented, set within a performative orientation: '*the purpose of doctrine is to enable one to be a competent participant—a reflective practitioner*'.[27] The ultimate aim, normed by the discourse of Scripture, is 'not simply to "picture" or conceptualize the divine drama but to *perform* it'.[28]

Language 'Alone'?

What role might music play in relation to the language of doctrine so understood? The first point worth making (here echoing Cook) is that like any medium, language never operates on its own. The formation and

[25] Vanhoozer, *The Drama of Doctrine*, 102. My italics.

[26] John Webster, *Word and Church: Essays in Christian Dogmatics* (Edinburgh: T & T Clark, 2001), 70. In fact, Webster is here speaking of 'dogmatics', but for our purposes at this point, the distinction is not crucial.

[27] Vanhoozer, *The Drama of Doctrine*, 103. Italics original. This is hardly the place for an extended discussion of the nature of doctrine, but it is perhaps worth adding that Vanhoozer's approach might be helpfully filled out and supplemented by Anthony Thiselton's treatment of dispositional accounts of belief, and the crucial importance of embodiment, time, and place: Anthony C. Thiselton, *The Hermeneutics of Doctrine* (Grand Rapids, MI: Eerdmans, 2007), chs 2–5, esp. 77–80.

[28] Vanhoozer, *The Drama of Doctrine*, 103. Italics original.

reception of theological speech and texts will always be to some extent affected and conditioned by non-verbal media. And very often music will be part of that non-verbal conditioning. In the Church's life that is most obvious in worship, where doxological and doctrinal languages are often intertwined in a context that includes music, even when the words are not directly set to music. A congregation's understanding of biblical texts—and in turn, doctrine—may well be influenced by the musical settings of these and other texts they have heard, whether in worship or not. Many will find it hard to hear Job's words 'I know that my redeemer liveth' without also hearing Handel's famous aria in *Messiah*, or some of the Psalms without also hearing the songs of U2. Of course, a non-verbal art can distort as well as disclose. But what needs questioning is the assumption that the more doctrinal language can be isolated from non-linguistic media, the more faithfully it will render theological truth. Apart from the fact that such isolation is impossible to achieve in any case, this implies a curiously narrow and mono-dimensional view of human perception and understanding. Language is no more 'alone' than music. A concern for the normative primacy of language is one thing, a quest for its quarantined purity quite another.

Unremarkable as this observation may be, and despite the massive influence of Ludwig Wittgenstein's thought on contemporary theology, with its pointed stress on the inextricability of language from 'forms of life', it remains the case that in discussions of 'interdisciplinarity', theological language is often spoken of as if it could first be treated as a quasi-self-contained entity, *to* which we then bring 'other' modes of perception and inquiry. Ironically, both those eager to recommend interdisciplinary activity and those suspicious of it can be prone to the same error (identified well by Cook): that of assuming these other modes will not have *already* had an impact on the forming and practical use of the primary language. The key question, we suggest, is not whether music (or any other medium) is able to exercise a role vis-à-vis doctrinal discourse, but rather what role it *has* played, *is* playing, and *could* or *should* play.[29]

Constructive Musical Theology

With limited space, we will focus here on the third part of that question: what role *could* or *should* music play in relation to doctrine, both to its formation and to its deeper 'indwelling' by the Church?

Picking up on our discussion of Cook, we propose a model according to which there is a perceived interaction between music and language such that

---

[29] There are some interesting parallels here with what Robin Jensen says about the relation of doctrinal statement to visual art; Robin Margaret Jensen, *Understanding Early Christian Art* (London: Routledge, 2000), 5–7.

the attributes of the former are 'made available' to the latter.[30] Here the primacy of the Church's normative texts and speech, in the sense already explained, need not be diminished or threatened: quite the opposite. Music—in, with, and through language—is capable of enabling a fuller participation in the realities which that language mediates and in which it is caught up. In the process, the distinctive capacities of music will be appropriated: in certain respects at least, music may actually be better equipped than language to allow some dimensions of the theological realities in question to disclose themselves. The perception thus generated will be more extensive than language could achieve without music, and at the same time greater than the sum of the parts—it involves more than one medium adding 'insights' or 'perspectives' to the other.

Here it is worth interjecting a remarkable passage from Augustine. Commenting on Psalm 32:8, he writes 'Sing *in jubilation*: singing well to God means, in fact, just this: singing in jubilation.' And what does that mean?

> It is to realize that words cannot communicate the song of the heart. Just so singers in the harvest, or the vineyard, or at some other arduous toil express their rapture to begin with in songs set to words; then as if bursting with a joy so full that they cannot give vent to it in set syllables, they drop actual words and break into the free melody of jubilation. The *jubilus* is a melody which conveys that the heart is in travail over something it cannot bring forth in words. And to whom does that jubilation rightly ascend, if not to God the ineffable? Truly is he ineffable whom you cannot tell forth in speech, yet we ought not to remain silent, what else can you do but jubilate? In this way the heart rejoices without words and the boundless expanse of rapture is not circumscribed by syllables. *Sing well unto him in jubilation.*[31]

Here we find a clear recognition of the limits of non-musical speech, in the face of both the need for a particular affective articulation of the heart and the need to respect the ineffability of the one in whom we take delight. In this context music can rejoice without words, the jubilus can 'say' the unsayable. Yet there is no suggestion that we are thereby suddenly absolved from responsibility to scriptural words, or from the need for clear articulation of speech to, or about, God.

Our immediate concern, however, is with doctrinal language. And here we seem to be confronted with a formidable obstacle. Doctrine, by its very nature, entails conceptual formation and clarification at its heart. Concepts, says John Webster,

---

[30] This of course may, and does, happen in the opposite direction, from language to music, but that is not our main concern here.

[31] Augustine, *St Augustine on the Psalms*, trans. Scholastica Hebgin and Felicitas Corrigan, vol. ii (Westminster, MD: Newman Press, 1961), 111–12.

have the modest task of ordering and arranging the church's thought and speech about Jesus Christ in such a way as to display its shapeliness, coherence and explanatory power. Concepts do not add to the confession, but work both from it and back towards it, starting from that which is well known in the sphere of faith and church, and returning to that sphere having undertaken their task.[32]

Music, however, does not deal in the kind of discrete, clearly bounded, and readily definable concepts that seem to be appropriate to language, and to 'ordering and arranging the church's thought and speech'. This suggests it inhabits a very different world from that of the theologian.

I recall once addressing a conference on theology and music, and being told very firmly by a respondent that my efforts were doomed to failure from the start, since music and theology were fundamentally incommensurable: one deals with the affective and connotational, the other with the conceptual. This kind of stark binary opposition crops up in many quarters. But things can hardly be this simple. Clearly, much depends on what we understand concepts to be. It is perhaps tempting to think of them as isolated mental units that are associated tightly and neatly with specific words and things (or groups of things) in the world. Words, concepts, and things-in-the-world thus become three distinct entities—concepts providing the link or bridge between word and world. However, just as representative or picture theories of language are to be eschewed, so also with parallel models of conceptualization. Kathleen Callow has proposed that instead of thinking of concepts as self-contained 'thought-capsules', we would be better understanding them as 'habitual events', habits of thought that order human experience in various configur- ations.[33] Concepts are 'thought-in-action'.[34] We do not attend thoughtfully *to* them; we attend *with* them, by means of them. So, for example, the concept evoked by the word 'vacation' is formed out of a huge variety of direct sensory experiences of holidays, as well as a complex of associations garnered from elsewhere—sun, time to read, family reunions, and so on. There may be something like a firm, central 'core' to the concept; however, the concept is not a mental picture of a tidily bounded object but pertains to the world- as-experienced—it is a socially formed, rule-governed, habitual way of organ- izing a multitude of experiences concerned with holidays. Callow writes: 'to give us the concept *dog* many experiences of dogs are overlaid on each other. Then, when we again think of, observe, or speak of dogs, our mind runs over

---

[32] Webster, *Word and Church*, 123–4.

[33] Kathleen Callow, *Man and Message: A Guide to Meaning-based Text Analysis* (Lanham, MD: Summer Institute of Linguistics and University Press of America, 1998), ch. 5.

[34] Callow, *Man and Message*, 53. Kevin Vanhoozer, to whose work I am much indebted in this part of the chapter, speaks of concepts as 'thought-acts'—parallel to the notion of 'speech- acts': Vanhoozer, *The Drama of Doctrine*, 89, and see the whole section 88–91.

the mental track already laid down. And this event is in turn absorbed into the concept, enriching its detail.'[35]

Taking this into theology: doctrinal concepts would be best considered not as mental units or images of discrete entities (though they may entail mental imaging) but as customary patterns of thinking, habits of thought that both shape and are shaped by the communal life of the Church, inseparably bound up with its manifold embodied 'forms of life'.[36] As with doctrinal language, concepts inevitably lack a certain kind of exactitude—they have 'fuzzy' edges. But this does not render them meaningless or infinitely pliable. The concept of God as 'Father' may not be amenable to hard-and-fast unambiguous definition: but it is semantically rich—potently so when oriented quite specifically towards God's self-revealing in Christ. Further, because of human sin and finitude, like doctrinal language, concepts can never achieve a final 'hold' on their primary object: 'they always stand on the threshold of breakdown, in the midst of the crisis of the fact of their own unsuitability for the task they have to perform'.[37] Further still, like doctrinal language,

> concepts and their use are to be judged appropriate if they resist the temptation to replace the primary modes of speech in which the Church's confession of Christ is expressed: homological, kerygmatic, doxological and aretological language and, above all, the prophetic and apostolic language of Scripture.[38]

To return to music: bearing all this in mind, there seems no prima facie reason to suppose that the practices of music-making and music-hearing, together with the distinctive types of cognition they involve and the language they entail and generate, cannot contribute to the formation of doctrinal concepts (as understood earlier) and to the reshaping of existing concepts, thus making its attributes 'available' to doctrinal language through the kind of interaction we have already described. Indeed, in the practical life of the Church and its worship there is every reason to believe this will be happening to some extent in any case.

---

[35] Callow, *Man and Message*, 56. Callow's account would appear to be related to what is sometimes called the 'abilities' view of concepts: that concepts are abilities characteristic of cognitive agents. See e.g. Anthony Kenny, 'Concepts, Brains, and Behaviour', *Grazer Philosophische Studien* 81, 1 (2010): 105–13. For discussion, see Eric Margolis and Stephen Laurence, 'Concepts', in Edward N. Zalta (ed.), *The Stanford Encyclopedia of Philosophy* [website] (2012): <http://plato.stanford.edu/archives/fall2012/entries/concepts/>, accessed 9 January 2013, sect. 1.2. It is worth noting that the extent to which concepts are dependent upon and tightly tied to language has been a matter of considerable debate. See Margolis and Laurence, 'Concepts', sect. 4.1.

[36] See Thiselton, *The Hermeneutics of Doctrine*, 88–91, and ch. 5 *passim*.

[37] Webster, *Word and Church*, 123.   [38] Webster, *Word and Church*, 124.

Two Examples

To flesh this out, two instances may be cited. The first we encountered earlier in the book. In Chapter 6, I addressed modernity's construction of freedom, showing that the theological discourse and conceptuality of freedom has frequently been fettered by an over-reliance on visual–spatial habits of thought, aided and abetted by certain habits of language. In effect, I was arguing that a particular feature of musical experience—the aural perception of simultaneously sounding and mutually resonating tones (something not possible in language)—can and should be 'made available' to the spatial discourse of theology. In this way, spatial language and concepts can be re-formed and massively enriched, so as to open up the possibility of a more penetrating and truthful theological apprehension of the shape and content of the freedom offered in and through the Gospel—fuller than would be possible without music, and richer than the sum of the particular capabilities of language and music. The spatial language already employed in doctrine ('above', 'immanence', etc.) takes on new depth, and fresh language is gener-ated ('resonance', 'harmony', etc.) that supplements and enhances the language already employed. The considerable errors so easily fostered by some default patterns of thought and speech are in the process exposed and corrected. None of this entails a compromising of the primacy of biblical texts—indeed, engaging music in this way enables the relevant texts to be perceived afresh, more profoundly and faithfully.

For a second example, we turn to Dietrich Bonhoeffer.[39] One of the most discussed metaphors in this Lutheran pastor's *Letters and Papers from Prison*[40] is that of musical *polyphony*. Bonhoeffer's immersion in Scripture and in the central doctrinal traditions of the Church cannot be in doubt, nor the priority he accords these texts throughout his writing. At the same time, in these letters he not only draws on music, but at many points appears to *think musically*. Conceptuality arising from music enables him to elucidate critical fields of doctrine.[41] Certainly, his lifelong experience of music (as singer, player, and

---

[39] The material that follows is a revised version of the section formerly published in Jeremy S. Begbie, *Resounding Truth: Christian Wisdom in the World of Music* (Grand Rapids, MI: Baker Books, 2007), 160–2.

[40] Dietrich Bonhoeffer, *Letters and Papers from Prison* (London: SCM Press, 1972).

[41] For discussion, see Andreas Pangritz, *Polyphonie des Lebens: Zu Dietrich Bonhoeffers, 'Theologie der Musik'* (Berlin: Alektor-Verlag, 1994); Andreas Pangritz, 'Point and Counterpoint—Resistance and Submission: Dietrich Bonhoeffer on Theology and Music in Times of War and Social Crisis', in Lyn Holness and Ralf Wüstenberg (eds), *Theology in Dialogue: The Impact of the Arts, Humanities and Science on Contemporary Religious Thought* (Grand Rapids, MI: Eerd-mans, 2002), 28–42; David J. R. S. Moseley, '"Parables" and "Polyphony": The Resonance of Music as Witness in the Theology of Karl Barth and Dietrich Bonhoeffer', in Jeremy S. Begbie and Steven R. Guthrie (eds), *Resonant Witness: Conversations Between Music and Theology* (Grand Rapids, MI: Eerdmans, 2011), 240–70.

listener) seems to have played a crucial part in preparing the way for these late theological reflections.[42] It is as if now that he is out of the political maelstrom, a major dimension of his own life, held in his memory, is given new and extra space to suffuse and sculpt his theological imagination.

Bonhoeffer coined the term 'polyphony of life' when his own sense of loneliness was at its most acute.[43] In May 1944, at a time of family reunion and celebration, and feeling intensely his separation from his fiancée, he acknowledges that his friend Eberhard Bethge (at the time a soldier in Italy, on temporary leave) has every right to want to live with, and live for, his wife and son. But there is a danger: in loving the polyphony of life our love of God might be displaced.

> God wants us to love him eternally with our whole hearts—not in such a way as to injure or weaken our earthly love, but to provide a kind of *cantus firmus* to which the other melodies of life provide their counterpoint. One of these contrapuntal themes . . . is earthly affection. Even in the Bible we have the Song of Songs; and really one can imagine no more ardent, passionate, sensual love than is portrayed there (see 7.6). It's a good thing that the book is in the Bible, in face of all those who believe that the restraint of passion is Christian.[44]

If the cantus firmus is secure we need not fear the other voices: 'Where the *cantus firmus* is clear and plain, the counterpoint can be developed to its limits.' Bonhoeffer reads the relation between the cantus firmus—love of God—and the surrounding counterpoint—earthly affection—in terms of the divine and human in Christ: 'The two are "undivided and yet distinct" . . . like Christ in his divine and human natures.' He asks: 'May not the attraction and importance of polyphony in music consist in its being a musical reflection of this Christological fact and therefore of our *vita christiana*?' A diversity of loves and desires can flourish around a firm cantus firmus, everything depending upon having the cantus firmus in place:

> I wanted to tell you to have a good, clear, *cantus firmus*; that is the only way to a full and perfect sound, when the counterpoint has a firm support and can't come adrift or get out of tune, while remaining a distinct whole in its own right. Only a polyphony of this kind can give life a wholeness and at the same time assure us that nothing calamitous can happen as long as the *cantus firmus* is kept going.[45]

---

[42] Pangritz, 'Point and Counterpoint'. John De Gruchy believes that 'it was music that provided him with most of his aesthetic categories and analogies when engaged in theological reflection': John W. De Gruchy, *Christianity, Art, and Transformation: Theological Aesthetics in the Struggle for Justice* (Cambridge: Cambridge University Press, 2001), 145.

[43] Bonhoeffer, *Letters and Papers from Prison*, 303. See De Gruchy, *Christianity, Art, and Transformation*, 158–60; David F. Ford, *Self and Salvation: Being Transformed* (Cambridge: Cambridge University Press, 1999), 253–9.

[44] Bonhoeffer, *Letters and Papers from Prison*, 303.

[45] Bonhoeffer, *Letters and Papers from Prison*, 303.

The same circle of ideas emerges in later letters. He notices how some of his fellow prisoners find it hard to harbour conflicting emotions at the same time:

> When bombers come, they are all fear; when there is something nice to eat, they are all greed; when they are disappointed, they are all despair; when they are successful, they can think of nothing else. *They miss the fullness of life* ... everything objective and subjective is dissolved for them into fragments. By contrast, *Christianity puts us into many different dimensions of life at the same time* ... life isn't pushed back into a single dimension, but is kept multi-dimensional and polyphonous.[46]

Bonhoeffer thus envisages a polyphonous kind of life for the Church in the world, a life of 'worldliness'—not the God-denying worldliness of the secularist, nor the worldliness of a certain kind of aesthete, fleeing responsibility, but 'a way of being *Christian* in the world which is *fully human, truly of the earth*'.[47] The fragments of life 'do not fly apart but find their coherence in Christ, in whom the broken themes of praise are restored'.[48]

Bonhoeffer's musical experience, specifically his aural experience of simultaneously sounding and mutually resonating tones—the phenomenon we examined in Chapter 6, but now extended in time and woven around a cantus firmus—is 'made available' to the theological conceptuality and language concerned with the multidimensionality of the Christian life. Our discernment of this reality as readers of Bonhoeffer's text is thus enriched and deepened, a discernment that goes further than language without these musical allusions could accomplish, and is greater than the sum of the capacities of language and

---

[46] Bonhoeffer, *Letters and Papers from Prison*, 310, 311. My italics.

[47] De Gruchy, *Christianity, Art, and Transformation*, 167. His italics.

[48] De Gruchy, *Christianity, Art, and Transformation*, 167. Bonhoeffer is by no means the only theologian to employ the language of polyphony in a theological context. See e.g. David S. Cunningham, *These Three are One: The Practice of Trinitarian Theology* (Oxford: Blackwell Publishing, 1998), 127–64; Thiselton, *The Hermeneutics of Doctrine*, 134–44; Juliana M. Claassens, 'Biblical Theology as Dialogue: Continuing the Conversation on Mikhail Bakhtin and Biblical Theology', *Journal of Biblical Literature* 122, 1 (Spring 2003): 127–44; Jostein Børtnes, 'The Polyphony of Bakhtin' on *Aarhus Universitet* [website] (2002): <http://www.hum.au.dk/romansk/polyfoni/Polyphonie_V/Bortnes5.pdf>, accessed 26 June 2012; Richard B. Hays, *The Moral Vision of the New Testament* (New York: HarperCollins, 2007), 187–9; Lundin, *Believing Again*, 162–71.

We should acknowledge, however, that despite the use of the polyphony model in the prison letters, in Bonhoeffer's earlier reflections on the nature of Christian community, written in the late 1930s, there is a robust recommendation of unison song as 'the essence of all congregational singing'. Here his concern is about music distracting us from the meaning of words. He sees singing in church as 'bound wholly to the Word'. The 'soaring tone of unison singing' is supported by the words sung, and hence does not need the musical support of other voices, which can only be a distraction. Bonhoeffer is scathing about singers who like the sound of their own voices, especially those who improvise different parts. Nonetheless, this is more than a matter simply of keeping music at bay: unison singing, through its 'simplicity and frugality', 'humaneness and warmth' can bring a 'joy which is peculiar to it alone': Dietrich Bonhoeffer, *Life Together*, trans. John W. Doberstein (New York: Harper & Brothers, 1954), 59–61.

music. And we are given new language and richer conceptuality in the process. We are also granted a deeper perception of the textual witness of Scripture and of classic texts of doctrine (in this case, the confession of Chalcedon concerning the divinity and humanity of Christ). It is important to underline that the key musical engagement here is with *music as heard*—even though for the imprisoned Bonhoeffer this could only have been in his memory. Music *performed* for him a Christian fullness of life, demonstrating an interweaving of lines in which none overwhelms the others and all prosper.[49]

A Glance Back at the Models

To make clearer what is entailed here, it is worth observing how useful Cook's account of the limitations of traditional models of multimedia is for illuminating the inadequacies of certain construals of interdisciplinary encounter between music and theology, and between music and doctrinal theology in particular. The model of *conformance* is patently unable to account for the kind of interaction we have been describing—for according to this model (applied in its 'unitary' form) the best music could ever do for a given doctrinal language would be to amplify or magnify what was already presumed to be wholly evident in, and transparent through, that language, ruling out any possibility of music deepening, correcting, or advancing our perception of doctrine's content and significance. The common reaction to this kind of picture, out of a keenness to give music its full sway, easily falls prey to the same unitary-conformance logic: music is enthroned as the supreme theological medium to which language must now bow the knee in every possible respect—the primacy simply switches from one medium to the other. This is why Cook's category of 'coherence' is so important, where words and music are regarded as elaborating *in different ways* a common reality.

What of the second model, *contest*? This would certainly draw attention to irreducible differences between doctrine and musical practices, but insofar as it suggests two or more media occupying entirely separate and wholly incommensurable zones, it is seriously deficient. Having said that, we also need to reckon with Cook's observation that at some level, conflict is unavoidable—to some extent, music is going to undercut and distort the modus operandi of language. This, of course, is one of the things that makes the anxious Protestant especially apprehensive—that revered texts will be rendered unintelligible through the music's inevitable distortion of speech patterns. But provided the conflict does not occur at every level, this does not have to be problematic. Much depends on what is intended or required. In musical text-settings at

---

[49] I owe this way of putting the matter to Dona McCullagh.

their best, the interaction of the incompatible elements can result in a richer perception of whatever the text is engaging or making accessible. And the same basic dynamic applies to less direct interactions between music and language. To return to the example of Bonhoeffer's appropriation of polyphony—and to make the point clearer, we will imagine this as wordless polyphony—there is a striking incompatibility between, on the one hand, the morphology of four different melodies sounding together, and on the other, the 'linear' syntax and grammar of an assertion about the many-layered, many-stranded character of the Christian life. In this respect, sounding music (even if only heard in the memory) and assertoric prose each mediate meaning in markedly different ways. Yet through their interaction, the attributes (or 'meaning-potential') of music (in particular, multiple sounds in the same heard space) are 'made available' to the prose, such that the significance, depth, and experiential power of the language are considerably deepened and extended as it is being read.

The inadequacy of thinking in terms of *complementation* (the third model) thus hardly needs spelling out. The model may help us recognize the distinctive capacities of music and language, and it allows for the different elaboration of theological truth by each. But it will undoubtedly tend to oversimplify the differences between the media, and—more seriously—will lead us to overlook the possibility of a substantial interplay between them. We have been advocating a dynamic that is interactive, pressing us towards fresh theological perception and articulation. So, for example, the musician who asks a theologian to consider aural musical spatiality and its potential impact on the use of traditional trinitarian language is inviting the theologian to consider reinterpreting and reconceiving such language, and perhaps even adding to it; the musician would be understandably irritated to find their contribution reduced to no more than an entertaining addition to the theologian's communicative or pedagogical toolkit.

It is worth adding here that what we are proposing is not limited to music: music is only one of many ways of enhancing and transforming dogmatic, conceptual expression—along with scientific practices and discourses, logic, poetry, and a myriad of other cultural forms.

Is Music Being Taken Seriously Enough?

Running through what we have said, then, is a concern to take music and musical discourse seriously in the contemporary arenas of theology. Looked at from a broad historical perspective, this is hardly a new plea. Modernity has witnessed a number of notable attempts to reinstate music's theological prestige in relation to language. However, it is perhaps worth distinguishing my own approach from at least some of the other options that have appeared and continue to appear.

We examined one of them in Chapter 5. For some of the pre-Romantics and Romantics, music's (relative) freedom from language and concepts was thought to give it huge metaphysical reach and theological promise—and there is undoubtedly a point to be taken to heart here about the irreducibility of music.[50] However, caution is needed not to overplay the potential of music in relation to the 'unspeakable'. It is common in some strands of postmodern thought to find a fierce insistence on a radical and unbridgeable incommensurability between language and world, to urge that all language and concepts inevitably do violence to the 'other' through a lust for mastery, the drive to enclose, delimit, and dominate, and—not surprisingly—that theological language is especially vulnerable to such coercive strategies. Music holds out hope here, it will be said, for of all art forms it is the least reducible to words and concepts and thus not only a paradigmatic model of what communion with God entails but a superlative vehicle of it. The fascination of some current scholarship with the quasi-theological connotations of 'ineffability' in relation to music is relevant here.[51] Accounts of this kind play hard on the distinctiveness of musical practices, their resistance to linguistic seizure. And understandably so. But by now the considerable weaknesses of this type of argument ought to be obvious. It radically overstates music's reducible, underplaying its *relative* commensurability with language (after all, the Romantics *wrote* huge amounts about music, and presumably thought they were doing something coherent and intelligible!). It also elides the inevitable intertwining of all music with language at some level. Most fundamentally, theologically, it tends to overlook the intrinsic role of language in the dynamic of God's salvific and reconciliatory action. Divine ineffability rather too easily becomes exalted a priori into a kind of abstract, methodological absolute, eliding the possibility that the inadequacy and dangers of speech about God has, so to speak, become *God's* problem long before it became ours. Rowan Williams's warning about some forms of 'negative theology' is apposite here:

> The risk of a negative theology in abstraction, the identification of the sacred with the void, is the purchase it gives to a depoliticized—or even anti-political—aesthetic, in which there is a subtle but unmistakable suggestion that social and linguistic order (as opposed to this or that questionable order) is what we need to be delivered from, and that a particular kind of artistic praxis can so deliver.[52]

---

[50] See Chapter 5 'Musical Apotheosis: Early German Romanticism' (p. 109) in this volume.

[51] See e.g. Vladimir Jankélévitch, *Music and the Ineffable*, trans. Carolyn Abbate (Princeton: Princeton University Press, 2003).

[52] Rowan Williams, *Wrestling with Angels: Conversations in Modern Theology*, ed. Mike Higton (Grand Rapids, MI: Eerdmans, 2007), 31.

There are, of course, other ways to argue for a more substantial place for music in relation to theological language. In the course of a helpful and stimulating book, Philip Stoltzfus has critiqued my writing—as well as that of Albert Blackwell and Heidi Epstein—for failing to do adequate justice to the 'performance dimension' of music-making and its implications for theology.[53] He contends that my approach to theology 'is not, in the first instance, a constructive one', by which he means that my models of musical performance 'serve to reinforce or reconceptualize the already existing, unexamined "*cantus firmus*" of "the triune God, definitively disclosed in Jesus Christ"'.[54] He asks: 'will the development of such aesthetic tools [as musical performance] lead to a constructive reassessment of theological method and reengagement with issues central to the tradition, such as the concept of God, or will it merely assist us in providing apologetic décor to previously articulated doctrinal positions?'[55] The question is well put, and I offer two responses. The first concerns the normative criteria that are presumed to shape a 'reassessment' of issues such as 'the concept of God'. If we allow music a role in such a reassessment, to what or to whom do we go to set any limits on the enterprise? I see no inherent or prima facie reason—if theology is to retain a sense of primary responsibility to the self-revealing triune God of Jesus Christ, which in turn means according some kind of normative role to Scripture—why this orientation should be relativized or radically revised by musical experience. What would give music the right to do this? The question can hardly be dodged.[56] Second, Stoltzfus's question well exemplifies the 'either/or' stipulations that can easily mar the theology and music dialogue—*either* we allow music a central and methodologically decisive role in revising the Church's doctrinal tradition, *or* music will be treated as mere gloss, 'apologetic décor'. It should be clear by now that these are not the only options. Our tendency to imagine that they are is due in large part, I suggest, to our dependence on the unitary conformance model (together with the assumption that holding to the primacy of certain texts necessarily entails unitary conformance), as well as a failure to work through the implications of an account of the Church's theological language of the sort I have tried to adumbrate.

But there is a further and rather more helpful thrust to Stoltzfus's criticism that needs addressing, for it provides an important opportunity for clarification. It concerns his plea to give due weight to performance. When we speak of

---

[53] Philip Edward Stoltzfus, *Theology as Performance: Music, Aesthetics, and God in Western Thought* (New York: T & T Clark, 2006), 14–16.

[54] Stoltzfus, *Theology as Performance*, 15.

[55] Stoltzfus, *Theology as Performance*, 16. I am presuming that the last clause is intended to represent my position.

[56] I am less convinced than Stoltzfus that we should follow Gordon Kaufman's methodological orientations (Stoltzfus, *Theology as Performance*, 10–12, 253–8), but to argue that would take us beyond what I have space for here.

the contribution of 'music' to the languages of theology, are we speaking of musical sounds as sung/played and/or heard (i.e. performed), or of discourse *about* music? At one level, of course, the question is empty. As Cook would remind us, there is no 'music alone'—it is always to some extent mediated by and with language. Nonetheless, from what I have said so far the critic could well be suspicious that in the last resort all we are recommending is the bringing together of two types of verbal language—musical and theological—along with their associated thought patterns; not two different media. William Dyrness, discussing my book *Theology, Music and Time*, writes:

> Begbie offers a helpful discussion of music as providing the conceptual tools to explore the temporal and interpenetrating dynamics of God's creation (217); it even helps us to see ourselves as shaped by this temporality. Nevertheless, on this view, music is still only a metaphor; it is a giver of insight.[57]

Dyrness wants to ask: 'Can [music] perhaps be a kind of icon, transparent to its eternal ground? Can it perhaps stop us in our tracks and make us aware of a Presence before which we may be transformed?' Dyrness's focused interest is in 'aesthetic practice' and its capacity to 'mediate God's presence'.[58]

Dyrness's questioning here is of considerable importance. At the very least, it prompts the following reflections. As stated in Chapter 1, I take it as axiomatic that music is first and foremost a matter of practices or activities—fundamentally, those of music-making and music-hearing. These possess their own singular character, overlapping with but not reducible to other practices (such as language). When we ask about the contribution of music to theology, at the most fundamental level it is these practices we are considering—music's 'performance' (which we take to involve both making and hearing music). This is the primary field to which we are aiming to do justice.[59] Further, as we have seen, these practices involve distinctive patterns of thought and language. At their worst, musical thought and language take on a life of their own, losing their roots in the physical business of plucking strings, blowing over reeds, hearing songs in a restaurant. At their best, they constantly return to musical practices so as to be shaped and reshaped accordingly. Although in *Theology, Music and Time* I was indeed concerned with the conceptual resources that music can generate, I explained there that this can only properly happen if music is allowed to 'perform possibilities' for theology.[60] All fruitful work in music and theology in the future must find

---

[57] William A. Dyrness, *Poetic Theology: God and the Poetics of Everyday Life* (Grand Rapids, MI: Eerdmans, 2011), 151.

[58] Dyrness, *Poetic Theology*, 151.

[59] Andrew Bowie writes: 'it is only in the active process of engagement with music that one can experience the open-ended challenge which it poses': Andrew Bowie, *Music, Philosophy, and Modernity* (Cambridge: Cambridge University Press, 2007), 137.

[60] Begbie, *Theology, Music and Time*, 272–3.

ways of integrating performance into its work. (It is perhaps worth adding the rather more obvious point: that music's benefits for the Church and theology range much more widely than simply generating conceptual or linguistic resources—'insight'—for the theologian!)

So, to return to Dyrness's questions: *can* music be 'transparent to its eternal ground'? *Can* music reveal the grace of the Creator directly? *Can* music without directly associated texts function as 'iconic' of the glory of God? The answer to all of these is, of course, yes. But we can hardly avoid adding: no such claims can be made with any integrity, let alone be justified, without recourse at some stage to language and concepts—indeed, at some level, to language and conceptuality regarded as normative. To judge this or that piece of music *as*, for example, 'transparent to its eternal ground' is not a language-free or concept-free activity; prior language about 'the eternal' and some related conceptual activity will of necessity be involved. Moreover, such assessments are logically dependent on assumptions about what is to count as reliable and warranted language and conceptuality concerning 'the eternal'. This is not to deny for a moment the possibility of musical performance mediating the divine; it is only to point out that contending for this possibility will immediately press us to ask what shapes and grounds such a contention. Otherwise, the claim is vulnerable to being dismissed as vacuous.

* * *

A final reflection. In Chapter 2, we commented on the way in which despite Calvin's reticence about wordless music, he pointed the way to a theological vision of the created world that can do justice *both* to the immense powers of language to engage fruitfully with the world we inhabit, *and* to a recognition that the created world possesses and makes possible forms of order not wholly transparent to the ordering power of language—such as music. This issue has cropped up many times in this book. A revered teacher of mine towards the end of his career often used to comment that if there is a central malaise of modernity it concerns the integrity of creation and our relation to it: an inadequate sense of the variegated order fashioned through God's grace within which humans have been granted a place as agents of the new creation. Although Calvin is by no means the only one who might orient us in the right direction here, I am inclined to think that if we are to understand the story of music's relation to language as part of the story of modernity, and explore the extent to which music can enrich the language of theology in the future, much will depend on how far our imaginations can encompass a unified vision of the cosmos that is able to ground the validity and viability of both the miracle of language and the no less astonishing miracle of music. In other words, I suspect that like many great teachers in their sunset years, my mentor saw—or heard—to the heart of the matter.

Bibliography

Ackerman, Diane, *A Natural History of the Senses* (London: Chapman, 1992).

Adams, Kyle, 'Aspects of the Music/Text Relationship in Rap', *Music Theory Online* [online journal] 14, 2 (May 2008): <http://www.mtosmt.org/issues/mto.08.14.2/mto.08.14.2.adams.html>, accessed 28 November 2011.

Adorno, Theodor W., 'Bach Defended Against His Devotees', in Theodor W. Adorno (ed.), *Prisms* (Cambridge, MA: Spearman, 1981), 133–46.

Adorno, Theodor W., 'On Popular Music', in John Storey (ed.), *On Record: Rock, Pop, and the Written Word* (New York: Pantheon Books, 1990), 301–14.

Agawu, Kofi, 'The Challenge of Semiotics', in Nicholas Cook and Mark Everist (eds), *Rethinking Music* (Oxford: Oxford University Press, 1999), 138–60.

Agawu, Kofi, *Music as Discourse: Semiotic Adventures in Romantic Music* (Oxford: Oxford University Press, 2009).

Alkier, Stefan, 'Intertextuality and the Semiotics of Biblical Texts', in Richard B. Hays, Stefan Alkier, and Leroy A. Huizenga (eds), *Reading the Bible Intertextually* (Waco, TX: Baylor University Press, 2009), 3–22.

Andersen, Hans C., *What the Moon Saw: And Other Tales*, trans. H. W. Dulcken (London: George Routledge and Sons, 1866).

Armitage, David, 'What's the Big Idea? Intellectual History and the Longue Durée', *History of European Ideas* 38, 4 (2012): 493–507.

Arthur, Richard, 'Space and Relativity in Newton and Leibniz', *British Journal for the Philosophy of Science* 45, 1 (1994): 219–40.

Augustine, *St Augustine on the Psalms*, trans. Scholastica Hebgin and Felicitas Corrigan, vol. ii (Westminster, MD: Newman Press, 1961).

Augustine, *Confessions*, trans. Henry Chadwick (Oxford: Oxford University Press, 1992).

Axmacher, Elke, *'Aus Liebe will mein Heyland sterben': Untersuchungen zum Wandel des Passionsverständnisses im frühen 18. Jahrhundert* (Neuhausen-Stuttgart: Hänssler-Verlag, 1984).

Bach, Johann Sebastian, *J. S. Bach's Precepts and Principles for Playing the Thorough Bass or Accompanying in Four Parts*, trans. Pamela L. Poulin (Oxford: Clarendon Press, 1994).

Bagchi, David V. N. and Steinmetz, David Curtis (eds), *The Cambridge Companion to Reformation Theology* (Cambridge: Cambridge University Press, 2004).

Bailey, Adrienne Thompson, 'Music in the Liturgies of the Reformers: Martin Luther and Jean Calvin', *Reformed Liturgy and Music* 21 (1987): 74–9.

Baker, Gordon, *'Philosophical Investigations* Section 122: Neglected Aspects', in Robert L. Arrington and Hans-Johann Glock (eds), *Wittgenstein's Philosophical Investigations: Text and Context* (London: Routledge, 1991), 35–68.

Balserak, Jon, *Divinity Compromised: A Study of Divine Accommodation in the Thought of John Calvin* (Dordrecht: Springer, 2006).

Balthasar, Hans Urs von, *The Glory of the Lord: A Theological Aesthetics*, vol. v. *The Realm of Metaphysics in the Modern Age*, trans. Oliver Davies et al. (Edinburgh: T & T Clark, 1991).

Barber, John, 'Luther and Calvin on Music and Worship', *Reformed Perspective Magazine* 8, 26 (25 June–1 July 2006): 1–16.

Barclay, John M. G., '"By the Grace of God I Am What I Am": Grace and Agency in Philo and Paul', in John M. G. Barclay and Simon J. Gathercole (eds), *Divine and Human Agency in Paul and His Cultural Environment* (London: T & T Clark, 2006), 140–58.

Barclay, John M. G., 'Introduction', in John M. G. Barclay and Simon J. Gathercole (eds), *Divine and Human Agency in Paul and His Cultural Environment* (London: T & T Clark, 2006), 1–8.

Barenboim, Daniel, 'Sound and Vision', *The Guardian* [online newspaper], Monday 25 October 2004: <http://www.guardian.co.uk/music/2004/oct/25/classicalmusi-candopera1>, accessed 28 September 2012.

Barenboim, Daniel, and Said, Edward W., *Parallels and Paradoxes: Explorations in Music and Society* (New York: Knopf Publishing Group, 2004).

Baridon, Michel, 'Le Concept de nature dans l'esthétique de Rameau', in Jérôme de la Gorce (ed.), *Jean-Philippe Rameau, Colloque international organisé par la Société Rameau, Dijon, 21–24 septembre 1983* (Paris: Champion Slatkine, 1987), 445–59.

Baron, Carol K. (ed.), *Bach's Changing World: Voices in the Community* (Rochester, NY: University of Rochester Press, 2006).

Barr, James, *Biblical Faith and Natural Theology* (Oxford: Oxford University Press, 1994).

Barry, Kevin, *Language, Music, and the Sign: A Study in Aesthetics, Poetics and Poetic Practice from Collins to Coleridge* (Cambridge: Cambridge University Press, 1987).

Bartel, Dietrich, *Musica Poetica: Musical–Rhetorical Figures in German Baroque Music* (Lincoln, NE: University of Nebraska Press, 1997).

Barth, Karl, *Church Dogmatics*, trans. Geoffrey W. Bromiley and Thomas F. Torrance, vol. iv/1 (Edinburgh: T & T Clark, 1958).

Barth, Karl, *The Epistle to the Romans* (Oxford: Oxford University Press, 1968).

Barth, Karl, *Church Dogmatics*, trans. Geoffrey W. Bromiley and Thomas F. Torrance, vol. i/1 (Edinburgh: T & T Clark, 1975).

Barthes, Roland, *Image Music Text* (London: Fontana, 1977).

Battles, Ford Lewis, 'God Was Accommodating Himself to Human Capacity', *Interpretation* 31, 1 (1977): 19–38.

Battles, Ford Lewis, *The Piety of John Calvin: An Anthology Illustrative of the Spirituality of the Reformer* (Grand Rapids, MI: Baker Books, 1978).

Bauckham, Richard, *The Theology of the Book of Revelation* (Cambridge: Cambridge University Press, 1993).

Bauckham, Richard, 'Time and Eternity', in Richard Bauckham (ed.), *God Will be All in All: The Eschatology of Jürgen Moltmann* (Edinburgh: T & T Clark, 1999), 155–226.

Bauckham, Richard, *God and the Crisis of Freedom: Biblical and Contemporary Perspectives* (Louisville, KY: Westminster John Knox Press, 2002).

Bauckham, Richard, 'Reading Scripture as a Coherent Story', in Ellen F. Davis and Richard B. Hays (eds), *The Art of Reading Scripture* (Grand Rapids, MI: Eerdmans, 2003), 38–53.

Bauckham, Richard, *Bible and Ecology: Rediscovering the Community of Creation* (London: Darton, Longman & Todd, 2010).

Bauckham, Richard, and Hart, Trevor A., Hope Against Hope: Christian Eschatology at the Turn of the Millennium (Grand Rapids, MI: Eerdmans, 1999).

Bauckham, Richard, and Hart, Trevor, 'The Shape of Time', in Marcel Sarot and David Fergusson (eds), *The Future as God's Gift: Explorations in Christian Eschatology: Explorations in Contemporary Theology* (Edinburgh: T & T Clark, 2000), 41–72.

Bauckham, Richard, and Mosser, Carl (eds), *The Gospel of John and Christian Theology* (Grand Rapids, MI: Eerdmans, 2008).

Begbie, Jeremy S., *Voicing Creation's Praise: Towards a Theology of the Arts* (Edinburgh: T & T Clark, 1991).

Begbie, Jeremy S., *Theology, Music and Time* (Cambridge: Cambridge University Press, 2000).

Begbie, Jeremy S., 'Through Music: Sound Mix', in Jeremy S. Begbie (ed.), *Beholding the Glory: Incarnation Through the Arts* (Grand Rapids, MI: Baker Books, 2000), 138–54.

Begbie, Jeremy S., 'Music, Word and Theology Today: Learning from John Calvin', in Lyn Holness and Ralf Wüstenberg (eds), *Theology in Dialogue: The Impact of the Arts, Humanities and Science on Contemporary Religious Thought* (Grand Rapids, MI: Eerdmans, 2002), 3–27.

Begbie, Jeremy S., 'Unexplored Eloquencies: Music, Religion and Culture', in Sophia Marriage and Jolyon Mitchell (eds), *Mediating Religion* (Edinburgh: T & T Clark, 2003), 93–106.

Begbie, Jeremy S., 'Theology and the Arts: Music', in David F. Ford and Rachel Muers (eds), *The Modern Theologians: An Introduction to Christian Theology Since 1918* (Oxford: Blackwell Publishing, 2005), 719–35.

Begbie, Jeremy S., 'Beauty, Sentimentality and the Arts', in Daniel J. Treier, Mark Husbands, and Roger Lundin (eds), *The Beauty of God: Theology and the Arts* (Downers Grove, IL: InterVarsity Press, 2007), 45–69.

Begbie, Jeremy S., *Resounding Truth: Christian Wisdom in the World of Music* (Grand Rapids, MI: Baker Books, 2007).

Begbie, Jeremy S., 'Created Beauty: The Witness of J. S. Bach', in Jeremy S. Begbie and Steven R. Guthrie (eds), *Resonant Witness: Conversations Between Music and Theology* (Grand Rapids, MI: Eerdmans, 2011), 83–108.

Begbie, Jeremy S., 'Pressing at the Boundaries of Modernity: A Review Essay on *Bach's Dialogue with Modernity: Perspectives on the Passions* by John Butt (CUP, 2010)', *Christian Scholar's Review* 40, 4 (Summer 2011): 453–65.

Begbie, Jeremy S., 'Openness and Specificity: A Conversation with David Brown on Theology and Classical Music', in Robert C. MacSwain and Taylor Worley (eds), *Theology, Aesthetics, and Culture: Responses to the Work of David Brown* (Oxford: Oxford University Press, 2012), 145–56.

Begbie, Jeremy S., 'Natural Theology and Music', in Russell R.e Manning (ed.), *The Oxford Handbook of Natural Theology* (Oxford: Oxford University Press, 2013), 566–80.

Begbie, Jeremy S., 'Time and Eternity: Richard Bauckham and the Fifth Evangelist', in Jonathan T. Pennington and Grant Macaskill (eds), *'In The Fullness of Time . . . ': A Festschrift for Professor Richard Bauckham* (forthcoming).

Begbie, Jeremy S., and Guthrie, Steven R. (eds), *Resonant Witness: Conversations Between Music and Theology* (Grand Rapids, MI: Eerdmans, 2011).

Beiser, Frederick C., *The Romantic Imperative: The Concept of Early German Romanticism* (Cambridge, MA: Harvard University Press, 2003).

Beller-McKenna, Daniel, *Brahms and the German Spirit* (Cambridge, MA: Harvard University Press, 2004).

Bender, Kimlyn J., 'Christ, Creation and the Drama of Redemption: "The Play's the Thing . . ."', *Scottish Journal of Theology* 62, 2 (2009): 149–74.

Bennett, Gerald, 'The Early Works', in William Glock (ed.), *Pierre Boulez: A Symposium* (London: Eulenburg Books, 1986), 41–84.

Bent, Ian, *Music Analysis in the Nineteenth Century*, 2 vols (Cambridge: Cambridge University Press, 1994).

Bent, Ian, (ed.), *Music Theory in the Age of Romanticism* (Cambridge: Cambridge University Press, 1996).

Bent, Ian, 'Plato–Beethoven: A Hermeneutics for Nineteenth-Century Music?', in Ian Bent (ed.), *Music Theory in the Age of Romanticism* (Cambridge: Cambridge University Press, 1996), 105–24.

Berger, Karol, *Bach's Cycle, Mozart's Arrow: An Essay on the Origins of Musical Modernity* (Berkeley and Los Angeles: University of California Press, 2007).

Berger, Karol, Newcomb, Anthony, and Brinkmann, Reinhold (eds), *Music and the Aesthetics of Modernity* (Cambridge, MA: Harvard University Press, 2005).

Berger, Wilhelm G., *Clasicismul de la Bach la Beethoven* (Bucarest: Editura Muzicala, 1990).

Bertram, Christopher, 'Language, Music and the Transparent Society in Rousseau's *Essai sur l'origine des langues* and the *Contrat social*', *Studies on Voltaire and the Eighteenth Century* 08 (2004): 175–82.

Bhaskar, Roy, *A Realist Theory of Science* (London: Verso, 2008).

Billings, J. Todd, *Calvin, Participation, and the Gift: The Activity of Believers in Union with Christ* (Oxford: Oxford University Press, 2007).

Blackwell, Albert L., 'The Role of Music in Schleiermacher's Writings', in Kurt-Victor Selge (ed.), *Internationaler Schleiermacher-Kongress 1984*, vol. i (Berlin: Walter de Gruyter, 1985), 439–48.

Blankenburg, Walter, 'Johann Sebastian Bach und die Aufklärung', in K. Matthaei (ed.), *Bach Gedenkschrift 1950* (Freiburg im Breisgau: Atlantis Verlag, 1950), 25–34.

Blankenburg, Walter, 'Calvin', *Die Musik in Geschichte und Gegenwart*, vol. ii (Kassel and Basel: Bärenreiter-Verlag, 1952), 653–66.

Blankenburg, Walter, 'Church Music in Reformed Europe', in Friedrich Blume (ed.), *Protestant Church Music: A History* (New York: W. W. Norton & Co., 1974), 509–90.

Blume, Friedrich, 'Outlines of A New Picture of Bach', *Music and Letters* 44 (1963): 214–27.

Blumenberg, Hans, *The Legitimacy of the Modern Age* (Cambridge, MA: MIT Press, 1983).

Blundell, Valda, Shepherd, John, and Taylor, Ian R. (eds), *Relocating Cultural Studies: Developments in Theory and Research* (London: Routledge, 1993).

Boersma, Hans, *Heavenly Participation: The Weaving of a Sacramental Tapestry* (Grand Rapids, MI: Eerdmans, 2010).

Bohlman, Philip V., 'Ontologies of Music', in Nicholas Cook and Mark Everist (eds), *Rethinking Music* (Oxford: Oxford University Press, 1999), 17–34.

Bohlman, Philip V., 'Herder's Nineteenth Century', *Nineteenth-Century Music Review* 7, 1 (2010): 3–21.

Bonds, Mark Evan, *Music as Thought: Listening to the Symphony in the Age of Beethoven* (Princeton: Princeton University Press, 2006).

Bonds, Mark Evan, 'The Spatial Representation of Musical Form', *Journal of Musicology* 27, 3 (2010): 265–303.

Bonhoeffer, Dietrich, *Life Together*, trans. John W. Doberstein (New York: Harper & Brothers, 1954).

Bonhoeffer, Dietrich, *Letters and Papers from Prison* (London: SCM Press, 1972).

Bonhoeffer, Dietrich, *My Soul Finds Rest: Reflections on the Psalms*, ed. and trans. Edwin Hanton Robertson (Grand Rapids, MI: Zondervan, 2002).

Børtnes, Jostein, 'The Polyphony of Bakhtin' on *Aarhus Universitet* [website] (2002): <http://www.hum.au.dk/romansk/polyfoni/Polyphonie_V/Bortnes5.pdf>, accessed 26 June 2012.

Bouma-Prediger, Steven and Walsh, Brian J., *Beyond Homelessness: Christian Faith in a Culture of Displacement* (Grand Rapids, MI: Eerdmans, 2008).

Bower, Calvin M., 'The Transmission of Ancient Music Theory into the Middle Ages', in Thomas Christensen (ed.), *The Cambridge History of Western Music Theory* (Cambridge: Cambridge University Press, 2002), 136–67.

Bower, Calvin M., 'Boethius' on *Grove Music Online* [website]: <http://www.oxfordmusiconline.com>, accessed 4 July 2012.

Bowie, Andrew, *Aesthetics and Subjectivity from Kant to Nietzsche* (Manchester: Manchester University Press, 1990).

Bowie, Andrew, 'Music and the Rise of Aesthetics', in Jim Samson (ed.), *The Cambridge History of Nineteenth-Century Music* (Cambridge: Cambridge University Press, 2002), 29–54.

Bowie, Andrew, 'What Comes After Art?', in John J. Joughin and Simon Malpas (eds), *The New Aestheticism* (Manchester: Manchester University Press, 2003), 68–82.

Bowie, Andrew, 'Romantic Philosophy and Religion', in Nicholas Saul (ed.), *The Cambridge Companion to German Romanticism* (Cambridge: Cambridge University Press, 2006), 175–90.

Bowie, Andrew, 'Romanticism and Music', in Nicholas Saul (ed.), *The Cambridge Companion to German Romanticism* (Cambridge: Cambridge University Press, 2006), 243–55.

Bowie, Andrew, *Music, Philosophy, and Modernity* (Cambridge: Cambridge University Press, 2007).

Bowie, Andrew, *Philosophical Variations: Music as 'Philosophical Language'* (Malmö, Sweden: NSU Press, 2010).

Bowie, Andrew and Tadday, Ulrich, *Musikphilosophie* (Munich: Edition Text + Kritik, 2007).

Bowman, Wayne D., *Philosophical Perspectives on Music* (New York: Oxford University Press, 1998).

Boyd, Malcolm, *Bach* (Oxford: Oxford University Press, 2000).

Brague, Rémi, *The Wisdom of the World: The Human Experience of the Universe in Western Thought*, trans. Teresa Lavender Fagan (Chicago: University of Chicago Press, 2003).

Braider, Christopher, *Refiguring the Real: Picture and Modernity in Word and Image, 1400–1700* (Princeton: Princeton University Press, 1993).

Briggs, Richard, *Words in Action: Speech Act Theory and Biblical Interpretation* (Edinburgh: T & T Clark, 2001).

Brillenburg Wurth, Kiene, *Musically Sublime: Indeterminacy, Infinity, Irresolvability* (New York: Fordham University Press, 2009).

Brown, Christopher Boyd, *Singing the Gospel: Lutheran Hymns and the Success of the Reformation* (Cambridge, MA: Harvard University Press, 2005).

Brown, Christopher Boyd, 'Devotional Life in Hymns, Liturgy, Music, and Prayer', in Robert Kolb (ed.), *Lutheran Ecclesiastical Culture, 1550–1675* (Leiden: Brill, 2008), 205–58.

Brown, David, *Tradition and Imagination: Revelation and Change* (Oxford: Oxford University Press, 1999).

Brown, David, *Discipleship and Imagination: Christian Tradition and Truth* (Oxford: Oxford University Press, 2000).

Brown, David, *God and Enchantment of Place: Reclaiming Human Experience* (Oxford: Oxford University Press, 2004).

Brown, David, *God and Grace of Body: Sacrament in Ordinary* (Oxford: Oxford University Press, 2007).

Brown, David, *God and Mystery in Words: Experience through Metaphor and Drama* (Oxford: Oxford University Press, 2008).

Brown, David, *Divine Humanity: Kenosis Explored and Defended* (London: SCM Press, 2011).

Burnham, Scott, 'Theorists and "The Music Itself"', *Journal of Musicology* 15, 3 (Summer 1997): 316–29.

Burnham, Scott, 'How Music Matters: Poetic Content Revisited', in Nicholas Cook and Mark Everist (eds), *Rethinking Music* (Oxford: Oxford University Press, 1999), 193–216.

Burnham, Scott, *How Music Matters: Poetic Content Revisited* (Oxford: Oxford University Press, 2009).

Burnham, Scott, 'Review of Karol Berger, *Bach's Cycle, Mozart's Arrow: An Essay on the Origins of Musical Modernity*', *Hopkins Review* 2, 2 (2009): 303–6.

Burrell, David B., *Freedom and Creation in Three Traditions* (Notre Dame, IN: University of Notre Dame Press, 1993).

Burrell, David B., 'Can We Be Free Without a Creator?', in L. Gregory Jones, Reinhard Hütter, and C. Rosalee Velloso da Silva (eds), *God, Truth, and Witness: Engaging Stanley Hauerwas* (Grand Rapids, MI: Brazos Press, 2005), 35–52.

Buszin, W. E., 'Luther on Music', *Musical Quarterly* 32 (1946): 80–97.

Butin, Philip Walker, *Revelation, Redemption, and Response: Calvin's Trinitarian Understanding of the Divine–Human Relationship* (New York: Oxford University Press, 1994).

Butler, Melissa A., 'The Quarrel Between Rousseau and Rameau', *Studies on Voltaire and the Eighteenth Century* 08 (2004): 183–91.

Butt, John, *Bach: Mass in B Minor* (Cambridge: Cambridge University Press, 1991).

Butt, John, *Music Education and the Art of Performance in the German Baroque* (Cambridge: Cambridge University Press, 1994).

Butt, John, 'Bach's Metaphysics of Music', in John Butt (ed.), *The Cambridge Companion to Bach* (Cambridge: Cambridge University Press, 1997), 46–71.

Butt, John, (ed.), *The Cambridge Companion to Bach* (Cambridge: Cambridge University Press, 1997).

Butt, John, 'Introduction', in John Butt (ed.), *The Cambridge Companion to Bach* (Cambridge: Cambridge University Press, 1997), 1–6.

Butt, John, '"A Mind Unconscious that it is Calculating"? Bach and the Rationalist Philosophy of Leibniz and Spinoza', in John Butt (ed.), *The Cambridge Companion to Bach* (Cambridge: Cambridge University Press, 1997), 60–71.

Butt, John, 'The Seventeenth-century Musical "Work"', in Tim Carter and John Butt (eds), *The Cambridge History of Seventeenth-Century Music* (Cambridge: Cambridge University Press, 2005), 27–54.

Butt, John, 'The Universal Musician', *The Guardian* [online newspaper], Monday 12 December 2005: <http://www.guardian.co.uk/music/2005/dec/12/classicalmusic-andopera.jsbach3>, accessed 27 December 2011.

Butt, John, 'The Postmodern Mindset, Musicology and the Future of Bach Scholarship', *Understanding Bach* 1 (2006): 9–18.

Butt, John, *Bach's Dialogue with Modernity: Perspectives on the Passions* (Cambridge: Cambridge University Press, 2010).

Callow, Kathleen, *Man and Message: A Guide to Meaning-based Text Analysis* (Lanham, MD: Summer Institute of Linguistics and University Press of America, 1998).

Calvin, John, *Commentary on the Book of Psalms*, trans. James Anderson, 5 vols, vol. i (Edinburgh: The Edinburgh Printing Company, 1845).

Calvin, John, *Commentary on the Book of Psalms*, trans. James Anderson, 5 vols, vol. iii (Edinburgh: The Edinburgh Printing Company, 1847).

Calvin, John, *Commentary on the Book of Psalms*, trans. James Anderson, 5 vols, vol. iv (Edinburgh: The Edinburgh Printing Company, 1847).

Calvin, John, *Commentary on the Book of Psalms*, trans. James Anderson, 5 vols, vol. v (Edinburgh: The Edinburgh Printing Company, 1849).

Calvin, John, 'Homiliae in primum librum Samuelis Cap. XIII–XXXI: Homilia LIX', in Guilielmus Baum, Eduard Cunitz, and Eduard Reuss (eds), *Ioannis Calvini Opera Quae Supersunt Omnia*, vol. xxx (Brunswick: C. A. Schwetschke, 1886) 171–84.

Calvin, John, 'Articles Concerning the Organization of the Church and of Worship at Geneva', in J. R. S. Reid (ed.), *Calvin: Theological Treatises* (London: SCM Press, 1954), 47–55.

Calvin, John, *Institutes of the Christian Religion*, ed. John T. McNeill, trans. Ford Lewis Battles, 2 vols, vol. i (London: SCM Press, 1960).

Calvin, John, *Institutes of the Christian Religion*, ed. John T. McNeill, trans. Ford Lewis Battles, 2 vols, vol. ii (London: SCM Press, 1960).

Calvin, John, *The Epistle of Paul the Apostle to the Hebrews and the First and Second Epistles of St Peter*, trans. T. H. L. Parker (Edinburgh: Oliver and Boyd, 1963).

Calvin, John, *The Epistles of Paul The Apostle to the Galatians, Ephesians, Philippians and Colossians*, trans. T. H. L. Parker (London: Oliver and Boyd, 1965).

Calvin, John, *Institutes of the Christian Religion 1536 Edition*, trans. Ford Lewis Battles (London: Collins, 1986).

Calvin, John, 'Foreword to the Genevan Psalter', in Elsie Anne McKee (ed.), *John Calvin: Writings on Pastoral Piety* (New York: Paulist Press, 2001), 91–7.

Cameron, Euan, 'Living with Unintended Consequences', *Historically Speaking* 13, 3 (June 2012): 11–13.

Campbell, Douglas A., *The Quest for Paul's Gospel: A Suggested Strategy* (London: T & T Clark, 2005).

Campbell, Douglas A., *The Deliverance of God: A Rereading of Justification in Paul* (Grand Rapids, MI: Eerdmans, 2009).

Campbell, Edward, *Boulez, Music and Philosophy* (Cambridge: Cambridge University Press, 2010).

Canlis, J., 'Being Made Human: The Significance of Creation for Irenaeus' Doctrine of Participation', *Scottish Journal of Theology* 58, 4 (2004): 434–54.

Canlis, J., 'Calvin, Osiander and Participation in God', *International Journal of Systematic Theology* 6, 2 (2004): 169–84.

Canlis, J., *Calvin's Ladder: A Spiritual Theology of Ascent and Ascension* (Grand Rapids, MI: Eerdmans, 2010).

Caputo, John D., and Scanlon, Michael J. (eds), *Transcendence and Beyond: A Postmodern Inquiry* (Bloomington, IN: Indiana University Press, 2007).

Carter, Chandler, 'The Rake's Progress and Stravinsky's Return: The Composer's Evolving Approach to Setting Text', *Journal of the American Musicological Society* 63, 3 (2010): 553–640.

Casati, Robert, and Dokic, Jerome, *La Philosophie du son* (Nîmes: Jacqueline Chambon, 1994).

Case, Jonathan P., 'The Music of the Spheres: Music and the Divine Life in George Steiner and Robert W. Jenson (Part II: Intersections)', *Crucible* [online journal] 3, 2 (September 2011): <http://www.ea.org.au/Crucible/Issues/Past-Issues/Vol-3-No-2-September-2011.aspx>, accessed 17 June 2012.

Chadwick, Henry, *Boethius: The Consolations of Music, Logic, Theology, and Philosophy* (Oxford: Clarendon Press, 1981).

Chafe, Eric T., *Tonal Allegory in the Vocal Music of J. S. Bach* (Berkeley and Los Angeles: University of California Press, 1991).

Chafe, Eric T., *Analyzing Bach Cantatas* (Oxford: Oxford University Press, 2000).

Chantler, Abigail, *E. T. A. Hoffmann's Musical Aesthetics* (Aldershot: Ashgate, 2006).

Childs, Brevard S., 'Speech-Act Theory and Biblical Interpretation', *Scottish Journal of Theology* 58, 4 (2005): 375–92.

Christensen, Thomas, 'Eighteenth-Century Science and the "Corps Sonore": The Scientific Background to Rameau's "Principle of Harmony"', *Journal of Music Theory* 31, 1 (1987): 23–50.

Christensen, Thomas, *Rameau and Musical Thought in the Enlightenment* (Cambridge: Cambridge University Press, 1993).

Chua, Daniel K. L., *Absolute Music and the Construction of Meaning* (Cambridge: Cambridge University Press, 1999).

Chua, Daniel K. L., 'Introduction', in Suzannah Clark and Alexander Rehding (eds), *Music Theory and Natural Order from the Renaissance to the Early Twentieth Century* (Cambridge: Cambridge University Press, 2001), 1–13.

Chua, Daniel K. L., 'Vincenzo Galilei, Modernity and the Division of Nature', in Suzannah Clark and Alexander Rehding (eds), *Music Theory and the Natural Order from the Renaissance to the Early Twentieth Century* (Cambridge: Cambridge University Press, 2001), 17–29.

Chua, Daniel K. L., 'Music as the Mouthpiece of Theology', in Jeremy S. Begbie and Steven R. Guthrie (eds), *Resonant Witness: Conversations Between Music and Theology* (Grand Rapids, MI: Eerdmans, 2011), 137–61.

Chung, Sung Wook, *Alister E. McGrath and Evangelical Theology: A Dynamic Engagement* (Grand Rapids, MI: Baker Academic, 2003).

Claassens, Juliana M., 'Biblical Theology as Dialogue: Continuing the Conversation on Mikhail Bakhtin and Biblical Theology', *Journal of Biblical Literature* 122, 1 (Spring 2003): 127–44.

Clark, Stuart, *Vanities of the Eye: Vision in Early Modern European Culture* (Oxford: Oxford University Press, 2007).

Clark, Suzannah, and Rehding, Alexander, *Music Theory and Natural Order from the Renaissance to the Early Twentieth Century* (Cambridge: Cambridge University Press, 2001).

Clark, Tony, *Divine Revelation and Human Practice: Responsive and Imaginative Participation* (Eugene, OR: Cascade Books, 2008).

Clayton, Martin, 'What Is Entrainment? Definition and Applications in Musical Research', *Empirical Musicology Review* 7, 1–2 (2012): 49–56.

Clayton, Martin, Middleton, Richard, and Herbert, Trevor (eds), *The Cultural Study of Music: A Critical Introduction*, 2nd edn. (London: Routledge, 2012).

Clive, H. P., 'The Calvinist Attitude to Music', *Bibliothèque d'humanisme et Renaissance* 19 (1957): 80–102.

Clouser, Roy A., *The Myth of Religious Neutrality: An Essay on the Hidden Role of Religious Belief in Theories*, rev. edn. (Notre Dame, IN: University of Notre Dame Press, 2005).

Coakley, Sarah, 'Feminism', in Philip L. Quinn and Charles Taliaferro (eds), *A Companion to Philosophy of Religion* (Oxford: Blackwell, 1997), 601–6.

Coakley, Sarah, 'Kenosis: Theological Meanings and Gender Connotations', in John C. Polkinghorne (ed.), *The Work of Love: Creation as Kenosis* (Grand Rapids, MI: Eerdmans, 2001), 192–210.

Coakley, Sarah, 'What Does Chalcedon Solve and What Does it Not? Some Reflections on the Status and Meaning of the Chalcedonian "Definition"', in Stephen T. Davis, Gerald O'Collins, and Daniel Kendall (eds), *The Incarnation: An Interdisciplinary Symposium on the Incarnation of the Son of God* (Oxford: Oxford University Press, 2002), 143–63.

Coakley, Sarah, 'Does Kenosis Rest on a Mistake? Three Kenotic Models in Patristic Exegesis', in C. Stephen Evans (ed.), *Exploring Kenotic Christology: The Self-Emptying of God* (Oxford: Oxford University Press, 2006), 246–64.

Coakley, Sarah, 'The Trinity and Gender Reconsidered', in Miroslav Volf and Michael Welker (eds), *God's Life in Trinity* (Minneapolis: Fortress Press, 2006), 133–42.

Cobb, John B., *A Christian Natural Theology: Based on the Thought of Alfred North Whitehead*, 2nd edn. (Louisville, KY: Westminster John Knox Press, 2007).

Cohen, David E., 'The "Gift of Nature": Musical "Instinct" and Musical Cognition in Rameau', in Suzannah Clark and Alexander Rehding (eds), *Music Theory and the Natural Order from the Renaissance to the Early Twentieth Century* (Cambridge: Cambridge University Press, 2001), 68–92.

Cohen, H. F., *Quantifying Music: The Science of Music at the First Stage of the Scientific Revolution, 1580–1650* (Dordrecht: D. Reidel, 1984).

Cole, Catherine J., 'From Silence to Society: The Conflicting Musical Visions of Rousseau's *Discours sur l'origine de l'inégalité and the Essai sur l'origine des langues*', *Studies on Voltaire and the Eighteenth Century* 08 (2004): 112–21.

Cook, Nicholas, *Analysing Musical Multimedia* (Oxford: Clarendon Press, 1998).

Cook, Nicholas, *Music: A Very Short Introduction* (Oxford: Oxford University Press, 1998).

Cook, Nicholas, 'Epistemologies of Music Theory', in Thomas Christensen (ed.), *The Cambridge History of Western Music Theory* (Cambridge, MA: Cambridge University Press, 2006), 78–105.

Cook, Nicholas, and Everist, Mark (eds), *Rethinking Music* (Oxford: Oxford University Press, 1999).

Corbin, Alain, *Time, Desire, and Horror: Towards a History of the Senses* (Cambridge: Polity Press, 1995).

Cox, Christoph and Warner, Daniel (eds), *Audio Culture: Readings in Modern Music* (New York: Continuum, 2004).

Cox, H. H. (ed.), *The Calov Bible of J. S. Bach* (Ann Arbor: UMI Research Press, 1985).

Crane, T., 'Intentionalism', in Brian P. McLaughlin, Ansgar Beckermann, and Sven Walter (eds), *The Oxford Handbook of Philosophy of Mind* (Oxford: Clarendon Press, 2009), 474–93.

Crisp, Oliver, 'Problems with Perichoresis', *Tyndale Bulletin* 56 (2005): 118–40.

Crisp, Oliver, *Divinity and Humanity: The Incarnation Reconsidered* (Cambridge: Cambridge University Press, 2007).

Cross, Ian, 'Music as a Communicative Medium', in Rudie Botha and Chris Knight (eds), *The Prehistory of Language* (Oxford: Oxford University Press, 2008), 77–99.

Cross, Ian, 'The Evolutionary Basis of Meaning in Music: Some Neurological and Neuroscientific Implications', in Frank Clifford Rose (ed.), *The Neurology of Music* (London: Imperial College Press, 2010), 1–15.

Cross, Ian, and Morley, Iain, 'The Evolution of Music: Theories, Definitions and the Nature of the Evidence', in Susan Hallam, Ian Cross, and Michael H. Thaut (eds), *The Oxford Handbook of Music Psychology* (Oxford: Oxford University Press, 2009), 61–81.

Cross, Ian, and Woodruff, Ghofur Eliot, 'Music as a Communicative Medium', in Rudolf Botha and Chris Knight (eds), *The Prehistory of Language* (Oxford: Oxford University Press, 2009), 77–98.

Cross, Richard, 'Duns Scotus and Suárez at the Origins of Modernity', in Wayne J. Hankey and Douglas Hedley (eds), *Deconstructing Radical Orthodoxy: Postmodern Theology, Rhetoric and Truth* (Aldershot: Ashgate, 2005), 65–80.

Cumming, Naomi, 'The Subjectivites of "Erbarme Dich"', *Music Analysis* 16, 1 (March 1997): 5–44.

Cunningham, Conor, *A Genealogy of Nihilism: Philosophies of Nothing and the Difference of Theology* (London: Routledge, 2002).

Cunningham, David S., *These Three Are One: The Practice of Trinitarian Theology* (Oxford: Blackwell Publishing, 1998).

Dadelson, G. von, *Beiträge zur Chronologie der Werke Johann Sebastian Bachs* (Trossingen: Hohner Verlag, 1958).

Dahlhaus, Carl, *The Idea of Absolute Music* (Chicago: University of Chicago Press, 1989).

Dammann, Guy, 'Review of John J. Joughin and Simon Malpas (eds), *The New Aestheticism* (Manchester: Manchester University Press, 2003)', *Journal of Applied Philosophy* 22, 2 (2005): 199–203.

Dammann, Guy, 'The Morality of Musical Imitation in Jean-Jacques Rousseau', doctrinal dissertation (King's College, 2006).

Dammann, Guy, '"Sonate, que me veux-tu?": Jean-Jacques Rousseau and the Problem of Instrumental Music', *Ad Parnassum* 3, 5 (April 2005): 57–67.

Dammann, Guy, 'Review of Andrew Bowie, *Music, Philosophy, and Modernity* (Cambridge, Cambridge University Press, 2007)', *British Journal of Aesthetics* 48, 4 (2008): 459–61.

Davenport, Anne Ashley, *Measure of a Different Greatness: The Intensive Infinite, 1250–1650* (Leiden: Brill, 1999).

Daverio, John, *Nineteenth-Century Music and the German Romantic Ideology* (New York: Schirmer Books, 1993).

David, Hans T., Mendel, Arthur, and Wolff, Christoph (eds), *The New Bach Reader: A Life of Johann Sebastian Bach in Letters and Documents* (New York: W. W. Norton & Co., 1998).

De Gruchy, John W., *Christianity, Art, and Transformation: Theological Aesthetics in the Struggle for Justice* (Cambridge: Cambridge University Press, 2001).

De Man, Paul and Godzich, Wlad, *Blindness and Insight: Essays in the Rhetoric of Contemporary Criticism* (London: Methuen, 1983).

Dearborn, Kerry, 'The Crucified Christ as the Motherly God: The Theology of Julian of Norwich', *Scottish Journal of Theology* 55, 3 (2002): 283–302.

Dell'Antonio, Andrew, 'Review of Nicholas Cook, *Analysing Musical Multimedia* (Oxford: OUP, 1998)', *Notes* 56, 3 (March 2000): 676–80.

Derrida, Jacques, *Of Grammatology*, trans. Gayatri Chakravorty Spivak (London: The John Hopkins University Press, 1997).

Deutsch, Diana, 'An Auditory Illusion', *Nature* 251 (1974): 307–9.

Deutsch, Diana, 'The Octave Illusion Revisited Again', *Journal of Experimental Psychology: Human Perception and Performance* 30, 2 (2004): 355–64.

Diderot, Denis and d'Alembert, Jean le Rond, *Encyclopédie ou Dictionnaire raisonné des sciences, des arts et des métiers (articles choisis)*, vol. xi (Stuttgart and Bad Cannstatt: Friedrich Frommann, 1988).

Dobbins, Frank, 'Bourgeois, Loys' on *Grove Music Online* [website]: <http://www.oxfordmusiconline.com>, accessed 2 July 2012.

Doede, Robert Paul, 'Polanyi on Language and the Human Way of Being Bodily Mindful in the World', *Tradition & Discovery: The Polanyi Society Periodical* 30, 1 (2003–4): 5–18.

Doede, Robert Paul, and Hughes, Paul Edward, 'Wounded Vision and the Optics of Hope', in Miroslav Volf and William H. Katerberg (eds), *The Future of Hope: Christian Tradition amid Modernity and Postmodernity* (Grand Rapids, MI: Eerdmans, 2004), 170–99.

Donelan, James H., *Poetry and the Romantic Musical Aesthetic* (Cambridge: Cambridge University Press, 2008).

Donovan, Siobhán and Elliott, Robin (eds), *Music and Literature in German Romanticism* (Rochester, NY: Camden House, 2004).

Doumergue, Émile, 'Music in the Work of Calvin', *Princeton Theological Review* 7 (1909): 529–52.

Dowey, Edward A., *The Knowledge of God in Calvin's Theology* (Grand Rapids, MI: Eerdmans, 1994).

Drake, C. and Bertrand, D., 'The Quest for Universals in Temporal Processing in Music', *Annals of the New York Academy of the Sciences* 930 (2001): 17–27.

Dreyfus, Laurence, *Bach and the Patterns of Invention* (Cambridge, MA: Harvard University Press, 1996).

Dryden, John, 'Preface to Purcell's *King Arthur*', in Montague Summers (ed.), *The Dramatic Works*, vol. vi (London: Nonesuch Press, 1931–2), 242.

Dryden, John, 'Preface to *King Arthur: Or, The British Worthy*', in Vinton A. Dearing (ed.), *The Works of John Dryden*, vol. xvi (Berkeley and Los Angeles: University of California Press, 1996), 3–8.

Düchting, Hajo, *Paul Klee: Painting Music* (Munich: Prestel, 1997).

Dugan, C. N. and Strong, Tracy, 'Music, Politics, Theatre and Representation in Rousseau', in Patrick Riley (ed.), *The Cambridge Companion to Rousseau* (Cambridge: Cambridge University Press, 2001), 329–64.

Dunning, Albert, 'Calvin, Jean' on *Grove Music Online* [website]: <http://www.oxfordmusiconline.com>, accessed 28 June 2012.

Dupré, Louis K, *Passage to Modernity: An Essay in the Hermeneutics of Nature and Culture* (New Haven: Yale University Press, 1993).

Dürr, Alfred, *Zur Chronologie der leipziger Vokalwerke J. S. Bachs* (Berlin: Evangelische Verlagsanstalt, 1958).

Dürr, Alfred, *Johann Sebastian Bach: St John Passion: Genesis, Transmission, and Meaning*, trans. Alfred Clayton (Oxford: Oxford University Press, 1988).

Dürr, Alfred, '"Ich freue mich auf meinen Tod": Sterben und Tod in Bachs Kantaten aus musikwissenschaftlicher Sicht', *Jahrbuch des Staatlichen Instituts fur Musikforschung Preussischer Kulturbesitz* (1996), 41–51.

Dürr, Alfred, *The Cantatas of J. S. Bach*, trans. Richard Jones (Oxford: Oxford University Press, 2005).

Dyer, Joseph, 'The Place of Musica in Medieval Classifications of Knowledge', *Journal of Musicology* 24, 1 (Winter 2007): 3–71.

Dyrness, William A., *Reformed Theology and Visual Culture: The Protestant Imagination from Calvin to Edwards* (Cambridge: Cambridge University Press, 2004).

Dyrness, William A., *Poetic Theology: God and the Poetics of Everyday Life* (Grand Rapids, MI: Eerdmans, 2011).

Einstein, Alfred, *Music in the Romantic Era* (New York: W. W. Norton & Co., 1947).

Eire, Carlos M. N., *War Against the Idols: The Reformation of Worship from Erasmus to Calvin* (Cambridge: Cambridge University Press, 1986).

Eldridge, Richard T., *Leading a Human Life: Wittgenstein, Intentionality, and Romanticism* (Chicago: University of Chicago Press, 1997).

Ellul, Jacques, *The Humiliation of the Word* (Grand Rapids, MI: Eerdmans, 1985).

Engel, Mary Potter, *John Calvin's Perspectival Anthropology* (Atlanta: Scholars Press, 1988).

Evans, Peter, *The Music of Benjamin Britten* (London: Dent, 1979).

Evernden, L. L. Neil, *The Social Creation of Nature* (Baltimore: Johns Hopkins University Press, 1992).

Fallows, David, 'New Musicology', in Alison Latham (ed.), *The Oxford Companion to Music* (Oxford: Oxford University Press, 2002), 834.

Fee, Gordon D., 'Exploring Kenotic Christology: The Self-Emptying of God', in C. Stephen Evans (ed.), *Exploring Kenotic Christology* (Oxford: Oxford University Press, 2006), 25–44.

Fergusson, David, 'Types of Natural Theology', in F. LeRon Shults (ed.), *The Evolution of Rationality: Interdisciplinary Essays in Honor of J. Wentzel van Huyssteen* (Grand Rapids, MI: Eerdmans, 2006), 380–93.

Fergusson, David, *Faith and Its Critics: A Conversation* (Oxford: Oxford University Press, 2009).

Feuerbach, Ludwig, *The Essence of Christianity*, trans. George Eliot (New York: Harper & Row, 1957).

Finney, Paul Corby (ed.), *Seeing Beyond the Word: Visual Arts and the Calvinist Tradition* (Grand Rapids, MI: Eerdmans, 1999).

Flatley, Jonathan, *Affective Mapping: Melancholia and the Politics of Modernism* (Cambridge, MA: Harvard University Press, 2008).

Ford, David F., *Self and Salvation: Being Transformed* (Cambridge: Cambridge University Press, 1999).

Forman, Miloš (director), Peter Shaffer (writer), Saul Zaentz (producer), *Amadeus* (Orion Pictures, 1984).

Frank, Manfred, *The Philosophical Foundations of Early German Romanticism* (Albany, NY: State University of New York Press, 2004).

Frisch, Shelley Laura, *The Lure of the Linguistic: Speculations on the Origin of Language in German Romanticism* (New York: Holmes & Meier, 2004).

Frith, Simon, 'Why Do Songs Have Words?', in A. L. White (ed.), *Lost in Music: Culture Style and the Musical Event* (London: Routledge & Kegan Paul, 1987), 105–28.

Funkenstein, Amos, *Theology and the Scientific Imagination: From the Middle Ages to the Seventeenth Century* (Princeton: Princeton University Press, 1986).

Garside, Charles, 'Calvin's Preface to the Psalter: A Re-appraisal', *Musical Quarterly* 37 (1951): 566–77.

Garside, Charles, 'The Origins of Calvin's Theology of Music: 1536–1543', *Transactions of the American Philosophical Society* 69 (1979): 4–35.

Geering, Arnold, 'Calvin und die Musik', in Jürgen Moltmann (ed.), *Calvin-Studien 1959* (Neukirchen: Neukirchener Verlag der Buchhandlung des Erziehungsvereins Neukirchen, 1960), 16–25.

Gelfand, Stanley A., *Hearing: An Introduction to Psychological and Physiological Acoustics*, 4th edn. (New York: Marcel Dekker, 2004).

Gellner, Ernest, *Reason and Culture: The Historic Role of Rationality and Rationalism* (Oxford: Blackwell Publishing, 1992).

George, Timothy (ed.), *John Calvin and the Church: A Prism of Reform* (Louisville, KY: Westminster John Knox Press, 1990).

Gerrish, B. A., *Grace and Gratitude: The Eucharistic Theology of John Calvin* (Minneapolis: Fortress Press, 1993).

Gibson, J. J., *The Perception of the Visual World* (Boston: Houghton Mifflin, 1950).

Gilbert, Shirli, *Music in the Holocaust: Confronting Life in the Nazi Ghettos and Camps* (Oxford: Clarendon Press, 2005).

Gillespie, Michael Allen, *The Theological Origins of Modernity* (Chicago: University of Chicago Press, 2008).

Girdlestone, Cuthbert, *Jean-Philippe Rameau: His Life and Work* (New York: Dover Publications, 1969).

Goehr, Lydia, 'Normativity Without Norms: Review Article of Andrew Bowie, *Music, Philosophy, and Modernity* (Cambridge, Cambridge University Press, 2007)', *European Journal of Philosophy* 17, 4 (December 2009): 597–607.

Goeser, Robert, 'Luther: Word of God, Language, and Art', *Currents in Theology and Mission* 18 (1991): 6–11.

Goldman, Jonathan, *The Musical Language of Pierre Boulez: Writings and Compositions* (Cambridge: Cambridge University Press, 2011).

Gorham, Geoffrey, 'Early Scientific Images of God: Descartes, Hobbes, and Newton', in Charles Taliaferro and Jil Evans (eds), *Turning Images in Philosophy, Science, and Religion: A New Book of Nature* (Oxford: Oxford University Press, 2011), 25–45.

Gorringe, Timothy J., *The Education of Desire: Towards a Theology of the Senses* (London: SCM Press, 2001).

Gossman, Lionel, 'Time and History in Rousseau', *Studies on Voltaire and the Eighteenth Century* 30 (1964): 311–49.

Gouk, Penelope, 'The Role of Harmonics in the Scientific Revolution', in Thomas Christensen (ed.), *The Cambridge History of Western Music Theory* (Cambridge: Cambridge University Press, 2002), 223–45.

Gourevitch, Victor, 'The Religious Thought', in Patrick Riley (ed.), *The Cambridge Companion to Rousseau* (Cambridge: Cambridge University Press, 2001), 193–246.

Gregory, Brad S., *The Unintended Reformation: How a Religious Revolution Secularized Society* (Cambridge, MA: Belknap Press of Harvard University Press, 2012).

Grewe, Cordula A., *Historicism and the Sacred Imaginary: Painting Religion in the Age of Romaniticism* (Aldershot: Ashgate, 2008).

Griffiths, Paul J., 'How Reasoning Goes Wrong: A Quasi-Augustinian Account of Error and Its Implications', in Paul J. Griffiths and Reinhard Hütter (eds), *Reason and the Reasons of Faith* (London: T & T Clark, 2005), 27–52.

Grimsley, Ronald, *Rousseau and the Religious Quest* (Oxford: Clarendon Press, 1968).

Grindal, Gracia, 'Luther and the Arts: A Study in Convention', *Word and World* 3 (1983): 373–81.

Gunton, Colin E., 'Transcendence, Metaphor and the Knowability of God', *Journal of Theological Studies* 31, 2 (1980): 501–16.

Gunton, Colin E., *Yesterday and Today: A Study of Continuities in Christology* (London: Darton, Longman & Todd, 1983).

Gunton, Colin E., 'The Human Creation: Towards a Renewal of the Doctrine of the *Imago Dei*', in Colin E. Gunton (ed.), *The Promise of Trinitarian Theology* (Edinburgh: T & T Clark, 1993), 104–21.

Gunton, Colin E., *The One, the Three, and the Many: God, Creation, and the Culture of Modernity* (Cambridge: Cambridge University Press, 1993).

Gunton, Colin E., *A Brief Theology of Revelation: The 1993 Warfield Lectures* (Edinburgh: T & T Clark, 1995).

Gunton, Colin E., (ed.), *God and Freedom: Essays in Historical and Systematic Theology* (Edinburgh: T & T Clark, 1995).

Gunton, Colin E., *The Triune Creator: A Historical and Systematic Study* (Edinburgh: Edinburgh University Press, 1998).

Gunton, Colin E., 'Election and Ecclesiology in the Post-Constantinian Church', *Scottish Journal of Theology* 53, 2 (2000): 212–27.

Gunton, Colin E., *Act and Being* (London: SCM Press, 2002).

Habets, Myk, 'Putting the "Extra" Back into Calvinism', *Scottish Journal of Theology* 62, 4 (November 2009): 441–56.

Habets, Myk, *Theosis in the Theology of Thomas Torrance* (Farnham: Ashgate, 2009).

Habgood, John S., *The Concept of Nature* (London: Darton, Longman & Todd, 2002).

Hallam, Susan, Cross, Ian, and Thaut, Michael H. (eds), *The Oxford Handbook of Music Psychology* (Oxford: Oxford University Press, 2009).

Halliwell, Stephen, *The Aesthetics of Mimesis: Ancient Texts and Modern Problems* (Princeton: Princeton University Press, 2002).

Halter, Carl and Schalk, Carl, *A Handbook of Church Music* (St Louis: Concordia Publishing, 1978).

Hamilton, Andy, *Aesthetics and Music* (London: Continuum, 2007).

Hamilton, Andy, 'The Sound of Music', in Matthew Nudds and Casey O'Callaghan (eds), *Sounds and Perception: New Philosophical Essays* (Oxford: Oxford University Press, 2009), 146–82.

Hansen, Collin, *Young, Restless, Reformed: A Journalist's Journey with the New Calvinists* (Wheaton, IL: Crossway Books, 2008).

Harper-Scott, J. P. E., *Edward Elgar, Modernist* (Cambridge: Cambridge University Press, 2006).

Hárran, Don, *Word–Tone Relations in Musical Thought: From Antiquity to the Seventeenth Century* (Neuhausen-Stuttgart: American Institute of Musicology, 1986).

Hárran, Don, 'Text Underlay' on *Grove Music Online* [website]: <http://www.oxfordmusiconline.com>, accessed 28 June 2012.

Hart, David Bentley, *The Beauty of the Infinite: The Aesthetics of Christian Truth* (Grand Rapids, MI: Eerdmans, 2003).

Hart, David Bentley, 'Freedom and Decency', in Thomas F. Torrance (ed.), *In the Aftermath: Provocations and Laments* (Grand Rapids, MI: Eerdmans, 2009), 69–82.

Hart, David Bentley, *In the Aftermath: Provocations and Laments* (Grand Rapids, MI: Eerdmans, 2009).

Hart, Trevor, 'Humankind in Christ and Christ in Humankind: Salvation as Participation in Our Substitute in the Theology of John Calvin', *Scottish Journal of Theology* 42 (1989): 67–84.

Hauerwas, Stanley, *With the Grain of the Universe: The Church's Witness and Natural Theology* (London: SCM Press, 2002).

Hawkins, Peter S. and Schotter, Anne Howland (eds), *Ineffability: Naming the Unnamable from Dante to Beckett* (New York: AMS Press, 1984).

Hawkins, Peter S. and Schotter, Anne Howland, 'Introduction', in Peter S. Hawkins and Anne Howland Schotter (eds), *Ineffability: Naming the Unnamable from Dante to Beckett* (New York: AMS Press, 1984), 1–4.

Hays, Richard B., *The Conversion of the Imagination: Paul as Interpreter of Israel's Scripture* (Grand Rapids, MI: Eerdmans, 2005).

Hays, Richard B., *The Moral Vision of the New Testament* (New York: HarperCollins, 2007).

Hebblethwaite, Brian, 'Finite and Infinite Freedom in Farrer and von Balthasar', in F. Michael McLain and W. Mark Richardson (eds), *Human and Divine Agency: Anglican, Catholic, and Lutheran Perspectives* (Lanham, MD: University Press of America, 1999), 83–96.

Heidegger, Martin, *The Question Concerning Technology, and Other Essays* (New York: Harper & Row, 1977).

Helmer, Christine, 'Schleiermacher', in David Fergusson (ed.), *The Blackwell Companion to Nineteenth-century Theology* (Oxford: Wiley-Blackwell, 2010), 31–57.

Hepokoski, James A., 'Verdi's Composition of *Otello*: The Act II Quartet', in Carolyn Abbate and Roger Parker (eds), *Analyzing Opera: Verdi and Wagner* (Berkeley and Los Angeles: University of California Press, 1989), 125–49.

Herl, Joseph, *Worship Wars in Early Lutheranism* (Oxford: Oxford University Press, 2004).

Hermand, Jost and Richter, Gerhard, *Sound Figures of Modernity: German Music and Philosophy* (Madison: University of Wisconsin Press, 2006).

Hoeckner, Berthold, *Programming the Absolute: Nineteenth-Century German Music and the Hermeneutics of the Moment* (Princeton: Princeton University Press, 2002).

Hoffmann, E. T. A., 'Beethovens Symphonie, No. 5', *Allgemeine Musikalische Zeitung* 12, 40–1 (4 July and 11 July 1810): cols 630–42, 652–9.

Hoffmann, E. T. A., 'Alte und neue Kirchenmusik', *Allgemeine Musikalische Zeitung* 16, 35–7 (31 August, 7 September, and 14 September 1814): cols 577–84, 593–603, 611–19.

Hoffmann, E. T. A., *Hoffmann's Musical Writings: Kreisleriana, The Poet and the Composer, Music Criticism*, ed. David Charlton, trans. Martyn Clarke (Cambridge: Cambridge University Press, 1989).

Hoffmann, E. T. A., 'Old and New Church Music', in David Charlton (ed.), *E. T. A. Hoffmann's Musical Writings: Kreisleriana, The Poet and the Composer, Music Criticism*, trans. Martyn Clarke (Cambridge: Cambridge University Press, 1989), 351–76.

Hoffmann, E. T. A., 'Review of Beethoven's Fifth Symphony', in David Charlton (ed.), *E. T. A. Hoffmann's Musical Writings: Kreisleriana, The Poet and the Composer, Music Criticism*, trans. Martyn Clarke (Cambridge: Cambridge University Press, 1989), 234–51.

Hollander, John, *The Untuning of the Sky: Ideas of Music in English Poetry, 1500–1700* (New York: W. W. Norton & Co., 1970).

Holloway, Robin, 'Stravinsky's Self-Concealment', *Tempo* 108 (1974): 2–10.

Holze, Heinrich, 'Luther's Concept of Creation: Five Remarks on His Interpretation of the First Article in the Large Catechism (1529)', in Viggo Mortensen (ed.), *Concern for Creation: Voices on the Theology of Creation* (Uppsala: Tro & Tanke, 1995), 49–52.

Honing, Henkjan, 'Without It No Music: Beat Induction as a Fundamental Musical Trait', *Annals of the New York Academy of the Sciences* 1252, 1 (2012): 85–91.

Hook, Julian, 'Exploring Musical Space', *Science* 313, 5783 (July 2006): 49–50.

Horne, Brian L., 'A Civitas of Sound: On Luther and Music', *Theology* 88 (1985): 21–8.

Horne, Brian L., 'Art: A Trinitarian Imperative?', in Christoph Schwöbel (ed.), *Trinitarian Theology Today* (Edinburgh: T & T Clark, 1995), 80–91.

Horton, Michael S., *People and Place: A Covenant Ecclesiology* (Louisville, KY: Westminster John Knox Press, 2008).

Horton, Michael S., 'Union and Communion: Calvin's Theology of Word and Sacrament', *International Journal of Systematic Theology* 11, 4 (October 2009): 398–414.

Hosler, Bellamy, *Changing Aesthetic Views of Instrumental Music in 18th Century Germany* (Epping: Bowker, 1981).

Huh, Paul Junggap, 'John Calvin and the Presbyterian Psalter', *Liturgy* 27, 3 (2012): 16–22.

Hull, John, *Touching the Rock: An Experience of Blindness* (London: SPCK, 1990).

Hulliung, Mark, 'Rousseau, Voltaire, and the Revenge of Pascal', in Patrick Riley (ed.), *The Cambridge Companion to Rousseau* (Cambridge: Cambridge University Press, 2001), 57–77.

Hunsinger, George, *How to Read Karl Barth: The Shape of His Theology* (New York: Oxford University Press, 1991).

Hunsinger, George, 'Karl Barth's Christology: Its Basic Chalcedonian Character', in John B. Webster (ed.), *The Cambridge Companion to Karl Barth* (Cambridge: Cambridge University Press, 2000), 127–42.

Hunsinger, George, 'Postliberal Theology', in Kevin J. Vanhoozer (ed.), *The Cambridge Companion to Postmodern Theology* (Cambridge: Cambridge University Press, 2003), 42–57.

Husbands, Mark, 'The Trinity Is Not Our Social Program: Volf, Gregory and Barth', in Daniel J. Treier and David Lauber (eds), *Trinitarian Theology for the Church: Scripture, Community, Worship* (Downers Grove, IL: InterVarsity Press, 2009), 120–41.

Hütter, Reinhard, 'St Thomas on Grace and Free Will in the *Initium Fidei*: The Surpassing Augustinian Synthesis', *Nova et Vetera* 5, 3 (2007): 521–54.

Hyer, Brian, 'Tonality' on *Oxford Music Online* [website]: <http://www.oxfordmusiconline.com>, accessed 9 November 2010.

Ilic, Ljubica, *Music and the Modern Condition: Investigating the Boundaries* (Farnham: Ashgate, 2010).

Ingold, Tim, *The Perception of the Environment: Essays on Livelihood, Dwelling and Skill* (London: Routledge, 2000).

Irwin, Joyce L., *Neither Voice Nor Heart Alone: German Lutheran Theology of Music in the Age of the Baroque* (New York: Peter Lang, 1993).

Irwin, Joyce L., '"So Faith Comes from What Is Heard": The Relationship Between Music and God's Word in the First Two Centuries of German Lutheranism', in Jeremy S. Begbie and Steven R. Guthrie (eds), *Resonant Witness: Conversations Between Music and Theology* (Grand Rapids, MI: Eerdmans, 2011), 65–82.

Isacoff, Stuart, *Temperament: How Music Became a Battleground for the Great Minds of Western Civilization* (New York: Alfred A. Knopf, 2001).

Israel, Jonathan I., *Radical Enlightenment: Philosophy and the Making of Modernity, 1650–1750* (Oxford Oxford University Press, 2001).

Israel, Jonathan I., *Enlightenment Contested: Philosophy, Modernity, and the Emancipation of Man, 1670–1752* (New York: Oxford University Press, 2006).

Israel, Jonathan I., *A Revolution of the Mind: Radical Enlightenment and the Intellectual Origins of Modern Democracy* (Princeton: Princeton University Press, 2010).

Ito, John, 'Looking for Bach', *Books and Culture* (January/February 2003): 8–9, 40–1.

Jameson, Fredric, *A Singular Modernity: Essay on the Ontology of the Present* (London: Verso, 2002).

Jameux, Dominique, *Pierre Boulez*, trans. Susan Bradshaw (London: Faber and Faber, 1991).

Jankélévitch, Vladimir, *Music and the Ineffable*, trans. Carolyn Abbate (Princeton: Princeton University Press, 2003).

Jarvis, Simon, *Adorno: A Critical Introduction* (Cambridge: Polity, 1998).

Jauss, Hans Robert and Roetzel, Lisa C., 'The Literary Process of Modernism from Rousseau to Adorno', *Cultural Critique* 11 (1988–9): 27–61.

Jay, Martin, *Downcast Eyes: The Denigration of Vision in Twentieth-century French Thought* (Berkeley and Los Angeles: University of California Press, 1994).

Jeffrey, David L., and Maillet, Gregory, *Christianity and Literature: Philosophical Foundations and Critical Practice* (Downers Grove, IL: IVP Academic, 2011).

Jenks, Chris, 'The Centrality of the Eye in Western Culture: An Introduction', *Visual Culture* (London: Routledge, 1995), 1–25.

Jensen, Robin Margaret, *Understanding Early Christian Art* (London: Routledge, 2000).

Jenson, Matt, *The Gravity of Sin: Augustine, Luther and Barth on 'homo incurvatus in se'* (London: T & T Clark, 2006).

Jenson, Robert E., '"The Father, He..."', in Alvin F. Kimel (ed.), *Speaking the Christian God: The Holy Trinity and the Challenge of Feminism* (Grand Rapids, MI: Eerdmans, 1992), 95–109.

Jenson, Robert W., *Systematic Theology: The Triune God*, 2 vols, vol. i (New York: Oxford University Press, 1997).

Jenson, Robert W., *Systematic Theology: The Works of God*, 2 vols, vol. ii (New York: Oxford University Press, 1999).

Jeske, Richard L., 'Bach as Biblical Interpreter', in Martin Heckscher et al. (eds), *The Universal Bach: Lectures Celebrating the Tercentenary of Bach's Birthday, Fall 1985* (Philadelphia: American Philosophical Society, 1986), 82–94.

Joby, Christopher R., *Calvinism and the Arts: A Re-assessment* (Leuven, MA: Peeters, 2007).

Johnson, Julian, *Webern and the Transformation of Nature* (Cambridge: Cambridge University Press, 1999).

Johnson, Julian, 'Review of *Music and the Ineffable* by Vladimir Jankélévitch (Princeton University Press, 2003)', *Music and Letters* 85, 4 (2004): 643–7.

Johnson, Julian, 'Between Sound and Structure: Music as Self-Critique' (unpublished paper delivered at Music and Philosophy, a study day at King's College London on 20 February 2010).

Jonas, Hans, *The Phenomenon of Life: Toward a Philosophical Biology*, 1st edn. (New York: Harper & Row, 1966).

Jones, Paul S., 'Calvin and Music', in David W. Hall and Marvin Padgett (eds), *Calvin and Culture* (Phillipsburg, NJ: P & R Publishing, 2012), 217–53.

Joughin, John J. and Malpas, Simon (eds), *The New Aestheticism* (Manchester: Manchester University Press, 2003).

Jüngel, Eberhard, *Christ, Justice and Peace: Toward a Theology of the State in Dialogue with the Barmen Declaration*, trans. D. Bruce Hamill and Alan J. Torrance (Edinburgh: T & T Clark, 1992).

Kagan, Andrew, *Paul Klee: Art and Music* (Ithaca, NY: Cornell University Press, 1983).

Kalb, F., *Theology of Worship in 17th-Century Lutheranism*, trans. H. P. A. Hamann (St Louis: Concordia Publishing, 1965).

Kallas, Endel, 'Martin Luther in Praise of Music', *Journal of Church Music* 25 (1983): 13–16.

Kant, Immanuel, *Critique of the Power of Judgment* (Cambridge: Cambridge University Press, 2000).

Kavanagh, Donncha, 'Ocularcentrism and Its Others: A Framework for Metatheoretical Analysis', *Organization Studies* 25, 3 (2004): 445–64.

Kelly, Christopher, 'Rousseau and the Case Against (and For) the Arts', in Clifford Orwin and Nathan Tarcov (eds), *The Legacy of Rousseau* (Chicago: University of Chicago Press, 1997), 20–42.

Kenny, Anthony, 'Concepts, Brains, and Behaviour', *Grazer Philosophische Studien* 81, 1 (2010): 105–13.

Kerman, Joseph, *Opera as Drama* (Berkeley and Los Angeles: University of California Press, 2005).

Kermode, Frank, *The Sense of an Ending* (Oxford: Oxford University Press, 2000).

Kevorkian, Tanya, *Baroque Piety: Religion, Society, and Music in Leipzig, 1650–1750* (Aldershot: Ashgate, 2007).

Kiernan, Colm, 'Rousseau and Music in the French Enlightenment', *French Studies* 26 (1972): 156–65.

Kimel, Alvin F. (ed.), *Speaking the Christian God: The Holy Trinity and the Challenge of Feminism* (Grand Rapids, MI: Eerdmans, 1992).

King, Jonathan, 'Text-setting' on *Grove Music Online* [website]: <http://www.oxfordmusiconline.com>, accessed 4 July 2012.

Kintzler, Catherine, 'Rameau et Rousseau: Le Choc de deux esthétiques', preface in Jean-Jacques Rousseau, *Écrits sur la musique* ([Paris:] Éditions Stock, 1979), ix–liv.

Kirk, J. Andrew, *The Meaning of Freedom: A Study of Secular, Muslim and Christian Views* (Carlisle: Paternoster Press, 1998).

Kivy, Peter, *Antithetical Arts: On the Ancient Quarrel Between Literature and Music* (Oxford: Clarendon Press, 2009).

Kleinberg-Levin, David Michael, *Modernity and the Hegemony of Vision* (Berkeley and Los Angeles: University of California Press, 1993).

Kleinberg-Levin, *The Philosopher's Gaze: Modernity in the Shadows of Enlightenment* (Berkeley and Los Angeles: University of California Press, 1999).

Kolb, Robert, *Lutheran Ecclesiastical Culture, 1550–1675* (Leiden: Brill, 2008).

Kraage, Jean-Denis, 'Luther: Théologien de la musique', *Études théologiques et religieuses* 58 (1983): 449–63.

Kramer, Lawrence, *Music and Poetry: The Nineteenth Century and After* (Berkeley and Los Angeles: University of California Press, 1984).

Krieger, Leonard, 'The Autonomy of Intellectual History', in Leonard Krieger and M. L. Brick (eds), *Ideas and Events: Professing History* (Chicago: University of Chicago Press, 1992), 159–77.

Kuyper, Abraham, *Lectures on Calvinism* (Grand Rapids, MI: Eerdmans, 1931).

LaCocque, André, and Ricoeur, Paul, *Thinking Biblically: Exegetical and Hermeneutical Studies*, trans. David Pellauer (Chicago: University of Chicago Press, 1998).

Lakoff, George, and Johnson, Mark, *Metaphors We Live By*, updated edn. (Chicago: University of Chicago Press, 2003).

Lamm, Julia A., 'Romanticism and Pantheism', in David Fergusson (ed.), *The Blackwell Companion to Nineteenth-Century Theology* (Oxford: Wiley-Blackwell, 2010), 165–86.

Lane, Anthony N. S., 'Calvin's Doctrine of Assurance', *Vox Evangelica* 11 (1979): 32–54.

Lash, Nicholas, 'Up and Down in Christology', in Stephen W. Sykes and D. Holmes (eds), *New Studies in Theology*, vol. i (London: Duckworth, 1980), 31–46.

Lash, Nicholas, 'Ministry of the Word or Comedy and Philology', *New Blackfriars* 68, 801 (January 1987): 472–83.

Lash, Nicholas, *Holiness, Speech and Silence: Reflections on the Question of God* (Aldershot: Ashgate, 2004).

Lash, Nicholas, 'Reflections on Where We Have Come From', *Modern Theology* 26, 1 (2010): 45–52.

Latour, Bruno, *Politics of Nature: How to Bring the Sciences into Democracy* (Cambridge, MA: Harvard University Press, 2004).

Le Huray, Peter and Day, James (eds), *Music and Aesthetics in the Eighteenth and Early-Nineteenth Centuries* (Cambridge: Cambridge University Press, 1981).

Leaver, Robin A., *Music as Preaching: Bach, Passions and Music in Worship* (Oxford: Latimer House, 1983).

Leaver, Robin A., *J. S. Bach as Preacher: His Passions and Music in Worship* (St Louis: Concordia Publishing, 1984).

Leaver, Robin A., *J. S. Bach and Scripture: Glosses from the Calov Bible Commentary* (St Louis: Concordia Publishing, 1985).

Leaver, Robin A., 'Music and Lutheranism', in John Butt (ed.), *The Cambridge Companion to Bach* (Cambridge: Cambridge University Press, 1997), 35–45.

Leaver, Robin A., 'Lutheranism', in Malcolm Boyd (ed.), *J. S. Bach* (Oxford: Oxford University Press, 1999), 277–8.

Leaver, Robin A., 'Eschatology, Theology and Music: Death and Beyond in Bach's Vocal Music', in Anne Leahy and Yo Tomita (eds), *Bach Studies from Dublin* (Dublin: Four Courts Press, 2004), 129–47.

Leaver, Robin A., 'Motive and Motif in the Church Music of Johann Sebastian Bach', *Theology Today* 63 (2006): 38–47.

Leaver, Robin A., *Luther's Liturgical Music: Principles and Implications* (Grand Rapids, MI: Eerdmans, 2007).

Lee, Robert E. A., 'Bach's Living Music of Death', *Dialog: A Journal of Theology* 24, 2 (1985): 102–6.

Lee, Yang-Ho, 'Calvin on Deification: A Reply to Carl Mosser and Jonathan Slater', *Scottish Journal of Theology* 63, 3 (2010): 272–84.

Leisinger, Ulrich, 'Forms and Functions of the Choral Movements in J. S. Bach's *St Matthew Passion*', in Daniel R. Melamed (ed.), *Bach Studies 2* (Cambridge: Cambridge University Press, 1995), 70–84.

Lerdahl, Fred, *Tonal Pitch Space* (New York: Oxford University Press, 2001).

Lerdahl, Fred, and Jackendoff, Ray, *A Generative Theory of Tonal Music* (Cambridge, MA: MIT Press, 1996).

Lester, Joel, *Compositional Theory in the Eighteenth Century* (Cambridge, MA: Harvard University Press, 1992).

Lester, Joel, *Bach's Works for Solo Violin: Style, Structure, Performance* (New York: Oxford University Press, 1999).

Lester, Joel, 'Rameau and Eighteenth-Century Harmonic Theory', in Thomas Christensen (ed.), *The Cambridge History of Western Music Theory* (Cambridge, MA: Cambridge University Press, 2006), 753–77.

Levinson, Jerrold, 'Musical Thinking', *Journal of Music and Meaning* 1 (Fall 2003): section 2.

Lewin, David, *Studies in Music with Text* (New York: Oxford University Press, 2006).

Lewis, Alan E., 'Ecclesia Ex Auditu: A Reformed View of the Church as the Community of the Word of God', *Scottish Journal of Theology* 35, 1 (1982): 13–31.

Lewis, Alan E., *Between Cross and Resurrection: A Theology of Holy Saturday* (Grand Rapids, MI: Eerdmans, 2001).

Lewis, C. S., *Studies in Words*, 2nd edn. (Cambridge: Cambridge University Press, 1967).

Lindlof, Thomas R. and Taylor, Bryan C., *Qualitative Communication Research Methods* (Thousand Oaks, CA: Sage Publications, 2002).

Lippman, Edward A., 'Theory and Practice in Schumann's Aesthetics', *Journal of the American Musicological Society* 17, 3 (1964): 310–45.

Lippman, Edward A., *A History of Western Musical Aesthetics* (Lincoln, NE: University of Nebraska Press, 1992).

Little, Meredith and Jenne, Natalie, *Dance and the Music of J. S. Bach* (Bloomington, IN: Indiana University Press, 1991).

Loewe, Andreas, '"God's Capellmeister": The Proclamation of Scripture in the Music of J. S. Bach', *Pacifica* 24 (June 2011): 141–71.

Loewe, Andreas, '"Musica Est Optimum": Martin Luther's Theory of Music' on *academia.edu (Melbourne College of Divinity)* [website]: <http://mcd.academia.edu/loewe/Papers/1074845/Musica_est_optimum_Martin_Luthers_Theory_of_Music>, accessed 7 July 2012.

Loewe, Andreas, 'Why Do Lutherans Sing? Lutherans, Music and the Gospel in the First Century of the Reformation', on *academia.edu (Melbourne College of Divinity)* [website]: <http://mcd.academia.edu/loewe/Papers/1614194/Why_do_Lutherans_sing_Lutherans_Music_and_the_Gospel_in_the_first_Century_of_the_Reformation>, accessed 7 July 2012.

Long, D. Stephen, *Speaking of God: Theology, Language, and Truth* (Grand Rapids, MI: Eerdmans, 2009).

López, José and Potter, Garry, *After Postmodernism: An Introduction to Critical Realism* (London: Athlone, 2001).

Lowe, Walter, 'Postmodern Theology', in J. B. Webster, Kathryn Tanner, and Iain R. Torrance (eds), *The Oxford Handbook of Systematic Theology* (Oxford: Oxford University Press, 2007), 617–33.

Lundin, Roger, *There Before Us: Religion, Literature, and Culture from Emerson to Wendell Berry* (Grand Rapids, MI: Eerdmans, 2007).

Lundin, Roger, *Believing Again: Doubt and Faith in a Secular Age* (Grand Rapids, MI: Eerdmans, 2009).

Luther, Martin, *D. Martin Luthers Werke: Kritische Gesamtausgabe*, vol. iii (Weimar: H. Böhlau, 1885).

Luther, Martin, *D. Martin Luthers Werke: Kritische Gesamtausgabe*, vol. xxx/2 (Weimar: H. Böhlau, 1909).

Luther, Martin, *D. Martin Luthers Werke: Kritische Gesamtausgabe*, vol. iv (Weimar: H. Böhlau, 1916).

Luther, Martin, *Luther's Works*, vol. i. *Lectures on Genesis Chapters 1–5* (Saint Louis: Concordia, 1958).

Luther, Martin, *Luther's Works*, vol. liii. *Liturgy and Hymns* (Philadelphia: Fortress Press, 1965).

Luther, Martin, *Luther's Works*, vol. liv. *Table Talk* (Philadelphia: Fortress Press, 1967).

Luther, Martin, *Luther's Works*, vol. xvii. *Lectures on Isaiah 40–66* (Philadelphia: Fortress Press, 1972).

Luther, Martin, *Luther's Works*, vol. xlix. *Letters II* (Philadelphia: Fortress Press, 1972).

McClary, Susan, 'The Blasphemy of Talking Politics During Bach Year', in Richard D. Leppert and Susan McClary (eds), *Music and Society: The Politics of Composition, Performance, and Reception* (Cambridge: Cambridge University Press, 1987), 13–62.

McCormack, Bruce L., 'What's at Stake in Current Debates Over Justification?', in Mark Husbands and Daniel J. Treier (eds), *Justification: What's at Stake in the Current Debates* (Downers Grove, IL: InterVarsity Press, 2004), 81–117.

McCormack, Bruce L., *Engaging the Doctrine of God: Contemporary Protestant Perspectives* (Grand Rapids, MI: Baker Academic, 2008).

McDonnell, Kilian, *John Calvin, the Church, and the Eucharist* (Princeton: Princeton University Press, 1967).

McDowell, John C., 'The Strange Word Creating Its Own Familiarity: A Response to Rodney Holder on Barth and Natural Theology', *Themelios* 27, 2 (2002): 32–44.

McFadyen, Alistair I., 'Sins of Praise: The Assault on God's Freedom', in Colin E. Gunton (ed.), *God and Freedom: Essays in Historical and Systematic Theology* (Edinburgh: T & T Clark, 1995), 32–56.

McGrath, Alister E., *The Genesis of Doctrine: A Study in the Foundations of Doctrinal Criticism* (Oxford: Blackwell Publishing, 1990).

McGrath, Alister E., *Luther's Theology of the Cross* (Grand Rapids, MI: Baker Books, 1990).

McGrath, Alister E., *Christian Theology: An Introduction* (Oxford: Blackwell Publishing, 1994).

McGrath, Alister E., *Thomas F. Torrance: An Intellectual Biography* (Edinburgh: T & T Clark, 1999).

McGrath, Alister E., *A Scientific Theology: Nature*, 3 vols, vol. i (Edinburgh: T & T Clark, 2001).

McGrath, Alister E., *A Scientific Theology: Reality*, 3 vols, vol. ii (Edinburgh: T & T Clark, 2001).

McGrath, Alister E., *A Scientific Theology: Theory*, 3 vols, vol. iii (Edinburgh: T & T Clark, 2001).

McGrath, Alister E., *The Open Secret: A New Vision for Natural Theology* (Oxford: Blackwell Publishing, 2008).

MacIntyre, Alasdair C., *Whose Justice? Which Rationality?* (Notre Dame, IN: University of Notre Dame Press, 1988).

McKee, Elsie Anne (ed.), *John Calvin: Writings on Pastoral Piety* (New York: Paulist Press, 2001).

McLain, F. Michael and Richardson, W. Mark, *Human and Divine Agency: Anglican, Catholic, and Lutheran Perspectives* (Lanham, MD: University Press of America, 1999).

McMahon, Darrin M., 'The Return of the History of Ideas?', in Darrin M. McMahon and Samuel Moyn (eds), *Rethinking Modern European Intellectual History* (New York: Oxford University Press, forthcoming).

McMaken, W. Travis, 'The Impossibility of Natural Knowledge of God in T. F. Torrance's Reformulated Natural Theology', *International Journal of Systematic Theology* 12, 3 (July 2010): 319–40.

McNeill, William H., *Keeping Together in Time: Dance and Drill in Human History* (Cambridge, MA: Harvard University Press, 1995).

MacNiven, Stuart A., 'Politics, Language and Music in the Unity of Rousseau's System', *Studies on Voltaire and the Eighteenth Century* 08 (2004): 166–74.

Malin, Yonatan, 'Review of Beate Julia Perrey, *Schumann's Dichterliebe and Early Romantic Poetics: Fragmentation of Desire* (Cambridge, Cambridge University Press: 2002)', *Music Theory Spectrum* 28, 2 (2006): 299–310.

Margolis, Eric and Laurence, Stephen, 'Concepts', in Edward N. Zalta (ed.), *The Stanford Encyclopedia of Philosophy* [website] (2012): <http://plato.stanford.edu/archives/fall2012/entries/concepts/>, accessed 9 January 2013.

Marissen, Michael, *The Social and Religious Designs of J. S. Bach's Brandenburg Concertos* (Princeton: Princeton University Press, 1995).

Marissen, Michael, 'The Theological Character of J. S. Bach's *Musical Offering*', in Daniel R. Melamed (ed.), *Bach Studies 2* (Cambridge: Cambridge University Press, 1995), 85–106.

Marissen, Michael, *Lutheranism, Anti-Judaism, and Bach's St John Passion* (New York: Oxford University Press, 1998).

Marshall, Robert L., *The Compositional Process of J. S. Bach: A Study of the Autograph Scores of the Vocal Works* (Princeton: Princeton University Press, 1972).

Marshall, Robert L., *The Music of Johann Sebastian Bach: The Sources, the Style, the Significance* (New York: Schirmer, 1989).

Marshall, Robert L., 'Truth and Beauty: J. S. Bach at the Crossroads of Cultural History', in Paul Brainard and Ray Robinson (eds), *A Bach Tribute: Essays in Honor of William H. Scheide* (Chapel Hill, NC: Hinshaw Music, 1993), 179–88.

Marshall, Robert L., *Luther, Bach, and the Early Reformation Chorale* (Atlanta: Pitts Theology Library, 1995).

Marsoobian, Armen T., 'Saying, Singing, or Semiotics: "Prima la Musica e Poi le Parole" Revisited', *Journal of Aesthetics and Art Criticism* 54, 3 (1996): 269–77.

Martin, David, 'The Handel Revolution: A Great Composer Reconceived', *Books and Culture* (March/April 2011): 11–15.

Masters, Roger D., 'Rousseau and the Rediscovery of Human Nature', in Clifford Orwin and Nathan Tarcov (eds), *The Legacy of Rousseau* (Chicago: University of Chicago Press, 1997), 110–40.

Melamed, Daniel R., *Hearing Bach's Passions* (Oxford: Oxford University Press, 2005).

Mellers, Wilfrid H., *Bach and the Dance of God* (Oxford: Oxford University Press, 1981).

Melzer, Arthur M., *The Natural Goodness of Man: On the System of Rousseau's Thought* (Chicago: University of Chicago Press, 1990).

Merleau-Ponty, Maurice, *Phenomenology of Perception* (New York: Humanities Press, 1962).

Miłosz, Czesław, *To Begin Where I Am: Selected Essays*, ed. and intr. Bogdana Carpenter and Madeline G. Levine (New York: Farrar, Straus and Giroux, 2001).

Minear, Paul S., 'J. S. Bach and J. A. Ernesti: A Case Study in Exegetical and Theological Conflict', in John Deschner, Leroy T. Howe, and Klaus Penzel (eds), *Our Common History as Christians: Essays in Honor of Albert C. Outler* (New York: Oxford University Press, 1975), 131–55.

Mithen, Steven J., *The Singing Neanderthals: The Origins of Music, Language, Mind and Body* (London: Phoenix, 2006).

Molnar, Paul D., *Incarnation and Resurrection: Toward a Contemporary Understanding* (Grand Rapids, MI: Eerdmans, 2007).

Molnar, Paul D., *Thomas F. Torrance: Theologian of the Trinity* (Farnham: Ashgate, 2009).

Moltmann, Jürgen, *God in Creation: An Ecological Doctrine of Creation* (London: SCM Press, 1985).

Moltmann, Jürgen, 'God in the World—The World in God: Perichoresis in Trinity and Eschatology', in Richard Bauckham and Carl Mosser (eds), *The Gospel of John and Christian Theology* (Grand Rapids, MI: Eerdmans, 2008), 369–81.

Mondzain, Marie-José, *Image, Icon, Economy: The Byzantine Origins of the Contemporary Imaginary* (Stanford, CA: Stanford University Press, 2005).

Monson, Craig A., 'The Council of Trent Revisited', *Journal of the American Musicological Society* 55, 1 (Spring 2002): 1–37.

Monti, Anthony, *A Natural Theology of the Arts: Imprint of the Spirit* (Aldershot: Ashgate, 2003).

Moore, Andrew, *Realism and Christian Faith: God, Grammar, and Meaning* (Cambridge: Cambridge University Press, 2003).

Moreno, Jairo, *Musical Representations, Subjects, and Objects: The Construction of Musical Thought in Zarlino, Descartes, Rameau, and Weber* (Bloomington, IN: Indiana University Press, 2004).

Morgan, David, *Protestants and Pictures: Religion, Visual Culture and the Age of American Mass Production* (New York: Oxford University Press, 1999).

Morgan, Robert P., 'Musical Time/Musical Space', *Critical Inquiry* 6, 3 (1980): 527–38.

Morgenstern, Mira, 'Jean-Jacques Rousseau: Music, Language and Politics', *Studies on Voltaire and the Eighteenth Century* 08 (2004): 62–74.

Morrow, Mary Sue, *German Music Criticism in the Late Eighteenth Century: Aesthetic Issues in Instrumental Music* (Cambridge: Cambridge University Press, 1997).

Morton, Timothy, *Ecology Without Nature: Rethinking Environmental Aesthetics* (Cambridge, MA: Harvard University Press, 2007).

Moseley, David J. R. S., '"Parables" and "Polyphony": The Resonance of Music as Witness in the Theology of Karl Barth and Dietrich Bonhoeffer', in Jeremy S. Begbie and Steven R. Guthrie (eds), *Resonant Witness: Conversations Between Music and Theology* (Grand Rapids, MI: Eerdmans, 2011), 240–70.

Muller, Richard A., *The Unaccommodated Calvin: Studies in the Foundation of a Theological Tradition* (New York: Oxford University Press, 2000).

Murphy, Raymond, *Rationality and Nature: A Sociological Inquiry into a Changing Relationship* (Boulder, CO: Westview Press, 1994).

Music, David W., *Instruments in Church: A Collection of Source Documents* (Lanham, MD: Scarecrow Press, 1998).

Nettl, B., 'An Ethnomusicologist Contemplates Universals in Musical Sound and Musical Culture', in Nils L. Wallin, Björn Merker, and Steven Brown (eds), *The Origins of Music* (Cambridge, MA: MIT Press, 2000), 463–72.

Nettl, Paul, *Luther and Music*, trans. Frida Best and Ralph Wood (New York: Russell & Russell, 1967).

Neubauer, John, *The Emancipation of Music from Language: Departure from Mimesis in Eighteenth-Century Aesthetics* (New Haven: Yale University Press, 1986).

Newton, Isaac, *Mathematical Principles of Natural Philosophy*, trans. A. Motte, vol. i (Berkeley and Los Angeles: University of California Press, 1962).

Newton, Isaac, *The Principia: Mathematical Principles of Natural Philosophy*, trans. I. Bernard Cohen and Anne Miller Whitman (Berkeley and Los Angeles: University of California Press, 1999).

Ngien, Dennis, *Gifted Response: The Triune God as the Causative Agency of our Responsive Worship* (Carlisle: Paternoster Press, 2008).

Nimmo, Paul T., 'Karl Barth and the Concursus Dei: A Chalcedonianism Too Far?', *International Journal of Systematic Theology* 9, 1 (2007): 58–72.

Norris, Richard, 'Chalcedon Revisited: A Historical and Theological Reflection', in Bradley Nassif (ed.), *New Perspectives on Historical Theology: Essays in Memory of John Meyendorff* (Grand Rapids, MI: Eerdmans, 1996), 140–58.

Nudds, Matthew, 'Experiencing the Production of Sounds', *European Journal of Philosophy* 9, 2 (2001): 210–29.

Nudds, Matthew, and O'Callaghan, Casey (eds), *Sounds and Perception: New Philosophical Essays* (Oxford: Oxford University Press, 2009).

Nussbaum, Martha C., *Upheavals of Thought: The Intelligence of Emotions* (Cambridge: Cambridge University Press, 2001).

O'Callaghan, Casey, *Sounds: A Philosophical Theory* (Oxford: Oxford University Press, 2007).

O'Callaghan, Casey, 'Auditory Perception', *The Stanford Encyclopedia of Philosophy* [website] (Summer 2009): <http://plato.stanford.edu/archives/sum2009/entries/perception-auditory/>, accessed 28 July 2011.

O'Callaghan, Casey, and Nudds, Matthew, 'Introduction: The Philosophy of Sounds and Auditory Perception', in Matthew Nudds and Casey O'Callaghan (eds), *Sounds and Perception: New Philosophical Essays* (Oxford: Oxford University Press, 2009), 1–25.

O'Dea, Michael, *Jean-Jacques Rousseau: Music, Illusion and Desire* (Basingstoke: Macmillan, 1995).

O'Donovan, Oliver, *Resurrection and Moral Order: An Outline for Evangelical Ethics* (Leicester: InterVarsity Press, 1994).

O'Regan, Kevin, 'Review of Daniel K. L. Chua, *Absolute Music and the Construction of Meaning* (Cambridge, Cambridge University Press: 1999)', *Music & Letters* 82, 2 (2001): 287–91.

Oakes, Kenneth, 'The Question of Nature and Grace in Karl Barth: Humanity as Creature and as Covenant-Partner', *Modern Theology* 23, 4 (2007): 595–616.

Oettinger, Rebecca Wagner, *Music as Propaganda in the German Reformation* (Aldershot: Ashgate, 2001).

Old, Hughes Oliphant, *Worship that is Reformed According to Scripture* (Atlanta: John Knox Press, 2002).

Ong, Walter J., *Ramus, Method, and the Decay of Dialogue: From the Art of Discourse to the Art of Reason* (Cambridge, MA: Harvard University Press, 1983).

Otto, Peter, *Multiplying Worlds: Romanticism, Modernity, and the Emergence of Virtual Reality* (Oxford: Oxford University Press, 2011).

Otto, Randall E., 'The Use and Abuse of Perichoresis in Recent Theology', *Scottish Journal of Theology* 54, 3 (2001): 366–84.

Owen, David, 'Wittgenstein and Genealogy', *Nordic Journal of Philosophy* 2, 2 (2001): 5–25.

Paddison, Angus, *Scripture: A Very Theological Proposal* (London: T & T Clark, 2009).

Pangritz, Andreas, *Polyphonie des Lebens: Zu Dietrich Bonhoeffers, 'Theologie der Musik'* (Berlin: Alektor-Verlag, 1994).

Pangritz, Andreas, 'Point and Counterpoint—Resistance and Submission: Dietrich Bonhoeffer on Theology and Music in Times of War and Social Crisis', in Lyn Holness and Ralf Wüstenberg (eds), *Theology in Dialogue: The Impact of the Arts, Humanities and Science on Contemporary Religious Thought* (Grand Rapids, MI: Eerdmans, 2002), 28–42.

Park, Chan Ho, 'Transcendence and Spatiality of the Triune Creator', doctrinal dissertation (Fuller Theological Seminary, published by Peter Lang 2005).

Patel, Aniruddh D., *Music, Language, and the Brain* (Oxford: Oxford University Press, 2008).

Patel, Aniruddh D., 'Experimental Evidence for Synchronization to a Musical Beat in a Nonhuman Animal', *Current Biology* 19, 10 (30 April 2009): 827–30.

Patel, Aniruddh D., 'Music and the Brain: Three Links to Language', in Susan Hallam, Ian Cross, and Michael H. Thaut (eds), *The Oxford Handbook of Music Psychology* (Oxford: Oxford University Press, 2009), 208–16.

Patterson, Steven W., ' "A Picture Held us Captive": The Later Wittgenstein on Visual Argumentation', *Cogency* 2, 2 (Spring 2010): 105–34.

Pattison, Stephen, *Seeing Things: Deepening Relations with Visual Artefacts* (London: SCM Press, 2007).

Paul, Charles B., 'Jean-Philippe Rameau (1683–1764), the Musician as Philosophe', *Proceedings of the American Philosophical Society* 114, 2 (13 April 1970): 140–54.

Paul, Charles B., 'Music and Ideology: Rameau, Rousseau, and 1789', *Journal of the History of Ideas* 32, 3 (1970): 395–410.

Pederson, Sanna, 'Defining the Term "Absolute Music" Historically', *Music and Letters* 90, 2 (2009): 240–62.

Pelikan, Jaroslav J., *Bach Among the Theologians* (Philadelphia: Fortress Press, 1986).

Perrey, Beate Julia, *Schumann's Dichterliebe and Early Romantic Poetics: Fragments of Desire* (Cambridge: Cambridge University Press, 2002).

Pfau, Thomas, 'Introduction—Reading Beyond Redemption: Historicism, Irony and the Lessons of Romanticism', in Thomas Pfau and Robert F. Gleckner (eds), *Lessons of Romanticism* (Durham, NC: Duke University Press, 1998), 1–37.

Pfau, Thomas, *Romantic Moods: Paranoia, Trauma, and Melancholy, 1790–1840* (Baltimore: Johns Hopkins University Press, 2005).

Pfau, Thomas, and Gleckner, Robert F., *Lessons of Romanticism: A Critical Companion* (Durham, NC: Duke University Press, 1998).

Pfau, Thomas, and Mitchell, Robert (eds), *Romanticism and Modernity* (London: Routledge, 2012).

Pickstock, Catherine, *After Writing: On the Liturgical Consummation of Philosophy* (Oxford: Blackwell Publishing, 1998).

Pietsch, H., 'On Luther's Understanding of Music', *Lutheran Theological Journal*, 16 (1992): 160–8.

Placher, William C., *The Domestication of Transcendence: How Modern Thinking about God Went Wrong* (Louisville, KY: Westminster John Knox Press, 1996).

Plantinga, Richard J., 'The Integration of Music and Theology in the Vocal Compositions of J. S. Bach', in Jeremy S. Begbie and Steven R. Guthrie (eds), *Resonant Witness: Conversations Between Music and Theology* (Grand Rapids, MI: Eerdmans, 2011), 215–39.

Plato, *Republic*, trans. Robin Waterfield (Oxford: Oxford University Press, 1993).

Polanyi, Michael, *Personal Knowledge: Towards a Post-Critical Philosophy* (New York: Harper & Row, 1964).

Polanyi, Michael, *The Tacit Dimension* (New York: Doubleday, 1966).

Polkinghorne, John C. (ed.), *The Trinity and an Entangled World: Relationality in Physical Science and Theology* (Grand Rapids, MI: Eerdmans, 2010).

Pollard, D. E. B., 'Picture Theory of Meaning', in Peter V. Lamarque (ed.), *Concise Encyclopedia of Philosophy of Language* (Oxford: Pergamon Press, 1997), 166–8.

Prickett, Stephen, *Narrative, Religion, and Science: Fundamentalism Versus Irony, 1700–1999* (Cambridge: Cambridge University Press, 2002).

Prickett, Stephen, *Modernity and the Reinvention of Tradition: Backing into the Future* (Cambridge: Cambridge University Press, 2009).

Quash, Ben, 'Real Enactment: The Role of Drama in the Theology of Hans Urs von Balthasar', in Trevor A. Hart and Steven R. Guthrie (eds), *Faithful Performances: Enacting Christian Tradition* (Aldershot: Ashgate, 2007), 13–32.

Rae, Murray, 'The Spatiality of God', in Myk Habets and Phillip Tolliday (eds), *Trinitarian Theology after Barth* (Eugene, OR: Wipf & Stock, 2011), 70–86.

Rahner, Karl, *Theological Investigations*, vol. i (Baltimore: Helicon Press, 1961).

Rahner, Karl, *Encyclopedia of Theology: The Concise Sacramentum Mundi* (New York: Seabury Press, 1975).

Rahner, Karl, *Foundations of Christian Faith: An Introduction to the Idea of Christianity*, trans. W. Dych (New York: Crossroad, 1978).

Rameau, Jean-Philippe, The Complete Theoretical Writings of Jean-Philippe Rameau, ed. Erwin R. Jacobi, 6 vols, vol. ii (Middleton, WN: American Institute of Musicology, 1967).

Rameau, Jean-Philippe, *The Complete Theoretical Writings of Jean-Philippe Rameau*, ed. Erwin R. Jacobi, 6 vols, vol. iii (Middleton, WN: American Institute of Musicology, 1967).

Rameau, Jean-Philippe, *The Complete Theoretical Writings of Jean-Philippe Rameau*, ed. Erwin R. Jacobi, 6 vols, vol. vi (Middleton, WN: American Institute of Musicology, 1967).

Rameau, Jean-Philippe, 'Erreurs sur la musique dans l'Encyclopédie', in Erwin R. Jacobi (ed.), *The Complete Theoretical Writings of Jean-Philippe Rameau*, 6 vols, vol. v (Middleton, WN: American Institute of Musicology, 1969), 309–30.

Rameau, Jean-Philippe, *Treatise on Harmony*, trans. Philip Gossett (New York: Dover Publications, 1971).

Rasch, Rudolf, 'Tuning and Temperament', in Thomas Street Christensen (ed.), *The Cambridge History of Western Music Theory* (Cambridge: Cambridge University Press, 2002), 193–222.

Rastier, François, 'A Little Glossary of Semantics', trans. Larry Marks, on *Texto! Textes & Cultures* [website] (2001): <http://www.revue-texto.net/Reperes/Glossaires/Glossaire_en.html#discourse>, accessed 31 December 2011.

Ratzinger, Joseph, *The Spirit of the Liturgy*, trans. John Saward (San Francisco: Ignatius Press, 2000).

Reed, Esther D., 'Revelation and Natural Rights: Notes on Colin E. Gunton's *Theology of Nature*', in Paul Louis Metzger (ed.), *Trinitarian Soundings in Systematic Theology* (London: T & T Clark, 2005), 203–15.

Rehding, Alexander, 'Rousseau, Rameau and the Enharmonic Furies in the French Enlightenment', *Journal of Music Theory* 49, 1 (2005): 141–80.

Reimann, Henry W., 'Luther on Creation: A Study in Theocentric Theology', *Concordia Theological Monthly* 24 (1953): 26–40.

Renwick, William, 'Of Time and Eternity: Reflections on "Das alte Jahr vergangen ist"', *Journal of Music Theory* 50, 1 (Spring 2006): 65–76.

Repp, Bruno H., 'Musical Synchronization', in E. Altenmuller, M. Weisendanger, and J. Kesserling (eds), *Music, Motor Control, and the Brain* (Oxford: Oxford University Press, 2006), 55–76.

Reuning, Daniel, 'Luther and Music', *Concordia Theological Quarterly* 48 (1984): 17–21.

Riasanovsky, Nicholas V., *The Emergence of Romanticism* (New York: Oxford University Press, 1992).

Richard, L., 'Bach as Religious Interpreter', in Martin Heckscher et al. (eds), *The Universal Bach* (Philadelphia: American Philosophical Society, 1985).

Richards, Robert J., *The Romantic Conception of Life: Science and Philosophy in the Age of Goethe* (Chicago: University of Chicago Press, 2002).

Rigby, Cynthia L., 'Divine Sovereignty, Human Agency, and the Ascension of Christ', *Quarterly Review* 22, 1 (2002): 152–65.

Rigby, Cynthia L., 'Taking our Place: Substitution, Human Agency, and Feminine Sin', *International Journal for the Study of the Christian Church* 4, 3 (2004): 220–34.

Roche, Anthony, 'Review of Kevin Barry, *Language, Music, and the Sign: A Study in Aesthetics, Poetics and Poetic Practice from Collins to Coleridge* (Cambridge, Cambridge University Press: 1987)', *Eighteenth-Century Ireland/Iris an dá chultúr* 4 (1989): 190–3.

Rolf, Sibylle, 'Luther's Understanding of *Imputatio* in the Context of His Doctrine of Justification and Its Consequences for the Preaching of the Gospel', *International Journal of Systematic Theology* 12, 4 (October 2010): 435–51.

Rorty, Richard, *Philosophy and the Mirror of Nature* (Oxford: Blackwell Publishing, 1980).

Rorty, Richard, *Contingency, Irony, and Solidarity* (Cambridge: Cambridge University Press, 1989).

Rosand, Ellen, 'Operatic Madness: A Challenge to Convention', in Steven Paul Scher (ed.), *Music and Text: Critical Inquiries* (Cambridge: Cambridge University Press, 1992), 241–87.

Rosen, Charles, *The Romantic Generation* (Cambridge, MA: Harvard University Press, 1998).

Ross, Barry, 'Challenges Facing Theories of Music and Language Co-evolution', *Journal of the Musical Arts in Africa* 6, 1 (2009): 61–76.

Rousseau, Jean-Jacques, 'Rousseau, Judge of Jean-Jacques: Dialogues', in *The Collected Writings of Rousseau*, ed. Roger D. Masters and Christopher Kelly, vol. i (London: University Press of New England, 1990).

Rousseau, Jean-Jacques, 'Discourse on the Origin and Foundation of Inequality among Men (Second Discourse)', in Roger D. Masters and Christopher Kelly (eds), *The Collected Writings of Rousseau*, vol. iii (London: University Press of New England, 1992), 1–95.

Rousseau, Jean-Jacques, 'Letter to Voltaire, II', in Roger D. Masters and Christopher Kelly (eds), *The Collected Writings of Rousseau*, vol. iii (London: University Press of New England, 1992), 108–21.

Rousseau, Jean-Jacques, *Essay on the Origin of Languages and Writings Related to Music*, ed. and trans. John T. Scott (Hanover, NH: University Press of New England, 1998).

Rupprecht, Philip Ernst, *Britten's Musical Language* (Cambridge: Cambridge University Press, 2001).

Samson, Jim (ed.), *The Cambridge History of Nineteenth-Century Music* (Cambridge: Cambridge University Press, 2001).

Sartre, Jean-Paul, *Being and Nothingness: An Essay on Phenomenological Ontology*, trans. Hazel Estella Barnes (New York: Philosophical Library, 1956).

Sauer, James, *Faithful Ethics According to John Calvin: The Teachability of the Heart* (Lewiston, NY: E. Mellen Press, 1997).

Schachner, Adena, et al., 'Spontaneous Motor Entrainment to Music in Multiple Vocal Mimicking Species', *Current Biology* 19, 10 (30 April 2009): 831–6.

Schalk, Carl, *Luther on Music: Paradigms of Praise* (St Louis: Concordia Publishing, 1988).

Schalk, Carl, *Music in Early Lutheranism: Shaping the Tradition (1524–1672)* (St Louis: Concordia Academic Press, 2001).

Schelling, F. W. J., 'Philosophie der Kunst', in Manfred Schröter (ed.), *Werke* (Munich: C. H. Beck, 1959), 142–55.

Schlegel, Friedrich von, *Literary Notebooks: 1797–1801*, ed. Hans Eichner (London: University of London, Athlone Press, 1957).

Schlegel, Friedrich von, *Dialogue on Poetry and Literary Aphorisms*, trans. Ernst Behler and Roman Struc (University Park, PA: Pennsylvania State University Press, 1968).

Schlegel, Friedrich von, *Kritische Schriften und Fragmente* (Paderborn: Schöningh, 1988).

Schlegel, Friedrich von, *Philosophical Fragments*, trans. P. Firchow (Minneapolis, MN: University of Minnesota Press, 1991).

Schleiermacher, Friedrich, *Christmas Eve: Dialogue on the Incarnation*, trans. Terrence N. Tice (Richmond, VA: John Knox Press, 1967).

Schleiermacher, Friedrich, *On Religion: Speeches to Its Cultured Despisers* (Cambridge: Cambridge University Press, 1996).

Schleiermacher, Friedrich, *The Christian Faith*, trans. J. S. Stewart (Edinburgh: T & T Clark, 1999).

Schmalfeldt, Janet, *In the Process of Becoming: Analytic and Philosophical Perspectives on Form in Early Nineteenth-Century Music* (Oxford: Oxford University Press, 2011).

Schmidt, Ricarda, 'From Early to Late Romanticism', in Nicholas Saul (ed.), *The Cambridge Companion to German Romanticism* (Cambridge: Cambridge University Press, 2006), 21–39.

Schneewind, J. B., *The Invention of Autonomy: A History of Modern Moral Philosophy* (Cambridge: Cambridge University Press, 1988).

Scholtz, Gunter, *Schleiermachers Musikphilosophie* (Göttingen: Vandenhoeck & Ruprecht, 1981).

Schoot, Henk J. M., *Christ the 'Name' of God: Thomas Aquinas on Naming Christ* (Leuven: Peeters, 1993).

Schreiner, Susan Elizabeth, *The Theater of His Glory: Nature and the Natural Order in the Thought of John Calvin* (Durham, NC: The Labyrinth Press, 1991).

Schroeder, David, 'Listening, Thinking and Writing', in Simon P. Keefe (ed.), *The Cambridge History of Eighteenth-Century Music* (Cambridge: Cambridge University Press, 2009), 183–200.

Schubert, Peter and Cumming, Julie E., 'Text and Motif *c.*1500: A New Approach to Text Underlay', *Early Music* 40, 1 (February 2012): 3–14.

Schwarz, Hans, 'Martin Luther and Music', *Lutheran Theological Journal* 39, 2/3 (August–December 2005): 210–17.

Schwöbel, Christoph and Gunton, Colin E. (eds), *Persons, Divine and Human: King's College Essays in Theological Anthropology* (Edinburgh: T & T Clark, 1991).

Scott, John T., 'Politics as the Imitation of the Divine in Rousseau's *Social Contract*', *Polity* 26, 3 (1994): 473–501.

Scott, John T., 'The Harmony Between Rousseau's Musical Theory and His Philosophy', *Journal of the History of Ideas* 59, 2 (1998): 297–308.

Scott, John T., 'Introduction', in Jean-Jacques Rousseau, *Essay on the Origin of Languages and Writings Related to Music*, ed. and trans. John T. Scott (Hanover, NH: University Press of New England, 1998), xiii–xlii.

Scruton, Roger, *The Aesthetics of Music* (Oxford: Clarendon Press, 1997).

Scruton, Roger, 'Sounds As Secondary Objects and Pure Events', in Matthew Nudds and Casey O'Callaghan (eds), *Sounds and Perception: New Philosophical Essays* (Oxford: Oxford University Press, 2009), 50–68.

Scruton, Roger, *Understanding Music: Philosophy and Interpretation* (London: Continuum, 2009).

Scruton, Roger, 'Effing the Ineffable', *Big Questions Online* [website] (2010): <http://www.rogerscruton.com/articles/1-politics-and-society/51-effing-the-ineffable.html>, accessed 27 July 2011.

Sennett, James F. and Groothuis, Douglas R., *In Defense of Natural Theology: A Post-Humean Assessment* (Downers Grove, IL: InterVarsity Press, 2005).

Seyhan, Azade, 'What is Romanticism, and Where Did it Come From?', in Nicholas Saul (ed.), *The Cambridge Companion to German Romanticism* (Cambridge: Cambridge University Press, 2006), 1–20.

Shaffer, Peter, 'Amadeus' on *Daily Script* [website]: <http://www.dailyscript.com/scripts/amadeus.html>, accessed 14 August 2012.

Sharpe, Kevin, 'Reformed Arts? Reformation and Visual Culture in Sixteenth-Century England', *Art History* 33, 5 (2010): 915–23.

Shattuck, Kathryn, 'Picasso, Who Let his Imagination Run from Art to Language', *New York Times* [online newspaper], 5 February 2009: <http://www.nytimes.com/2009/02/08/nyregion/connecticut/08artsct.html?_r=1>, accessed 2 June 2010.

Shepherd, John and Wicke, Peter, *Music and Cultural Theory* (Cambridge: Polity Press, 1997).

Shults, F. LeRon, *Reforming the Doctrine of God* (Grand Rapids, MI: Eerdmans, 2005).

Simon, Julia, 'Music and the Performance of Community in Rousseau', *Studies on Voltaire and the Eighteenth Century* 8 (2004): 192–200.

Simon, Julia, 'Rousseau and Aesthetic Modernity: Music's Power of Redemption', *Eighteenth-Century Music* 2, 1 (2005): 41–56.

Smaill, Peter, 'Bach Among the Heretics: Inferences from the Cantata Texts', *Understanding Bach* 4 (2009): 101–18.

Smallman, Basil, *The Background of Passion Music: J. S. Bach and His Predecessors* (London: SCM Press, 1957).

Smith, James K. A., *Speech and Theology: Language and the Logic of Incarnation* (London: Routledge, 2002).

Smith, James K. A., *Introducing Radical Orthodoxy: Mapping a Post-Secular Theology* (Grand Rapids, MI: Baker Books, 2004).

Smith, James K. A., *Letters to a Young Calvinist: An Invitation to the Reformed Tradition* (Grand Rapids, MI: Brazos Press, 2010).

Söhngen, Oskar, 'Fundamental Considerations for a Theology of Music', in Theodore Hoelty-Nickel (ed.), *The Musical Heritage of the Church*, vol. vi (St Louis: Concordia Publishing, 1963), 7–16.

Soper, Kate, *What is Nature? Culture, Politics and the Non-Human* (Oxford: Blackwell Publishing, 1995).

Soskice, Janet Martin, *Metaphor and Religious Language* (Oxford: Clarendon Press, 1985).

Stacey, Peter F., 'Towards the Analysis of the Relationship of Music and Text in Contemporary Composition', *Contemporary Music Review* 5, 1 (1989): 9–27.

Stapert, Calvin, 'Bach as Theologian: A Review Article', *Reformed Journal* 37 (1987): 19–27.

Stapert, Calvin, 'Christus Victor: Bach's *St John Passion*', *Reformed Journal* 39 (1989): 17–23.

Stapert, Calvin, *My Only Comfort: Death, Deliverance, and Discipleship in the Music of Bach* (Grand Rapids, MI: Eerdmans, 2000).

Stapert, Calvin, *Handel's Messiah: Comfort for God's People* (Grand Rapids, MI: Eerdmans, 2010).

Steinberg, Michael P., *Listening to Reason: Culture, Subjectivity, and Nineteenth-Century Music* (Princeton: Princeton University Press, 2004).

Steinberg, Michael P., 'Music as Thought', *Beethoven Forum* 14, 2 (2007): 182–6.

Steiner, George, 'Schoenberg's *Moses und Aron*', in George Steiner, *George Steiner: A Reader* (London: Penguin, 1984), 234–45.

Steiner, George, *Real Presences: Is There Anything in What We Say?* (London: Faber & Faber, 1989).

Steiner, George, *Errata: An Examined Life* (London: Phoenix, 1997).

Steinitz, Paul, *Bach's Passions* (London: Elek, 1979).

Stevenson, Robert, 'Bach's Quarrel with the Rector of St Thomas School', *Anglican Theological Review* 33 (1951): 219–30.

Stiller, Günther, *Johann Sebastian Bach and Liturgical Life in Leipzig*, trans. Herbert J. A. Bouman, Daniel F. Poellot, and Hilton C. Oswald (St Louis: Concordia Publishing, 1984).

Stoltzfus, Philip Edward, *Theology as Performance: Music, Aesthetics, and God in Western Thought* (New York: T & T Clark, 2006).

Strong, Tracy B., 'Music, the Passions, and Political Freedom in Rousseau', in Christie McDonald and Stanley Hoffmann (eds), *Rousseau and Freedom* (Cambridge: Cambridge University Press, 2010), 92–109.

Strunk, W. Oliver, *Source Readings in Music History: The Romantic Era*, 5 vols, vol. v (London: Faber & Faber, 1981).

Sudduth, Michael, *The Reformed Objection to Natural Theology* (Farnham: Ashgate, 2009).

Swain, Joseph Peter, *Musical Languages* (New York: W. W. Norton & Co., 1997).

Sweetman, Robert, 'Univocity, Analogy, and the Mystery of Being According to John Duns Scotus', in James K. A. Smith and James H. Olthuis (eds), *Radical Orthodoxy and the Reformed Tradition: Creation, Covenant, and Participation* (Grand Rapids, MI: Baker Books, 2005), 73–87.

Taliaferro, Charles and Evans, Jil (eds), *Turning Images in Philosophy, Science, and Religion: A New Book of Nature* (Oxford: Oxford University Press, 2011).

Tamny, Martin, 'Newton, Creation, and Perception', *Isis* 70, 1 (1979): 48–58.

Tanner, Kathryn, *God and Creation in Christian Theology: Tyranny or Empowerment?* (Oxford: Blackwell Publishing, 1988).

Tanner, Kathryn, *Jesus, Humanity and the Trinity: A Brief Systematic Theology* (Edinburgh: T & T Clark, 2000).

Tarry, Joe E., 'Music in the Educational Philosophy of Martin Luther', *Journal of Research in Music Education* 21 (1973): 355–65.

Taruskin, Richard, 'Stravinsky's "Rejoicing Discovery": In Defense of His Notorious Text-Setting', in E. Haimo and P. Johnson (eds), *Stravinsky Retrospectives* (Lincoln, NE: University of Nebraska Press, 1987), 162–99.

Taruskin, Richard, *The Oxford History of Western Music: Music in the Early Twentieth Century*, 5 vols, vol. iv (Oxford: Oxford University Press, 2009).

Tatlow, Ruth, *Bach and the Riddle of the Number Alphabet* (Cambridge: Cambridge University Press, 1991).

Tatlow, Ruth, 'Number Symbolism', in Malcolm Boyd (ed.), *J. S. Bach* (Oxford: Oxford University Press, 1999), 320–2.

Taylor, Barry, *Entertainment Theology: New-Edge Spirituality in a Digital Democracy* (Grand Rapids, MI: Baker Academic, 2008).

Taylor, Charles, *Philosophical Arguments* (Cambridge, MA: Harvard University Press, 1995).

Taylor, Charles, 'Rorty and Philosophy', in Charles B. Guignon and David R. Hiley (eds), *Richard Rorty* (Cambridge: Cambridge University Press, 2003), 158–80.

Taylor, Charles, *A Secular Age* (Cambridge, MA: Harvard University Press, 2007).

Taylor, Charles, *Sources of the Self: The Making of the Modern Identity* (Cambridge, MA: Harvard University Press, 1989).

Taylor, W. David O., 'John Calvin and Musical Instruments: An Investigation', ThD paper (Duke Divinity School, 2010).

Thiselton, Anthony C., '"Behind" and "In Front Of" the Text', in Craig G. Bartholomew, Colin J. D. Greene, and Karl Möller (eds), *After Pentecost: Language and Biblical Interpretation* (Grand Rapids, MI: Zondervan, 2001), 97–120.

Thiselton, Anthony C., *The Hermeneutics of Doctrine* (Grand Rapids, MI: Eerdmans, 2007).

Thomas, Downing A., *Music and the Origins of Language: Theories from the French Enlightenment* (Cambridge: Cambridge University Press, 1995).

Thomas, Stephen, *Deification in the Eastern Orthodox Tradition: A Biblical Perspective* (Piscataway, NJ: Gorgias Press, 2007).

Toews, John, 'Integrating Music into Intellectual History: Nineteenth-Century Art Music as a Discourse of Agency and Identity', *Modern Intellectual History* 5, 2 (2008): 309–31.

Tomlinson, Gary, *Metaphysical Song: An Essay on Opera* (Princeton: Princeton University Press, 1999).

Torrance, Alan J., 'Response by Alan J. Torrance', in Hilary D. Regan and Alan J. Torrance (eds), *Christ and Context: The Confrontation Between Gospel and Culture* (Edinburgh: T & T Clark, 1993), 192–200.

Torrance, Alan J., *Persons in Communion: An Essay on Trinitarian Description and Human Participation* (Edinburgh: T & T Clark, 1996).

Torrance, Alan J., '*Creatio Ex Nihilo* and the Spatio-Temporal Dimensions, with Special Reference to Jürgen Moltmann and D. C. Williams', in Colin E. Gunton (ed.), *The Doctrine of Creation: Essays in Dogmatics, History and Philosophy* (Edinburgh: T & T Clark, 1997), 83–104.

Torrance, Alan J., '*Auditus Fidei*: Where and How Does God Speak? Faith, Reason, and the Question of Criteria', in Paul J. Griffiths and Reinhard Hütter (eds), *Reason and the Reasons of Faith* (London: T & T Clark, 2005), 27–52.

Torrance, Alan J., 'The Theological Grounds for Advocating Forgiveness and Reconciliation in the Sociopolitical Realm', in Daniel Philpott (ed.), *The Politics of Past Evil: Religion, Reconciliation, and the Dilemmas of Transitional Justice* (Notre Dame, IN: University of Notre Dame Press, 2006), 45–85.

Torrance, James B., 'Covenant and Contract: A Study of the Theological Background of Worship in Seventeenth-Century Scotland', *Scottish Journal of Theology* 23 (1970): 51–76.

Torrance, James B., *Worship, Community and the Triune God of Grace* (Carlisle: Paternoster Press, 1996).

Torrance, John, *The Concept of Nature* (Oxford: Clarendon Press, 1992).

Torrance, Thomas F., 'Knowledge of God and Speech About Him According to John Calvin', in Thomas F. Torrance (ed.), *Theology in Reconstruction* (London: SCM Press, 1965), 76–98.

Torrance, Thomas F., *Space, Time and Incarnation* (London: Oxford University Press, 1969).

Torrance, Thomas F., *Space, Time, and Resurrection* (Grand Rapids, MI: Eerdmans, 1976).

Torrance, Thomas F., *The Ground and Grammar of Theology* (Charlottesville, VA: University Press of Virginia, 1980).

Torrance, Thomas F., 'The Transformation of Natural Theology', in Thomas F. Torrance (ed.), *The Ground and Grammar of Theology* (Charlottesville, VA: University Press of Virginia, 1980), 75–109.

Torrance, Thomas F., *Divine and Contingent Order* (Oxford: Oxford University Press, 1981).

Torrance, Thomas F., 'Natural Theology in the Thought of Karl Barth', in Thomas F. Torrance (ed.), *Transformation and Convergence in the Frame of Knowledge: Explorations in the Interrelations of Scientific and Theological Enterprise* (Belfast: Christian Journals, 1984), 285–302.

Torrance, Thomas F., *Transformation and Convergence in the Frame of Knowledge: Explorations in the Interrelations of Scientific and Theological Enterprise* (Belfast: Christian Journals, 1984).

Torrance, Thomas F., *Trinitarian Perspectives: Toward Doctrinal Agreement* (Edinburgh: T & T Clark, 1994).

Torretti, Roberto, 'Space', in Edward Craig (ed.), *Routledge Encyclopedia of Philosophy*, 10 vols, vol. ix (London: Routledge, 1998), 59–66.

Towne, G., 'A Systematic Formulation of 16th-Century Text Underlay Rules', *Musica Disciplina* 44 (1990): 255–87; 45 (1991): 143–68.

Trautmann, C., 'J. S. Bach: New Light on his Faith', *Concordia Theological Monthly* 42 (1971): 88–99.

Treitler, Leo, 'Medieval Music and Language', in Leo Treitler (ed.), *With Voice and Pen: Coming to Know Medieval Song and How It Was Made* (Oxford: Oxford University Press, 2003), 435–56.

Trocmé-Latter, Daniel, 'The Psalms as a Mark of Protestantism: The Introduction of Liturgical Psalmsinging in Geneva', *Plainsong and Medieval Music* 20, 2 (October 2011): 145–63.

Trueman, Carl, 'Metaphysics, the Middle Ages and the Birth of Protestantism', on *Reformation 21* [website] (2 April 2012): <http://www.reformation21.org/blog/2012/04/metaphysics-the-middle-ages-an.php>, accessed 31 December 2012.

U2, 'The Fly', on *Achtung Baby* [CD] (Island, 1991), track 7.

Van Inwagen, Peter, *An Essay on Free Will* (Oxford: Clarendon Press, 1983).

van't Spijker, Willem, 'Bucer's Influence on Calvin: Church and Community', in David F. Wright (ed.), *Martin Bucer: Reforming Church and Community* (Cambridge: Cambridge University Press, 1994), 32–44.

VanderWilt, Jeffrey T., 'John Calvin's Theology of Liturgical Song', *Christian Scholar's Review* 25, 1 (1995): 63–82.

Vanhoozer, Kevin J., *Is There a Meaning in This Text? The Bible, the Reader, and the Morality of Literary Knowledge* (Leicester: Apollos, 1998).

Vanhoozer, Kevin J., 'Scripture and Tradition', in Kevin J. Vanhoozer (ed.), *The Cambridge Companion to Postmodern Theology* (Cambridge: Cambridge University Press, 2003), 149–69.

Vanhoozer, Kevin J., *The Drama of Doctrine: A Canonical–Linguistic Approach to Christian Theology* (Louisville, KY: Westminster John Knox Press, 2005).

Vanhoozer, Kevin J., *Remythologizing Theology: Divine Action, Passion, and Authorship* (Cambridge: Cambridge University Press, 2010).

Varwig, Bettina, 'One More Time: J. S. Bach and Seventeenth-Century Traditions of Rhetoric', *Eighteenth-Century Music* 5, 2 (2008): 179–208.

Varwig, Bettina, 'Death and Life in J. S. Bach's Cantata *Ich habe genung* (BWV 82)', *Journal of the Royal Musical Association* 135, 2 (2010): 315–56.

Varwig, Bettina, 'Metaphors of Time and Modernity in Bach', *Journal of Musicology* 29, 2 (2012): 154–90.

Veit, Patrice, *Das Kirchenlied in der Reformation Martin Luthers: Eine thematische und semantische Untersuchung* (Stuttgart: Franz Steiner Verlag, 1986).

Verba, Cynthia, *Music and the French Enlightenment: Reconstruction of a Dialogue, 1750-1764* (Oxford: Clarendon Press, 1993).

Verhey, Allen, *Nature and Altering it* (Grand Rapids, MI: Eerdmans, 2012).

Vogel, Steven, *Against Nature: The Concept of Nature in Critical Theory* (Albany, NY: State University of New York Press, 1996).

Volf, Miroslav and Katerberg, William H. (eds), *The Future of Hope: Christian Tradition amid Modernity and Postmodernity* (Grand Rapids, MI: Eerdmans, 2004).

Voorhees, Matthew, 'Melodic Communities: Music and Freedom in Rousseau's Political Thought', *History of Political Thought* 32, 4 (2011): 617–44.

Waeber, Jacqueline, 'Jean-Jacques Rousseau's "unité de mélodie"', *Journal of the American Musicological Society* 62, 1 (Spring 2009): 79–143.

Wallace, Ronald S., *Calvin's Doctrine of the Word and Sacrament* (Edinburgh: Oliver and Boyd, 1953).

Wallace, Ronald S., *Calvin, Geneva and the Reformation: A Study of Calvin as Social Reformer, Churchman, Pastor and Theologian* (Edinburgh: Scottish Academic Press, 1988).

Walser, Robert, 'Rhythm, Rhyme, and Rhetoric in the Music of Public Enemy', *Ethnomusicology* 39 (1995): 193–217.

Ward, Graham, 'The Future of Protestantism: Postmodernity', in Alister E. McGrath and Darren C. Marks (eds), *The Blackwell Companion to Protestantism* (Oxford: Blackwell Publishing, 2006), 453–67.

Ward, Timothy, *Word and Supplement: Speech Acts, Biblical Texts, and the Sufficiency of Scripture* (Oxford: Oxford University Press, 2002).

Watson, Derek (ed.), *The Wordsworth Dictionary of Musical Quotations* (Ware: Wordsworth Editions, 1994).

Weber, Édith, 'L'Humanisme musical au XVIe siècle et ses répercussions sur le chant d'Église protestant et catholique', in Charles Kannengiesser and Yves Marchasson (eds), *Humanisme et foi chrétienne* (Paris: Beauchesne, 1976), 239–54.

Weber, Édith, 'Martin Luther, poète, musicien et hymnologue', *Unité chrétienne* (November 1983): 100–8.

Weber, Max, *The Rational and Social Foundations of Music* (Carbondale, IL: Southern Illinois University Press, 1958).

Webster, John, *Word and Church: Essays in Christian Dogmatics* (Edinburgh: T. & T. Clark, 2001).

Webster, John, 'The Church and the Perfection of God', in Mark Husbands and Daniel J. Treier (eds), *The Community of the Word: Toward an Evangelical Ecclesiology* (Downers Grove, IL: InterVarsity Press, 2005), 75–95.

Weeda, Robert, *Itinéraires du Psautier huguenot à la Renaissance* (Turnhout, Belgium: Brepols, 2009).

Wellmer, Albrecht, 'On Music and Language', in Jonathan Cross et al. (eds), *Identity and Difference: Essays on Music, Language and Time* (Leuven: Leuven University Press, 2004), 71–131.

Wencelius, Léon, 'L'Idée de modération dans la pensée de Calvin', *Evangelical Quarterly* 7 (1935): 87–94, 295–317.

Wencelius, Léon, *L'Esthétique de Calvin* (Paris: Belles Lettres, 1979).

Werbeck, Walter, 'Bach und der Kontrapunkt: Neue Manuskript-Funde', *Bach-Jahrbuch* 89 (2003): 67–95.

Westermeyer, Paul, 'Grace and the Music of Bach', *Christian Century* 102, 1 (1985): 291–4.

Wheeler, Samuel C., *Deconstruction as Analytic Philosophy* (Stanford, CA: Stanford University Press, 2000).

White, Thomas Joseph, *The Analogy of Being: Invention of the Antichrist or the Wisdom of God?* (Grand Rapids, MI: Eerdmans, 2010).

Whittall, Arnold, *Romantic Music: A Concise History from Schubert to Sibelius* (London: Thames and Hudson, 1987).

Wiedmann, August K., *Romantic Roots in Modern Art: Romanticism and Expressionism: A Study in Comparative Aesthetics* (Woking: Gresham Books, 1979).

Wiedmann, August K., *Romantic Art Theories* (Henley-on-Thames: Gresham Books, 1986).

Wieninger, Fritz, 'Die Musik im pastoralen Konzept Martin Luthers', *Diakoni* 14 (1983): 372–7.

Wigmore, Richard, *Schubert: The Complete Song Texts* (London: Gollancz, 1988).

Williams, Bernard, 'The Makropulos Case: Reflections on the Tedium of Immortality', in Bernard Williams (ed.), *Problems of the Self* (Cambridge: Cambridge University Press, 1976), 82–100.

Williams, Peter F., *Bach: The Goldberg Variations* (Cambridge: Cambridge University Press, 2001).

Williams, Peter F., *The Life of Bach* (Cambridge: Cambridge University Press, 2004).

Williams, Rowan, *Grace and Necessity: Reflections on Art and Love* (London: Continuum, 2005).

Williams, Rowan, *Wrestling with Angels: Conversations in Modern Theology*, ed. Mike Higton (Grand Rapids, MI: Eerdmans, 2007).

Winn, James A., *Unsuspected Eloquence: A History of the Relations Between Poetry and Music* (New Haven: Yale University Press, 1981).

Wittgenstein, Ludwig, *Philosophical Investigations* (Oxford: Blackwell Publishing, 1953).

Wittgenstein, Ludwig, *Notebooks 1914–1916* (Oxford: Basil Blackwell, 1979).

Witvliet, John D., 'Images and Themes in John Calvin's Theology of Liturgy', in John D. Witvliet (ed.), *Worship Seeking Understanding: Windows into Christian Practice* (Grand Rapids, MI: Baker Books, 2003), 127–48.

Witvliet, John D., 'The Spirituality of the Psalter in Calvin's Geneva', in John D. Witvliet (ed.), *Worship Seeking Understanding: Windows into Christian Practice* (Grand Rapids, MI: Baker Books, 2003), 203–29.

Wokler, Robert, *Rousseau on Society, Politics, Music, and Language: An Historical Interpretation of His Early Writings* (New York: Garland Publishing, 1987).

Wolff, Christoph, *Johann Sebastian Bach: The Learned Musician* (New York: W. W. Norton & Co., 2000).

Wolterstorff, Nicholas, *Art in Action: Toward a Christian Aesthetic* (Grand Rapids, MI: Eerdmans, 1980).

Wolterstorff, Nicholas, *Divine Discourse: Philosophical Reflections on the Claim that God Speaks* (Cambridge: Cambridge University Press, 1995).

Wolterstorff, Nicholas, 'Beyond Beauty and the Aesthetic in the Engagement of Religion and Art', in Oleg V. Bychkov and James Fodor (eds), *Theological Aesthetics after Von Balthasar* (Canterbury: Aldershot, 2008), 119–34.

Wood, David, 'Topologies of Transcendence', in John D. Caputo and Michael J. Scanlon (eds), *Transcendence and Beyond: A Postmodern Inquiry* (Bloomington, IN: Indiana University Press, 2007), 169–203.

Wood, Gillen D'Arcy, *Romanticism and Music Culture in Britain, 1770–1840: Virtue and Virtuosity* (Cambridge: Cambridge University Press, 2010).

Woolf, Virginia, *A Room of One's Own* (Norwalk, CT: The Easton Press, 2003).

Wörner, K. H., *Schoenberg's Moses and Aaron* (London: Faber & Faber, 1963).

Wright, David F., 'Calvin's Pentateuchal Criticism: Equity, Hardness of Heart and Divine Accommodation in the Mosaic Harmony Commentary', *Calvin Theological Journal* 21 (1986): 33–50.

Wright, David E., 'Calvin's Accommodating God', in Wilhelm H. Neuser and Brian G. Armstrong (eds), *Calvinus Sincerioris Religionis Vindex* (Kirksville, MO: Sixteenth Century Journal Publishers, 1997), 3–19.

Wright, Steve, 'The Creator Sings: A Wesleyan Rethinking of Transcendence with Robert Jenson', *Heythrop Journal* 52 (2011): 1–11.

Youens, Susan, 'Words and Music in Germany and France', in Jim Samson (ed.), *The Cambridge History of Nineteenth-Century Music* (Cambridge: Cambridge University Press, 2002), 460–99.

Zachman, Randall C., *John Calvin as Teacher, Pastor, and Theologian: The Shape of His Writings and Thought* (Grand Rapids, MI: Baker Academic, 2006).

Zachman, Randall C., *Image and Word in the Theology of John Calvin* (Notre Dame, IN: University of Notre Dame Press, 2007).

Zbikowski, Lawrence M., 'Music, Language, and What Falls in Between', *Ethnomusicology* 56, 1 (Winter 2012): 125–31.

Zenck, Martin, 'Reinterpreting Bach in the Nineteenth and Twentieth Centuries', in John Butt (ed.), *The Cambridge Companion to Bach* (Cambridge: Cambridge University Press, 1997), 226–50.

Zon, Bennett, 'Bedazzled by Breakthrough: Music Theology and the Problem of Composing Music in Words', *Journal of the Royal Musical Association* 136, 2 (2011): 429–35.

Zuckerkandl, Victor, *Sound and Symbol: Music and the External World* (London: Routledge & Kegan Paul, 1956).

Zuckerkandl, Victor, *The Sense of Music* (Princeton: Princeton University Press, 1971).

Zuckerkandl, Victor, *Man the Musician* (Princeton: Princeton University Press, 1973).

Zuidervaart, Lambert and Luttikhuizen, Henry (eds), *Pledges of Jubilee: Essays on the Arts and Culture, in Honor of Calvin G. Seerveld* (Grand Rapids, MI: Eerdmans, 1995).

Index

References to a definition or to the principal treatment of a subject are in **bold**. Page numbers in *italics* denote illustrations.

Printed and bound by CPI Group (UK) Ltd, Croydon, CR0 4YY